I CHANGE WORLDS

ANNA LOUISE STRONG

I CHANGE WORLDS
The Remaking of an American

with an introduction by
BARBARA WILSON

The Seal Press   Seattle

First Seal Press edition
November, 1979
Introduction Copyright © 1979 by Barbara Wilson

Photos Courtesy of
University of Washington Manuscript Collections,
Seattle, Washington and Mr. Tracy Strong.

Library of Congress Cataloging in Publication Data

Strong, Anna Louise, 1885-1970
  I change worlds.

  Reprint of the 1935 ed. published by H. Holt, New York,
with a new introd.
  Includes index.
  1. Strong, Anna Louise, 1885-1970. 2. Journalists—
United States—Biography. 3. Communism—Russia
4. Russia—Description and travel—1917- I. Title.
PN4874.S74A3 1979   070'.92'4 [B]   79-23128
ISBN 0-931188-05-9

The Seal Press
P.O. Box 13
Seattle, WA 98111

Printed in U.S.A.

Acknowledgements

The reprinting of Anna Louise Strong's autobiography has been a monumental task for a small three-woman press. Much thanks is due the friends and supporters without whom this project could not have taken shape. We would especially like to thank Martha Boland, Doug Honig, David Henderson, Richard Contreras, Sue Davidson, Mary Pond, Sybil James, Craig Hanks, Marjorie Nelson and Victor Steinbrueck. Debbie Gay supplied us with an annotated bibliography in the early stages, and Stephanie Ogle was kind enough to discuss with us her doctoral thesis on Anna Louise Strong. We would also like to thank Tracy Strong, Ken Davidson and the staff of the University of Washington archives for their advice and encouragement.

September, 1979

Rachel da Silva
Hylah Jacques
Barbara Wilson

List of Illustrations

Introduction

by Barbara Wilson

"And that is why we say that we are starting out on a road that leads—NO ONE KNOWS WHERE!" . . . So Anna Louise Strong ended an article written in 1919, just before the Seattle General Strike. She was speaking of the problems that might arise when and if Labor took over the city's management, but the quote could just as well serve as an epitaph to her entire life. That Anna Louise Strong was on a road somewhere she never doubted; but where she was going and why were problems she often grappled with, though rarely publicly.

In the course of her long writing career she authored countless articles and more than twenty-five books, yet her autobiography is the only volume in which she specifically addresses the direction of her own life, the reasons why she broke away from her middle-class upbringing to embrace Revolution in its many and various forms.

I Change Worlds covers a period of approximately fifty years—from Strong's birth in 1885 in Friend, Nebraska, to the early Thirties when she was still living in the Soviet Union. Three-fourths of the book takes place in the USSR. Stong gives rather short shrift to her life before she was thirty-five. It must have seemed, when she was writing her autobiography, that everything up to the day she first set foot in post-revolutionary Moscow was pale and uninteresting. Yet those formative years are what may prove to be most absorbing to those of us who wonder about the process of radicalization.

Anna Louise Strong's parents were middle-class liberals heavily involved in the Congregational Church and missionary work. Her mother, Ruth Tracy Stong, was one of the first women to graduate from an American college. An outgoing, ambitious woman, she accompanied her husband on his missions until she died in Africa at forty-one, when Anna Louise was nineteen. She imparted to the oldest of her three children many basic values, including some that her daughter would later strive to overcome. Independence, fearlessness, love of writing—all these Strong credits her mother with instilling in her, along with a troublesome belief in the innate goodness of humanity. Strong describes her childhood moral education with some irony: "Children must never know the meaning of harshness and injustice. Even more than most children of my class and time, I had what was called the good fortune of a completely protected childhood . . . I grew up expecting justice and kindness as natural rights of man; if anyone treated me with unkindness, I assumed it must be through my fault."

Her father, Sidney Strong, was to prove an even more decisive influence in her life. Descendant of Anglo-Saxon pioneers, he was a Congregationalist minister, a progressive deeply involved with labor unions, peace organizations and civic reform. Anna Louise was always his favorite; with the death of his wife he came to depend more than ever on his daughter's support. Yet he encouraged her independence and her political development, giving her the courage to risk unpopularity in defense of her ideals. Strong compares her father at one point to Tolstoy, but he was considerably more of a puritan than the Russian novelist. His combination of high ideals and strong moral standards acted as a restraint over Strong's emotional life. Although she sometimes found herself in conflict with her father, she ended by absorbing his puritanism about relationships. Significantly, she did not marry until her forties, a few years before her father's death.

Strong was intellectually precocious. Graduating at fifteen from high school, she spent a year studying in Germany before she was eligible for college. She relates that when she was only two, she corrected the grammar of a fellow train passenger; by her teens she was already writing poetry and publishing stories in *Youth's Companion.* After college, which she finished at only twenty, she took a job as a writer for *The Advance,* a religious magazine in Chicago. Using four pseudonyms, she covered women's news and ministers' conventions, as well as wrote book reviews and children's stories and poems.

Strong was out to impress the editor and let herself be exploited. It would not be the last time. The words she uses to describe her productivity and her desire to make herself indispensable are almost the same as she later employs in describing her stint on *The Moscow/News.* "I was only eager to do more work for my salary than anyone else could do," she writes of her job on *The Advance;* while of *The Moscow News:* "I worked, flushed with fever or shaking with exhaustion but my brain worked clear, doing everything that nobody else had time for . . . Let them produce a communist who could drive himself harder than I!"

Hard work, however, as Strong was to learn in both cases, was not always the key to advancement or success. She was fired after only five months on *The Advance* because it was the custom for the editor to use new graduates to boost circulation and then drop them. Partly in order to "save face," she decided to attend graduate school at the University of Chicago. There she took a Ph.D. in philosophy. Her thesis was published as *The Psychology of Prayer.* After she finished it, Strong writes, she never opened a book of philosophy again. Unlike most women with advanced degrees, Strong did not consider a career in academia. College and graduate school had been, for her, a means of passing time until she decided what to do.

Meanwhile her father had moved to Seattle as the minister of the Queen Anne Congregational Church, and Strong joined him there after completing her degree. She wasn't in Seattle long, however, before she was tapped to help organize a series of national Child Welfare Exhibits. She traveled across the country, attending to all aspects of the exhibits, from publicity to bulletin board design. She was enthusiastic about working with local people and helping them express their ideas about children's welfare.

In the course of organizing one exhibit in St. Louis, Strong met and fell in love with Roger Baldwin, who would later found the American Civil Liberties Union. Their relationship was tangled and unhappy, in part because Sidney Strong objected to Baldwin's lack of religion. Later she became involved with another man, David Thompson, on the East Coast, but she apparently did not reciprocate his affection, and this involvement, too, was broken off. Strong is extremely reticent about specific men in her life—neither Baldwin nor Thompson is mentioned in *I Change Worlds*, only a nameless married man in Seattle. She never even refers to her husband, the Russian journalist Joel Shurbin, by name, nor indicates much about him.

This is not to say she was not often preoccupied in her biography with questions of love and marriage. She is candid in her analysis of her motivations: "It was really a god I wanted, a boss, a master, a parent who would continue infancy for me. People told me that it was feminine to want this; and I believed in my soul, a soul already molded by the emotions of religion into the mood of adoring dependence that they were right . . . I reconciled these contradictory cravings for a boss and for freedom by telling myself that I would not give myself till I found somebody worth it . . ."

It was during her years as a progressive organizer that Strong first discovered socialism. In Kansas City she came to the realization that when the exhibit closed down, she would be in the position of firing a draftsman who depended on this job to support his family. She was placed in the kind of inherently unfair position her mother had never warned her about. She came to condemn capitalism, not through "any oppression endured by me personally," but through her desire to be, as she put it, an efficient organizer. However, she soon found that in the socialist world she felt excluded because of her class background and privilege. She was not yet ready to embrace the concept of "class struggle."

Thirty years old, independent and still respectably liberal in spite of her brush with socialism, Strong returned to Seattle in 1916 to take up housekeeping with her father. Not the least of her reasons for returning to the Northwest was an awakening love of mountain climbing. She organized the first winter expedition up Mt. Hood and barely came back alive; later she put together summer camps in the mountains. She grew to look forward to her summers out of the city as she became increasingly embroiled in Seattle politics.

Pre-World War I Seattle was still the frontier then, pro-labor and progressive, especially in the matter of public ownership of utilities. Strong's first political ventures were predictably liberal. She spoke on issues of peace and anti-conscription. In 1916 she ran for the legislature to emphasize her opposition to the ballot issues, and then, when she lost, for the Seattle School Board. She was the only woman, and won easily because of her reputation as an organizer for the Child Welfare Exhibits.

Three days after the School Board elections, the Everett Massacre occurred, an event which had repercussions all over the country, perhaps for no one as much as Strong. At the time, however, she felt herself an impartial observer, reporting the events for *The New York Evening Post*.

Everett, thirty miles north of Seattle, was, as it is today, a lumber town, controlled almost entirely, as Strong would say, by "interests." The fight against them was led by the Industrial Workers of the World, popularly known as the Wobblies. Sparked by a wage strike against the owners of the shingle mills, the Everett Massacre was class struggle at its rawest, and as such, typical of the fights that were going on throughout the western states. The mill owners hired scabs and organized groups of

x

vigilantes to keep the Wobblies out of town. On November 5, 1916 the Wobblies met in Seattle and chartered two boats to take them to a rally in Everett, knowing that they couldn't get through by road. When the Wobblies reached the Everett docks they found them covered with vigilantes. Gunfire broke out and seven Wobblies died; seven more were missing and twenty-seven were wounded. But it was the Wobblies who were put on trial for the deaths of two vigilantes, later found to have been killed by their own companions.

If the Everett Massacre was Strong's first introduction to the realities of class warfare, other events over the next three years pushed her firmly leftward. 1917 saw the entrance of the United States into war and the outbreak of the Bolshevik Revolution. Strong's respectable friends began to desert her as she first became a witness in the well-publicized trial of Hulet Wells for anti-conscription activities, and then befriended a young anarchist, Louise Oli.vereau, on trial for mimeo-graphing pacifist tracts. Strong was finding new friends, however, among the workers pouring into Seattle's wartime shipyards. They increasingly became the audience she wrote for in the radical paper *The Seattle Daily Call.*

Her connection with the paper was still not widely known, however, when the movement to recall her from the Seattle School Board began. It grew instead out of a general indignation over her participation in the two anti-conscription trials. On one side Strong was supported by the Seattle Central Labor Council, on the other derided and maligned by the city's establishment. When she was finally recalled in 1918, by a vote of 27,000 to 21,000, Editor Blethen of *The Seattle Times* wrote: "Anna Louise Strong, in spite of the consolidation on her behalf of every IWW, every Red Socialist, every pacifist, every man and woman who disapproves of the recall principle and the large numbers who came to her aid through the mistaken sympathy for a woman, was ejected from office with creditable neatness and dispatch . . . The sound of the door locking behind her will be music in the ears of the Seattle boys who have already reached the trenches in France."

Strong saw the vote differently. Not only was she glad to have been relieved of her duties on the school board, but she found in her recall an affirmation of her new radicalism. The workers had come out in her support; there was a new political alignment in the city. *The Seattle Daily Call* folded, but in its stead came a new, more financially stable daily, *The Seattle Union Record.* Strong became the features and magazine editor; under the pen name "Anise" she wrote poetry, a column ("All Outdoors") and a series of articles on City Light, in addition to regular features under her own name. At this time she also helped to issue a pamphlet with a speech of Lenin's, edited and with subtitles to make it easy and interesting reading for workers eager to know more about the Russian Revolution.

This pamphlet sold hundreds of copies and was seen everywhere; it may well have been a factor in the Seattle General Strike of 1919. That year, in February, the entire city shut down for three days in solidarity with a shipyard workers' strike. Emergency services were administered by the Strike Committee and carried out by union members. It was the first time in U.S. history, and the last, that workers tried to take over the functions of a city government, and the results were heady and confusing.

As Strong wrote later, during that time one saw:

"The Milk Wagon Drivers consulting late into the night over the task of supplying milk for the city's babies;

"The Provision Trades working twenty-four hours out of the twenty-four on the question of feeding 30,000 workers;

"The Barbers planning a chain of co-operative barber shops;

"The Steamfitters opening a profitless grocery store."

There was no outbreak, as had been feared, of crime and lawlessness. Essential services ran surprisingly smoothly. Yet neither the Strike Committee nor the strikers had a strong sense of direction. They had meant to make a point—their support for higher wages for shipyard workers. Now they found themselves in control of Seattle. At the same time, there was never any real indication that the strike might continue indefinitely or that force might be necessary to maintain the workers'leap to power. The labor leaders, many of whom had been out of town at a conference when the strike began, announced the end of the strike after three days, and Mayor Ole Hanson took credit for subduing the "Bolshevist" menace.

Strong herself played a journalist's role, writing up an account of the strike afterwards in a booklet put out by the Strike Historical Committee, analyzing the events, the reasons for failure and the lessons learned. She was not an organizer, yet she was emotionally involved in the Seattle General Strike, more so than she ever would be again in any form of direct political action. The events of February, 1919 touched her deeply, and she would continue to hark back to them throughout her restless career as an onlooker to revolution.

By 1921 Anna Louise Strong was in the Soviet Union, on the advice of her friend Lincoln Steffens, the muckraking journalist who had proclaimed, "I have seen the future and it works." She used a job with the American Friends Service Committee in Poland to get to the mecca every red-blooded American radical dreamed of—Moscow. That same year anarchist leader Emma Goldman bitterly turned her back on post-revolutionary Russia, citing authoritarian bureaucracy, and the failure of an ideal. Strong, however, embraced the whole spectrum of life in the new Soviet Union with rapture. The books she wrote during this period all have the flavor of the newly converted: *First Time in History* (1924); *Children of Revolution—the story of the John Reed Colony* (1925); *The Soviets Conquer Wheat* (1931).

For the most part, these books are naive and enthusiastic propaganda, full of facts and heart-warming, revolutionary conversations. It is only in her letters and, hesitantly, in her autobiography, that Strong begins to discuss what was difficult for her about living in the Soviet Union. It was neither typhus nor the famine, both of which she survived during her first year, but instead the conflict between (her own) American "efficiency" and Soviet bureaucracy. Although she refers often and disparagingly to her efficiency in earlier sections of *I Change Worlds*, it wasn't until she arrived in the Soviet Union that she found a society where "getting things done" wasn't consistently praised and rewarded. The conflict is best illustrated in the two projects which Strong undertook over a ten-year period and to which she devotes obsessive pages in her autobiography attempting to understand what she did wrong.

The first was the concept of the Russian-American Club, an organization designed to bring together Americans new to the USSR, to provide support for them as they attempted to donate their skills, money and labor to the new regime. In the beginning everyone, especially the bureaucrats, seemed enthusiastic about her idea; promises of money and a building to house the club were freely given. As time went on, a subtle tone of discouragement began to permeate the project, and it finally had to be abandoned. No one ever really told Strong why it would not work; she was expected to know.

But Strong was not a particularly subtle person, nor did she ever understand power politics on a personal level. As an idealist turned socialist, she could only conceive of struggle between the capitalists and the people, not between "comrades." So she tried to please everyone, incorporating the ideas of Trotsky, the foreign businesspeople and the ruling bureaucrats, as to what the Russian-American Club should be— and ended by pleasing no one. She had dreamed of being an organizer in the Soviet Union; after this failure she returned to journalism, somewhat bitterly noting that the Soviet government seemed to prefer her to write for the capitalist press than to work for them.

Strong refers to this episode as "My First Great Failure." Her second great failure came with *The Moscow News,* a paper published in English for foreigners living in the Soviet Union. Her self-confidence no doubt received a boost at being asked to organize this venture; she involved writers from the United States and threw herself into the project with her usual energy. She hadn't reckoned, however, with censorship and other problems connected with publishing American-style journalism in a country like the Soviet Union. A comic piece in the first issue about Americans in Moscow was blue-penciled until she explained that American humor was "different." The editor, T.L. Axelrod, tended to prefer tedious party-line translations. There were constant questions about the nature of the audience; was the paper for workers or for diplomats or for businesspeople? These questions were not easily resolved as the editors shifted; Axelrod moved on to found the competing *Workers' News,* and the new editor gave Strong less and less to do.

Strong tended to blame herself for the problems. She felt guilty both at disappointing her fellow writers and at not understanding the kind of paper required. She berated herself over an individuality that rebeled at the collective process. And yet, she couldn't help thinking sometimes that she could put out a lively socialist paper, if only they would let her.

What comes across painfully in all these descriptions of enthusiastic plans and failures is Strong's desire to be used in the service of the country . . . but on her own terms. It is not surprising, then, that she spent a good deal of her time "in Russia" traveling. She made yearly trips back to the United States; she covered revolutionary developments in Mexico, Poland and Spain; she wrote articles and books about nearly everything she saw. She was increasingly interested in China and visited that country six times from the Twenties to the Forties, each time traveling widely and making detailed notes on everything from women's groups to conversations with generals to descriptions of the countryside. At least half of her literary output during those years relates to China: *China's Millions* (1928, 1935); *Red Star in Samarkand* (1949); *Road to the Grey Pamir* (1931); *The Chinese Conquer China* (1949).

Like Agnes Smedley, another American journalist who lived and wrote in China at that time, Strong found the Chinese character much to her liking. Certainly she found the political situation in China more to her taste than the Russian. She was always drawn to the drama of revolution, empathizing with every insurgency, reliving her own radicalization, her own understanding of class warfare. In the Thirties and Forties the Soviet Union could no longer be considered revolutionary, struggling with economic and social problems under Stalin's increasingly iron grip, but heroic China did battle with real villains—the landlords, the Japanese, Chiang Kai-shek.

In China, Strong met and interviewed Mao; she was the first western journalist to whom he used the phrase "paper tiger" in referring to his enemies. Strong's book *The Chinese Conquer China* includes her visits to the caves of Yenan and is distinctly pro-Maoist. It was in galley proofs when she was unceremoniously expelled from the Soviet Union in 1949 while waiting for a visa to China. The book's stance of warm admiration for the Chinese communists may have conceivably been Strong's downfall.

Whatever the reasons for the charges against her of being an American spy, for the next six years Strong was to exist as a pariah among the American left. The check she wrote to the defense fund for Smith Act victims was endorsed "For the American Communists who are getting as raw a deal from American justice as I got from the USSR, from a fellow victim of the Cold War." It was returned by a member of the Civil Rights Congress as "tainted money."

Nevertheless, she refused to give up her beliefs, to join the chorus of disillusioned ex-Communists in writing anti-Soviet propaganda. In her letters she blamed the American left for abandoning her, but she kept most of her criticism to herself. She lived quietly in California, putting out a small newsletter, *Today,* and waiting patiently for the day when she would be rehabilitated. Although it was never made official, after the public revelation of Stalin's crimes in 1956, she was quietly taken back into the fold. She had never been a party member, however, and she still did not join.

Strong immediately began a full speaking tour after her exoneration and became involved in a suit against the government for denying her a passport. When the Supreme Court finally decided in her favor, she took herself and her passport to Moscow, where she was warmly greeted, and then to China, where she was to spend the remaining decade of her life.

She lived in Peking, in the foreigner's compound, occasionally sharing dinners with an old friend, Rewee Alley, a New Zealand poet. Friends said she was happy, had slowed down, was accepting life more graciously. She resumed her old newsletter, now called "Letter From China," in response to the growing rift between China and the Soviet Union. Mao, who sincerely liked her and protected her during the tumultuous days of the Cultural Revolution, saw her newsletter as a valuable means of explaining China's position to the West. In Peking she was well thought of, respected and listened to; though she still thought of returning to the United States, she put off her departure, until in March of 1970 she died. She left behind a second volume of autobiography which, so far, has remained in China.

* * *

*"Our individuality is partial and restless; the stream of conscious-
ness that we call 'I' is made of shifting elements that flow from our group
and back to our group again. Always we seek to be ourselves and the herd
together, not one against the herd."*

For most of her life Anna Louise Strong felt herself an outsider.
From her earliest years as a too-intelligent girl to her various
ostracisms—from polite Seattle society, from the Soviet Union, from the
American left—she often felt, or was made to feel, that she did not
belong. Not surprisingly for her class and generation, she never laid the
blame on a patriarchal society which accorded her only a grudging
respect. Although she supported the suffragists and early on dedicated a
portion of her talents to organizing a traditionally women-oriented
project—the Child Welfare exhibits—Strong more often identified with
the male world of journalism and international politics. She portrayed
her isolation as a contrast between the individual and society, not from
the vantage point of a woman who must constantly prove herself, a
woman isolated in a world of men.

Consequently, she often appeared to others as invulnerable. In an
article written after her death, "The Classic Fellow Traveler," Nym
Wales, an acquaintance from the early China years, summed up Strong's
personality in the following manner: "She was self-sufficient, self-
centered, self-esteemed. She was encased in Athenian armor, safe from
emotional injury." There is no recognition in this statement that a woman
who wanted to succeed in a predominantly male field might have need to
"encase" herself emotionally. Strong's parents had given her love and
self-confidence; she was slow to learn that society did not reward strength
and energy in a woman but instead sought to ostracize and/or trivialize
her.

Strong did not adopt a feminist analysis; instead she continued, like
many women on the left, to hope that communism would bring about a
new equality, where even "intellectual idealists" like herself would find a
place. The interim was often lonely, as Strong makes abundantly clear in
her autobiography. Never quite sure who to blame for her unhappiness
and inability to fit in, she found it easiest to fault her own individualistic
tendencies. Yet, paradoxically, it was her "difficult" and tenacious
character which often helped her to surmount the traditional biases
against her sex.

Early in *I Change Worlds,* Strong writes of the ways in which she
attempted to overcome her isolation: "From this haunting feeling of not
being wanted . . . I found two ways of escape . . . One was the invention of
gods, the other was personal efficiency in work."

It is evident from her schoolgirl letters that her first "gods" were women. She had crushes on female teachers long before she discovered Stalin and Mao. Florence Fitch, an Oberlin professor, acted as a role model for a successful, intellectual woman; likewise Jane Addams and Florence Kelly. Strong may have been looking for maternal replacements; later she would attempt to become a "normal" woman and subjugate herself to a man she could admire. This desire led, in its most sinister form, to her admiration of Stalin. The chapter in *I Change Worlds* where Stalin solves the problems of *The Moscow News* would be ludicrous if it were not so tragically mistaken—and so typical of the way Stalin was viewed at that time by a number of foreigners. Later, in her letters, Strong was to express a growing alarm at the court trials and the disappearances of Russian acquaintances; she maintained a public display of confidence, however, that it was all for the best. In self-protection, perhaps, she was already switching her political allegiance to the Chinese communists, Mao in particular.

Politics, for Anna Louise Strong, was imbued with personality. And perhaps indistinguishable from it. The finer points of theory were lost on her; action and struggle were what she found most absorbing. It is conceivable that she never even read Marx; only late in her autobiography does she admit that there might be a need for a "scientific approach." For the most part abstract analysis reminded her too much of philosophy, too much of her useless degree from the university. Her political journalism is remarkable for being free of abstraction and pompousness. Her style varied from ironic to panegyric; she was always committed, often biased, rarely sectarian. More than anything she was concerned with making politics understandable and exciting to the common reader. One of her greatest gifts was being able to convey the excitement that she felt in the presence of change.

Although Strong was by birth and education a Midwesterner, she identified strongly with the West and with a pioneering tradition. Perhaps because she came of age, politically speaking, in Seattle, she often saw social struggle in terms of the "interests" or the ruling class against the people for control of natural resources and economic self-determination. It seems clear, in the one book she wrote about the United States, *My Native Land,* that she was a populist, a Jeffersonian, who spoke far more often of "democracy" than "communism." She was well-schooled in the American political tradition, and it influenced her thinking when she traveled to observe other countries. She sought always to identify with the vitality of the little people standing up to the capitalists, of the common people creating their future.

When Anna Louise Strong was not yet two years old, she was blown by a Midwestern cyclone from the front lawn to the cow pasture. According to family tradition she remained unperturbed and even curious. That was characteristic of her life as a whole; she changed worlds, and often, but always she retained her curiosity and her imperturbable optimism in the face of twentieth-century upheavals.

Her enthusiasm for life expressed itself in a thousand different ways. "Motor-minded" she calls herself and other Americans like her who act first and think later. Strong's energy and confidence enabled her to see and do things, to take part in history in a way closed to most women of her time. Yet her enthusiasm also led to blindness about the realities of power, to reliance on male leaders and to insensitivity to the price to be paid for change. Naive, ambitious and often desperately lonely, Strong carried to the end of her life a desire for justice, a longing for personal and political freedom, if only to find out what it would mean.

Near the end of her autobiography, she tells Lincoln Steffens, "I'm reporter enough to know that there is no absolute truth. Truth is for each of us our picture of the world. When I say I want to tell the truth, I mean I want to paint my picture."

In *I Change Worlds* Anna Louise Strong has painted not only her own picture of a changing world but the self-portrait of a remarkable woman.

TO
ALL OF THOSE AMERICANS
WHO STAND WHERE I STOOD FIFTEEN YEARS AGO
AND TO
ALL THOSE RUSSIAN COMMUNISTS
WHO WANT TO UNDERSTAND AMERICA

If your book lands on your public as it does on us, it will be a triumph. And it will clear up so many incomprehensibles. And so much good. It is especially convincing and clearing at the points where you, the writer, are still unclear, where it is plain that you have not yet completed the journey from one world to the other.

You have a big subject, you know. To make and cross a bridge from one age to another, from one whole united philosophy to another is something that was never done in any other transition in history—not by a single generation. You are making the passage that will take us over here decades to go through; you are speeding through it.

You are reporting the chapters of your progress from our old Christian-Greek culture to the communist culture which will probably prevail for the next two thousand years. The only person I ever met who seemed to have made the trip completely is a Russian boy, about twenty-one, a Moscow University student at Hollywood, who was born so late that he did not understand our United States. He was serene, simple, without any hypocrisy at all; he thought and acted together. He was wonderful. He was a unit. You and I will never get where he is, but he, on the other hand, will never know about the trip you are describing, never know how they got from one world to the other.

Every single thing in the world is changed by the process of history that you are describing your way through. That's what most of my liberal friends cannot see—that Time is a dimension as it really is. They say to me: "Right is Right, isn't it?" I answer: "When?" Which seems the height of absurdity to them. And it is now in these United States. But not in Russia. There, Time is of the essence of Right. Treason to the tsar wasn't a sin; treason to communism is. . . .

The truth from now on is always dated, never absolute, never eternal. Your opportunity to tell this story is for this one day only and for our generation alone. A rare tale you are telling.

L. S.

IT has done more for me, this book, than it will do for any of my readers. We motor-minded people think in action, and I, a writer, think by writing. Not till I have it down on paper do I firmly grasp what I know. By the months of this writing, rereading old files of letters, recalling old fights that had long been forgotten, the tangled mass of many years of struggle has grown to an organic whole.

When I began to write there were years I feared to touch, so sore they were with old defeat and pain. They kept rising up, more and more years that I had buried, dividing themselves into months and days. So many of those days seemed to have been battles which turned out twisted and wrong, hopes that flamed and burned to ashes and left life desolate and gray. How could I have survived so many and each time begun anew?

But as I lived through in the writing those years that I feared to touch, I was amazed to find that the pain had vanished, long since for many years. I was glad to remember and learn, before turning to new tasks.

Every one of those years has been fruitful: not one was a defeat. Nor was a single one of them a victory. There were no defeats and no victories but an ever-continuing struggle, and out of every phase of it something grew. Never exactly what I purposed, yet something in which my purpose played a part. As I saw this, my energy increased and a weariness which had seemed to be growing with age disappeared. I was ready to launch into battle again: I felt so happy and young.

Here in the Soviet Union our life is such that struggles and failures no longer fall to the ground and die, unnoticed or noticed by chance by some other man, as has been the way of life since time began. They begin to be welded into a common experience from which all of us learn. Our human history is in part the story of increasing ability to share the experience of other men. From early animal cries to human speech, from secret handicrafts to machinery shared with ten thousand men, from picture writing to Shakespearean dramas and formulæ of Einstein—thus we advance. Already in modern days science and technical skill have in all lands a common tongue. Here in the Soviet Union our many-millioned mass attains this privilege of scientist and engineer: that what we strive and do or fail to do is correlated into the planned experience of the rest.

This is our new stage in man's advance. This is the collective power that sweeps a backward land so swiftly from its half-nomad, half-patriarchal past to the practical possibility of socialism tomorrow. Nothing in the Soviet Union can be exclusively mine, not even the achievements and failures of my own life and work. Capitalists may create an institution and possess it, but not we. Nothing can be mine to exploit for profit, nothing to possess and exploit for fame, nothing to establish or ruin by my unchecked will. . . .

"Nothing is mine," said Morosov, "but all shall be ours." . . . There is not even private property in mistakes.

Like the pioneers of old I fled from myself and the complexities of our human struggle. I found my same self and the same complexities of struggle with a less familiar face. I found more than I knew how to ask, more pain, more joy. For I had the incredible good fortune to be born in an epoch when the whole earth is tortured by the pangs of birth.

Not to have been the most favored person in all the forty centuries of past history would I give up the life that I have had and have. Not to have any rewards those forty centuries held in their keeping or the present capitalist world can offer, of fame or luxury or power or admiring friends and lovers.

Nor do I even greatly envy, as once I did, the youth of this Soviet generation, which will live to new achievements of which we now cannot dream. Certainly I should like to be starting all over, to be twenty again with a future on this emerging earth. But I know that, at a new height in the spiral, they will again face our old human problems, of comradeship and allegiance, of love and work. Though they reach heights to me unattainable, I also have a joy they cannot know. I have seen and been and intimately experienced—both chaos and the forming world.

I have built myself into this new land by choice and struggle. Yet such is the paradox of my flight here that the more I know and love the Soviet Union, the less may I ask to stay.

For there is another land whose workers have the right to claim that I deserted the struggle which I with them began. In times and ways and to an extent yet undecided, I recognize their right to call me back. My life must be henceforth as I have made it, a link between two lands.

It is to you I write, the comrades I deserted, that thus my desertion may serve you, sending back my gain from the new land. For your struggle has grown now to a mighty conflict, torturing in its complexity, vicious in its brutality, while I remained apart.

This is the word I send you, as I look both backward and forward from the ridge of a great divide: Nearly everything that made my life had to be broken, yet I have found new life.

Yet? No! THUS I found it.

A. L. S.

CONTENTS

xxv

CONTENTS

CHAPTER I

A GIRL IN A GARDEN

The older Americans ask me: "What ever made you go to Moscow?" The younger Americans say: "Can you get me a job if I come over; I want to pioneer in the new world?" All of them want to ask, but hardly dare to phrase it: "What is it really like in that strange world beyond the border? You must know; you have lived there more than thirteen years. Is it really something new for which the world is waiting? Or is it just one more of life's old disillusions? What have you found there; what has it made of you—you who were just like us some fifteen years ago?"

This is my attempt to answer their deeper question, to analyze, for them and for myself, the best I have learned from life. I must begin not with autumn of 1921 when I crossed the Russian border; I must begin far back. Before the Bolshevik Revolution, before the war even. I cannot remember how far back began this journey, which millions have been making with me, which I think all the world is making. Towards Moscow and beyond Moscow. For Moscow is not the end, if indeed there be a final end to our journey. But I, like a million others, did not know where I was going in Seattle some fifteen years ago.

I am one of those who never knows the direction of my journey until I have almost arrived. There are others like me; I think most Americans are like me. Psychologists call us motor-minded, which means that we think not in terms of visual or auditory images, nor in terms of graphs and plans, but in terms of actions. Perhaps it is our pioneer life that made us so, its journeying into a West which we could neither visualize nor hear nor plan but only march to. Perhaps it is the effect upon our nervous system of the machines which we, unlike the rest of the world, are almost born knowing. Or perhaps it is

1

not American at all, but primitively human, since consciousness always arises, in individuals as in history, out of the clash of actions, which always precede thought.

In any case, we act; and afterwards, if we survive and still have time to reason, we know why we have acted. I remember years ago in a different world, my college, an estimable dean of women reproved me for some thoughtless act in these words: "For what is our reason given us, if not to govern our actions?" I told her it gave my reason a full time job to explain my acts after I had done them, and I hadn't any reason left for other work! . . . This wasn't quite as flippant as she thought it.

How I have sometimes envied those people who plan out their lives beforehand; who know when they are young just what they intend to be. Yet when I look back, it seems that my life also has followed, if not a plan, at least a consistent direction. It was never one of which I was clearly conscious. I never laid it down in advance to follow. It grew from day to day by the unplanned interaction of what for want of a name we call "myself," which my parents and the far-back unre-membered past had made me, and the impact of new forces out of which I picked what suited me. It seems we motor-minded folk also arrive. In the words of our national proverb, we don't know where we're going, but we are, like the rest of the world, on our way.

It saves much toil and pain to know where one is going. For though I feel quite sure that the goal which I am approaching is the goal I should have chosen if I could have clearly planned it years ago, I cannot forget how many started as blithely as I did, and wandered off to disillusion and despair. Nor can I forget the wasted strength of my own years of bewildered, con-flicting emotions, due to the fact that I never clearly under-stood my way. Others perhaps may learn from the chart of my road to avoid its detours. For I think my road is the road of millions.

. . . .

My unremembered past is the story of a continent and of old migrations overseas. I come of the tribes that drove stead-ily westward from the motherland of men in the heart of Asia, westward over the plains of Europe down into Rome and Gaul and Britain for more than two thousand years. Then they leaped the sea, no longer by tribes but by groups and families; they settled the American seaboard and kept on driving west. Farther into the wilderness with each new generation.

The new lands know these men as pioneers and conquerors; the old lands knew them as the Men Who Fled! Behind them in the old lands rose the triumph of the victor and the groans of the oppressed. They were squeezed out by great social struggles; they were the surplus middle class of successive generations. They were tribes crowded out of pastures but strong enough to seize new lands; tradesmen who failed but had strength to begin anew in a simpler world; workmen without jobs but with funds for one last journey; adventurers to whom a settled society offered insufficient gain; idealists and religious men who were unable either to enforce or renounce their views.

Neither their fortune nor their brains had made them masters and they disdained to be slaves. They chose the wilderness to conquer, finding it easier than man. They left the complex problem of human society to the men who served oppressors and the men who were oppressed. They chose the simpler task: to conquer the earth and hold it. Thus they held each new bit of earth for a generation, till human society arose with its struggles around them and drove them to the wilderness again. Hope was their claim upon the new land; it was the converse of an old despair. But they buried the despair in alien graveyards and kept the hope for their sons. Thus they went down in history as conquerors of the West.

From this life came their virtues and their weaknesses. They were proud of physical strength, of daring optimism, of resourceful invention, of quick adaptability to new conditions. They rejoiced in the power to survive in isolation which they called "independence," and in agility to flee and change, which they called "freedom." They were "practical men" with little use for "theory"; for they shrank from analyzing those social and economic forces by which other men from a distance controlled them, cast them into the wilderness and

entangled them again. Having neither the shrewdness which
serves oppressors, nor the guile that lawlessly outwits them,
nor the solidarity that in the end destroys them, they lived by
faith—and evasion. As they gave up old lands to tyrants,
they dreamed always of new lands without slaves or masters.
From the German tribes that overran imperial rotting Rome
for the stronger, more imperial papacy, to the settlers who
won the west for Jim Hill's railroads, they were daring and
free and equal—and easily deceived. For they substituted
energy for thinking, and optimism for analysis. Cast forth
by great struggles of classes, they refused to believe in classes,
but had faith that somewhere "beyond the ranges" men might
be free and equal still. But they never clearly analyzed how
this could happen.

Thus came into being Americans—of all men strongest in
subduing nature, most inventive in the use of machinery, most
determined to optimism, most naïve and credulous in social
relations. . . .

.   .   .   .

Thus came the youth John Strong in 1630 to Massachusetts
and in 1635 to settle the Connecticut Valley, yet before old
age overtook him he found Connecticut too populous and
moved north to settle Northampton, where he became a notable
man, founder of a family and a town. A century after his
death another John Strong went farther north to the wild
hills of Vermont; he left them after twenty years and took
his family of ten to Ohio where he founded the town of
Strongsville. This settler for whom the town was named was
my father's grandfather. My mother's forebears, the Tracys
and Lords and Russells, came also in 1630 to America and
followed a similar westward track by a route somewhat more
southern.

In a land of advancing colonists they were farmers, preach-
ers, educators, artisans, engineers, tradesmen, governors.
There was Captain David Strong, a fighter in the War of
Independence, whose mother, Sarah Warren, carried him back
to the *Mayflower*. There was Lieutenant Thomas Tracy, a

founder of Norwich, Connecticut. There was John Russell, who founded the town of Hadley and who bragged in his old age of the years when he had hidden in his house the two regicides, Goffe and Whalley, when the king of England's officers were seeking them. In the library of his son, Samuel Russell, Yale College was started. There was Russell F. Lord, engineer, who built the Delaware and Hudson canal and the first American railroad out of Honesdale. From old John Stoughton Strong, who herded cattle at the age of eighty over six square miles of Ohio wilderness to my grandmother's sister, Lizzie Lord, who married President Harrison and lived in the White House, they expressed the many-sided life of an advancing land.

The direct line of my ancestry was always "progressive" which meant that they kept on going, though to what goal was not always clear. They were builders of towns, railroads and colleges, which they left to build anew. They had faith that humanity inevitably advances with each generation and that new things are usually best. Were they not justified by the American expansion of three centuries where energy and optimism made good?

They were similarly progressive in ideas. My father was one of the first in his generation to embrace the doctrines of Darwinism and evolution and many struggles it cost him some fifty years ago. My mother was one of that first generation of women anywhere in the world to receive a college education. There were in her youth only two universities in the world open freely to women, Mt. Holyoke in the east and Oberlin in the west. It was in Oberlin, of anti-slavery traditions, whose very college motto is "learning and labor" from the days when students built the college with their hands, that she met my father. Their marriage followed the new progressive tradition that wives are not only partners in pioneer hardships but equals in brains.

In part because of her inspiration and perhaps still more because of his own remarkable tenacity of purpose, my father became a man of Christian ideals which he held against all batterings of fact and fate. I have read of Tolstoi, but not seen him; my father, I think, is like him. From love of "God and man" he hated war; and he preached against it during the greatest war that has yet shaken the earth. Like a stalwart "independent" he held staunchly while the whole organization of his life, his work, his friendships fell in ruins around him. In old age he launched forth to Geneva to "see what is happening to peace." He survived even that disillusion. He is perhaps the only man I ever knew who almost follows the ethics of Jesus; he can die for a faith but cannot renounce an ideal. By words and life he taught me that neither money nor fame nor human opinion are to be counted against being "right" in one's soul. If he could not quite teach me how to learn what "right" is, he seemed to say to me as years went by that it is whatever is for the greatest good of the greatest number of people; and if this is not always concretely applicable, it was clearly the best that was known to his generation. I owe much to his indomitable will which served without wavering whatever he found good and true.

My father was the pioneer of his family; every American family in those days had one or more. It was he who went west. He went west spiritually also. The small family inheritance divided among his brothers gave each of them a couple of thousand dollars. One of them invested in land and became a solid local farmer; one invested in bank shares and became the local banker. My father spent his inheritance on a grand wedding trip. His was the ideal American romance: strong and intelligent youth in the glad, free choice of a first mating. Four years he waited for my mother while they finished their education. They celebrated properly when the marriage came. They took the "grand tour" through Europe and Greece and Palestine and Egypt. "It will be a fine memory for all our lives, our first year of comradeship before we begin the cares of work and children," was the reason they gave to their protesting relatives.

On that gorgeous jaunt of joy and culture, defying the property traditions of their world, my unconscious life was formed on the borders of Africa and Asia and carried back across the ocean to be born in the prairie town of Friend, Nebraska, a few months after their return.

I have no memories of Friend, Nebraska. Family tradition tells that in this, his first job as a rural preacher, my father had one house for home and one for study, and each was a shack of a single room. Tradition tells also of the great cyclone which blew me, a baby not yet two, from the front yard to the cow pasture, a considerable distance away. When they found me I was somewhat worried by the cows but not at all by the cyclone; clearly I continued the pioneer tradition and found the storms of nature friendlier than the whims of living creatures.

There is another tradition with which they pestered my youth. When we moved from Friend to Mt. Vernon, Ohio, and I was not yet two, it is recorded that I corrected the grammar of a woman on the train, saying: "My mother says you mustn't say 'ain't.'" . . . It was my mother, it seems, who destined me for an editor from the beginning.

Into my conscious years she increased this training. She read me to sleep with the rhythm of classic poetry, "Lady of the Lake," "Marmion," the poetry of the Bible and many old ballads. It was this training, I think, rather than any unusual talent, which caused me to write verses from the age of six and seven and to issue a book of verse (typewritten and bound by a proud Uncle Del) at the age of thirteen. At an early age she enthralled me with Robert Ball's "Starland," an excellent description of the stars for children. It was one of my early treats to be allowed to stay up at night to place the constellations. When my younger brother and sister grew into our study circle, my mother had games at mealtimes where we learned new words and their uses, their correct pronunciation and spelling. It is probably this early training which made me a writer.

My mother also made us independent; for she was a modern progressive mother, unlike the clinging mothers of the past. From the age of seven I was taught to go downtown in the perilous city of Cincinnati, to which we had just moved. On one of the crowded crossings, a neighbor heard me repeating my mother's careful lesson: "First look up, then look down; then run." . . . It is a lesson which adult Russian peasants still need to learn on Moscow streets! . . . At the age of eight I was sent on an overnight railway journey alone. I do not know what instructions may have been given the conductor, but I know that I handled my ticket, gave a tip to the porter, got off at Mansfield at dawn and took a cab to my grandmother's house, where I proudly arrived for breakfast. It was my big day of independence.

My mother determined to make us fearless. The thunderstorms of the west, which rage across the prairie and are feared by many children and even by timid adults, were cleverly made by her our special treats for good behavior. We were allowed, as a great prize, to sit on the porch and watch the next thunderstorm. Once I sat thus while five gorgeous bursts of lightning struck within two blocks of our home. I was quite aware that this lightning would finish me if it hit me, but this only added to the excitement and the grandeur of the sight. I think it is due to this training that in later life when death has actively threatened, when a storm has caught me in a small boat far out in lake or ocean, or a blizzard has surprised me on a mountain, I have not known fear; I have known increased capacity for cool action, and even a thrill of joy in the power of the storm which I defied.

The northern part of Ohio, where my mother grew to womanhood, had led in the fight against Negro slavery; her college, Oberlin, held the proud tradition of being the first university to admit Negroes, as it had admitted women, on the basis of a common humanity. When we moved to the southern town of Cincinnati, my mother carried her traditions with her and fought for them. A neighbor came in horror to inform her that her oldest daughter, Anna Louise, was constantly playing with the two children of the Negro washwoman. My mother told her, and told me also (I was six years old) that if children were good children, well-mannered, kindly and using no bad language, I could play with them if I chose and should not mind the color of their skin. Tradition says that I, hurt by the uppish attitude which my white playmates copied from their mothers, clung to the washwoman's "Guppy" and whimpered that I "liked the colors best." But Guppy is a tradition before my conscious days.

It was and is the theory of the American middle class that their children should see no evil in the world. None of the great battles of man should enter the home to "take the bloom from youth." Children must never know the meaning of harshness and injustice. Even more than most children of my class and time I had what was called the good fortune of a completely protected childhood. There was real love in our family, real kindness and intelligence. My mother was a very beautiful and able woman; she divided herself into the tasks of being comrade to her husband, educator to her children, yet she found time for the social work permitted by the period, which was organizing women's societies. She did all these duties graciously and well. From neither of my parents did I ever hear a harsh or unjust word: if they blamed or punished, it was only after careful inquiry showed me the reason for my punishment. I grew up expecting justice and kindness as natural rights of man: if anyone treated me with unkindness, I assumed it must be through my fault.

I still remember the bewildered shock when I met the harshness of the public school in Cincinnati, where a teacher jerked my ear and shook me violently for the crime of having on my own initiative filled my inkwell when it was empty. My mother hastened to save me from a repetition of such shocks: she arranged for a private school. Whether through my own reputation for cleverness or the standing of my father's church or my mother's personal persuasiveness I was accepted as "guest pupil" in the best private school of Cincinnati where, with excellent individual instruction, I promptly finished eight grades in four years and even acquired a smattering of French. I chiefly remember from this school the remark which Miss Nourse, its director, made to my mother:

"Your daughter is a real 'love-child'; she has evidently always known kindness. She always expects people to like her and assumes that they have kind motives. Even when girls are unkind she invents better excuses for them than they can invent themselves."

My mother clearly considered that she had received a great compliment; influenced by her tones I also took it as a compliment for myself. Not for nearly a lifetime did it occur to me that it may be a dangerous thing to launch into life expecting only kindness, and always inventing plausible good motives for acts that are clearly evil.

. . . .

Even the family kindness which surrounded me could not protect me from the human loneliness which befell one day in a garden and which set a recurring problem for nearly forty years of life. For as I try to answer the question what took me to Moscow and what it is that I found, I seem to trace the beginning of all my conscious seeking in the little girl, eleven years old, who played on a perfect day in spring near lilac bushes on a parsonage lawn in Oak Park.

I think there was, or had been, a dog. It may have been after Noiro died of distemper and Tiger was poisoned and we gave up having dogs. I think there was, or had been, a game of hide-and-seek. But I know for one long eternal moment there was no living creature there at all. Then, whether it was the blue and gold perfection of the day, or the intoxication of the lilac-laden air, or the exquisite curve of one white spray against the purple blooms—suddenly the little girl knew that she was a hard, round soul and that all the spacious springtime was outside. She could look at it and smell it and love it, but she couldn't be it: she could never, never be it. She couldn't get out and nothing could get in through the shell of that hard, round soul.

She threw her arms around the lilac bush, but the lilac bush remained aloof, tantalizingly beautiful and never to be reached. She threw herself on the ground and clutched the roots, digging her face into the soft grass of spring. There was comfort in the hardness of the earth but the essential desolation remained. The ecstasy of the day was like a pang from which a naked red baby is born. For the first time she knew herself

an individual creature, cut off from the world of which she
had been a part. She painfully wanted to get back.

I do not know what psychologists now teach about that
loneliness of the human soul with which philosophers begin
and poets end. But I have thought, in recent years, its pain-
fulness may have a very simple reason. We humans are herd
animals of the monkey tribe, not natural individuals as lions
are. Our individuality is partial and restless; the stream of
consciousness that we call "I" is made of shifting elements
that flow from our group and back to our group again. Always we seek to be ourselves and the herd together, not One
against the herd. And we cannot, for the herd itself is split
by struggles, which change in form with the ages: slave against
owner, serf against baron, worker against capitalist and the
myriad complex conflicts that derive from these.

So at high moments, when our life is keenest, striving to lose
itself in wider life beyond us—each in his own way by art, religion, patriotism, love, comradeship or work—we lose ourselves
in something larger. Yet each success is brief and partial as
Beauty, Country, God, the Loved One or the Cause absorbs
us and leads again to conflict with some alien Beauty, Country
or some other God. . . . Not till the human herd that breeds
and forms us wins its oneness, and acts with conscious will to
rule its future, may any man of it find rest.

.   .   .   .

The way out of human loneliness—this was the search that
began for me a lifetime ago in a garden.

CHAPTER II

THE GODS OF THE GARDEN

THE pangs of isolation are brief in healthy childhood. I
swiftly created worlds of my own contriving to make up for
the world from which I had been cast. There were fairy-
worlds told in bed at night to a younger sister; they grew more
complex with the years. There was the burning of Troy
played with a gang of admiring followers who had not read
the Iliad, and so allowed me to improvise as I chose; we burned
Troy and rescued Helen across charred grass of prairie fires.
Somehow I cannot remember being Helen; I seem to have been
a more active figure. I was at least a highly respected and
welcome person in all those worlds.

There was a period, but whether it lasted weeks or months
I cannot recall, when the world I built became continuous with
new structures added nightly in the interval before sleep.
Once when a girl chum spent the night with me, we both admitted in the sheltering dark that we spent long hours in a
quite different world, a much more exciting world than our
ordinary life, but a world of which we would tell nobody.
When after many pledges of mutual disclosure and secrecy,
she admitted that she thought of boys and I that I thought of
heaven, I am not sure which was the more ashamed. I was
younger than she; I had not begun to think of boys. I privately thought her very silly, but I thought myself sillier still
for having told.

In truth it was the same thing we thought about, a wider,
more thrilling life, whose content changed with the years. It
was natural that as a minister's daughter, surrounded by
stage properties of church and Sunday-school, I should have
called it heaven. From the very first I discarded all harps,
crowns and angels, and created a heaven after my own desire.
One could fly anywhere by merely wishing and speak to any-

12

one by merely thinking. It was in short a world of the airplane and radio just before these things existed. It was the adventure of being everywhere and seeing everything and communicating with everybody at once that thrilled my childhood days.

As adolescence deepened, heaven grew more personal. It acquired companionship more intimate and perfect than any-thing afforded by earth. My first contacts with the world outside my home had shown me that by no means everybody loved me. My parents had told me to be good and love everybody, and then everybody would love me. But they didn't; certainly not everybody. Sometimes it was the older girls who plainly didn't want me about; sometimes it was boys. A painful feeling began to grow of being generally not wanted. I felt in terms of great generalities. I wanted everybody to like me; I felt that nobody did. My standards were too demanding; if they were less kind than my mother, I thought they didn't like me at all, and that something was the matter with me.

This absurd feeling recurred unanalyzed for decades, till it was suddenly punctured on my trip through the Pamirs when I was forty years old. I complained to the head of our expedition that the other woman in the party didn't like me and that two of the men seemed to feel me a burden because they had to help me on my horse. "What do you expect," said the genial Professor Nikitin. "If in our party of ten one likes you and two are reasonably friendly and six are indifferent while one dislikes you, isn't that a fair average? That's human society, isn't it?" . . . It is; but I had been led from childhood to expect that if I were good, everybody would like me.

From this haunting feeling of being not wanted, which remained a recurrent haunt through life, I found two ways of escape, both of which in changing form also persisted. One was the invention of gods, the other was personal efficiency in work. My early heaven was commanded to furnish companionship—and did. It offered raptures of thought transference. Words were so difficult; they never gave my exact meaning. How wonderful if one could think and have the exactness of the thought repeated to a loved person far across the world!

I was introduced to a disapproved form of mysticism by a novel of Marie Corelli's *The Romance of Two Worlds*, one of the few books my mother ever prohibited. We hid it under school-books and discussed it with bated breath. Somewhere in the dark past or the dim future, somewhere on a whirling planet in one of the many million solar systems, one had a perfect "soul mate." The chances were clearly against meeting for the next million years, but exceptional souls might sometimes pull their soul-mates down across great voids of ether. We never really believed it, but it was thrilling to imagine soul-mates on Sirius, whom we could summon in dreams.

When high school courses demanded specialization in study, I abandoned soul-mates in favor of "living a thousand lives." It was stupid to be just one person; one person could never do all the interesting things there are to do. I wanted to be a North Pole explorer, and an airman, and a great writer, and a mother of ten—one child wasn't worth the time! There were at least ten lives that I simply had to live, and I knew if I started to think, I could make it a thousand. Yet all these lives must be linked into one person who could know and enjoy them all. I gave it up; it was too complicated.

The organized religious life around me soon took these dreamings and molded them into an approved form of mysticism which lasted many years. God became the Great Companion. There were really two kinds of God, though they had the same name. The one most preached by my elders was a very practical God, who wanted me to be good. I would ask him for strength to do things I thought I ought to do, but I considered myself above the level of those acquaintances who asked him for bicycles and parties. I turned to him to correct my inefficiencies; we were taught to examine our souls for trivial sins. Impoliteness, rough words, slight errors in manners were matters over which to brood; they were important to the universe. Since there were many such matters on which I needed correction I became very friendly with "God."

This first God fitted the moods when I was energetically improving myself and wanted to be sure I would succeed. But there was another God for whom my need was greater. When I was succeeding I could get on alone. But when I felt broken and baffled, in a world where I didn't fit, there was a God so beyond all human understanding, that nothing I did could greatly matter. I might smash; I might go to pieces; but God remained infinite in space. They even told me that this God loved me; he loved everybody, even when they failed. It was very consoling. Even into college years and the first years of working life I escaped from defeats by climbing to a roof under starlight or spreading a golf cape on the snows of the campus, staring at stars till I lost track of time, adoring the universe. Perhaps nobody on earth wanted me; but the universe did. I swung from one of these emotional generalizations to the other, blindly striving to continue that loving world which had surrounded my childhood into the rougher world which asked me to be grown-up. Thus I held on to infancy.

I loved these gods without distinguishing them. I never knew that there had ever lived people to whom religion meant fear. I did not even know what it had meant to my father when he encountered Darwinism in his youth. It seemed to him to conflict with the religion he was preaching, which was based on the Bible. He solved his problem by concentrating on "the ethics of Jesus" and avoiding controversial questions, in the optimistic faith that the "inevitable law of progress" would bring everybody around to Darwin.

By the time I came to conscious thought my father's optimism was justified; this problem had ceased in our surroundings. I lived in a comfortable family in a comfortable suburb —it was now Oak Park, near Chicago—where nobody was very poor. There were thousands of these residential suburbs in American life. In them lived not only the well-to-do, but also people of moderate means, among whom we were classed. "Workers" also lived there, skilled building workers, railwaymen, other skilled trades. No one in these suburbs ever spoke of distinctions of class, but only of good society, into which all were pushing. We didn't see men of the steel towns or textile mills.

In this comfortable suburb all our religions, under names which ranged from Roman Catholic to Christian Science, were really much alike. They were a comfortable religion suited to our class and time. Hell had died out; only uneducated people took the Bible literally, but there were still enough of these uneducated people so that one must not openly and impolitely denounce their views. Our world was going from better to better, guaranteed by an omnipotent God. The exact extent to which he would interfere for individuals, and the ways of accomplishing this, might be matter for debate. But certainly one could always get from him justice and often mercy, and sometimes even prosperity.

The only contact I remember with the terrible gods of the past was a discussion I had with another girl on "the unpardonable sin." This was years earlier; I could not have been more than eight. She posed the intriguing problem whether, if I positively knew I must die within twenty-four hours, I should prefer to get it over at once or wait the whole day. After some thought I replied that I should wait to say good-by to my mother and friends; I was a sociable soul who hoped for tears of farewell. Then she beat me by choosing immediate death, since she didn't think she had yet committed the unpardonable sin, but she might do it if she waited, and then she would go to hell. Neither of us knew what the unpardonable sin was; but she just felt she hadn't committed it. Even the pang I felt at her superior depth of soul could not make that unpardonable sin seem real. My parents had taught me to avoid all such unpleasant things.

So deeply do habits of childhood condition our after days that even today I disbelieve evil that lies right under my eyes. I see it, am horrified by it and then I forget it; my mind will not take it in. I find it difficult to believe in spies and wreckers, even when I see them spying and wrecking; I catch myself always assuming that capitalists and workers wish the same kind of "decent world." I feel it incredible that the world moves towards war, even when I can follow the moves. I slip always into the great American religion that if you think good and expect good, then good will come. Sometimes it does in personal relations; many people hate to disappoint a child. But many others wish to exploit a credulous fool. I learned to live in heaven but not the way to make heaven. It gave me that frame of mind which, multiplied by many millions, enabled whole hosts of youth to slip steadily into the World War, never believing it possible until it killed them.

That indeed was one function of all that opium of my youth, a function my kind parents never knew. It lulled and quieted us for the slaughter; it kept us "good" and polite while the competitive capitalism of our day moved towards imperialism and prepared to kill us.

.   .   .   .

I was still in my early teens when I discovered the poverty of Chicago's west side; I went there to teach sewing in settlement classes. I was told that this poverty was due to ignorance; these people were not yet developed. I never thought of them as a different "class." They were just immigrants from a more backward world who had not yet attained the polished prosperity which America gave. They would go to schools (my sewing classes were such schools) and play in the city playgrounds which Chicago so magnificently built. Then they, or at least their children, would be American like us. Clean, contented, efficient, prosperous was what "American" meant. America was "God's country," a country without classes, the best and freest country in the world.

As I grew somewhat older, some perplexities invaded our home from the trips my mother made to organize women's societies in the southern parts of Illinois. There she saw mining towns, real Americans in some cases who suffered and went on strike. She gave me no details but I remember her depression when she came home on one occasion and said: "There is much injustice in the world; it is hard to understand it. Some people are very hard and greedy and grab much more than their share; they refuse to hear the rights of others. Many people suffer because of them, yet nobody punishes them. You must never, never grab more than your share." I think now that she must have tried to argue with some mine-owner about the condition of the miners and come face to face with a naked capitalism that bewildered her.

I clearly remember about this time—it was in my middle teens—my mother rushed up to a colored woman and embraced her on the street, telling me that this was Molly Church, one of her best-loved classmates from Oberlin College. I showed no great warmth over the introduction; my early love for "the colors" had evaporated under the influence of schoolmates. I had even written a poem for the high school paper, "Remember the *Maine*"; it was the time of the Spanish War and I was on the high road to becoming a young imperialist. As soon as the woman left, my mother reproved me, saying that if I had any feelings against people on account of the color of their skin, these were bad feelings which I must at once overcome. She added that bad people made it very hard for Negroes to get education and equal rights and that when a Negro succeeded in doing it, as her classmate had, she had shown much more courage than I had ever shown or than most white people possessed. She was therefore entitled to special honor. I wished that the classmate might come back that I might show how splendid I now understood her to be.

It was about this time that I read Bellamy's *Looking Backward*. Entranced by this Utopia of the year 2000, which bore marked resemblances to my early heaven, I was also impressed by its economic basis in publicly owned wealth and equal division of goods. I discussed it with my mother, and through her gentle voice the theory of her class and generation answered "Yes, it would be a beautiful world," her voice was also wistful, "but when you understand human nature you will realize that if all goods were divided equally today, inequalities would recur in ten years because some people are abler and more grasping than others. Besides, public ownership has been tried in some cities and is very inefficient. Perhaps some day, when people are better, it can happen."

Like all the women of her generation, even the progressive, educated women, mother knew little about economics or classes, except that there had been classes in Europe. People were all to her individuals, who were entitled to the rewards of income, fame and affection according to their just deserts of efficiency, morality and kindness. Yet she saw that the world was not just; that the grabbing by "bad people" handicapped others. Her remedy was that we must all strive to be just; thus the world would slowly become just, since God was on the side of justice and would help. . . . No, we must be better than just, for our idea of justice might not be enough. We must love people, love the world even when it hurt us. If we loved people, it would be easy to give without thinking too much about return. Then people would love us also. . . .

It certainly never occurred to her that she might be encouraging us to be willingly exploited and to kiss the hand of our oppressor. Nor did her intelligence ever reconcile the different ethical views she gave me. The world had taught her the justice of the honest trader; she herself added the cherishing care of a mother and the courage of a pioneer. These she gave not only to us but to as many individuals as she reached, trying to believe in a human equality which would come some day, she did not guess how—when we were all "good enough."

. . . .

It was after my mother's death that I first questioned my father's religious theories. He had preached a children's sermon on "cheap girls," meaning girls who gave their caresses too easily to boys, without waiting until they were sure they had discovered the chosen one, who would properly prize them. He had preached it earlier in a different city when I was younger and it had impressed me. But now I was in my late teens and I discovered discrepancies in his views.

"I don't think this talk about cheap girls goes well with Christian ethics," I told him. "Jesus tells us to love everybody and to give all we have to the world without questioning the return, and when people injure us we are to forgive 'till seventy times seven.' But now you say girls are to hold back and not give themselves until they are properly prized. I see very well one mustn't be easy with one's kisses. All the same, it would be really more Christian to be 'easy.' It wouldn't be safe to be quite Christian."

My father was worried. "I am only trying to save you from ruin," he answered.

"That's another difference between us," I persisted. "You think there are just two things that can ruin a girl, either an unhappy marriage or a love affair without marriage. Well, I think either of those would be a horrible tragedy but I wouldn't let either of them ruin me permanently. I'd get out of it somehow. I don't think either of them is what the novels call 'worse than death,' for when you are dead, you are finished."

My father shrank from my lightness. Though he had become unusually broad-minded for his generation on the question of divorce and fallen women, for his own family he accepted the view that the first sexual experience of a girl either establishes her or ruins her. He had rejected property marriage with disdain, yet he cherished uncritically the ethics derived from it.

Nor did I myself escape those ethics. In spite of my protest that "nothing a man could do to me could permanently ruin me" I really thought of marriage as the great decisive choice of life which would determine all my future and to which any previous schemes of my own must be sacrificed.

I even chose my future work with reference to its possible subordination in marriage. Writing seemed to me an admirable occupation because it could be done in any part of the world to which my husband might take me, and could even be accomplished in odd moments at home. I tried to avoid having opinions which were too fixed and definite, which might some day have to be changed to fit a married state. I reasoned that I must have some work of my own and save a little money in order to be independent in case I should disagree with my husband, and not be a burden on him in case we happily agreed. If I did all these things then when the master of my fate at last arrived, I should be ready to adapt myself to anything he might demand.

That I really looked on such a future husband as the master of my fate is clear from a conversation I had when I was already twenty with some highly sophisticated members of the

faculty of the University of Chicago. By this time I was going about with older men who were attracted and amused by
my combination of youthful freshness with noticeable brains.
One of them teased me as an "unmastered girl who doesn't
want a master."

"Oh, but I do," I cried. "I want to find someone who will
tell me just what I must do about everything and then I will
do it. I will never have to decide for myself again."

"Good heavens, child," he cried, sobered by the impact of
my feeling. "It isn't a husband you want. You want God."

Yes, it was really a god I wanted, a boss, a master, a parent
who would continue infancy for me. People told me that it
was feminine to want this; and I believed in my soul, a soul
already molded by the emotions of religion into the mood of
adoring dependence, that they were right. Yet against this
mood there warred the contradictory demand for freedom,
which I was winning through the personal efficiency taught in
the schools. My own life, my own work, my own career already threatened to become interesting and to make me less
adaptable, less ready to give them up at the whim of some
male. I reconciled these contradictory cravings for a boss and
for freedom by telling myself that I would not give myself till
I found somebody worth it, somebody sufficiently important
and wonderful so that I should not mind putting all my life
into one parcel and handing it over to him.

The girls of my day discussed the word "obey" in the stricter
forms of church marriage, alternately adoring it and shivering
away from it. Although the changing times caused me to talk
of sex equality and of comradeship in marriage, yet a marriage in which the wife did not "look up" to her husband
seemed to me to lack the authentic emotion. The emotion
which I really sought was not that of equal friendship, but
that of adoration. For decades this unconscious craving alien-
ated the only type of man that my developing conscious personality could really desire.

Thus the traditions around me and the religious emotions
I had cherished prepared me not only to seek a master but to
love and reverence him when discovered. If I should not be

chosen in marriage I was equally well prepared to become the highly skilled and very devoted servant of some man in an office, treating him also as a god whose whims could never be wrong for me. It is the fate of hundreds of thousands of girls prepared as I was. But if I should be chosen in marriage by some man who was not quite god, I was ready with a cloud of ideals with which to enthrone him.

For I clearly remember when President Thomas of Bryn Mawr College told us in college assembly that education was useful to women because, if they did not find happiness in marriage, they would have outside interests. I said to myself, outraged: "What horrible cynicism! Marriage *must* be happy: one must never admit to oneself that it could fail to be happy. One must expect the best; then one will get it."

By all these gods of my youthful garden I was turned out fit for any kind of exploitation. Fit even to like being exploited or at least to pretend to myself till death that I liked it. I was "ready for life" as a well-brought-up girl of pre-war America.

CHAPTER III

THE TOOLS FOR LIFE

WHILE the gods of the garden were preparing my emotions to enjoy or to endure the life which presumably lay ahead, the justly admired efficient schools of America were sharpening in my mind the tools with which I must work to the end of my days. The gentle private school in Cincinnati, whose pupils were almost entirely daughters of the wealthy, continued my family tradition of refinement and kindness, preparing me and the others for the life of a well-to-do woman, from whom good manners are expected, to be rewarded by smiles. But when we moved to Oak Park, a growing suburb of Chicago on the flat, untamed western prairie, and I entered at the age of eleven her excellent high school, I encountered the standardizing process which was to fit me for the struggle of life in real America—America of the developing industrial west.

The chief aim of school for the serious students was to outstrip the others; for the less serious it was to have a good time and get by with bluff. We had marks; we compared them; I shone in these marks. I did not shine in the good times. I was from three to five years younger than the others: the home training and private school had done this for me. Consequently I did not react normally to the teasing approaches of the boys; I got embarrassed, pleased or angry at the wrong times. I was entirely too young to take to dances; I actually deferred to my mother who wouldn't let me go. So I wasn't popular; it hurt me not to be wanted. This route out of loneliness denied me, I found the other: I became efficient, with the highest marks in the class.

The paths of love and work are indeed the twin paths out of loneliness for all generations of men; but always they are conditioned by the environment of class and time. As my surroundings had diverted my hunger for love to invent gods and

23

masters, so they diverted my need for work to the game of "beating the others." I was soon aware that this did not make me at all popular; students of riper age, boys especially, were very much annoyed when the highest marks went to the youngest girl. They even put down my "characteristic" in the publication of the school graduation annual as "I know a trick worth two of that," implying that I always thought I could beat them. Well, I did think so, and I could. If it made me still less popular and led to occasional heart-aches, at least it made me noticed; this recognition grudgingly accorded blunted the edge of loneliness a bit.

I remember once in the class on Roman History we touched the story of the rape of Lucrece. The girls had wondered, shivering, whose task it would be to have to tell that embarrassing tale; they giggled across the room at the boys who knew just why they giggled. The teacher knew also why they giggled; she herself was worried by what might happen in the class during the coming recitation; so she picked me out to see her through. She thought I would handle the story best because I wouldn't understand it; she thought I was too young to know about sex. I was just as embarrassed as the others but I called to my aid an excellent memory and went through the tale of rape in the exact, chaste language of the text-book in which the Tarquin "has his will with her." I was certainly noticed that time, most embarrassingly noticed. Questioning glances passed between the pupils as to whether I really knew what I was talking about. I haughtily ignored them. If I couldn't get through in one way, I could in another. I was becoming efficient.

That indeed was the aim of all our education, which was admirably adapted to its purpose. We were to be turned out energetic and efficient, not especially qualified for any particular work, but eagerly seeking any kind of work available and able to make ourselves fit it. There was also a secondary aim of education—to kill time till we were old enough for work. The rapid improvement in the processes of production in the world around us meant that fewer workers were needed, and especially fewer of the higher qualified administrators and

salesmen which we intended to be. It was therefore desirable
that youth should spend as long as possible in school. I finished high school so early that I spent a year in Germany and
half a year in Switzerland studying languages before I was
considered old enough for college. I studied a year in Bryn
Mawr, graduated in Oberlin and took postgraduate work leading to a doctor's degree in the University of Chicago, partly
because I finished so soon that I wasn't old enough for a good
job. Yet none of all the courses I took was any very exact
preparation for anything I might intend to do. None of us
knew what the world would make us do (we called it "what
we expect to do"). We knew only that we intended to get
ahead in the world. This everyone in America intended. One
got ahead by efficiency.

To supplement efficiency there was bluff. It was even a
form of efficiency; for some it seemed the most important form.
The problems of production in the world around us were
changing to the problems of selling, so the salesman's ability
to put on a good front became important. We were not conscious that this affected us; but it did. A sprightly confident
manner which convinced teachers that we knew more than we
had really mastered, an easy choice of words which made the
most of our small knowledge—these we admired. I was quite
apt in this; it seemed I could almost guess from the teacher's
glance what she wanted, and give it to her at once. Sometimes
I asserted my independence and gave her what I knew she
didn't want, but never in such a way as to lessen my standing.

We slightly disapproved of using bluff to cover an utter
vacuum; that was almost lying, we thought. Yet we had a
sneaking admiration for the clever guys who went through
whole courses without opening a book. They did to illegal
limits what all of us did less daringly. (Thus long afterwards
I found Russian peasants admiring successful thieves.) But
normal bluffing was proper; it was even a virtue. To make a
little learning seem much; to sell ourselves to the world at a
price higher than was justified by the quality of our goods—
this salesman's ethic was our ethic. We called it "making the
most of ourselves." The post-war generation calls it frankly

"selling yourself"; even under this cynical description it remains the ideal.

Those who were most successful came out of the university sharp and polished swords. With no deep knowledge but flourishing well what they had. With no great passion for science but quick to maneuver and keen. With no technical specialty; early specialization was considered bad. It was really bad for our flexibility in a salesman's world which needs to put a good front on everything and know nothing too much. Even today when young Americans come to Moscow they do not know why Russians ask: "What is your specialty—chemistry, mining, literature, metallurgy, art?" Our professors said we should not be practical too soon, but get a varied course on liberal cultures of mankind. But we didn't specialize on old cultures or do even our varied courses well. We really specialized, but not on any course. We specialized on rationalization, personal efficiency, and bluff.

For this great purpose I learned as much from my jobs as from my studies. Most of us did; it was an accepted theory in the western colleges that to earn at least part of one's living while studying was a way of showing practical efficiency which would be later approved in the business world. There was some prejudice against this in those eastern schools which trained the sons and daughters of the well-to-do; I noticed it in Bryn Mawr. But in Oberlin and later in the University of Chicago we had no prejudice against any kind of work. Girls did housework in professors' homes and did not lose caste. Cleverer students sold things during vacations. That we were being prepared to become the kind of easily shifted replaceable part of industry which the growing mechanization of American production demanded did not occur to us.

I came to one decision in Oberlin days which deeply affected my later habits of life. When I saw how easy it was to give one's main attention to education, while earning a living in various odd jobs, I grew contemptuous of those people who, the moment they finished school, used all the rest of their life just making a living. Often they took jobs which they hated in order to pile up dollars. This seemed to me a confession of inefficiency, the more amazing since during their untrained youth they had been freely choosing education, and earning their living as an afterthought. Why did they exchange freedom for slavery? I believed it was their dependence on an increasing standard of comfort and luxury, needing more dollars.

I therefore resolved to keep myself independent by never becoming habituated to a soft standard. I would choose my own path in life and do whatever I found interesting whether it paid me anything in money or not. If necessary I could always earn money at odd jobs; had I not done so in school? It is a method I recommend to other Americans who wish to revert to the frontiersman's ideal of independence. It has given me a vivid life. Carleton Beals followed it into Mexico, refusing a good high school post to roam Indian villages. He said to me: "For an intelligent man in these days it is hard to become a millionaire and equally hard to starve." . . . This ideal of mine was less usual than the prevailing one of heaping up dollars. But in both these aims personal efficiency was the actual ideal.

The first test of my personal efficiency came in the nine months between my undergraduate and graduate studies, when I had a real job. I was invited to become associate editor of the *Advance*, a weekly paper of Protestant fundamentalism in Chicago. The salary was small but the editor warmly assured me it would grow with experience. It seemed a wonderful chance to start on the path of becoming a writer and editor. I had already published a small volume of verse called *Storm Songs;* this offer of a job was the recognition. The *Advance* advertised me to their readers till it seemed I was the coming author of the world. Even for me it was impossible to believe that I was as good as they openly said in print, but I thought I might be some day. I wanted most devotedly to make good to justify their amazing faith.

I therefore wrote tirelessly. Every weekly issue contained fairy tales by me on the children's page, stories on the women's page with a good moral for youth, reports on the Ministers'

Federation and the Women's Church organizations, half a dozen book reviews, an original column called "From a Woman's Window," expressing an ironic feminist viewpoint, and another column of boiled-down items from the press entitled "More About Women." I had four pseudonyms to cover my various kinds of work. I knew that the purpose of this was to bluff our readers into thinking we had a big, expensive staff, but this already seemed to me clever. As for their exploitation of myself, I was only eager to do more work for my salary than anyone else could do; this seemed the road to advancement.

I also wrote poems in many of the numbers. Mystical poems, poems about nature but chiefly poems about the city —"City Lights," "City Comradeship," "The Call of the City," expressing the fascination one felt in this ruthless monster and the joy of being swallowed by thousands of men. I was among those who thus deified the modern city; I was feeling the spirit of the age. I published a thin book of poems, *The Song of the City;* even now I think their technique not bad. Some of them have been copied into revolutionary anthologies, but I had no thought of revolution. It was "City Comradeship" that I expressed. I published also a rather useless short drama, "The King's Palace," describing the shocked idealism of a young girl who sees the world and refuses to enter it— this was after I went back to the university.

I was on my way to becoming a famous writer; not twenty yet and I had published books! I was justifying the faith the *Advance* had had in me; nobody else could possibly have done so much work for them before. So I was the more startled when five months after I had begun they suddenly fired me; the editor said vague things about unsatisfactory work. I took it hard. Not that I cared for the job; it bored me already and I was thinking of going to the university for graduate work. But they cast such a horrible doubt on my estimate of my own competence; if I hadn't that, I had nothing left.

The business manager was kinder than the editor. Observing my demoralized spirits in that last month after notice was given he quietly said: "Don't tell the editor I told you. It's the old man's habit to take on a new associate each autumn and give them a terrific boost so as to get subscription renewals for the winter. By March the subscription campaign is over and he chucks the associate out. It saves half a year of salary and gets the first energy of youth. He's making a mistake on you; I told him so. You write so much that you more than save your salary on contributors. But the old man's got the habit."

I did not pause to generalize on this horrible rape of youth, rousing devoted loyalty and taking the bloom and throwing them out—deflowered. Awakening self-confidence and then killing it—that still seems to me the worst. Sexual rape could not have been more cruel. I never thought of attributing it to a social system. It was just—a rotten old man. But my chief feeling was relief in learning that I hadn't been doing bad work. I had thought I could write; now I knew it. The business manager admitted that I wrote more than anybody else had done. This gave me strength again. But I also had learned that writing alone did not satisfy me; after a certain time I grew restless and wanted to act. Thus I was already in my first job after college; thus I have always been.

I returned to the university partly because it seemed the easiest thing to do, and partly because it "saved my face" in the loss of my job on the *Advance*. The ruin which that editor must have spread annually among young graduates who had no university to which to return and who had to seek another job with one expulsion behind them, still seems to me appalling. I had a way of escape; scholarships paying at least my tuition were an easy thing for a student of my record to obtain. I would work my way through to a graduate degree. It was as easy as hunting a job and distinctly more honorable. It should lead to a better job later; just what kind I did not know.

I decided to specialize in philosophy chiefly because I had liked the religious emotions which accompanied that subject in Oberlin, where one got the sense of discovering an infinite world. After the first six months of the dry philosophy of the University of Chicago, with its logic and theory of knowledge, I knew that I hated it. Nevertheless I stuck; I was growing alarmed at my frequent shifting from school to school and from school to jobs. I wanted to prove to myself and the world that I could stick to something. This was the form my personal efficiency took; it led me even to do away with bluff. A doctorate of philosophy was a sure proof of efficiency; nobody could call you shallow after that. So I worked my brain till I could feel it ache, twisting around new problems which seemed to me to have no connection with life.

Gradually I observed that each professor, after the dry dust of the earlier part of the course, would come to the philosophy in which he himself really believed. Then his eyes would glow, his words would become less cautious and more fervent, and I would catch a glimpse of that same religious emotion that had thrilled me in Oberlin. With one it was a theory of ethics, with another it was social psychology, with a third it was art as the unifier of those divisions which logic engendered. I also perceived that logic divided them all into different theories, but that in this sudden emotion about the universe they were all akin. So I shared this emotion every time one of them had it; I enjoyed it. For a few days I let myself believe as he did; the professor would catch my glowing eyes and rejoice in his convert. But I was already aware that the next professor would just as easily prove the opposite. This debauch of emotions was called "learning to look on all sides of a question"; it has its uses in a laboratory when nothing is yet proved. It is, however, a deadly quality in a battle. It was sharpening my mind to cut round and round inside itself, yet to avoid any final decision which might hew a path through life.

Meantime my jobs taught me something more useful. I supported myself by a dozen kinds of work: typing, tutoring young students, making college pennants. This forced me to rationalize my time. I usually carried a heavy program of studies; four instead of the ordinary three. I took my degree of doctor of philosophy in two and a half years instead of three. During this time I not only supported myself but at times lived an hour's ride away on the West Side of Chicago where my father did settlement work.

I did it by careful planning of every ounce of strength. My most energetic hours of early morning must go to Kant's *Critique of Pure Reason*, or whatever was my heaviest course. By doing the hardest work when I was fittest, I cut down the needed time. Less vigorous hours went to my English courses; they didn't need such a clear head. Only when I was already tired would I turn to typing, choosing jobs of copy-work at home. When I was too exhausted to type correctly I made and sold college pennants.

I rationalized also my making of pennants. By making many at once and modifying the design to use all material to best advantage, I cut the cost one half. By division of labor— cutting them all first, then drawing and cutting all the letters, then basting them all, then sewing them all, I cut the cost again. I learned to make banners so rapidly that I earned on them a dollar and a half an hour. I figured that making banners paid better than any of the other work I was doing—provided I sold the banners. But since I might not sell them all, I must have other lines. I also discovered that the speed I put on banners would exhaust me if I did it too many hours. I therefore decided that variety of work was better, in order to "get the most out of myself."

Thus I became personally efficient—the highest characteristic known to any American. This rationalization was in the air I breathed. I did it better than many; I had health and a good brain. But all of us did it somewhat, except those who wasted themselves in dissipation. The serious students had a horror of waste. Waste was the devil; efficiency was God. By efficiency one got ahead in the world. That there might exist on earth other peoples who had other gods than these, old dynasties who prefer gaudiness to efficiency, old aristocracies who exalt leisure above work, many-millioned peasant peoples who never rationalize their time, never entered our young minds. That there might arise other people who would think in other terms than every individual shoving himself ahead

forever—this also we could not dream. We were fitting ourselves to get ahead in prewar America. That was the world to
us, the world as it had been and would be.

I came to my last year of graduate study and took as subject for the thesis on which the granting of my degree of doctor
of philosophy depended "A Study of Prayer from the Standpoint of Social Psychology." This emotional material attracted me. For a whole year I read and classified the devo-
tional literature of the centuries. It was characteristic of the
liberal theology around me that religion should not fear
science. I gave theoretical form to that difference in gods I
had felt for years, and classified prayers into "esthetic prayers" of the Christian mystics and the Buddhists, who seek ob-
livion in the infinite, and "practical prayers" in which more
energetic people use God to get anything from a job to moral
strength. I related these two forms of prayer to basic needs of
the human soul—the need to forget despair, more felt by the
contemplative peoples of the east, and the need for assistance in
work, felt by the practical peoples of the west. It never occurred to me that it was the suppressed peoples who tried to
forget despair, and the imperialist peoples who asked God's
blessing on their work. The thesis was published as a book by
the University of Chicago Press.

So I took my degree as doctor of philosophy. My subject
was so interesting that the university revived an unusual tradition and made me "defend my thesis" before the combined
philosophical and theological faculties of Chicago University.
Three hours of such argument before such people was no easy
task for a girl of twenty-three. I worked my brain with great
pressure and won my degree *magna cum laude*, analyzing and
proving the derivation of various forms of prayer from the
savage fetish to the Buddhist prayer-wheel. I was the youngest student to have taken such a degree from Chicago.

Then I left the lecture hall and grabbed my golf cape and
rushed to an open square of darkness on the "Midway" to
throw myself down on the snow. I dug my face into the cold,
white softness till I reached the buried grass, and I turned and

threw a kiss to the stars. "You Loveliness," I cried. "I've been proving the funniest things about you. I hope you enjoyed that nice debate." I felt a little worried lest I find my stars receding, lest God might be annoyed at the impertinent freedom with which I had "had to" treat him to win that discussion. So I put a good face on it—bluffing God!

This was what the efficient American universities had made of that lonely girl in a garden. Her parents made her fearless and independent, yet wanting to win love by being good. Her gods made her a seeker for masters whom she was ready to serve and adore. Now her education made of her mind an efficient two-edged tool, able to cut in any direction but not to choose a direction. She was now really a high-priced article worth a good salary; not only her highly rationalized labor power but her sharpened mind and emotional soul were fit implements for a dozen well-paid purposes of capitalism. She could believe almost anything emotionally and induce you to believe it; she could disprove it, disbelieve it, and believe it again. She was fit to become a salesman fervently praising any products, or a lawyer-politician convincingly pleading any cause, or a writer juggling words in any direction, or a social worker curing sores and forever hiding from herself the causes, or a teacher of "truth" through philosophy. All such jobs were open to her. But would she ever herself know for ten days consecutively what she herself believed?

If she had said that beneath all this complexity there was still a lonely girl who passionately wanted not only to be "good" and to be loved, but even to know and serve the "truth" so that at the end of life she should not have lived in vain, would you not be right in laughing? Would you not be wise in scanning suspiciously anything she might ever say again? An industrial worker might try to deceive you but he would not easily be able, but we trained intellectuals, even without trying, bluff both ourselves and our gods.

I was vaguely aware of a faint inconsistency as I analyzed God and then adored him. But even for this I had my answer pat. "Reality is apprehended both through the contradictions of logic and the unity of the esthetic emotion!" . . . There, what is there wrong with that? . . . But I was conscious chiefly of a great relief to be "through with philosophy" and to feel the earth and the stars draw near. I lay in the snow long after I began to shiver, finding in the aching cold a tonic from the heat of lecture halls. I felt no love for the philosophy on which I had ground my mind for two and a half years to prove that I could do it, and which I had now triumphantly conquered: I hated it. To this day I have never willingly opened a book on philosophy.

Twenty-three, older than men who died in the trenches during the whole World War. Older than Chinese students who overthrew cabinets, or German youth who are killed for opposing Hitler, or Soviet youth that made the revolution and build socialism today. The age which, having made the physical adjustments of adolescence, has had for years the fresh explosive power and daring allegiance which shatter and build worlds. In America they confine this power by barriers of dreams in gardens or divert its punch into football matches lest it wreck the system which does not want it. They call it protecting youth a little longer from the world's roughness. Is it not rather protecting their world a little longer from the rough demands of youth?

These were the characteristics I brought with me out of the garden where the custom of my class and time confined me until the age of twenty-three:

Loneliness and a great wish to escape it;
Pride in personal efficiency as my right to existence;
Hunger for a world where I might create and be wanted;
An agile brain and skill in words which could bluff myself as well as others and make brief worlds to my taste if I did not find them.

In creating these private worlds I was led by vague beliefs derived from my early religions: belief that my emotions were important to the universe, alternating with the sick sense that they were important to no one; belief that by pretending good and wishing good I could make good appear; faith that inevitable progress would somehow save me.

Note well these characteristics and beliefs. You have seen them before; you will see them again. They have conditioned all my days.

CHAPTER IV

I DISCOVER THE WORLD

ONE's first responsible job is the great revealer—far more than school.

After taking my doctor's degree in Chicago I went home to Seattle (my father had moved to that city) and invented with him the idea of "Know Your City" Institutes. We had lectures and discussions on civic institutions, followed by excursions. These grew popular in the far west country where citizens were newly arrived and had begun to be city-conscious. But the first serious challenge to my personal efficiency came in the New York Child Welfare Exhibit, a vast, chaotic attempt to show all forces in the city which affect the welfare of the child. Its organizer was a dreamer who conceived but could not put it through. During long reorganizations the efficient ones came to the top. I began in a minor capacity but was asked to remain as secretary of the administration, which consisted of the new director and myself. Our job was to put the whole thing over. We did it. I rode on top of the whirling world.

Then I began to notice subtle changes. The director who first introduced me as "my associate" began to speak of me as "my secretary" and at last ceased to introduce me at all. I felt myself slipping. I had no time to analyze the causes; we were all so hard at work. Part of it seemed to be the jealousy of the director's wife; part clearly came from an old man in a small job who envied my success and who hurt the whole exhibit through me.

This glimpse of the cause did not help me. Was that old man cleverer than I? Surely not. Then why could he destroy me by his oddly inefficient acts? I began to worry about my working efficiency; it was almost a harder blow than when, a few months earlier, I had fallen in love with a married man and had a nervous breakdown from the strain of repelling him. That was just a ghastly accident that might happen to anyone; but my personal efficiency was the law by which I had permit to exist. Whoever attacked that took away my right to life. It is this that kills the courage of America's unemployed.

Through all my after years I remembered the wise, kind words of Leonard Ayres, whom I had met in a previous job with the Russell Sage Foundation. He understood my predicament and took me out to lunch. "I'll tell you how you can stop any man who undermines your position," he said. "You are clever enough to do it, but I think you won't."

I sensed in the words a challenge. "Just tell me how," I cried.

"In every great job," he said slowly, "when hundreds are honestly at work, it is always possible for one petty man to cause considerable wrecking, far more than his ability would indicate. It is usually some man who knows himself a failure, and slakes the malice of his ego by hurting those who succeed. He sits back, studies the organization that is working, and sees just where to pull wires. Then he pulls them; one little wire here, one there. And the hundreds of honest workers, who haven't time to study those wires, feel jerked out of position; they function inaccurately; the whole machine works badly."

"Yes, yes," I cried, "you describe it exactly. How do I beat him?"

"All you need to do," said Ayres, "is also to sit back and study the wires, and spend your time watching him pull them. Then you can pull other wires. You can beat him; you are more intelligent than he."

"But the work wouldn't get done," I almost shouted in dismay.

"No," he smiled, "the work wouldn't get done."

"But I couldn't do that," I cried.

"I told you you wouldn't," he smiled. "But now you know what you are doing. It is one of the first choices anyone who organizes has to make."

Those words I have kept in mind for twenty-five years. Ayres was a great educator: he taught me in the New York

Child Welfare Exhibit the law by which I was to understand the vast wrecking in Soviet Russia in later years. "Men who know they have failed, and slake the malice of their ego by hurting those who succeed." Sometimes one must stop productive work altogether to root out wreckers; it was done in the Russian civil war; sometimes one must ignore them to push through the slightly twisted work. Sometimes one must have men who specialize in finding and checking wreckers, and who thereby injure their own chances for comradeship in production. Always one must analyze one's choice and understand it.

In New York and Chicago Child Welfare Exhibits I was secretary or associate; in Kansas City I was for the first time director. I came at the beginning; I helped the organization take form. It came into being, as New York had not done, and as Chicago had only partly done, in a new democratic form determined by my traditions and those of Kansas City—traditions of the pioneer west. Starting with chaos I formed committees on health, housing, education, play, child labor—every subject connected with childhood. I tried to find out in the committees what was the dream of each member's life, what he really most desired to do for the city's children, the desire that he had forgotten for years under a mass of angry detail. When he got this out, I helped express it by photograph, chart and model; people grew enthusiastic, committees grew enthusiastic. Rapidly in each committee a program for children appeared, a plan on health, on housing, on education, on play, on the fighting of child labor, on mothers' pensions and minimum wage.

Slowly at first, then ever faster and faster, from chaos this collective plan took form. Then we aroused Kansas City behind it. Charts, exhibits, demonstrations, thousands of children displaying gymnastic feats and folk dances drew thousands of interested parents. Through the greatest building in the city there passed in a week a hundred thousand people, all with a great desire for improving the children's life. It startled the city politicians; they began to take seriously the dozen or more laws, reforms, new institutions we advocated. It was what we call in America "the power of public opinion."

How much was real power and how much was organized bluff it is hard to tell at this distance. It certainly bluffed the politicians into voting funds for several institutions and passing several new laws.

I was in the center of this whirling life; I was making the whole organism run smoothly. I shifted a man to a committee where he could function more harmoniously; I helped a woman express the best thought of her soul in effective words, till it seemed I could feel the pulse of Kansas City to its furthest suburbs, as far as it was concerned with children, throbbing through my pulse and helped to expression by me.

It was then I said one evening to Ruth White, a girl in her twenties like me, who ran the "Standards of Living and Minimum Wage Committee" and had become my closest friend: "There isn't any God now; but there's going to be one. If you mean by God something so far above us that he is the Great Unknowable, then it doesn't pay even to think about what you never can know. He's out of our world and no more to be considered than the comet that may some day crash the earth. Unknowable things may hit us some day and finish us, but we plan our lives without reference to comets.

"But if you mean by 'God' a consciousness anything like ours, which understands and takes account of every person and directs them to the best good of all—then it's perfectly clear that we don't have anything like that in the world. But the world *could* be run that way! Bit by bit we human beings will make such a super-consciousness. We will make it as we made the exhibit in Kansas City, drawing out the deepest wills of people for joint purposes and fitting them all together, till more and more people feel more and more of the world, and think it and plan it. Some time we'll get a combination of consciousnesses that will take account of everybody and have everybody's power to use for the best good of all. That will be a God worth having; but such a God doesn't exist today."

Thus I discovered the world in the Child Welfare Exhibit of Kansas City, in 1911. I saw it forever after in terms of my first responsible job. The very same week I discovered socialism.

I had known the word socialism from my brief youthful dream inspired by Bellamy's *Looking Backward*. But now in Kansas City I came to socialism backward as an employer of labor. The architectural draftsman who helped draw plans for the booths and central court of our exhibit came to me in the midst of the crowds of the opening and asked how much longer we would need him. . . . "Not that I want to leave but I ought to know. As far as I can see, there's nothing for me to do after Saturday."

"No, there's nothing after Saturday," I answered. Actually his work was already over; I was giving him the grace of an extra week. It was one of the forgotten details of the opening.

That night I found it was not forgotten. We motor-minded people know moments that seem turning-points; when waters that have slowly gathered behind a dam, unnoticed, reach the top and break over to a new channel. That night was such a time for me. Joyously weary with the opening, I could not sleep. The words of the draftsman came back in their full meaning. I knew he had a wife and two small children and had been without a job for months. I knew the prospects for his future work were poor. How did it chance that I, a girl in my twenties and in no way related to this man, had the power to refuse him the right to a living? His wife, his babies had nothing to say about it; but I, an outsider, had. What monstrous thing was this?

Hour after hour through a sleepless night I traced it back, calmly, unemotionally, till I saw how the capitalist world is organized. I couldn't give the man a job; I had my "duty to the budget." My committee couldn't give him a job; our exhibit was over. Who could give him a job? I looked for that job for him—a sure job for him and for everybody willing to work—through the entire United States, through the whole world. It didn't exist. The world was horrible chaos, insecure. Not one of the reforms I had ever been told about would fix it; I tried them all that night. The only remedy would be a world quite differently organized, where work and jobs and wages were public matters, and everything that conditioned them was publicly owned, where society organized assignment of work and cut everybody's hours to fit work and looked after all workers, and all children learning to work and all old people after their work was done. That was common sense; it was efficiency; it was abolition of chaos and waste. I knew enough to know that such a society was called socialism, and that I must be a socialist.

Thus I came to condemn capitalism, not through any oppression endured by me personally, but through that very deification of efficiency which capitalism had taught me, for its own purposes. It is a road not understood, a road which must be studied, for many more will arrive by this road. Just as the mass production of capitalism prepares the organized working class which conquers capitalism, so the standards of efficiency which capitalism sets up in the minds of technical men and administrators lead many of them to condemn capitalism in the end. But when I took that road, it was neither charted nor acknowledged.

I rushed to Ruth White next day with my discovery. I learned that she had discovered the same on a trip to Madison from which she had just returned. She had told her friends the conditions she had found among working girls in Kansas City and they had reproved her: "You talk just like a socialist." . . . Suddenly, with a great lift of heart, she knew she was one and told them that she was.

Never had we felt so happy as we did in the next few days. Ruth and I had discovered what to do with our lives; we must spend them making socialism come true. Why did so few people think of it, when it was so very clear? After the first days of ecstasy we looked around for other socialists to join; we must get together with others to reorganize the world. We knew there were socialists somewhere in Kansas City, but the only person we had ever heard mention socialism was Dante Barton on the Kansas City *Star*, reputed to be a socialist who made compromises for a living.

We went to Dante Barton to ask him where to join. He looked at us quizzically, savoring our young enthusiasm. I still remember how the western sun came through his window

on the high floor on that decisive day. "Socialists, are you?
Believe in the class struggle?"

Can anyone in Europe or in the Soviet Union believe that
we answered blankly: "Class struggle? What's that?"

I had been through a university, taken a doctorate in philosophy, lived in a social settlement and organized two years for
reform, yet I didn't know what Dante Barton meant. Such
was American university life in those days that it insulated
me almost completely from such conceptions. If I had ever
heard of Marx at all, the whole set-up of my student life was
arranged to make me minimize and forget him. They did not
argue against him; they merely ignored him. If I ever had
heard of the Paris Commune it can only have been by vague
references to riots at the end of the Franco-German War of
1870-71; even years later when I heard of it in Russia, I
thought they were talking of the French Revolution. Not
only college but all American middle class life was thus protected against knowledge. I may have heard of socialism on
the west side of Chicago; but if so, it passed lightly over an
already insulated surface.

When Dante Barton told us what class struggle meant, of
course we didn't believe it. It seemed a monstrous thing. We
had found out how to organize a good world; we wanted to
proclaim it high and low. We wanted to join all others who
agreed, and help explain things to the world. Why should
anybody oppose us? Who would want to live in the rotten
world of capitalism if he knew of a better? Maybe a few
grasping "bad men," and a few natural wreckers like the man
who thwarted organization in New York. But they would be
easily handled.

But class struggle? Going out to organize workers to hate
—and maybe kill? How could we, born as we were, brought
up as we were, believe in that?

Dante Barton told us no Socialist Party would let us in.
He told us this class struggle was keeping "lots of people
out." He said the chief discussion in the Socialist Party was
how literal and bloody this class struggle was: whether it
only meant strikes and political fighting; or whether it meant

armed uprising. The more he said, the more we were appalled. Even the mildest socialism meant struggle, not just reorganizing the world.

We made one last attempt. We got from Dante Barton the address of the Socialist Party headquarters and went to find it—a rather dirty room on a back street, full of spittoons and dust and papers. We talked to a pale-faced man of a type we had never dealt with, who sat at his desk in soiled shirt-sleeves and spat tobacco. None the less there was something about him that impressed us—a wistful, dogged persistence. By day he worked in a printing-shop, by night he ran this office. He was clearly working himself ill for this socialism we believed in. But he didn't seem very hopeful either of us or of anyone. We got no response to our simple plan of explaining things to the world.

He was polite and patient. But he told us our place. It was outside the Socialist Party among the useless ones who must be overthrown. We were not at all cheered by the fate he offered. The world where we made investigations and ran Child Welfare Exhibits, and were grown-ups with jobs instead of rejected children, seemed—with all its shortcomings—better.

There were experiences in my own job that might have shown me class struggle, if I had known how to understand. A bit of enlightenment came once from Leonard Ayres. I was running a Child Welfare Exhibit in Louisville when he stopped on his way through to give me a warning. He began in his quizzical style when we were half through dinner.

"I have bad news for you—they are noticing your exhibits in New York." I smiled; I was happy to know it; "bad news" was just his joke.

"Yes, the Russell Sage Foundation is starting a Department of Surveys to standardize the social investigations of the country, and in view of the wide interest aroused by these Child Welfare Exhibits, they have decided to include them too. The new 'Department of Surveys and Exhibits' is organized."

"What a fine idea," I exclaimed. "We can do it on a wider scale."

"I don't think you quite realize," continued Ayres with a

smile, "how you're getting people stirred up. Did you know
that exhibit of Ruth White's on minimum wage is the first time
minimum wage for women has been advocated in public—outside small committees of socialists? You are rather chaotic:
one city wants minimum wages, and one wants mothers' pensions and a third wants something else. They get excited about
it. They are getting out of control. For they're not always
advocating the correct things. The Sage Foundation, for instance, doesn't believe in mothers' pensions or minimum wages
for women." . . . Again he eyed me, to see if I understood.

"How fine to have help," I declared, "from a central organization. Already I manage to pass the best ideas of one city to
the next. I tell them in Louisville what Kansas City wanted;
sometimes they want it too. Sometimes they are too backward
to want it, but have good ideas of their own. A central organization can be a reservoir of all the best ideas and push them
all, with much more authority than I can."

Leonard Ayres leaned back to look at me. "That isn't quite
the idea," he said. What was the menace that lurked behind
his smile? "They think the local people should be told what
to want." There was grimness in that word "told."

"You can't quite tell them what to want," I answered. "You
would know that if you worked in the cities. You can tell them
what Kansas City wanted and how she got it; you can tell them
about a dozen places and who succeeds the best. But when
you've told all this, if they don't want it, you have to drop it,
and let them want something else. Unless they know what they
want themselves, they'll forget it as soon as you leave the city,
and nothing will be done. So it's better to let them demand
in the exhibit the things they are ready to fight for, if these
lead in the right direction, than the most advanced ideas New
York can think of." It was the first time I had so clearly
formulated my work.

"It might not be the most advanced ideas," said Ayres, mus-
ingly. "Sound and proper ideas, put up on standard charts
and sent around to cities, with an organizer from the central
office to fit a few local charts into the scheme. It will be ad-

vertised as much less expensive than your present method; that
will make it the coming form."

"But the life will die out of it," I said, dismayed. "The
local people will create nothing."

"Yes, the life will die out of it," he nodded. "That was
what I stopped in Louisville to tell you. And also this. . . .
You will be offered a chance to be one of their organizers, rec-
ommended by them to cities that apply. They might even give
you a continuous salary, more than you are sure of now. They
would charge the cities for your services. Between assignments on which they sent you, you would stay in New York and
study exhibit methods and learn the proper things for local
cities to think."

"Dependent on New York to suppress the local cities, and
not on the local cities whose life I try to express?" I cried in
horror. I saw it now. Leonard Ayres nodded. "That," he
smiled, "is what I stopped in Louisville to say."

I have often wondered at Leonard Ayres' kindness in stopping in Louisville to tell me that. He was a man I always
liked to talk with, but in no sense were we intimate friends.
Was it the flair of an old educator, guarding young life? Or
had he himself had early aspirations and found himself
trapped? He was then holding a high post in the Sage Foundation; he later went from educator to statistician and thence
to banker—a big name in the capitalist world. But he understood the person I was, and he stopped in Louisville to warn
me, that my choices might be clear.

From this personal experience I might have deduced class
struggle if I had not been long trained to think in other terms.
I merely deduced—as we westerners usually did, that "New
York was trying to hog things," and that I would remain independent. I was glad that I had always adopted a standard of
living which was so far below my income that I could stand a
big drop in engagements. This would make me independent
in any boycott by New York. It did; I remained independent
and hardly observed that even in my independence the life of
exhibits died out. More and more even I was sent for not to
arouse new cities to democratic planning, but to give good

technical form to old ideas. Certainly this was the case when I was invited to Ireland, not by a great city, but by Lady Aberdeen. But even in America my exhibits seemed to lose vitality; I thought I was growing stale. The democracy of the West, the initiative of the frontier life was dying; the exhibits that expressed it died too. I thought myself still independent when I took a post as exhibit expert with the Children's Bureau in Washington, to create standard exhibits of Child Health. I only vaguely realized that I was choosing between the two remaining bosses; there was no room for independents left.

During all these years, as I followed my job from city to city, and even across the sea to the viceregal lodge in Dublin (where I also wrote a booklet on "Home Rule" and a war song for "Irish Volunteers"), and back to a post in Washington, while I became known as chief specialist on child welfare exhibitions, I knew in recurring flashes of pain that the quest of my soul was defeated. I had seen capitalism as a horrible way of organizing the world; I had decided to spend the rest of my life making socialism come true; and the socialists wouldn't let me. I consoled myself that my work for children was of permanent use, since even under socialism cities must organize child care. I cheered myself with the sense of new cities coming briefly to organized life; this must be part of socialism too. I remember I explained this on the steamer on my way to Ireland to an amazed man who had no interest in socialism and no idea why a successful exhibitor invited to put on a health exhibit by Lady Aberdeen, wife of the viceroy of Ireland, should need consolation.

I was as much alone and shut out of the bright world I had found as I had been that day long past by lilac trees in a garden. From those others who had cornered socialism I was separated—by a flaming sword!

CHAPTER V

I LOSE "MY AMERICA"

It was not I who found the class struggle at last, but the class struggle which found me—as it found steadily during the first fifteen years of our century more and more Americans, who saw their country change from a land of "free and equal" colonists on an advancing frontier to the greatest imperial power on earth. What the Spanish War began the World War accomplished: America became the world's banker, and ceased to be the world's pioneer!

Gone were the days when a round copper cent for licorice drops was counted a childhood treat, when laborers got a dollar a day and hoped to be millionaires, when energetic millions of earth's dispossessed flooded through Ellis Island to be welcomed, exploited and Americanized in the melting pot of the world. Earth's most efficient industries rushed into being, based on great natural riches and created by the mixing genius of energetic sons from all the tribes of earth. Increasing goods piled up, creating new problems. The ideals of youth shifted from the frontiersman to the great industrialist, last of all to the supersalesman. More and more products on the one hand, fewer jobs on the other.

The fight for the treasure trove of forests and mines swiftly created alignments among the pioneer folk. Not the class lines which had barred me from the socialist fold, but a fight between the "people" and the "interests" who robbed them. Great titans, railway kings and lumber barons seized public wealth, and common citizens found their rights too circumscribed. We ordinary folk of Seattle, striving for parks, playgrounds, swimming resorts to make our city fit for Americans to live in, found the shores of our lakes and of Puget Sound held on perpetual franchise by the twin railroads of Jim Hill. Our new struggling industries, fighting to compete with other

47

towns, were strangled by the high rates which the Seattle Electric, our hated local "octopus," charged for light and power.

Similar fights marked the entire life of the developing American West. The popular novels of the period reflected these struggles. The hero was some valiant independent whose energetic daring used every legal, and sometimes a few illegal, means to overcome the octopus—the powerful villain financed from New York. The hero always won, but whether he later himself became an octopus, the story didn't tell; it ended discreetly, as the sex fiction of the time also did, at the altar.

I came to Seattle during the early years of the World War, while the peoples of Europe writhed in the agony of new forms of death, and America stood aloof. My father had gone there earlier, during my last year of graduate work in Chicago; my mother was long since dead. I had been organizing Child Welfare Exhibits around the country for years. But the exhibits were becoming standardized under the U. S. Children's Bureau and the Russell Sage Foundation, which told the folk of the provinces what to believe. The thrill of feeling a whole community come into organized life was gone. I ran one last exhibit of the U. S. Children's Bureau at the Panama Pacific Exposition in San Francisco in 1915, organized an "exhibit-investigation" of "Children's Interests" in Portland, Oregon, where children displayed toys, pets and hobbies, and then refused to return to the deadening life of Washington, D. C.

On the Pacific Coast to which my job had taken me, I had found a new solace for human isolation—the companionship of the hills. Long hikes on Tamalpais from San Francisco were followed in Portland by trips with the Mazamas, a mountaineering organization which conquered the tangled jungles of western forests and climbed the glaciers of Mt. Hood. This new-found wilderness became for me a passion; I began to seek more and more difficult climbs, new peaks to conquer. I organized in November the first winter climb of Mt. Hood, in which we four participants were all but swept away in an unexpected blizzard. All night under a starless sky we felt our way downward while storm clouds darkened the upper air and swept the peak which we had quitted just in time.

On our return to Portland less venturesome members of the Mazamas berated us for the foolhardy risking of lives. "If there had been a scientific end to be gained! What did you go for? Just a record!" I retorted that we had at least found out whether the upper slopes were snow or ice in winter, which had not been known before. But this was not the reason that had driven me. How could I explain that ecstasy that arose out of physical pain and exhaustion which the human will subdued, that new mysticism of the adventurer, conquering the unconquerable forces of desolate nature. The expanding social life which I had felt in Child Welfare Exhibits, and which I had first called "making God," and later a "part of socialism," had died inexplicably and left me again in isolation. Now I embraced isolation and called it freedom, as my forefathers did through a long line of pioneers. I loved these savage wastes which the strength of my youth could conquer, and from which I wrung far vistas of blinding beauty; the knowledge that advancing age or weakness must in the end betray me to a death on some cliff or glacier only added to the fascination of these dark gods of nature. For the next five years this was my new form of opium.

Love of the western mountains added to a belated sense of duty to my father made me decide to settle in Seattle. I had saved adequate funds from several years of exhibits, where my intention of independence kept me living on about one-half my very adequate salary. I had the confident belief of the unbeaten pioneer that I could always find myself a job if I should need one. Meantime I would keep house for my father and take part in Seattle's growing life.

The Seattle to which I came in the second year of the World War rated as a progressive city. The populace invariably voted against the "reactionary interests" who represented capital imported from New York. There were two organizations of business men. The Chamber of Commerce was composed of big business, the "interests," by which we meant the great timber and power companies. There was also a cheerfully democratic Commercial Club, of the young and progressive business men. They organized excursions and beach parties and clam-bakes to get acquainted with the surrounding farmers; together with these farmers they demanded municipal ownership of docks, warehouses, power, street cars, in order that independent business and farming might thrive under the shelter of cheap and benevolent public utilities. They were supported in these demands by the equally progressive Central Labor Council, the delegate body representing the trade unions of the city, whose slogan was a city of high wages and sound homes.

In every hard election fight, when the populace was really aroused, it was certain to beat the interests. Other cities might settle down under corrupt government, but not we. Political candidates always refused endorsement from the Chamber of Commerce and from its spokesman the Seattle *Times;* to accept financial contributions from the interests was a sure path to defeat. The population of young business men and respectable American skilled workers achieved one venture of municipal ownership after another; City Light was successfully competing with the power trust, the municipally owned docks were out-distancing in spectacular size the privately owned docks. Seattle was becoming a paradise of public ownership, visited by delegations from other cities.

Yet somehow, in spite of all the progressive victories, the Seattle Electric, alias the power trust, still flourished, and was even making money. One began to hear that Seattle Electric cheerfully left to City Light the costly task of lighting the far-flung homes of citizens, scattered over a hundred square miles of hills, which publicly owned City Light could not refuse; while Seattle Electric took the juicy central industries, selling them power at a price mutually agreeable. The big municipal docks had to handle farmers' perishable products at cost and insure them against waste, while the private docks picked the profitable customers. When after repeated fights the progressives won the city street cars, the price in city bonds paid for the old street railways gave the former owners more than they could have hoped to make by retaining the properties in the rapidly dawning era of motor cars and busses. But still the progressive citizens of Seattle kept struggling, saying that "eternal vigilance is the price of liberty," and hoping that by everlasting attention they could find public servants who for a few thousand dollars in salary would be as clever as private firms that had millions at stake. We found a few such public servants, but not enough to matter.

The progressive forces asked me to run for the School Board; for many years they had wished to have a woman on that board, which had been for two decades a self-perpetuating committee of bankers and business men. The chief plank in our platform was the wider use of school buildings for all sorts of public meetings, a demand close to the heart of all small clubs, societies, coöperative organizations, liberal and radical associations, which wished a respectable and inexpensive place in which to meet.

Fresh from my work with the U. S. Children's Bureau, with the degree of doctor of philosophy and two or three books to my credit, I was easily the most acceptable candidate in town. University clubs supported "a really educated woman against those self-made men of business." Labor organizations supported "schools run by teachers and mothers, instead of by capitalists." I was not a little helped by the wide popularity of my father. He had induced the Ministers' Federation to exchange fraternal delegates with organized labor, and had supported certain local strikes. The school election was at that time a sleepy affair attended by a few citizens and usually controlled by the self-perpetuating board through their pressure on the teachers. I easily captured the election.

We progressives were elated; we had elected a woman to the School Board for the first time in twenty years; we had beaten the interests. The interests were indeed distinctly annoyed at our temerity in thrusting an unwanted newcomer into their well-oiled School Board; they remembered it against me for the future. But they were not seriously worried, for I was only one member in five. The others allowed me, as a courtesy to a new member, to put through in modified form a resolution for the wider use of school buildings by all sorts of citizens' meet-

ings. Once by judicious use of publicity I succeeded in stopping the use of our high schools to recruit under-age volunteers for the war. Otherwise the machine rolled over me
weekly, voting appropriations for matters about which I understood little. Questions of education they never dealt with;
they referred them to the superintendent. The interest of the
board members was in gas and heating contracts, new buildings for important new areas, the spending of public funds.
I could not even know, after a year in which I sat at their
meetings, whether there was any graft in their assignment of
contracts. There need not have been; it was enough for them
to determine the location of new public improvements; information like that was money. For me those sessions were the
most completely boring hours of my existence, spent in long
debate over various makes of electric switches or plumbing
fixtures, with never a word on the aims or methods of education.

Meantime into the life of Seattle new forces were oozing,
in the dank lowlands below Yesler Way where respectable people seldom went. Great lumber trusts, which had stolen or
otherwise acquired hundreds of thousands of acres from the
public domain surrounding Seattle, were stimulated by the war
into extended logging operations. Lumberjacks, a rough and
ready type of hard-fighting, hard-working, and hard-drinking
labor, agitated and struggled with varying success for decent
conditions in the woods. They drifted with winter into the
cheap lodging houses near Seattle's vice district, and became
the natural prey of prostitutes, employment sharks, vote-
seekers and agitators. They had a hall of their own, occasionally raided, where hoarse-voiced yells for justice alternated
with social evenings. It was thus we respectable progressives
of Seattle first saw the I.W.W., the Industrial Workers of the
World.

These newcomers took little part in politics; they were
nomad labor, deprived of lawful vote. If this floating population voted at all, it was at the behest and with the illegal con-
nivance of politicians who paid for their ballots. As such they
became a "menace to good citizens." Yet they were true

Americans, truer than most of the settled citizenry. They were direct inheritors of the fighting pioneer. Like him they were men of brawn and daring, proud of their strength to fell the forest, drive the new railroad, reclaim the trackless waste. They did these things no longer for their own homes on the frontier, but under orders of railroad and lumber kings. Into their ballads there crept the bitter irony of men who "build all the homes of the world, and never have home of their own." They called their I.W.W. hall the "home of the homeless." Yet even their hate for their exploiters had in it a touch of condescension, the disdain which men of the open air feel for the mean shrewdness of cities even when it bests them in their struggle. Their hero remained Paul Bunyan, the giant mythical logger, never the industrialist or banker, whom they disdained. They had none of the serf traditions of Europe, and none of the sense of class struggle as an ingrained law of developing society, which grew out of those serf traditions.

Yet they had class struggle, the struggle of men once free and expecting freedom, but now slowly, inexplicably, irretrievably enslaved. This struggle stalked with them into Seattle streets. It was no longer the slow, bargaining struggle of trade union business agents for a share in increasing profits through increasing wages; it was a stark, bloody fight for elementary human rights. It borrowed some of its thought and language from the workers' struggle of all ages: vague theories of syndicalism, the word "international," the "Workers of the World, Unite." It borrowed fully as much from American pioneer traditions, their mood of grim jesting with hardship and death, their admiration for physical strength, their individualism, impatient of discipline, but capable of brave joint fighting, passionate and brief.

With these American traditions the I.W.W. often cut across class lines in the prewar West, and won adherents from the champions of democracy and free speech in all classes. In the smaller lumber towns the settled citizenry were chiefly dependents and hangers-on of lumber companies and therefore fought these industrial workers ruthlessly as class foes. But in larger commercial cities, like Seattle, there were many smaller business men who depended on the trade of the lumberjacks, and were themselves oppressed by big business. In such cities the fighting lumberjacks got a hearing. They carried on free speech fights, defying the lawless tactics of police by getting themselves arrested in such numbers that they flooded the local jails and broke the machinery of local courts with the number of cases. Such tactics brought grins of approval from large numbers of ordinary citizens who had not forgotten the courage and grimness of the pioneer.

The hunger of war-torn Europe for lumber and the rising costs of living increased the battle in the woods around Seattle. Suddenly we were startled by the "Everett massacre" in a neighboring port a score of miles away. The police of that city made a practice of expelling I.W.W.'s brutally; the workers retorted with a free speech fight; scores of I.W.W. members in nearby cities and lumber camps hastened to Everett to speak on her streets and be arrested. They were driven out by clubs and shotguns; they promptly announced a meeting in a prominent Everett square and since roads and railroads were patrolled by the Everett authorities, the workers charted the steamer *Verona* in Seattle, and went over *en masse*. They were met at the dock by armed men; some of the workers had arms. A clash ensued which left many dead on the decks of the *Verona* and on the docks. The *Verona* pulled out for Seattle where all its passengers were arrested and brought to trial.

The press of America took interest; I covered the trial for the New York *Evening Post*. I was not consciously taking sides in any struggle; I merely sent the news. The news, which still had power to horrify the average American believer in fair play, was that at every stage the Everett police and private lumber guards took the initiative in beating and shooting workers for speaking in their streets. The lumber guards on the dock had begun the shooting and continued firing as the *Verona* pulled away; yet none of them were arrested. The men on trial for murder were not individually shown to have even possessed a gun; it was enough that someone on their ship, a comrade or an *agent provocateur*, had fired. The New York *Post* printed my articles as a description of raw injustice on the Pacific Coast; Seattle progressives drew morals about the wickedness of the interests and were more determinedly progressive than ever.

Among the conservative members of the School Board I was already marked as a radical. My election to the board against the clique of business men, my articles for the *Post* on the Everett trial, my increasing visits to the I.W.W. headquarters and championship of their leaders—were listed against me. We progressives resented the term "radical"; we were not digging anything up by the roots; we were merely continuing the good old American tradition of inevitable progress, a country getting better and better forever—a tradition which the interests had attacked.

Towards the end of 1916 it became evident that strong forces were pushing America towards the battle trenches of Europe. Yet "our America's" pioneer traditions were against "entangling alliances." To supplement this negative aloofness we had a positive faith. Men of all nations and races, the best and most energetic, had come to our America seeking freedom. We must preserve freedom and democracy for the world. God, or Nature, or Fate had given to these seeking men of all races the last free lands on earth, the last frontier. Here were great riches, and a prosperous free people; unless WE could fight off oppressors, the world was doomed. Doomed to be gobbled up by the interests, who had already swallowed all of Europe and turned her into a hell, and who pushed on us from New York through the timber trusts and Seattle Electric. Meantime our fight was clear—keep America out of the war.

I threw myself into the Anti-Preparedness League, the Union Against Militarism, the Emergency Peace Federation—all that rapidly shifting galaxy of organizations with which pacifists, liberals, radicals and progressives fought America's advance towards war. These organizations sprang up in the East, New York, Washington or Philadelphia, with varying and perhaps conflicting leadership: socialists, bourgeois, pacifists of all kinds. We of the Pacific provinces never distinguished between the different leaderships. We all met together—all who opposed war, and of these there was a goodly number—in regular luncheon meetings once a week in a cafeteria, and in occasional Sunday mass meetings enthusiastically attended. We accepted speakers, campaigns, pamphlets from any national society that chose to send them.

The only debate on method that occurred among us was whether we should raise the American flag above our mass meetings. There were a few socialists who argued against this "reverence for the flag," and a few I.W.W.'s who openly flouted it as the "flag of the profiteers." We told them they were too easily discouraged. The flag was our flag, which had been sought by the oppressed of the earth. The profiteers were trying to grab it; we must not let them. There were bad conditions in America, but these were temporary; there were bad men in America, but they must be overthrown; there were the interests in America, but they challenged the vigilant activity of all free citizens. "Our America" was a democratic republic, ruled by the will of its citizens, a land of free and equal people, the pioneer land of the world.

We won our point; we waved the flag at pacifist mass meetings. Our America would not enter the war; she stood for peace. Our America elected Wilson on the slogan "he kept us out of war."

When after Wilson's accession, the war pressed ever nearer, we decided to "strengthen the hands of the President" against it. We conducted informal plebiscites all over the country. I organized one in Seattle. We sent hundreds of people into the streets and markets and factories with questionnaires asking: "Are you irrevocably against participating in the European War under any conditions?" Ninety-five percent of them shouted "Yes." I sent the daily report of these votes to Congress, keeping the wires hot with telegrams. Other cities were doing the same: we were informed of their struggle. We knew that Congress was informed.

Then this America whose populace protested war and whose profiteers desired it, left us and marched into the war with all of Europe. As the war approached, our local branch of the Anti-Preparedness Committee, the American Union against Militarism, the Emergency Peace Federation, dwindled; the respectable members were turning to war work. The presidents of women's clubs were "swinging in behind the President"; the head of the Parent-Teachers organizations, who spoke so valiantly for peace in the mass meeting which featured the flag, found other duties now. The weekly cafeteria meetings grew smaller. After the actual declaration of war we held one meeting. I was still secretary of the organization and I glanced bitterly at the empty tables. "Only a handful of socialists and wobblies left," I said. "All the people of prominence have deserted. Nobody left who can do anything."

The meeting reorganized as the "Anti-Conscription League," and voted to communicate with organizations of that name arising in the East. I asked them to elect another secretary. "Anti-conscription is a man's fight," I said. "My summer camps in the mountains are soon starting and I shall not be in town."

I left in truth because my courage and my heart were broken. Nothing in my whole life, not even my mother's death, so shook the foundations of my soul. The fight was lost, and forever! "Our America" was dead! The profiteers, the militarists, the "interests" had violated her and forced her to their bidding. I could not delude myself, as some did, that this was a "war to make the world safe for democracy"; I had seen democracy slain in the very declaration of war. The people wanted peace; the profiteers wanted war—and got it. There had been a deep mistake in the whole basis of my life. Where and how to begin again I had no notion.

I turned like a wounded beast to the hills for shelter. Like the pioneers of old I fled to the simpler wilderness from the problems of human society that I could not face. Week after week on the high slopes of Rainier I was busy with problems of pack-trains, commissary, cooking, hikes. Eight or ten hours a day I led parties on the glaciers. Few newspapers reached me; I did not read them. I shrank from every mention of the war. I drugged myself with forests, cliffs and glaciers. I exhausted myself with twenty-four-hour climbs. It was the end of youth, the end of belief, the end of "our America." I could not face the ruins of my world.

CHAPTER VI

SIGNALS FROM MOSCOW

Across the flaming battle lines of Europe, across two seas and two continents, we also, in the far north woods of America, building ships of war in Seattle shipyards, began to see signals from Moscow, which we seized and used to suit our local needs. Out of the murderous division of war, there came to all the earth a knowledge of the oneness of our planet; no land could stand aloof, no ports but were swept by participation in the ruthless struggle—China, Japan and the islands of the Pacific, no less than the trench-scarred fields of Europe. But if World War broke forever for us Americans the fetish of our uniqueness and peaceful isolation, we had our recompense; we also became joint heirs of the World Revolution.

The fall of the tsar passed lightly over me; I was chiefly annoyed at the way it was seized by our patriots to justify America's participation in the war. I was too far removed from any large Russian populations to note the flocking of revolutionists back to Petrograd, or to understand its importance. The first signal from the revolution which I caught was the call for a conference in Stockholm to discuss terms of "a democratic peace without annexations or indemnities."

It came to me in the mountain camps by the glaciers. Towards the end of summer a new newspaper began to appear in camp occasionally—the Seattle *Daily Call*. Four pages, poorly written, badly printed—it said what I wanted to say about the war. It said them in harsh words and poor English —the things that respectable folk had ceased to say. It jeered at the Wilson slogans, at "war to end war," at "world safe for democracy." It declared that America went into the war to protect her loans to the Allies and to make money for war profiteers. It demanded conscription of profits to balance conscription of men. It published the call to the Stockholm conference, from a land in revolution beyond both seas. "Let the workers of all lands get together and end this war," said that message.

The raw, red words of the Seattle *Daily Call* were balm on the wounds of my soul. The call for the workers of all lands to get together to end war gave me a reason for coming back from the mountains; it gave me a home again among men. As soon as the summer camp season ended I found the office of the *Call* and offered them my services as a writer. Thereafter I wrote almost a page of the paper a day. I covered "class war" trials in the courts; I already called it that when socialists and I.W.W.'s were railroaded to jail for demanding normal American rights. I covered local city hall grafts, local jail conditions, local labor, the newly forming Loyal Legion of Lumbermen, which was being organized to undercut the I.W.W. I covered also whatever we could get of national and world affairs. Lacking a cable service, we combed the socialist press of all cities for news and features to copy or rewrite. Lacking a staff, we worked fourteen to sixteen hours a day. Editorials, news, features, satirical poems were pounded out by me at white heat while I shivered from the cold cement floors of our unheated offices. Only twice again in my life was I ever able to work like that: in my first five weeks of Soviet Russia, and again in my first five weeks of organizing the Moscow *News*. There are times when one compresses a year of life and work into a few weeks.

The staff had two other full-time members: Lena Morrow Lewis who was a member of the socialist party, and Mauritzen, who I think was an I.W.W. Somewhere in the background there was a committee which tried to raise money for our existence. I think we were never an official organ for any organization; I never thought to inquire. Chiefly we ran on the good-will of our printer, William Piggott, who got all the money that came in while his bill against us grew and grew; he eventually had his plant wrecked for printing us. Sometimes Lena wanted to change my editorials; she said I didn't know a thing about Marxism. She was quite correct; it didn't occur to me that Marxism mattered. If she thought it did, I let her change the editorials. Usually none of us had time to edit the other; we saw and felt and wrote. We had only one policy; to use everything and especially all the contradictions of the war to expose and lash the capitalists who had caused it and who lied about it still.

We tried more or less to formulate these attacks inside the law; but we didn't worry much. In those first months of America at war one could say almost anything. Traditions of free speech were not immediately suppressed. Seattle was a city of big shipyards, rapidly expanding under war orders; it was a strong trade union town and the unions were also expanding at the rate of hundreds of members a week in the metal trades. The government in Washington did not want trouble with Seattle shipyard workers. The *Call* was popular in the shipyards; so the authorities occasionally harassed it, but did not quite dare suppress it openly. Suppression when it came was done by organized hooligans who wrecked the presses.

Most of our paper dealt with local problems, but we watched hopefully that Russian land beyond the seas where, even the capitalist press admitted, the workers were tired of war. We seized news from distorted press cables and guessed at what was behind them, helped by occasional interpretations from stray socialists or Russians. It was hard to get real knowledge. There were scattered socialists in Seattle, but practically no party. No one told us of differences between Bolsheviks and Mensheviks; we heard that Kerensky was leader of the socialists; later we heard that Lenin was. Long afterwards I was told by a Russian Bolshevik that our Seattle *Daily Call* was the first paper in America which cheered the new workers' state whole-heartedly. From very naïveté we did it, while the older socialist press of the eastern states debated theoretical distinctions. We knew no theory; we knew that on the other side of earth Russian workers had used the war to seize power and throw out kings and capitalists and that this was the right idea for all the workers in the world.

The arrival of a ship from Vladivostok after the October Revolution showed that many workers of that city knew scarcely more than we did. The vessel left Russia under the rule of Kerensky; it arrived in our port in the era of Bolshevik rule. Somehow a soviet of workers had been elected on board the ship under which the captain functioned. This caused some consternation among Seattle port authorities. To receive it as a normally managed ship was clearly impossible; but one could not arrest a crew for mutiny when the lawful captain was still on duty. The ship was finally allowed to land her cargo, but guards were set to prevent the crew from going ashore.

Sailors have ways of agreeing with longshoremen to evade regulations, and all Seattle's workers, stimulated by the *Call*, were avid for news from Vladivostok. A sailor from the ship was smuggled into the city; we questioned him all night at the home of a member of the I.W.W. through an amateur interpreter. The sailor had never heard of Kerensky, and hardly of Lenin. He talked about "soviets" in Vladivostok; our interpreter turned "soviets" into "councils" and we didn't know what kind of councils they were. We concealed our disappointment over the small amount of knowledge by sharing our emotions; for the first time I heard the Revolutionary Funeral March, played after midnight on a tinny piano—the march that I was to hear again in famine-stricken Samara, in teeming cities of China, on wind-swept plains of Mongolia, and played by symphony orchestras before great congresses of delegates standing with bowed head in Moscow. I wrote in the *Call* a long ironical ballad about the reception of this ship in our harbor.

Meantime class lines in Seattle were forming around a more personal struggle. An anti-conscription leaflet which had been authorized in that last meeting I had attended after the declaration of war had led to the arrest of four men, of whom the best known was Hulet Wells, socialist, former president of the Seattle Central Labor Council. As soon as I returned from the mountain camps he came to see me (he was out on bail) and asked for names of the former American Union Against Militarism, of which as secretary I still retained the membership list. He explained that the prosecutor was shaping his case on evidence of stool pigeons and disreputable elements who would try to prove that the leaflets were subsidized by "German gold." The defense intended to assert their right as American citizens to oppose European entanglements and conscript armies; they would list the many prominent Americans who had openly agreed with them only a few months ago.

"If that is your method of defense," I said, "you should call me as witness. I can connect you not only with people prominent in Seattle, but with famous names in the East. I will tell of the cafeteria meeting where we voted to print that dodger and show that it was paid for by well-known Americans, from funds which I personally handled."

Wells wanted to spare me; he knew better than I what would be the result for me personally. We consulted Vanderveer, attorney for the defense. He also displayed some conscience towards my future. "Young lady," he said with a warning smile, "my advice to you personally is that you need a guardian to keep you out of this; but my statement as attorney for the defense is that you offer us our best chance of winning."

Across eight columns of Seattle's front pages flamed the news when the woman member of the School Board took the stand in the "treason case." Vanderveer staged it well. He let the prosecutor display the evidence of police court agents, creating an atmosphere of cellar conspiracies. Then he called, as his unexpected first witness, the best known among all the respectable women of Seattle, the woman member of the School Board, connected with mothers and children and with progressives. My connection with the Seattle *Daily Call* was not yet widely known among the workers who read it.

This highly respectable young woman said: "Certainly we printed that dodger! What's wrong with it except its rotten style? Are you arresting for mistakes in grammar? I could have written it better; but I only gave money to print it. All of us did. Who? The American Union Against Militarism, affiliated in the East with Jane Addams, Lillian Wald, all the real patriots who hated this war as un-American. What's unlawful about that dodger? Printed before the conscription law was passed, wasn't it, when nine-tenths of this country thought conscription un-American? Even if it hadn't been, who prevents free-born Americans from attacking an oppressive law?" . . . It finished the trial; it gave us a hung jury. It can be done once—that approach of outraged respectability; it can be done by the same person only once. After it I was the best-known woman in Seattle; I was no longer among the most respectable.

For the defendants my testimony changed little in the end. The district attorney tried them again a few months later when we no longer had the weapon of surprise. He got his conviction easily the second time, and the socialists went to jail. The real result of that first trial lay in the agitation it caused, and in my own changed status. The political hangers-on of the Chamber of Commerce seized the chance to start a recall to remove me from the School Board.

The recall was a weapon of popular government forged by the progressives to make officials responsible to public demand. It was first used in Seattle by the reactionaries; they even violated the law in using it, since they paid salaries to circulators of petitions. Yet at first they got so few signatures that the recall languished and almost died. A friend of mine was passing the recall headquarters on a prominent thoroughfare and was asked by a woman who had stopped to observe the placards: "What are they recalling her for? What has she done?" . . . "She's against the war," said my friend. . . . "My God, who isn't?" grunted the woman and moved on. Opposition to war was no bar to popularity in Seattle, even seven months after America had joined the Allies.

My own fault revived the recall. I "befriended" an anarchist, Louise Olivereau, who was arrested for sending seditious literature to soldiers. She was one of those poetic souls to whom war never became a statistical movement of forces, but always vividly remained torn flesh, scattered brains and blood. She heard in her soul the shrieks of each murdered victim and hated war with emotion. Yet her acts were singularly futile. She spent her meager salary as typist in the I.W.W. hall to buy paper and postage; she collected statements against war by the wise and great of all ages, Tolstoi, Lincoln, Thoreau, the Bible; she mimeographed these and sent them to lists of drafted soldiers. The mimeographing was so badly done that one could hardly read it; there was nothing to prove that a single drafted soldier had been influenced from his allegiance.

Louise Olivereau refused an attorney; she declared herself an anarchist before a staid Seattle jury; she rushed on jail as a moth on a flame. Nothing that we of the *Call* could say could dissuade her from this demonstration. She asked me to sit beside her in court so that in intervals at noon and evening she might have a friendly word to relieve the soul-crushing atmosphere of American justice. I went, and I was neither prepared nor unprepared for the eight column headlines which greeted the fact that the woman school director, already under attack for recall, had befriended an anarchist.

The dying recall came swiftly to life. American troops were already in French trenches and Seattle's temper had changed. Former supporters of mine began to sign the recall. But simultaneously new forces rose to support me. A class that had never taken part in Seattle politics began to speak as a class. Absorbed in the campaign, I had not begun to analyze the new political alignment until a neighbor spoke to me.

"All your old friends have denounced you," he said. "The Federation of Women's Clubs has come out against you, and the Parent-Teachers, and the University Women's Club and the Municipal League. The Ministers' Federation won't discuss the question, but you know they are against you. Is anyone on your side?"

"Oh, yes," I said eagerly, "I've lots of the biggest organizations in the city. The Boilermakers Union with over seven thousand members is working enthusiastically. The blacksmiths, the longshoremen, the machinists, the electricians and lots of others. I think the whole Metal Trades Council is going to pass a resolution for me, though it's against their constitution to take part in politics. Even the Building Trades Council, which never takes part in politics, has been cheering me; I can count on most of them. We really have a chance to win."

"That's a funny lot of roughnecks," he said, "to be backing a girl like you."

I pondered his words, looking at the lights of Seattle's many hills from the height of Queen Anne Hill where he left me. I remembered the thousands of new comrades I had met in the few weeks of campaign, the cheering masses of men from forge and foundry, builders of ships. I did not greatly care about the outcome of the recall; I hated those meetings of the School Board; I was happy to be fighting shoulder to shoulder with this crowd. Not till long after did I really understand what had happened. The old Central Labor Council which joined the Municipal League and Commercial Club in endorsing progressive candidates was no longer the only spokesman for labor. From the war-expanded shipyards thousands of new members had poured into the great unions of the metal trades, new men, pioneers, some of them former I.W.W.'s, all of them impatient of tradition.

The Seattle *Daily Call* with its frank, rough speech had become their organ. They hated the suppressions of war-time; no strike or election gave them a chance to express this.

Suddenly they were given a chance. A young woman of education and culture was under attack by the profiteers for defending working men in their right to free speech. It aroused the resentment of the pioneer against suppressors of freedom; it aroused the protective chivalry which the homeless conquerors of the West feel for a "decent woman comrade"; it blended these emotions with the class feeling rising in the shipyards. With such an issue we invaded union after union of these new men, impatient of old rules. And blacksmiths, machinists, longshoremen, boilermakers, union after union, cheered and took up the fight on a political issue in defiance of federation custom.

That election expressed and helped create a new political alignment in Seattle. Instead of the time-honored division between "progressives" and the "interests" in which the progressives won most of the offices while the interests remained unscathed in the industries, a bitter battle ensued between "good citizens" and "reds." The good citizens raised the issue and fixed the day of election, combining the recall with a regular municipal election in hope of a more smashing victory. But, though no word of our side was printed for three months by any newspaper except the Seattle *Daily Call*, yet when the votes were counted, the good citizens who had expected a ten to one victory over a "handful of traitors," won by only some two thousand votes in a total of eighty-five thousand. They actually lost the city council to the "reds" who had intelligently prepared a whole slate, while the patriots had emotionally concentrated on the recall and the mayor. The patriots were momentarily crushed into silence; they were actually worried. We celebrated our "victorious defeat" in the Central Labor Council.

By a strange irony this first class alignment in a Seattle election was centered around a girl who had been unable to believe in the class struggle. It was the recall rather than the mayoralty and councilmen that won the headlines in that fray. It was the recall that sharply raised the class division. Thereafter for years Seattle elections divided the city into "good citizens and patriots" on the one hand, and "reds, pro-Germans, damned Bolsheviks" on the other; and the "reds" won regularly from forty to forty-five percent of the votes. We proudly knew that we had an actual majority in the city, if the newly arriving shipyard workers had all possessed electoral rights.

After nine months of living on debts and on the printing shop of William Piggott, the Seattle *Daily Call* expired, and the press which had printed it was wrecked by a gang of "patriots." The paper was almost immediately replaced by the Seattle *Union Record*, a much stronger newspaper, owned and controlled by the trade unions of the city. It was more respectable than the *Call*, more restrained in its discussion of war and less devoted to I.W.W.'s and anarchists, whose "right to free speech" it defended "without supporting all their ideas." It was far more powerful than the *Call*, for it was backed not only by the radical elements in the shipyards but by the united trade unions of the city, proud of being the first local unions in America to own a daily paper. They were too strong for either the city government or the distant American Federation of Labor to take lightly. Our editor, Harry Ault, had been for years a socialist, and if the possession of a good job and pleasant home had softened the belligerence of his youth, he could still give socialist theory far better than any of the young enthusiasts. Unlike the *Call*, which ran on debts and paid nobody, the *Union Record* was a solid concern with regular salaries.

I was offered my choice of jobs on the new paper and became feature editor. Most revolutionary news thus came in my province, for little of it arrived by cable. It came by chance lecturers, by men escaped across borders; it was dug out of letters, translated from pamphlets or culled from illegal bulletins which drifted to us across the world. In spite of the disadvantage of distance, we carried more columns about Soviet Russia than appeared in socialist papers of the East. There were indeed occasional protests from older trade union members that we devoted more attention to "those Bolsheviks" than to the legitimate problems of carpenters and painters. But our most vociferous readers were the shipyard workers and they wanted "Russian stuff." Still cheerfully unaware of the theoretical basis of Russia's revolution, and ready to cheer any workers who had taken power, we remained, in the period before the American Communist Party was organized, perhaps the only newspaper in America that was consistently pro-Soviet. But our cheers were based on feeling rather than knowledge.

After many months we suddenly came upon knowledge, from the greatest master of all. Lenin's address in April 1918 to the Congress of Soviets on the next tasks of organizing power made its way across the blockade to New York where it was translated and published with foreword and footnotes by Alexander Trachtenberg of the Rand School of Social Science. Not many copies circulated in the eastern states; the Rand School was harried by the Department of Justice and socialists were strictly watched. Moreover, the pamphlet itself was issued in a small edition and in a form meant for students of socialist theory.

A copy reached us in Seattle and we promptly reprinted it for popular circulation among workers. We discarded Trach-

tenberg's scholarly foreword with its puzzling explanations
about Mensheviks and Social Revolutionaries and other people
who didn't seem to matter, and inserted a foreword of our own
which I innocently and blithely wrote, explaining in vivid,
simple terms that this document was a "description of the problems faced by a working-class government on coming to
power," and therefore should be read by all workers who expected to take power. I also added "headlines" above each
paragraph, summarizing their contents in short phrases so
that workers, accustomed to reading newspaper headlines,
might quickly grasp what each section described.

This Lenin pamphlet was seized by workers eager to know
how the workers of Russia were running their new state. We
issued an edition of twenty thousand and sold them immediately in Seattle and a few cities of the northwest. The
workers' organizations of Vancouver, British Columbia, using
my foreword and headlines, reprinted another twenty thousand
for Canada; these circulated from Vancouver to Winnipeg.
For some time these little pamphlets were seen by hundreds
on Seattle's street cars and ferries, read by men of the shipyards on their way to work. Seattle's business men commented on the phenomenon sourly; it was plain to everyone
that these workers were conscientiously and energetically studying how to organize their coming power.

Already workers in Seattle talked about "workers' power" as
a practical policy for the not far distant future. Boilermakers,
machinists and other metal trades unions alluded to shipyards
as enterprises which they might soon take over, and run better
than their present owners ran them. These allusions gave life
to union meetings, uniting us with the rising tide of workers
around the globe. Every Wednesday night the Central Labor
Council sat till midnight listening to emissaries of suppressed
and rebelling peoples: Indians, Irish, Chinese, Koreans. We
were stirred by the seizure of factories in Germany, by the
mutiny of French troops in Odessa, by the rising of soviets in
Hungary and Bavaria. Workers all over the world were
rising to rule; it would be our turn soon. How this power

would be obtained we were completely ignorant; events everywhere seemed to be thrusting it into the workers' hands.

Reporters who had seen the Russian Revolution occasionally drifted to Seattle on lecture tours. They also cared little for theory, but dealt in picturesque anecdote and practical success. Thus came Raymond Robins, Louise Bryant, Wilfred Humphries, Albert Rhys Williams. We heard of women's freedom, of the equality of backward races, of children rationed first when supplies were scant; these things strengthened our enthusiasm. We heard conflicting tales of workers' rule in factories and amazing stories of rough common sense in revolutionary tribunals which cut across the wrongs of ancient law; these were stimulating but not quite comprehensible. I spent hours, sometimes days, with each of these lecturers, and wrote whole series of articles from what they told me. Fleeing across the sea from Japan came the wife of Krasnoschekoff, president of the Far Eastern Republic, who had been driven out by the Japanese. We got from her some knowledge of Soviet schools and care of children before we helped her on her way to the East.

I admired these messengers as privileged beings who had seen the center of the world. Yet not once in those years did it occur to me to leave Seattle. Friends have accused me since of being a natural nomad incapable of settled home. But when the whole journalistic world went to Europe's battle-fronts, to Versailles, to Moscow, to various revolutions, I was content in a far-away city of the Pacific Northwest. The reason is simple: the revolution had begun in Moscow, but was not in Moscow alone. It was world revolution which took us in. Its messengers crossed all seas, from India, Ireland, Germany, Hungary. It had begun in Moscow, but it was coming to Seattle; and Seattle was our battle-post. We also were part of this new world.

For every part of it we felt quite undiscriminating emotion. If we published Lenin, we also published manifestoes of the British Labor Party which had a new postwar program for obtaining "socialism in our time." Some of us thought they sounded stodgy and slower than the Russians, but others thought them more practical and much less bloody—"Anglo-Saxon, like us; that's how we'll do it." For myself, it seemed to me that all these movements were pushing ahead in the same general direction and no one could tell which would get there first. The Russians had seized power but they were having a great deal of trouble. Perhaps the workers in some other nation would find an easier way. Anyway, it was all inevitable; we would arrive by all these many roads.

Among the various roads suggested to the rising energy of Seattle's workers were workers' enterprises, coöperatively owned. Dr. Warbasse came from New York to tell us that this was the painless, profitable way to workers' ownership; we listened also to him. Various forms of coöperative enterprise sprang up. The Mutual Laundry was the first of these; it was launched by organized labor as a union-owned laundry which could harbor the organizers for all other laundries. This became a regular tactic; in any small industry where the bosses opposed trade unions, the unions would start an enterprise which could give jobs to all the agitators who were thrown out of other plants. We owned a motion picture theater, a number of coöperative stores, a mutual savings bank as well as our big newspaper. We began to conduct enterprises of direct trading with the farmers, and were entangled in some rather unsavory complications. The methods of financing all these enterprises were vague; some were consumers' coöperatives, some were stock companies whose shares were taken by trade unions. We reached a stage where even a privately owned enterprise started by a "friend of labor" seemed a workers' enterprise on the path to socialism. Nobody criticized any new scheme; those were boom days of workers' enterprises, when jobs were plentiful, wages high and everything succeeded.

I remember when Louise Bryant returned from the revolution in Russia to dazzle the smoke-laden air of the close-packed longshoremen's hall with her gorgeous amber beads and the glamor of the forbidden border. She said to me after the meeting: "You mustn't think they are pacifists over there because they withdrew from the war. They believe in armed uprising." . . .

I answered, "Of course"; but I felt a vague discomfort. It seemed we had forgotten something in Seattle. Where were our arms?

The discomfort soon vanished. Nobody had arms in Seattle; the only arms were out at Camp Lewis where "the boys" were being rapidly demobilized and where the *Union Record* had friends and readers. Did one really need arms to take the shipyards from Skinner, when we already had a majority of Seattle's population? There was occasional discussion whether it would be simpler to pay for the shipyards with a bond issue or just to take them. But I was among those who saw no reason for hurting Skinner; he could be retired on a pension to get him comfortably out of the way. We had a majority in Seattle; the tide was rising to give us a majority in the world.

If our theory was vague, our emotional loyalty was authentic. Seattle longshoremen led the strike against supplying arms to Kolchak, and it spread up and down the coast. They had just won by their wartime strength their first collective agreement with the shipping companies; under this longshoremen were hired through the union and waited their summons in comfortable union halls. This replaced the old barbaric method whereby men competed for jobs at the docks, waiting in sun and rain till the owner came to pick the strongest. Hardly was the ink dry on the agreement when the workers discovered that arms were in the sealed cases that were being shipped to Kolchak. They knew what they risked when they voted to strike, thus breaking the collective agreement which they were never again able to renew. But they knew also that British workers struck against sending arms to the intervention in Russia, that French soldiers mutinied, that workers struck in solidarity all round the world. Thus they did their part against Kolchak, their share in the world revolution.

Out of this emotion of solidarity, in a whirl of conflicting and yet unanalyzed theories, came the Seattle general strike, our local "revolution."

CHAPTER VII

OUR SEATTLE "REVOLUTION"

FROM coast to coast in January 1919 went the report that revolution was imminent in Seattle. A general strike had been called in sympathy with the shipyard workers and nobody knew how it might end. Government officials in Washington announced that Bolshevism had made its appearance in the northwest of the United States.

The tension in Seattle before the strike is difficult to exaggerate. Business men took out riot insurance and purchased guns. Citizens laid in supplies as for a long siege; kerosene lamps were dragged from storage to sell at high prices in case the strike should involve City Light. Some of the wealthy families took trips to Portland to be out of the upheaval. The press appealed to strikers not to ruin their home city. Later they changed their tone and demanded threateningly: "Which flag are you under . . . if under the American flag then put down Bolshevism in your midst."

Ours was the first general strike, involving all the workers in a city, that ever took place on the North American continent. For years the I.W.W. had talked of the general strike, declaring that the power of the workers' folded arms would bring the collapse of capitalism. Few of them claimed to know concretely what would happen when such a strike started. It was like pulling the trigger of a gun without knowing with what ammunition it was loaded. Government officials and local business men said it was loaded with revolution. All our labor leaders busily denied this.

The strike would probably not have occurred at all if the "labor leaders" had been in town. Most of them were absent at the Mooney convention called in Chicago to demand freedom for Mooney. They were terrified when they heard that a general strike had been voted. They discussed it on the train on

the way back to Seattle. Ten days earlier they had left an energetic, progressive but properly constitutional labor movement. To what were they returning?

I also was on that train from Chicago to Seattle. I rated
now as a leader of Seattle workers. Within that movement I
was considered one of the "progressives," which meant that I
stood for industrial unionism (to be attained through a process
of federating the craft unions), for political action by labor
(we were developing a farmer-labor party against the reactionaries of the American Federation of Labor), and for
eventual rule of the world by its workers, without specifying
how or when.

From the day when I had walked into the offices of the *Call*
to offer my services as writer, I had found both comradeship
and freedom so naturally mingled that I never analyzed these
blessings till long after they had gone. I planned and carried
through my own work, and seemed to do always the things I
most desired. Yet instinctively when new questions arose I
consulted with others, our editor Harry Ault, the secretary of
the Central Labor Council, Jimmy Duncan, whom we regularly
sent as delegate to meetings of the American Federation of
Labor to cast the single exasperating vote against Gompers
which prevented his election as president from being unani-
mous. My mind—all our minds—were being made by the same
past, the same events, the same comrades, by complaints from
the shipyards and letters from the mines. Thus formed, my
mind functioned easily with the others, with a sense both of
personal liberty and joint achievement.

My writing was winning reputation outside Seattle in the
labor and socialist press of America. Under the pseudonym
"Anise" I published daily satirical short-line verses, which
were widely copied and even translated into the workers' press
of other countries. As I read them now I see through them a
picture of what our left-wing of Seattle was in those days.

There are verses sharply aware of the inconsistencies and
cruelties of capitalism, satirizing the campaigns of local
patriots, the absurdities of spy scares, the economic waste of
saw-mills, mines and factories, and the world-wide chaos of post-

war Europe. The faults of capitalism we saw quite clearly. Other verses have a fine glow of optimism dealing with futures, "new worlds," "new freedom," the marching progress of the world's workers. But I search in vain for any positive plan or theory concerning the organization of this march. We seem to have seen world revolution as a sealed packet which God, or the inevitable laws of human progress, would give us, a marching into a golden West which nobody could foreshadow. We passionately believed that a Great Change was coming, but when or how we did not know.

And now, when we faced on the train from Chicago to Seattle the first signs of actual change, we were frankly frightened. A general strike was unleashed power. It might easily smash something—us perhaps, our well-organized labor movement. Yet we could not repudiate action taken by sixty thousand workers. The cynical reactionaries of the American Federation of Labor often repudiated rank and file action, but we left-wing idealists stuck with the workers. Having no theory or plan for handling a general strike, we must study the situation and "follow" where it led us, hoping that we might eventually get out without a crash. Thus from the beginning the leaders wavered between an open support of the strike and an unadmitted wish to stop it.

The general strike thus thrust upon unwilling leaders grew out of a strike of thirty-five thousand shipyard workers for wage adjustments. Throughout the war wages had been fixed by government boards in consultation with national presidents of craft unions. They bribed the highly skilled workers and cut the pay of the unskilled, which ran counter to the "solidarity" policy of our local Metal Trades Council. Discontent smoldered for a year and a half of war-time, ready to burst into flame when restraints should be removed.

Double-dealing by Mr. Piez, the head of the Emergency Fleet Corporation, supplied the torch for the bonfire. His frequent public statements that our workers had the right to bargain directly with their employers even during war-time, were undermined by his private telegrams to the shipyard owners threatening to cut off the supply of steel or to cancel contracts if they changed the wage-scales. Through the "mistake" of a messenger boy one of these telegrams was delivered not to the Metal Trades Association (the employers) but to the Metal Trades Council (the workers). The anger of the shipyard workers was thus directed against Washington; they struck and asked all unions of the city to support them by a general strike. Such a strike—as a political protest—was against the policy of the American Federation of Labor.

Yet swiftly union after union violated its constitution, flouted its national officers and sacrificed hard-won agreements to join the strike. The conservative typographical union, the property-holding carpenters union, the weak hotel-maids union, the staid musicians, the fighting longshoremen and teamsters—swung united into line. Japanese unions, existing in Seattle but barred from the American Federation of Labor, voted to strike and sent fraternal delegates; so did I.W.W. organizations. Miners from nearby coal-fields sent greetings and asked for instructions. Even the small business men of Seattle, annoyed by the interference of the East in our local affairs, agreed with the workers on several details in the conduct of the general strike. The only unions which did not join were some government employees; the postal clerks' representatives came to the meeting of the General Strike Committee to ask for instructions, saying that they were threatened with jail if they struck. For the first time Seattle workers faced the fact that the government ownership for which they fought so valiantly might suppress workers more than private owners dared. The General Strike Committee was "loyal"; it did not advise jail.

This General Strike Committee, composed of more than three hundred delegates from one hundred and ten unions, met all day Sunday, February 2, 1919. They faced and disregarded the national officers of craft unions, who were telegraphing orders from the East. They met the threats of the Seattle Health Department to jail drivers of garbage wagons if garbage was not removed, by agreeing to permit the collection of "wet garbage only" on special permit under the strikers' control. They rejected as strike slogan the motto "We have nothing to lose but our chains and a whole world to gain," in favor of "Together We Win." For they reasoned that they had a good deal to lose—jobs at good wages with which they were buying silk shirts, pianos and homes. They wanted solidarity but not class war. Then so little did they realize the problems before them that they fixed the strike for the following Thursday at 10 A.M. and adjourned to meet on Thursday evening after the strike should have started, meantime referring any new problems that might arise to a rather hastily elected "Committee of Fifteen."

This Committee of Fifteen became by the next morning the unintentional but actual rulers of Seattle. They were not organized for power; they strove to evade power; but power was thrust upon them. To "walk off the job" was not simple when it involved all activities of a city. Should streets be plunged into darkness? Should water-works stop? How would three hundred thousand people eat? If life was not to be made unbearable for the strikers as well as for the others, the simple order to quit work must be replaced by problems of exemption and management.

These workers who suddenly came face to face with the complexity of a modern city of which they and their families were part were men proud of their city, proud of its municipally owned light and water systems, its publicly owned port. For many years they had fought against "the interests" to secure these evidences of municipal ownership; they did not wish to wreck them now. They did not, in fact, wish to wreck anything, not even the privately owned shipyards. They wished to rebuke Mr. Piez and to show solidarity for unjustly treated shipyard workers. The sight of workers seizing power in other countries had stirred their emotions and aroused a faith that some day it might be their turn to supersede the capitalists in managing the world. Now suddenly they had to manage.

From hundreds of requests for exemptions I take a few:

King County Commissioners ask for janitors for City County Building—Refused.

F. A. Rust asks for janitors for the Labor Temple—Refused.

Coöperative Market asks for janitors because of the food they handle for strike kitchens—Granted.

Teamsters Union asks permission to carry oil for Swedish hospital—Approved.

Retail Drug Clerks ask for instructions in view of medical needs of city. Referred to public welfare committee which decides that certain prescription counters remain open, but the drug stores are not to sell any other merchandise.

Trade Printery asks exemption to print leaflets for unions. Refused, but Trade Printery is asked to put its plant at the disposal of the Strike Committee, its workers to be accepted as volunteers. This is agreed.

Auto drivers are allowed to answer emergency calls from hospitals and funerals, if these are made through the Auto Drivers Union.

Telephone girls requested to stay on the job temporarily.

Bake ovens at Davidson's allowed to operate, all wages to go to the strike fund.

Longshoremen ask permission to handle government mails, customs and baggage. Permit given for mails and customs but not for baggage.

Plumbers Union given permit to keep seven plumbers on duty for emergency calls. Street Car workers given permission to appoint six watchmen to safeguard car barns.

C. R. Case, chief of street department, and backed by mayor, requests that street lighting be allowed "to check hooliganism and riots." Confused discussion over this due to the technical difficulty of separating light from power; City Light finally allowed to run.

Robert Bridges, who was elected to presidency of the public port by votes of progressive workers, appeals on behalf of farm products in cold storage, saying: "The big companies store in private warehouses, getting power from Seattle Electric which your strike cannot touch. Do not ruin the small farmers, who store in the public warehouses with power from City Light." . . . This also influences the retention of City Light in full operation.

Such are a few of the activities of a modern city, which the strikers of Seattle glimpsed through demands for exemptions, the power to grant or refuse which lay with them. Besides these there were several important activities where the workers were forced to take the reins of organization.

The question of hospital laundry was such a problem. Would the strikers injure sick people by stopping hospital laundry work? Several conferences were held between the Laundry Workers Union, the Laundry-Drivers Union, the hospitals, and the Laundry-Owners Association. A plan was evolved whereby one laundry remained open for hospital laundry only, while the wagons allotted to carry this hospital laundry were marked "exempt by strike committee." This plan, accepted by owners as well as workers, was approved by the Committee of Fifteen.

A similar plan was made for the milk supply of children. The Milk Wagon Drivers established thirty-five milk stations in various parts of the city, to which the nearby farmers were sent with their wagons and from which families with children were permitted to secure milk. The owners of dairies were allowed to open one pasteurizing plant, operating it with their own hands, and pasteurizing for hospital use some milk which came to the city by train. One auto-truck was marked "exempt" for this purpose.

The Strike Committee organized "labor guards" to help the police keep order. Mayor Hanson offered to deputize these labor guards and give them "stars and guns." This offer was refused by F. A. Rust, their organizer. He chose for these labor guards men who had returned from the war, who were also trade unionists. "Let Seattle be assured of their patriotism," he said. "We can keep order in our own ranks without need of guns. If there is shooting done, it will not be by us. We think it will reassure the public to be told that labor has no guns."

In the few days between the announcement of the strike and its actual beginning it seemed to me at first that we were rushing headlong on catastrophe. We were closing the Seattle shipyards in order to attack Mr. Piez. But our strike might only help the competing shipyards of Hog Island in which Mr. Piez was reputed to be personally interested. Were we blindly playing into the hands of our enemies? My hope began to grow as I saw the power which the strike was putting into the hands of the workers. I remembered the pamphlet by Lenin on the problems faced by a workers' government on coming to power. It seemed to me that at last even we began to face such problems. Two days before the strike I wrote:

> We are undertaking the most tremendous move ever made by labor in this country, a move that will lead—No One Knows Where! We do not need hysteria! We need the iron march of labor!
>
> Labor will feed the people. . . .
> Labor will care for the babies and the sick. . . .
> Labor will preserve order. . . .
>
> Not the withdrawal of labor power, but the power of the workers to manage, will win this strike. . . . The closing down of our industries as a mere shut-down will not affect those eastern gentlemen much. But the closing down of the capitalistically-owned industries of Seattle while the workers organize to feed the people, care for babies and maintain order—this will move them, for this looks too much like the taking of power by the workers. . . .
>
> If the strike continues, labor may feel led to open more and more activities under its own management.
>
> That is why I say that we are starting on a road that leads— NO ONE KNOWS WHERE!

This editorial, quoted from coast to coast as an official expression, was hailed by our local progressives as the "first constructive explanation." "You have shown us something to gain from this strike—education in management." But did sixty thousand workers strike for education? Later when I was arrested, this editorial was one of the counts against me. Its very vagueness saved me. "No one knows where"—the prosecution claimed this threatened anarchy. The defense retorted that it merely admitted the fact that the future is unknown. Neither gave the real essence of those words. They appealed to the faith of the pioneer in inevitable progress; they stirred the passion of the march to the undiscovered West. Yet they carefully evaded battle. We shook the threat of workers' power in the face of our enemies, but made it plain that we intended only a threat. "This looks too much like the taking of power. . . ." "Labor may feel led to manage more activities. . . ." Not once did we say that labor "would" or "should." We consoled ourselves with good incidental work of organization, milk stations, feeding kitchens, but in all our ultimate policy we actually bragged that "no one knew where" we were going! . . . We had, in short, the mood of the New Era sixteen years ahead of Roosevelt!

"On Thursday at 10 A.M." sixty thousand workers went off their jobs in Seattle. The organized life of the city fell into their hands. They themselves hardly knew it; the sense of power was merely an extra fillip to the joyous solidarity felt among the workers. They laughed: "Our first vacation in three years." The union leaders bragged: "Sixty thousand out and not even a fist fight." They were proud of their pacifism and self-control. With smiling words the labor guards dispersed all crowds that gathered, lest someone provoke a riot. Strike bulletins urged workers to stay off the streets, to patronize libraries and dig in home gardens to "make the most of your leisure," as this is "fine weather for vacation." The feeding of down-town workers was done by the provision trades, in twenty-one special dining-rooms, opened for the duration of the strike. By the end of the strike they were serving thirty thousand meals a day. Thus the fighting solidarity of Seattle's workers was carefully shepherded into a demonstration of law and order. Years later I saw this happen again in the British General Strike, whose workers boasted of their ball games with the police. In Seattle the ordinary police court arrests sank far below the average, so careful were the workers to avoid all fights.

In spite of this pacific attitude of the workers, the business men who scanned the "exempt" signs on Seattle's public services, or who asked for tickets to eat in the strikers' kitchens, knew that power had slipped from their hands into the keeping of these new, unconscious men. Their exasperation grew hourly; it became wrath and thirst for blood. They pressed upon the mayor, upon Washington; they bought guns from hardware stores and demanded rights as deputies. Two thousand four hundred "citizens," not workers, thus received the stars and guns which the labor guards had refused. Troops from Camp Lewis were marched into the city and stationed in the armory to be "ready for trouble."

Ole Hanson, real estate promoter by profession and mayor

of Seattle at the time, was an amiable politician and a good
bluffer, as both his trade and his avocation demanded. When
the strike was announced he took some of the labor leaders to
lunch in Rippe's café and pled with them: "Boys, I want my
street lights and water supply and hospitals. I don't care if
you shut down all the rest of the city." He came to the *Union
Record* office to cajole us; he admired the material of my dress
and asked where his wife could get one like it. Ole was no
revolution-buster in those days; he was trying to conciliate the
revolution. He was a small town politician, all things to all
comers, a weather-cock in the wind. Yet by such weather cocks
one may tell whence wind is blowing. When Ole turned against
us on the second day of the general strike, we should have
guessed that he had discovered our weakness. When he began
to mail hundreds of copies of his own photographs to newspapers all over the United States as the man who smashed the
revolution in Seattle, we should have known that we had lost
the battle.

Ole didn't dare make that announcement in Seattle. When
word came back to us from other cities that Ole called our
strike an attempted revolution which he had already put down,
Seattle workers laughed. Not a union had gone back to work
at Hanson's orders, issued suddenly after a conference with
business men on the second day of the strike. We took pictures of Seattle's busiest corners on the morning after Ole
had "quelled" us; they showed empty streets. The national
officers of many trade unions had already arrived in Seattle
to call off the strike, but they were meeting with strong opposition from the rank and file.

Suddenly on the fourth morning the strike was called off by
a resolution which declared that there had been no defeat but
that everyone should return to work on the following day. It
was a muddled resolution in which the only thing that was
clear was that the strike was over, and that nobody could tell
exactly why. Its confused tone was echoed almost exactly
years later by the resolution which ended the British general
strike.

Shall one blame the yellow leaders who sabotaged the strike

and wished to end it? Such a charge is easy to make—and true. But it is more to the point to ask why it happened that as soon as any worker was made a leader he wanted to end that strike. A score of times in those five days I saw it happen. Workers in the ranks felt the thrill of massed power which they trusted their leaders to carry to victory. But as soon as one of these workers was put on a responsible committee, he also wished to stop "before there is riot and blood." The strike could produce no leaders willing to keep it going. All of us were red in the ranks and yellow as leaders. For we lacked all intention of real battle; we expected to drift into power. We loved the emotion of a better world coming, but all of our leaders and not a few of our rank and file had much to lose in the old world. The general strike put into our hands the organized life of the city—all except the guns. We could last only until they started shooting; we were one gigantic bluff. That expert in bluffing, Ole Hanson, saw this on the second day of the struggle.

We did not see it; not even when the strike was over. We would not admit it lost. One naïve newsboy said in disappointment: "I thought we were going to get the industries." If any of the leaders had had such thoughts half-consciously, we promptly forgot or denied them; we bluffed ourselves and the workers with phrases of victory. We had "shown the strength of labor"; we had "turned the attention of a continent on Mr. Piez' deceit"; we had "learned more about the administration of a city than any workers in America knew before." We had organized a city milk supply and the feeding of thirty thousand people. We had "come close to the problems of management." We persuaded ourselves that this was what the strike had been for. And the workers believed us, or half-believed us, and went back to work with a sense of having gained something, they were not sure just what.

With determined optimism and almost mystical idealism, I was writing editorials which declared: "If by revolution is meant violence, forcible taking of property, killing of men, surely none of our workers dreamed of such action. But if by revolution is meant that a Great Change is coming over the face of the world which will transform our methods of carrying on industry—then we do believe in such a Great Change and that our general strike was one step towards it."

A history committee was elected to produce a collectively authenticated account of our experiences that "the workers of the world may learn from our mistakes as well as from our successes." I was historian, submitting everything first to the committee and then through the columns of the *Union Record* to the workers' comments. We tried to analyze what we had hoped to gain and how we should have gained it. Was it a strike to demonstrate solidarity? Then we should have fixed a definite termination. Was it a strike for shipyard wages? Then we should have made this clear. Was it a strike for revolution? Then we should have been prepared to hold and organize power. "But we did not have the past experience or the intentions on which revolution is built."

So much we saw and wrote, passing quite unconsciously over the whole problem of the conquest of power. The gaps in our understanding would be to me now incredible had I not seen since then the dream called "technocracy" and the dream of Los Angeles workers that small worker-owned industries might lead to socialism, and that out of faith and emotion there may dawn a better world. To all those beautiful mists of hope our dreams were kin.

Frank Vanderlip, former president of the National City Bank of New York and a far-seeing capitalist, passed through our city, and I interviewed him for the *Union Record* on the economic situation in Europe, his intelligent views on which were being flouted by the diehard capitalists. He read our history of the general strike and said to me: "I expected only slogans but this is important history. It frightens me; I did not dream that such forces were alive in America."

The capitalists of America were not dreaming. Nor was the government in Washington asleep. We had jarred them rudely awake and they acted, far more effectively than we. We had shown strength and then failed to use it; they resolved that there should be no repetition of that strength. Their cruder steps took the form of raids and arrests of socialists and I.W.W.'s who had supported the strike. They even grew bold enough to arrest the chiefs of the *Union Record*. I was writing at home when Harry Ault telephoned me: "A deputy is here in the office to arrest you; better hurry down and get it over." So I hurried down and signed the receipt for the indictment which a rather embarrassed deputy gave me, and I waited in the district attorney's office while the Boilermakers Union went to the bank for bail.

But these arrests were hasty and ill-considered. They chiefly worried the Democratic Party of the state of Washington which sent a protesting delegate East. "My God, these folks are backed by forty thousand votes, the votes that changed to Roosevelt and then to Wilson. Now you will lose them all to the Farmer-Labor Party." . . . So our case was quietly dropped behind the scenes. But the votes went Farmer-Labor anyway as the next stage in progress.

We were marching on to victory, ever on! We were a light to the workers in the eastern states; we were a fighting part of the world's workers! So we were—until the shipyards closed! The war was over, they said; there was no more need of ships. Was it by accident that the Seattle shipyards closed a year earlier than the yards of Hog Island and San Francisco, which also worked on government orders? Or were there shrewd men in the East who decided that "red Seattle" must be tamed? We never knew; how could we ever know?

We knew that the economic crisis of 1920-21 came to us a year before it came to others. And that our shipyard workers drifted to other cities to look for work. The young, the daring, the best fighters went. The family men who were tied by payments on little homes could not so easily go. So the composition of our labor movement changed. The life died out of a dozen "workers' enterprises" which were part of our "inevitable road to socialism." Overexpanded coöperatives went bankrupt in a storm of recriminations. Business firms which had courted the *Union Record* with advertisements to capture the workers' trade now sensed our weakness and pressed for control of our columns. Workers fought each other for jobs and not the capitalists for power.

Out of the conflicts that raged around the *Union Record,* loneliness and confusion grew for me. As once I had clung to the hollow form of independence while eastern monopoly took control of my child welfare exhibits, so now I clung to the outworn form of comradeship, though the old comrades called each other traitors. There began to arise again in me the longing of the pioneer to escape from insoluble problems of the human society around me. Whither could I flee from the empty dissensions, from the deadening yet bitter reaction in which the exultant faith of our Seattle "revolution" so unaccountably had perished?

CHAPTER VIII

AN EXCHANGE OF WORLDS

It was Lincoln Steffens who released me to come to Moscow, in Blanc's café, in Seattle, some fifteen years ago.

It was one of those moments in life which occur to us motor-minded people, when we veer in a sharp direction that seems unrelated to the old, yet which is already determined by a hundred unnoticed influences which have heaped themselves within us. And then some chance event, a phrase, the sight of a new face releases us to our new, already destined path, and the moment of change seems a great, decisive moment, forever engraved on memory.

So I shall always remember those words of Lincoln Steffens and the little ill-lit booth in Blanc's café in Seattle where my Moscow life began. In those days of 1920, Blanc's dingy little basement was the place to which Seattle artists, authors and members of the left-wing generally—despite our "revolution" we still called ourselves "progressives"—used to take important visitors whom we wished to favor with good food and quiet talk without digging too deeply into our not very wealthy pockets.

So when my old friend Steffens, the admired reporter of my youth who had covered the "shame of the cities" and all the muck-raking reforms which tried to keep America democratic, came back from the war-torn lands of Europe to lecture about the Bolshevik Revolution, it was to Blanc's I took him for those personal additions to his lecture which we merciless friends of the lecturer always exact. He had seen half a dozen revolutions from Mexico to Moscow; he had attended the making of the Versailles treaty of peace which was no peace, and, far more exciting to all of us, he had helped influence President Wilson to send a special emissary, Bullitt, to Russia on the first official quest to that Soviet

land about which the whole world wondered. He himself had
gone with Bullitt; he was lecturing about it across America
and granted a day to Seattle.

I poured out upon him the tale of our local troubles. "All
the old comradeship is torn to pieces. All the old friends are
calling each other traitors."

"When did it start?" asked Steffens.

"It's been getting worse for months," I answered. The
Central Labor Council meetings that used to have such fine
speeches from workers all over the world have turned into nasty
wrangles between carpenters and plumbers for control of little
jobs. I think it began when the shipyards closed and the
metal trades workers began to leave. These workers' enterprises of which we were so proud began to go to pieces. And
everybody who took part in them got blamed. Now some of
the members of our staff are attacking Harry Ault, our editor,
most horribly; one of them said that if I didn't join the attack, they would 'rub my name in the dirt.' It was a man
I used to like who threatened me."

"So you are siding with Harry?" asked Steffens.

"Well, no, I can't exactly side with Harry." Under the
questions I began to analyze. "I think it's terrible the way
our paper is going. We are beginning to be bossed by advertisers. When the labor movement was united business firms had
to advertise in our paper. But now they are creeping up on
us and making us soften our tone. Harry is between the devil
and the deep sea. I think he's not bold enough; he ought to
defy these advertisers even if we have to have a smaller paper.
But the paper is his child; he dreamed of it when he used to
work as a small boy in a printing office and sleep on the table
at night. He gave his best years to make this paper; I hate
to see these upstarts call him traitor. But I can't agree with
Harry either; he's begun to say the workers are ungrateful.
One can't say that."

"If you only knew," said Steffens, "how this fight of yours
in Seattle is repeated all over the world. Your Harry reminds
me of the German social democrats who have knifed the revo-

lution in the back. You must drop him; he'll sell you out to
the advertisers."

"I oppose him all the time in our editorial meetings," I
answered. "But I oppose him in a friendly way because I
understand his troubles. I can't join these wolves who tear
him to pieces."

"You must join one or the other soon," said Steffens
gravely, "or be torn in pieces by both."

"They threaten from both sides already," I answered ruefully. "Not Harry; he's still friendly. But his conservative
friends, the old line trade unionists, can threaten as nastily as
these hot-heads who don't care what they wreck. I can understand both sides somewhat; I must help get them together.
They were such good comrades before; and we all went ahead
so rapidly. They must be good comrades again."

"Never," said Steffens. "Never! The gulf will grow wider!
It is growing all over the world."

His words dismayed me. We began to talk of Moscow,
which Steffens had recently seen, that glamorous, adventurous
country which was building a new world behind the old world's
blockade, Moscow, whose pamphlets I had seized and reprinted
yet which I had never thought of visiting. Now suddenly I
cried, meaning it as much and as little as one always means
such phrases: "Oh, I'd give anything if I could go there."

"Why don't you then?" asked Steffens calmly. It brought
me up short. Were the words I had said just words or did I
mean them? What was there to hold me in Seattle? Money?
I had saved up enough from my salary to live anywhere for a
couple of years. My job? But my job was now a disillusion.
Family ties? My father's household wants were cared for by
a Japanese school boy, and his reconciliation with old friends
after the war-time separation caused by his pacifism, was re-
tarded rather than helped by his radical daughter.

By a lightning flash four words of Steffens' revealed that
everything which held me in Seattle was completed; only inertia kept me now. Yet I might have remained much longer
—inertia can hold for years and even for lifetime—had it not
been for that question which challenged my words.

"How does one go?" I asked him, and this time I was serious. "There are two kinds of persons accepted past the blockade," he answered. "There is the new, illegal party of American communists now forming in the eastern states; they manage. But since you have no connections with them, but many connections with respectable social workers, your best chance would be the Quakers. They do relief work in Moscow and Petrograd, as in every war-ravaged land of Europe. They are the only civilians legally permitted by any capitalist government to enter Russia and the only bourgeois admitted by the Bolsheviks."

That evening I sent off a letter to the American Friends' Service in Philadelphia, proposing to make a three months' tour of their stations in Europe, including Russia, and write a book about them. I thought in terms of a correspondent's trip for which I would get a leave of absence from the *Union Record*, and from which I would return a cleverly informed person knowing just what to do to heal our troubles. The American Friends' Service answered that they sent people to Europe only on nine months' contract and that only one American relief worker was at present permitted in Moscow.

Several months passed. A summer vacation spent in my coöperative camps on Mt. Rainier took me temporarily out of the struggle; but even they were changing the name "Coöperative Campers" to "Washington Alpine Club," since "coöperative" smacked too much of radicalism! I needed rest after those camps, which I never had needed after camp before. I got leave of absence and went with my father to California and came back again to the fight. Then suddenly early in 1921 the American Friends' Service sent a telegram asking me to do nine months' publicity work in Poland. Nine months? I could not leave my job nine months, inertia still informed me. Poland? Who wants to go to Poland anyway?

Another decisive chance now hastened my future. It was a Saturday noon in the offices of the Seattle *Union Record*—in the new building obtained by clever financing but to which we had carried all the old internal dissensions that were soon to tear the labor paper asunder forever. With that hair-trigger habit of decision to which we motor-minded folk are addicted, and which makes us restless if our desks are piled with unfinished papers, I wrote a telegram of refusal and gave it to the telephone girl to send. She had called Western Union and was reading the first words to Philadelphia when the door of the office opened to a friend I had not seen for three years, who had been doing relief work in Vienna for the Friends' Service.

Swiftly I snatched back my telegram. What mania for speed had made me answer so quickly? In any case that office of God-fearing folk in Philadelphia would be closed till Monday morning. I had till Sunday evening to decide. I consulted with my more experienced friend and with others and sent an altered message, which after fourteen years I remember clearly: "Is assignment confined to Poland or will there be chance to visit other fields including Russia? Is publicity only for money-raising or will general articles promoting better international relations be permitted?" This, I think, was just to warn them of my intentions. Somehow I knew already I would go.

The American Friends' Service ran a smooth, sophisticated office—idealism tempered to the methods of this world. They replied in a noncommittal manner from which I might glean anything, mentioned the difficulty of securing a Russian visa and the great importance of money for relief. It was clear they expected me to stay chiefly in Poland and to use my writing talents for the raising of funds. It was equally clear that they would not say this explicitly, and that nothing in their letter forbade me to dream. Not that their forbidding would have stopped it; I had begun my preparations before I got their letter.

If I thus made use of the Friends' Service to reach in the end a purpose alien to their will, they similarly made use of me and of all their staff in Poland. Most of the members of their mission in Warsaw had originally applied to go to Russia, which to all us young left-wing idealists was our land of dream. They had been rather indefinitely led, as I was, to hope that Warsaw might be a gateway to Moscow, if, and

when, the blockade broke. But of them all I was the first
who made it.

I do not think that our ulterior purpose injured at all our
conscientious work in Poland. The reverse was rather true;
we strove by swift faithful labor under hard conditions to prepare ourselves for the greater goal beyond. Our mission chief,
Florence Barrow, was a gentle Englishwoman who had worked
among war refugees in Russia along the Volga till the blockade
and the orders of the Allied governments compelled her retreat.
Bolsheviks were to her neither the world's destroyers nor its
saviors, but human beings trying to organize a war-ruined
land under difficult conditions imposed by the hatred of great
nations. She hoped, in her gentle fashion, that hates would
die down and that the Bolsheviks would succeed without any
more upheavals in restoring industry and farming and in giving people food. Amid revolutions and counter-revolutions
she placidly held her all-inclusive human attitude; it was to
this I was to owe my early chance to leave Warsaw for Moscow.

Meantime in her gentle, smiling fashion she used my burning
hopes to warm the daily duties of my tasks in Poland. I recall
one night when we slept in an open field of a malarial village
near the eastern border, and another night when we did not
even try to sleep because the bedbugs in Baranowice railway
station were so thick that even sitting down was torment and
we walked the platform all night long. Florence Barrow
smiled at me: "Getting your Russian training," and my will
revived, as long ago on mountain climbs, to make of torturing
hours an ecstasy of triumph. Exhaustion, vermin, dysentery
were birth pangs to joy, the initiation to that chaos where a
new world was being born beyond the border.

Meantime with others of the Friends' Mission in Warsaw
I made myself acquainted with the new Soviet Embassy recently arrived in Poland. Its secretary, Mitchel Rubenstein,
knew of me; he had lived some years in New York and had
read my "Anise" verses copied in the New York *Call*. He
offered me the greatest prize he possessed, a visa to Soviet
Russia, and was somewhat affronted when my bourgeois sense

of honor refused to abandon the Quakers and go. I begged him to hold that visa for my first opportunity.

Events themselves were marching to release me. My newspaper training had seized the vivid new material which the Friends' stations in Poland afforded and swiftly turned out a mass of articles, news items and pictures which was almost more than they could use. I even sent a lantern slide lecture complete with more than a hundred photographs. I had covered all their stations and was ready to leave the last one, Lodz, for Warsaw when there occurred the final chance which gave me Moscow. Into my room on the last evening in Lodz came an American Red Cross girl fresh from New York. She was frankly bored by her first ten days in Poland and was praying that a kind God would send her with the Hoover relief just organizing to carry food to the Volga famine in Russia.

"They are up at Riga now," she told me. "Americans are going in; I hope one of them will be me."

"What makes you want to go to Russia?" I asked her, since her conversation had shown not the slightest interest in labor problems or revolutions.

"It's so much bigger; there's so much more to do," she answered. "Here in Poland is no different from working in the slums at home. Only dirtier. Over there is a famine to fight—something big!"

All night her words repeated themselves in my mind and would not let me sleep. I seemed to hear America speaking with her fresh, naïve young voice. America was ready for a new view of Russia. The old slanders which made the Bolsheviks the world's worst demons, nationalizing women, taking all children from their mothers, ravaging and slaying—those views were ready to perish. This girl hadn't mentioned them at all. America would not admit that she was mistaken; what nation ever admits? She would simply forget those old views if she could be sufficiently excited by a new obsession of mercy; she would be interested enough in saving the Russians to forget that they were devils.

News! News of the famine and with it news of the new world beyond the border. This American Red Cross girl wanted it; millions like her in America wanted it. I would send it. I went next morning to Warsaw and said to Florence Barrow: "The most important thing any reporter can do now for world peace and good understanding between nations is to send true news from the Russian famine. You see how the French reactionaries raise the cry: 'Let the Russians starve till they throw out the Bolsheviks.' We must fight that idea. The Quakers in Moscow have facts; other facts can be quickly ascertained. Someone must break this blockade of silence that relief may flow."

I asked for three weeks' leave of absence to go as far as the Volga; I asked the right to cable New York and form connections with a press agency. I brought out for all it was worth the promise of a Russian visa made by Rubenstein. "I can go more quickly than anyone else," I said. "There is no work holding me just now in Poland."

After a day Miss Barrow gave her decision. "You need not take a leave of absence. You can go for our Warsaw mission," she said. "We had determined to close our relief in eastern Poland. But the Volga famine is flooding us with refugees. We must know what to expect; will they come by hundreds of thousands or by millions? How fast and in what condition will they come? On this depends our future work in Poland.

"Go therefore as far as Moscow, and if you can manage it, as far as the famine areas. Report to the Friends' Mission in Moscow; if they need you, their demands take precedence of ours. If they do not need you, do not bother them but carry out our assignment. I do not forbid your connection with any American press agency that will take your cables. I have consulted our American vice-chairman and I have cabled London; they do not object since you get your visa outside our quota. Perhaps," she hesitated, "perhaps I should ask Philadelphia also."

My heart stood still. The Philadelphia headquarters had never forbidden Russia; but something told me their caution would oppose my trip. But I faced Miss Barrow calmly, knowing that I was on the road to Moscow and some day, now or later, would arrive. "The weekly train to Moscow goes to-morrow," I reminded her. "Answers from Philadelphia by cable take three or four days." Such was indeed the state of the postwar communications.

Did Miss Barrow also suspect Philadelphia? She was too wise a chief to let me know. She paused, then gave her placid answer, with that persistent, all-including humanness for which she would quietly withstand the world: "We send members of our staff to Berlin and Vienna without asking Philadelphia," she said calmly. "I don't know that one need assume that Moscow is out of the world."

For this she was later to receive a reprimand. How severe it was I do not know; she never mentioned it. It was from others that I knew. The great American Relief Administration for the Russian famine was being at that time organized under Hoover, who used its power of food to enter and attempt to dominate the Russian scene. The Russians were well aware of this; when Hoover's representative in Riga demanded for all relief workers full diplomatic privileges, which would allow his emissaries to investigate the sorest spots of the Volga and send out confidential information without control, Litvinoff answered bitterly, as he acceded: "Bread is a weapon." Bread was the next weapon by which the imperial powers of earth would probe the depths of Soviet Russia, guns having failed. American bread had helped to overthrow soviets in Hungary, and deterred revolution in Germany.

Hoover organized control of this weapon; he demanded that all American gifts go through the American Relief Administration; he asked this of the Quakers. Since the Friends' Service was an international organization, fully as British as American, the American Quakers even tried, with that unconscious conceit which comes so natural to us Americans, to give Hoover control over the British too. The British Quakers objected; the American Quakers were compelled to accept dictation from Hoover; this for a time caused a technical split in all the Russian relief of the Friends' Service. The Americans, for instance, had to buy all their grain in America, to help the American farmer; the British got theirs much more

quickly from Rumania. Hoover also demanded and secured
from the American Quakers the pledge that all the personnel
they sent to Russia should be approved by him. He didn't
want "reds" going there to sympathize with Bolsheviks.

So it worried our Philadelphia office when I suddenly appeared in Moscow, and traveled as far as the Volga, sending
out daily cables to the Hearst papers, which had snatched at
the chance to have me cover the famine. I made it quite plain
that the Friends had done relief work in Moscow long before
Hoover, and that the food I personally took to the Volga
reached Samara two weeks before the Hoover shipments arrived. I made it equally plain that the Soviets themselves were
contributing, by heroic sacrifice, far more relief to the famine
than they got from abroad. I showed an orderly world of
health departments, school departments, local authorities fighting a natural catastrophe, instead of anarchy brought into
order by Americans.

It was not a picture that suited Hoover. If the Friends'
Service in Philadelphia had cared to fight for independence,
as we did in the old days against the octopus, the picture
would have helped them greatly. But they did not choose;
they had agreed already with Hoover. They told Washington
that I had gone to Moscow without their will. This picture
of me as an irresponsible person who had jumped my job to
join the Russian reds, added to the picture already in Washington of a left-wing labor writer who had taken part in the
Seattle "revolution," led the American consul in Warsaw to
detain my passport which, meticulously following instructions,
I left with him when I went to Moscow. I had been in this
act more law-abiding than any other correspondent who went;
it cost me in the end some waiting and some legal fees in
Washington till I proved through Miss Barrow how I had
gone.

All this lay far in the future. So fast was I moving when
once I left Warsaw behind me that I was to live through
weeks of famine relief, varied by correspondent's cables, and
fight for life with typhus, and write many pamphlets for the
Friends' Service from my sick-bed in Moscow, and journey

slowly out to a Warsaw convalescence—before I even knew that I had no passport. If I had known, I doubt if it would have detained me. For as I approached the border where the two worlds divide—the line in those days was sharp as a drawn sword—I said to myself quite calmly that if the scarcely opened blockade were closing again and I must choose either to turn back and never see the Soviet land or to go forward and know I could never return—I would not risk even an hour to say farewell.

So swift and so far had I already traveled towards Moscow from that moment when four words set me free.

CHAPTER IX

MY UTOPIA IN RUINS

My Utopia to which I had been admitted was in ruins; famine and pestilence swept the land. We in Seattle had reasoned, when we observed the graft and exploitation of capitalists, that as soon as these were abolished widespread comfort would begin. We had allowed a few months, possibly even a few years for necessary reorganization; in our Seattle revolution the handling of milk by the drivers' union did not run smoothly till the third day. But we never allowed for the backwardness of a non-industrial country like Russia, for the Asiatic standards of vast populations, for the lack of surplus goods. Most of all we never allowed for the ravages of intervention and blockade of which we had no adequate conception. My two months in Poland had somewhat prepared me for the ruins of war, but not for the greater attrition of intervention.

Seven years of foreign and civil war had been followed by two years of drought in the Volga valley. Throughout recorded history this central plain between Europe and Asia has been subject to periodic famines. In the slow retreat of earth's last glacial age it is steadily drying; its once great inland lakes have shrunk to salt seas of which the Caspian and Aral seas are chief. Its rivers shift in sandy beds which grow steadily shallower; the mighty Volga itself is doomed some day to extinction unless man finds a way to conquer nature.*

Peasants of tsarist Russia knew no such way. They scratched the soil with wooden plows into shallow furrows; they relied on prayer and religious processions for rain. The chances of callous nature gave them food one year, and hunger the next. This had been their lot through all the years of tsardom, as it is still the lot of similar regions in China. But

---

* See page 369 for the Soviet war against Volga drought.

the drought of 1920 followed by a worse drought of 1921 found a Volga valley whose farm equipment was worn out and whose horses were diminished by seven long years of war.

From this workers' republic which I so eagerly entered hundreds of thousands of people were fleeing, panic-stricken before pestilence and hunger. All eastern Poland was clogged with these refugees. They were the peasants and townsmen who had been driven eastward six years before in the great 1915 retreat of the tsar's armies. Now, with the blockade for the first time lifted, they were flooding back with famine driving behind them to seek their former homes in what had become, since their departure, the new republic of Poland. Lucky were those who found even a shell of a house remaining; for most there were ashes of buildings in desolate fields.

I saw them by the thousands in the Polish quarantine of Baranowice, sleeping, eating, giving birth and dying under the sun and rains of heaven, a miserable louse-ridden horde in the same hairy sheepskins they had worn in their flight six years before. With the lice went typhus, smiting the travelers down as they journeyed. On the long road to Minsk—a few hours' journey now, but then taking more than a day on the war-ruined tracks—I saw through the dark the lights of their campfires where they huddled in dugouts, in ruined shacks, in holes in the ground or under scant shelter of trees. No one could list their number or know when death claimed the stragglers. For a thousand miles their road of death was marked with abandoned graves.

More orderly were those refugees who came by train to the border. These were listed as they passed Moscow and Minsk and disinfected as well as they could be without chemicals, soap or clean underwear. I tried to talk to some of them about the workers' country from which they were fleeing in panic. The peasants among them had seen in the revolution only odd jobs, fighting and fleeing. There were a few workers who had seen factories in Sverdlovsk or Samara. They said it was true that there were no more bosses or landlords; nobody ran things but workers. But the factories were broken down, the machines worn out; there was no food, no clothes, no oil, no raw materials.

Their wages, they said, had been a pound of bread daily till the famine. What more, I asked; they said nothing except occasionally herring and potatoes. Paper rubles were not worth collecting. Some of them told of looting factories and trading old iron for potatoes and cabbage, but the factories were so dismantled that even this resource failed. The famine had stopped even the daily pound of bread, so they were fleeing.

It was hard to believe that my Utopia was so ruined, despite what they said. I was happy when I saw the caps of the railway workers, bearing the crossed hammer and monkey-wrench, railway insignia which I took for the Soviet hammer and sickle. These were a sign that orderly factories existed somewhere, turning out caps. I gayly opened my basket of foodstuffs—it was my largest piece of baggage and I had been warned that it was irreplaceably precious—and began giving out bars of chocolate to trainmen who had those insignia. Those were the first things I saw that had been made since the revolution; I wanted the railway workers who wore them to know that I was a comrade of theirs going to Moscow. They stared at me as if I were crazy but they took the chocolate. After the fifth or sixth time I stopped; their stares made it so clear that they considered me a lunatic.

Vividly I recall the first contacts of that journey. A furtive Jew approached me as I sat on the Minsk platform near my food-basket, asked in bad German if I "had anything," and shuffled away quickly as a Red Guard approached; only then did I realize that he was a speculator-smuggler seeking to trade. The Red Guard himself was barefoot, affable, dangling his rifle by a piece of rope, while the spruce Polish official in our train sneered at the sight and I thought of Washington and Valley Forge and loathed that Pole. Peasant women with enormous food-sacks tried to get on the train in order to sell at famine prices in Moscow the grain that was relatively plentiful in the wet lands of White Russia.

A barefoot boy collecting for famine relief came into our train at Minsk. His shirt and trousers were of homespun linen and it was clear that he had no garments under them.

With fewer and worse clothes than any American beggar, he held himself with dignity as a regular official and presented a paper with the seal of the city showing that he was a member of the Young Communist League, entitled to collect for the Volga famine. It was clear that he did not consider himself in need; he was helping others. For the first time I knew, what the propaganda outside Soviet Russia obscured, that this hard-pressed country was collecting help from the poor to feed the starving. The famine relief from Soviet citizens was far more, I later learned, than all the foreign relief from the wealthiest lands of earth.

A dour man in a shabby uniform got on at Minsk and briefly shared my compartment. At sight of my foreign baggage he grunted a few words in German, and I began to tell him of my happiness in visiting a workers' country. He grumbled that it was a rotten, hungry country and that if I had a passport with which to escape I was lucky and had better get out. Was there no one at all, I wondered, who felt enthusiastic? Then I talked to the Soviet courier going from Warsaw to Moscow, an elderly worker who had seemed a rather dull person till I had caught him stroking the joint of his ring finger with a smile.

"My wedding ring was there," he explained, noting my glance. "My finger seems strange without it. We communists decided to give all our gold to the famine. I have been married thirty years; the ring never left my finger. I had a son who died on the Polish front. But my wife and I—she is waiting in Moscow—we do not need a ring."

No, there was no enthusiasm; that emotion was long since worn down into a grim war with ruin. Nor were all the citizens loyally helping that war. In place of the united country of convinced socialists defying the world which I had expected to find as soon as I crossed the border, I found grumbling, ill-fed folk, many of them barefoot, many cheating the government, most of them discontented. But there were people here and there—I began to note them—who quietly, doggedly and even cheerfully disregarded their own lack and gave their thought to keeping the country alive. Most of them, I began to see, were communists. There were not many of them; they seemed drowned in the chaotic, disgruntled masses; but their common purpose kept them moving forward and enabled them to move those inert others forward. The class struggle, then, was not over under this workers' dictatorship; it was, if anything, more open and bitter. Those who held together were the conquerors. Even they had no energy left for enthusiasm; they needed their energy for struggle.

I had come from America, a sentimental country with large reserves of emotion. I could not at once grasp the grim mood of these people who had experienced such extremes of conflict that death had become a minor event. On my arrival in Moscow, I came breezily into the Foreign Office; its press department was located then in the far corner of the Metropole Hotel and Weinstein was in charge. I confided to him first of all, almost before I presented my credentials, that I hoped to stay in Russia indefinitely and wanted to begin to live on the Russian ration; if others could stand it, I could. He showed no interest in my desire to be part of the country; he merely commented, "The Russian ration these days is a thin one which doesn't keep up efficiency. If you want to do good work, take what food the Quakers give you."

Somewhat dampened, I showed my credentials as correspondent for the International News Service and blithely offered to send all the "statements" he wished. Hadn't I been told that Russians wanted to send out propaganda? "Your side has never been told to the American people," I unnecessarily informed him. "State it to me and I will send it by cable, quoting you at length about the revolution or the famine." He looked more embarrassed than pleased by my offer.

"Stick around and see things, and you'll soon know what to send," he remarked kindly. "I'm no correspondent to write your cables for you." That was all I got for my attempts to be comradely! It is one of the sharp impressions of those first days in Moscow.

Equally sharp was my impression of the Health Commissariat, to which Arthur Watts, head of the Friends' Service in Moscow, sent me on the first day. He had no interpreter

for me, but I was so eager to begin that he smilingly agreed
to my request to try without one.

"Would you like to take the first cars of foreign food to the
Volga?" he asked. "The big American Relief is sending in-
vestigators to travel the whole length of the Volga before they
plan their work. This is a serious delay; we know the heart
of the famine is Samara. People flee from Samara by tens
of thousands. We Quakers have two cars of food to spare
from our children's work in Moscow—not balanced rations,
but canned milk, cocoa, fats and sugars to supplement the
government bread. Actually it won't go very far but I think
it would be psychologically effective to throw it into Samara;
it would let the people know that foreign relief is coming.

"Here's the address of the Health Department, written in
Russian and English. Find Dr. Tregubov, chief of their
transportation. He speaks only Russian but he has doctors
who speak German. Take him this list of food products, written in Russian. Ask if he wants them all for Samara or some
for Saratov. Find if he has trucks to deliver to the station
or if we must deliver. Get directions for finding the cars.
Ask if the cars will go attached to a Health Department feeding train, and if so, whether you can go along."

By waving my paper at men in the street I found the
Health Commissariat; it was at Petrovka 15, a giant building
pierced by an archway, my first experience of the Russian
"house" where one number covers a dozen entrances. I tried
two main entrances and three separate floors. Every floor was
jammed with clerks at tables, but not a single clerk would look
at my list of food products. I was outraged; here were Soviet
officials, sitting in a Health Commissariat. Yet they didn't
care enough about cars of food to turn their faces from the
pale yellow tea they were sipping, or to lift my paper in their
hands. I know now that they were the clogging bureaucratic
officials inherited from tsardom, who had sat idly in those seats
through all the revolution; moreover they were exhausted with
the hunger of years. They were the raw material the communists had to use for the mechanism of government.

Since I was fresh, full-fed, and very eager, by the time I

had reached the fourth floor of that apathy I had reasoned that even if the clerks were unresponsive there were men higher up who would gladly grab the food. This time I did not try to speak to the clerks but walked right past them, opening every inner door I could find as if I knew where I was going. Nobody stopped me; nobody cared. I came to an inner office where three men sat at a table in conference; they stared as I entered and I mutely handed them my paper.

I had guessed right; these men jumped into action at a list of food products. They tried me in Russian, French and German, and having established a mutual language, one of them said: "Dr. Tregubov is in quite a different office, and I cannot go with you since we have an important conference. I will give you a doctor who knows German and who will take you to Tregubov." We had to climb a dozen complicated flights of stairs and seek through several offices for the busy chief of transport; but the doctor found him and did my interpreting, so that less than half an hour after I entered the building I left it with a written order for our shipment of food to Samara and the promise that I might go with it, on a feeding train of the Commissariat of Health.

I learned that day a lesson I never forgot. Moscow did not have offices like those to which I was accustomed in America where every underling makes brisk and affable motions of efficient service in the interest of a man in the inside office who comes to work leisurely and late, and who leaves detailed work to subordinates. Russian offices were chaos, clogged with sluggish people who made no pretense of being interested. But somewhere behind them were men in the inner offices, working early and late, wearing themselves out, men who made the whole thing work. These men did not merely care, like those clerks, for their own cup of tea, their own food, their own jobs; to them every job of the Soviet Power was close and dear.

I had thought the revolution was loved by everyone; I had thought to find a brave new world beyond the border; I found the collapse of an old world under whose ruins men were dying. But living among those ruins were men who were building a

new world from the broken pieces under which all the armies
of earth had sought to bury them. The armies had made
chaos; but there were creators in chaos! They were men like
flames in the mist, signaling each other till fog dissolves in
light!

My desire for this new land strengthened into a passion.
Here was a real job, the biggest job in the world. I was
going to be one of those creators in chaos; I had a chance to
begin right away by taking food to the famine area. That
was only the beginning; I must at once learn Russian and see
what I could do next. I remembered a statement of Lenin's
in that report to the Soviet Congress which we had circulated
in Seattle; he had said that the country's chief lack was just
conscientious, efficient workers. He was certainly right, if
that Health Commissariat was a sample. Here was the place
for me.

The trains from Moscow to Samara take now some forty
hours as normal schedule. In the famine year of 1921, the
special health train on which I traveled took ten days. It
was a wonderful train equipped with kitchen-car to prepare
five thousand rations, with a bake-car that made a ton of
bread at a baking, a dispensary car and a first-aid car, as
well as living quarters for a fair-sized staff. It carried also
some thirty cars of food materials, besides my two cars of
Quaker food. It was one of many such trains operated by
the Health Commissariat for the famine; it bore a special
mandate instructing station masters to speed it on its way.
But we spent our time waiting on sidings. We waited for
engine repair, for the cutting of wood fuel, for trains of famine
refugees, even more broken than our train, to drag themselves
past towards Moscow. We made four hundred miles in the
first five days! With my American impatience I went nearly
crazy; I thought everyone would die before we got there!

When we moved the window openings were alight with
sparks that swept past from the damp wood fuel. The medical head of our train was a young "felcher," a half-trained
assistant doctor. The wars and epidemics had used up the
doctors of Soviet Russia; those who were left were needed for

serious diseases, not wasted on feeding trains and ordinary first-aid. The train commandant asked if it were possible for our foreign relief to give him winter clothes for his train crew who did the heavy open-air work. "We have twenty-four men; last winter the government could give us six pairs of boots and ten coats for the lot; this year they've given nothing. How can we feed five thousand children daily through the winter unless we have clothes in which our train crew can go outdoors? . . . Samara has the greatest extremes of heat and cold of any city on the European continent."

The wife of a train official, playing with her small child of three and expecting another shortly, was wondering where by any chance she could get a piece of warm material for the new baby's underwear. Near her a pleasant, gray-haired woman, head of the Bureau for Motherhood and Infancy in the city of Orenburg, was returning from a trip to Moscow in quest of underclothing, not for one baby but for hundreds. The government had given her cotton material, but she had no blankets nor anything warm. Fats also she wanted; the babies shriveled before her eyes. Nearly all of them died; there was nothing to give them. . . . Inside our car the cry of a baby arose. Its mother had laid it on our car-steps at one of our halts, crying: "Take it. Otherwise I must leave it in the market-place. I have no food; without the baby I may fight my way to regions of bread." We took the child and told her to look for it, if she lived, through the health authorities of Samara.

Thus every person in the train represented some dire need. When I turned to look out of the window, I heard the cry of hundreds of gaunt, dirty children: "Bread, for the love of God, a crumblet, a little crust of bread!" Their thin legs hardly supported them; they raised thin hands and wailed in thin voices. Huddled for warmth against the night in tiny stations I saw throngs of peasants, men, women, children, all armed with government transportation permits in lieu of tickets, all waiting for trains to take them to regions of bread, and dying as they waited.

"How can you fight a famine this way?" I burst out impatiently. "The engines need repairing every few miles, the cars are inspected daily and some are always removed from the train, the fuel is damp wood that is cut while we wait, and there are only a few of these broken-down railway lines across tens of thousands of square miles of burned desert where harvest has failed! All the rest of Russia—workers, officials, everyone —is underfed and underclothed and inefficient from malnutrition. It is ghastly! It is utterly impossible!"

"There is nothing impossible," said Sonia in clear, firm tones. Sonia shared my cabin; she was the interpreter they had found for me in Moscow, a communist giving her month's vacation to famine work. She was born in England of Russian exiles and came to Russia with the revolution. England made her a textile worker; Russia made her a soldier on the Polish front and a commissar in a military hospital. Twice she had been wounded in battle; she had had typhus, smallpox and malaria. She had had a husband, and left him to fight at the front. She had always carried with her a tiny revolver "in case they capture me and find out that I am a woman.

"I also have thought in the past that there were impossible things," continued Sonia. "For eight months I ran a typhus hospital where a thousand men lay on wooden floors that could not be disinfected. The men had been in dirt so long that we had to cut the clothes from them; they were rotten with filth that crumbled in your hands. The lice were imbedded in their flesh; you had to scrub hard or use a razor to get them off. We had no beds, no mattresses, no sheets, no blankets, no soap. The doctors and nurses came down with typhus regularly in fourteen days; there was no possible way to protect them; when they took hold of those men you knew they would most of them be sick with typhus in two weeks.

"I thought it was impossible. But always something can be done. We commandeered a big school-building—the only building big enough for our sick. We took a great wooden tank that was used for washing clothes, and we scrubbed the men in it. We sent word throughout the city (it was a town of thirty-five thousand souls) asking every family to bring us one suit of underwear for the men who were left naked when we cut their clothing off. From most it was a free gift, but communists, of course, were not permitted to refuse. They must give, even if they have no underwear left for themselves. We communists are making the revolution; we must do whatever is demanded." She spoke of the revolution not as a violent upheaval in the past, but as a process yet unfinished.

"The best of my help came from the department in charge of deserters. We didn't shoot deserters; we got good use out of them. We detailed them to hospital work. It was really more dangerous than the front, but it didn't worry them so much. They were used to death in dirt and disease but not to death from guns. They would do any work quite fast and obediently to avoid being sent to the front. Every two weeks I would send for twenty deserters and in two weeks they would be down with typhus and I would send for twenty more. I never knew why I didn't get sick myself. They thought I was immune. I got my typhus later after my time at the front. I must have been weaker; I had been wounded twice. Also I was dirtier—covered with lice for weeks. Then I came down with everything, typhus, smallpox, malaria.

"But I learned that there is nothing impossible. There is always a way. There may not be an easy way, or a way that is sparing of life, but there is always a way through. This famine is nothing to the wars of intervention, except that we're much more tired. But we've the oil of Baku back. We've the coal of the Donetz back. We've more than a thousand of the railway bridges repaired, even the big bridge over the Volga at Samara, blown up by the intervention. Think what it would be if we had to fight the famine without that bridge! We've the borders open now, the blockade broken. That means we can buy food abroad; there are gold and jewels still in our country. Now that we've beaten the intervention, don't think this famine can stop us."

"Millions will die," I said to Sonia.

And Sonia answered: "Millions have already died."

I wondered if she was thinking only of the millions who died in the wars of intervention, out of whose deaths had been won the independence of the revolution, or also of the millions who had died in Europe, to no end but the profits of war-lords and the ghastly peace of Versailles. Millions would die; but these communists who held together would win through. But Sonia had ceased to think of the millions. This Sonia of the hard-won philosophy was only a girl in her twenties; she was ten years younger than I. In the grisly heart of famine, with children wailing outside the windows, she pulled out a novel to read by a single candlelight, and said to me casually: "I should like a couple of babies more than anything, but we have plenty of children in Russia and not many women who can work like I can."

She read herself to sleep, and I blew out the candle.

CHAPTER X

THE FAMINE FRONT

GRAY and slow the dawn came creeping over the wasted planet outside our car windows, a misty dawn leaving its mockery of autumn dew on soil already burned to death by the summer's drought. We were in the heart of the famine where the earth cracked open with dryness; we were approaching the Volga. The wailing of children outside our windows had hushed with this hour of dawn. Outside I saw a village of thatched roofs, gray in the morning.

Just beyond the village as we crept slowly onward, I saw the lands of the peasants, already plowed, already springing green with the first shoots of winter rye for the harvest of the coming year. To this stricken district where all grain had died the Soviet government had sent seed, gathered with what effort I could imagine, sent by what difficulty along this broken railroad. The hungry peasants of this district, whose own children wailed for food, had gone, disciplined and controlled, to plow and feed the earth with government seed. Before next harvest many would be dead; those who were left would gather grain.

Then I knew the story I must send by cable to a full-fed land beyond the sea. I knew the wild tales spread in the press outside Russia of hospitals burned in panic, of peasants rioting as they fled. I knew the correspondent who had rushed to the Volga, saying: "Blood, show me blood! Show me corpses eaten by dogs." Mine must be a greater story—the tale of this disciplined control that made men sow the seed they could not live to gather. I must tell of life that went on though millions perished—of a barefoot boy in Minsk collecting not for himself but for others; of a food train where a crew without shoes or overcoats toiled in winter blizzards to feed five thousand children. I must tell of a vast land—ruined by long

109

war, by civil war in every city and village, where trains still halted on the emergency wood fuel enforced by the blockade, and moved forward with exasperating slowness on tracks not yet fully repaired—a land which nevertheless organized its cities and disciplined its peasants to concentrate what life was left on one united struggle, and whose fighting youth, even its girls, held nothing impossible.

I must tell it to the men of the great plains and cities in the American West. I must use very simple words. I must avoid the politics of Moscow and not speak of Bolsheviks or communists or often of soviets, since these words aroused in many minds strange and confused storms of hate. I must speak of "Health Department" trains, of children's homes under the "Board of Education," of "relief work by local authorities or central authorities"—the phrases America knows. I must tell it so that men and women of prairies and mountains and cities in the land I knew so well across the sea would feel it not as a strange tale of oddly different people dying in an alien country, but as something that might have happened in their own land, had the struggle and the heroism been the same.

For the next four weeks that was the story I sent. I left Sonia with the food train at Sizran, and went by swifter post train overnight to Samara, armed with a basket of personal provisions and a letter of introduction. I waved the letter at the first man in the Samara station who had a red cross on his cap; when Sonia came with the train three days later I was already installed in a second food train, which operated regularly in Samara station, and I had made with the local health and educational authorities tentative arrangements for the distribution of food. Sonia was horrified; she warned me that even doctors and teachers were robbers and must be properly controlled by the Samara Executive Committee, who would check on every pound of food they got. She arranged it; she also arranged for a horse and cart for our personal use for a few hours daily, so that we could visit the children's institutions. She arranged for the official seal on my telegrams which enabled them to be sent through the desultory postoffice of Samara.

I lived in a food train in Samara station, and awakened every morning with the murmur of five thousand children in my ears. They waited patiently from dawn till midday for the one meal of porridge or soup or bread and cocoa which kept them alive. Pregnant and nursing mothers also waited in line and were fed for the children they carried. They were mostly the women and children of peasants who were camped about the station, fleeing from dying villages, waiting for some transport to go to regions of bread. They included refugees bound for far-distant Poland. These peasants crammed all trains; they rode on the roofs of cars and of locomotives; they were swept from their hold by fatigue and hunger and died. The children and the women carrying children were the weakest and held the hope of the future; therefore they were fed by the health department which could not feed all.

Daily I struggled through the thousands who clogged the station—it was not possible to protect oneself against their lice even by washing daily. I went to the offices of health and education departments, to children's homes and hospitals, arranging the disposal of the cars of Quaker supplies. We had chiefly condensed milk, cod liver oil, sugar, cocoa and similar food. Much of it went to children's hospitals and the homes for small babies, run by the health department; some of it went to supplement rations in children's homes, which were run by the educational authorities. We had some hundreds of pounds of soap which was as much desired as food. Everyone agreed that this should go to the terrible "receiving stations" which handled, quarantined and distributed the hundred or more children that were daily picked up in Samara's streets— brought from distant villages and abandoned by parents who could not feed them. The Samara authorities had hastily organized emergency receiving stations in broken buildings, whose walls and windows still bore traces of the Czecho-Slovak intervention, and whose floors were still heaped with débris of broken woodwork. Into these went starving children by thousands, sick with cholera, typhus, dysentery; they had no soap nor change of underwear or clothing; they littered the floor with filth. Into these stations went, as into a ravenous maw, our hundreds of pounds of soap.

Out of these stations were organized, after quarantine, normal children's homes divided according to ages. That stricken, starving city had to organize almost one such children's home per day. Without mattresses, sheets, books or clothing—yet in these normal homes there was already order. I saw a home that had been two months organized; regular classes for children went on daily. The first class was learning to speak Russian; the famine had uprooted villages of a dozen nationalities, untouched since the great migrations of the Middle Ages. There were six different nationalities in that home, Mordva, Chuvash and others. The older classes learned to read from stray books picked up in the débris of Samara; only the very highest class learned writing; there were just six pencils in that school.

Yet the educational authorities of Samara had the daring to say to me, when they saw my list of products: "Those chocolate bars are too few to make a real addition to the food supply; let us use them for a problem in education. Let all our children's homes work out in their arithmetic classes the number of pieces of chocolate that fall to their share, according to the number of children in the children's homes of Samara; then every home will choose delegates to go to your train and get the chocolate with a written order made out by the school committee for the proper amount."

Two mornings later came pale but proud young delegates, each with the signed and stamped credential from his school. We followed the chocolate into the homes and saw the children divide it; nowhere did any child ask for more than his rationed share. I marveled how the organized life of human society persisted through death and chaos. Normal life asserted itself through discipline and education; and the forms it took were the new forms, fixed by the revolution. Fixed by those creators in chaos who held nothing impossible, and whose organizing will held on through famine.

Every night I sent the story of the day to America via the Internews. I saw my cables go into a bewildered and lazy postoffice where nobody understood English but where one clerk knew the Latin alphabet and spelled the messages over the wires blindly. The office seemed so disorganized and indifferent that I was not sure they sent the cables at all. No reassuring answer ever returned from the far-off west, nor from Moscow, not even when my relief work was finished and I telegraphed for further orders. I felt as much alone and as inaccessible as if I were signaling from Mars. Only months later did I hear that my cables reached America and that the western press in particular featured these "reports of an American girl in the famine-stricken heart of the Soviets."

Day after day in Samara I met new creators in chaos. There was Dr. Blaznansky, a woman physician who had organized and equipped a maternity hospital in a city where boards and nails were scarcely to be had; with what energy and care she salvaged bed-springs, plumbing pipe and old iron from heaps of débris outside war-ruined buildings. There was a factory manager who acted as my interpreter when Sonia returned to Moscow at the end of her "vacation." He was a homely Russian Jew from New York's East Side, but how his face lit up when he showed me the two broken buildings where he had created a sash and door factory to repair Samara's ruined houses.

Most of all I remember Puriayeff, chairman of relief in a little village near Samara. Is he alive now or did he die in the famine? When I met him he was already gaunt with hunger, not swollen like most famine victims. He refused to stay his stomach with substitute bread filled with ground bark and straw which others were eating and which bloated their bodies; he still had respect for his intestines which helped him control the pangs of hunger. I saw the firm support he had in his village and his carefully compiled lists. Of 1,700 souls, more than 200 had wandered away since the famine; there were left 1,477, of whom 79 had bread for a month and nobody had bread till Christmas. "There are 1,333 souls now eating bread from grass and leaves and bark mixed with a little grain," he told me, showing me the harsh dark samples of this "bread." "We had a piece of real bread in my house four days ago," he added.

I distributed the last of some Quaker clothing in Puriayeff's village; I sat in the room of the village soviet while the clothes were apportioned. The committee went down the list of all the village families, and assigned one garment here, one there. Peasants wandered in, listened, went out again; anyone who desired might hear and comment. Some of them complained: "We also have unclothed ones on our ovens. Isn't there enough for all?" . . . "There is not enough for all; we give to the poorest," said Puriayeff. After this there was no more complaint.

We invited Puriayeff to eat with us that evening; we had an enormous loaf of bread. "I should prefer to take home the bread you intend to give me," he said, after a brief hesitation. We learned that he shared it with his sister and her children; there could not have been more than a few mouthfuls each. Months after, when I heard of chairmen of relief who starved at their posts, obeying the iron law which sent rations only to children, I remembered Puriayeff. After a few chairmen died, that iron law was relaxed by the American Relief, and the personnel of relief stations were given food. Was it relaxed in time to save Puriayeff? His will, I think, would not relax even for death.

A second visit I made to Puriayeff's village as organizer of feeding kitchens for the American Relief Administration. My Quaker food was finished but while I awaited orders from Moscow, the great Hoover relief arrived in Samara with carloads of food, and began to form its local organization for distributing the relief. Though every Russian village had its relief committees, its lists of breadless families and its houses commandeered for kitchens, this was not acceptable to the Americans. They demanded special committees of their own in every village on which the local priests must be represented together with the local officials. It startled the villages but they did it. "Bread is a weapon!" Since the American Relief was short of organizers and I had time available, I went in their auto-truck to villages strategically placed in five townships, and organized the first local committees as examples, giving to each an order for food from the ARA supplies in Samara. . . . For one of my examples I chose Puriayeff's village, and he came to Samara for the food.

It was thus I saw him last, the most vivid of all my memories of him, in a large hotel room of faded splendor occupied by a man of the ARA who had come up the Volga from the Caspian, investigating all the way. This man had nothing to do with local relief; he reported conditions to Washington. Full fed and aggressively content he sat in the best rooms Samara afforded, consuming a copious meal of borsch, chicken and wine. On the floor beside him were great baskets of hams, canned goods, wines and stronger drinks with foreign labels.

Puriayeff looked not at the food; he looked at the man's uniform—an officer's uniform of fine cloth with shining buttons and epaulets, well brushed as if for parade. Puriayeff's own gaunt body was clothed in the patched linen homespun and ragged sheepskin in which he had fought in the Red Guards against the armies of intervention. He had seen such uniforms before, similar in magnificence of woolen cloth and shining decoration, if not in color. He had seen them on the tsar's officers and on the officers of the intervention. He had overthrown the men who wore them. Now he saw the uniforms come back on Americans who in the name of food traveled the length of the hard-won Volga, observing, reporting, yet protected by the Soviets.

Then Puriayeff looked down at the hampers of food and wine; in his eyes was the look not of hunger, but of worried contempt. Was that old world he had helped overthrow coming back to rule the Volga? What did this man portend? Then he looked at me, still puzzled. Who was I who sat in his village soviet that morning, and in the room of this officer tonight? I, who had given him a gladly received order for food which he had followed to this strange end? What was I doing between two worlds?

It was my last sight of Puriayeff. It was almost my last sight of either of those warring worlds or of any world at all.

After the whirlwind of those four weeks in Samara, working as relief organizer by day and as correspondent by night, I was suddenly stricken with typhus which turned me from a would-be "creator in chaos" into a mere consumer of food and hospital space, the two most precious articles in Samara.

CHAPTER XI

FEVER AND STORM

I WAS relieved when the doctor said I had typhus. Typhus excuses everything.

It excused the five days of horrible headache which kept me from working. It excused the disgraceful weakness and the whole hospital room which I occupied for myself and my nurse, a room that might have held three children. I was so weak that I wept in the night because I could not sleep and in the morning because I could not wash my face nor comb my hair. No Russian nurses had time to bother with hair-combing; they put a basin of water on a chair near my bed and gave me a towel, which I promptly dropped on the floor, weeping because I could not hold it. I was a useless person, worse than useless; I was hampering the action of others.

I thought in shame: why couldn't I get out before this happened? If I could only have held out one day more! A thousand miles back in Moscow and Warsaw they awaited my report. The long-expected telegram had come ordering my return, my ticket was bought for the evening train, my clothes were almost packed. For the first time in weeks a special car carried correspondents and relief workers from Samara to Moscow. Then the headache struck me down and I had not strength to go. "If there were a doctor on that train or even another woman, we would carry you to it," they said, "for Samara is not a good place to be sick in. But you may not be able to rise from bed tomorrow." They were right: I couldn't; not for weeks.

On the fifth day the doctor tried to show me the little black marks on my arm that meant typhus. I lied and said I saw them to avoid discussion. Actually it was too much trouble to focus my eyes. I do not know to this day what typhus looks like. But I sighed with relief as I sank back into typhus as

117

into a great sheltering excuse. This was no penalty for over-work or stupidity which care might have avoided; no influenza which I might have had at home. It was the lice-borne typhus, child of war and famine. I had come too late for war; my privilege of Quaker food protected me from famine. Typhus was my share in chaos; my initiation fee to join those other builders.

The doctor seemed annoyed at my sigh of relief. "It's a very serious disease," she reproved me, not knowing that it was just this seriousness that allowed me to relax into shameful inaction. "Do many people die of it?" I asked her. "Oh, no," she hastily beat a retreat. "You must not think of dying." So I thought of it lazily and long in the daze of the headache and decided against it. Nothing would come of dying way off in Samara, not even a propaganda funeral. I couldn't die after just six weeks of life.

Seven days and nights that horrible headache kept me sleepless, despite the sedatives that the doctor gave me. On the eighth night she gave something different. "Something you can't resist," she told me. All night a nightmare of wild Cossacks pursued me, shouting "You can't resist" as I tottered over desert sands. I woke in utter rage of exhaustion. What was the use of a doctor who couldn't give you even a night of decent sleep? "It would serve that doctor right if I went crazy," was my last vindictive thrust of consciousness. Almost immediately I did go crazy, escaping from Samara in a soft, warm airplane.

I dropped in the Coliseum in Chicago and began to tell thou-sands of people about the famine. They must hurry, hurry with the food! I saw my sister's face in the meeting but I could not stop to see her; I must take my report to London. I couldn't land in Fetter Lane in front of the Quakers' office; the streets were too dangerous with taxis. So I hunted for Miss Frye on the third floor of her country house, but the labor troubles on the second floor made it hard to get up and down. The water made my throat taste cottony; I was sur-prised that they had such bad water in England. Once they gave me a lemon that cut deliciously through the cotton; they brought it in a suitcase from London. But when I asked for more they told me the transport was blocked to Turkestan. What crazy excuse was that?

It was better on the wall outside Samara. Like the great Chinese wall we built it to keep back hosts of famine that howled like wolves in the darkening steppe. Were they wolves, or an army with waving banners, catching last gleams of sun? They were advancing; they stretched their lines southward and northward; they surrounded us in all directions. But they would not take the city. We were too much for them, we were too much for them, I knew quite cheerfully. To us there was nothing impossible!

Our wall was huge and thick and very long; far off to left and right it rose in turret after turret athwart the darkening plain. Every turret held by another lonely watcher; far off, till you could not see them for the night. At my feet the wall dropped sheer to a wide moat filled with human bones. Flashes of lightning showed the bones and the distant circling host. But they could not pass us; they could not pass our wall!

I crossed the Arctic Circle by airplane at a place called Nansen City; it was last land, a tiny bay with beetling cliffs. Over the northern sea the Polar Night marched southward, an inexorable wall of black. The little ships scudded for harbor recklessly; they evaded reefs and cliffs. One little ship was caught by the Polar Night and swallowed in blackness. I didn't like that Polar Night; I wouldn't go to the Pole! The airplane drifted south to sunlit air; the world swept past beneath me.

Suddenly I heard a cruel voice: "Where do you think you are?" . . . No, I wasn't, I wasn't in Samara. Not in that desolate city where the doctor wanted my room for three sick children. I had left Samara years ago and wouldn't go back. But America and Europe and the round globe of the world spun glassily smooth beneath me, and the airdrome reached up and caught me at Samara. I opened my eyes reluctantly in a hospital room with glass walls. They told me I had been wandering seven days.

As strength came back I began to notice the people around

me. There was a neatly-moving person who always had drinks of cold water on time and brushed my bed out properly and turned me over before I knew she had touched me. She was the English nurse sent down by the Quakers from Moscow; she arrived on the tenth day of the typhus with a warm down coverlet and a lemon in her bag. I was ashamed that I did not know her name after she had cared for me so long, washing me and coaxing me to eat. I tried to learn her name by asking the doctor; I repeated it over and over, "Pattison, Pattison," trying to remember. It was no use. I forgot her name as soon as she entered the room. What would she think of me for being so ungrateful?

There was another nurse about whom I never worried. I forgot or remembered as I chose. She wouldn't care; she would expect nothing. She was a peasant girl from the German Republic on the Volga, who had learned English in America. She was as strong and quiet as brown earth at harvest. When she touched me with firm hands, life flowed into me. She curled on a little cot in my room; it did not matter where she slept or what she ate. It was clear she liked touching people. I came alive at her touch without even bothering to be grateful.

After many days I asked her name and why she was always silent. She told me the doctor did not wish her to annoy me with her story. Naturally I insisted on hearing it. She said her father was a skilled carpenter in Marxstadt on the Volga. There were eight in the family; they had been to America but returned to the Volga just before the war. They had known misery ever since. There was no food in Marxstadt so she had set out with friends to make her way to Germany or Tashkent or anywhere that had bread. Then she would send for her family. Did I know where a skilled carpenter could find a job? She could not get a place in the train in Samara. Winter had come and she had no coat. She could not travel without a coat.

Later that day a relief worker came to see me. I asked what it was like in Marxstadt. "Very bad," he said, "mostly dead or gone away."

The doctor was right; I should not have heard that story. The girl was no longer comforting as brown earth at harvest. When she came into the room I turned my face to the wall and tried to think where a carpenter with six children could find bread. Only after many days did my nerves grow strong enough to forget her suffering. Nerves must grow callous if one is to live through famine. Never again could I quite relax in her presence. It was my fault that she had become human and not a comfortable green tree.

Steadily as I lay in Samara slowly recovering, the famine deepened around me. I heard of it from the English nurse and from relief workers who passed through Samara to Buzuluk, where the Friends' relief was now stationed. I heard of the train of thirty-five cars of food that came all the way from Manchuria, inscribed: "Harbin Relief Committee for Hungry Russia." I learned of the diplomatic train that bore the first Afghan ambassador to Moscow, traveling from Tashkent through Samara. I learned of the emergency hospital at the railway station which turned away a hopeless line of people with the words: "You are not ill; you are only starving." Young men from the villages who staggered with hunger, children carried in arms because they were too weak to walk, were dying from an ailment for which there was no medicine; the only thing to cure it was food.

Through the glass inner walls of the hospital in which I lay, I saw in the next room a young woman doctor, who was convalescing from typhus, go crazy at the news her mother brought. They had sold household treasures and bought one hundred pounds of flour and ten of sugar; but robbers had broken into the house and stolen the flour. The doctor went into hysteria; she rose and rushed out to seek the flour, though she had as yet no strength for walking. This was the meaning of bread even to doctors on government rations.

The Friends told of the relief in Buzuluk. There were receiving stations for children like the refuges in Samara. The Friends helped these stations, but soon they were asked to stop. For peasants, learning that there was food in the stations, began abandoning their children in such numbers that they could not be housed. "Feed the villages first and keep them at home," said the authorities. But the horses fell from hunger and could not draw the food. No horses came at all from several distant centers. A man from a distant village staggered into Buzuluk to report that all the members of his famine committee were dead or sick with typhus and no horses were available anywhere. He was taken to the hospital burning with fever. The Friends began to buy hay from Tashkent for horses, lest transport fail utterly.

A letter came to me from America enclosing a menu from a trans-Atlantic steamer. We read it aloud in the hospital and laughed and wept; we kept it for a week and showed it to everyone who came. It did not arouse envy; it was too much like a mad dream. It aroused incredulous hate and unholy mirth. It started with olives and pickles and two or three kinds of soup; it went on through three varieties of fish and three entrées to incredible luxuries of meats and fowl and salad. It finished with many desserts and five kinds of cheese. On the second day we noticed that one thing was omitted from that menu. Bread! It was taken for granted! Again we laughed and wept that people existed who took bread for granted.

Some time during winter my hospital room in Samara was exchanged for a bed in the Quaker flat in Moscow, to which I was carried by the special relief train on which Nansen traveled. Thrombosis had set in after typhus. I required several months in bed. I went on a stretcher through the Samara station, now white with snow, and by ambulance through the snow-bound Moscow streets. Life resumed its routine of famine news brought to my bedside, but I was no longer helpless. On a board across my knees I placed a portable typewriter and ground out stories for the Quaker relief campaigns in England and America. They were published in many thousand copies and read aloud at meetings.

As winter deepened the famine deepened also into yet greater horror, which came to us in glimpses through the storm. Often the Quaker flat was crowded with relief workers arriving from London and unable to travel east because the railway was blocked by blizzards. We sent off trains of food-cars which disappeared towards Samara behind a white curtain of storm. No news came back except occasional telegrams that another of our workers was down with typhus.

I awoke suddenly one midnight. A voice in the next room was saying: "The ARA man went crazy. He tried to count the corpses in the barn but he couldn't get beyond forty-eight. There were hundreds of corpses but he kept saying 'forty-eight, forty-eight' the rest of the day. No, he didn't have to stop work; he was all right next morning."

I sat up suddenly; I went into the next room. Hecker, one of our workers, had left us three weeks before to get news of the famine; he had been behind the storm and returned. When I saw his face, I cried: "Are you ill?" He laughed at that. "Not ill, only snowed in ten days without food, fuel or water. The Tashkent train for which you've been waiting."

He told of dead bodies piled in warehouses, stripped of clothes which were needed by the living. "There is no strength to bury them in the frozen soil," he said. "Those who survive will bury in the spring." He told of wailing children who fought with dogs for crusts of bread. "I saw starving men with exasperated nerves strike children, and they fell down spiritless, just moaning. The dogs also, if struck, crawled off and made no resistance. If there was food for which to fight, the dogs and children would struggle a little."

He had passed through many villages; the only signs of life were around the relief stations. He had seen men arrested for cannibalism; they had killed and eaten a young boy. Other cannibals did not kill, but stole corpses. Someone asked the prisoners how human flesh tastes, and they said: "Quite well; you don't need much salt." They were half-witted people.

The worst difficulty, he said, was transport; railway transport had been disrupted by the long wars, local transport by the death of horses. Refugee trains waited for days on sidings while their crowded cars were thinned by death. The fast relief train on which he traveled had been blocked for ten days by a blizzard between Buzuluk and Orenburg where winds sweep unchecked for hundreds of miles south of the Urals. "The cars shook as though they would be overturned," he told us.

"On the second day it quieted a little and one hundred of us started down the track to dig out our engine which had gone to help a freight train and been blocked by snow itself. Twelve of us reached the engine; we cleared a little space. We came back, always falling into snowdrifts and getting up with great effort. One of the men died of exhaustion before morning; another died a few days later when we dug out the freight train.

"Ten days we lived in the train, telegraphing madly to Orenburg and Samara and getting no reply. We published a little newspaper, the *Empty Alarm*, with all the news we wished were true. The worst was not the hunger, nor the cold and darkness (we had no lights in the cars); the worst was the thirst. We never had fuel enough to thaw all the snow we needed to drink. We were restless with thirst always.

"At last a turbine snow-sweeper arrived from Orenburg while a train of 1500 demobilized soldiers went through from Samara, digging out tracks on their way. As they approached we sent our baggage-car miles down the track and hid it, locking ourselves in our cars all day. Our deliverers were hungry as wolves and 1500 strong, and we feared they would want the last bits of food we had left. We were afraid even of those who saved us.

"When we reached Ryazan and had a straight six hours' run to Moscow we went hysterical with joy. Everyone began singing, the sick ones from their bunks and the well ones tramping up and down the corridors and shouting. Silly little songs, nonsense songs at first, then folk songs and songs of revolution. So we pulled into Moscow with twenty typhus cases in our isolation car, with two dead and two dying, and all the rest of us, sick and well, shouting and singing."

Such was the story Hecker brought from behind the white storm curtain that hung between us and the east. Next evening another train started for the famine area bearing many of our workers. Two days later storm began again and we waited again ten days for trains. Thus it was from week to week the whole winter long. The war against famine went on throughout the Volga valley on a vast plain of drifting whiteness behind a curtain of storm.

"It may be," said a woman in Moscow who shall be nameless, for in the fine work she does today she would not wish her discouragement of those days recalled, "it may be that they will beat us. It may be that we Russians are too backward, too utterly poor, too exhausted to build communism. It may be that we shall pass into history like another Paris Commune, serving only as a signal to the future, so that some day out of our bloody doom the working class of some more advanced western nation shall draw the lessons they need for victory."

While some idealists like her killed themselves thinking the revolution was beaten, while communists fought and died on the famine front in storm and fever, the first capitalists of the New Economic Policy invaded the red capital. Along the streets little shops of private trade sprang up like mushrooms, the market-places resounded with the shouts of speculators, and hard-faced profiteers with their jeweled women held high revel in the night cafés of hungry Moscow.

CHAPTER XII

THE COMMANDING HEIGHTS

I HAVE often been asked what drew me back to Russia, which I saw first in its utterly darkest days. Four months of the first five I spent on a sick-bed; the traces they left on my body will never entirely pass. In all that mighty country I found no slightest comfort of living; in those five months I never tasted fresh water and never enjoyed fresh milk. I had met no important people, but nurses and doctors and peasants and minor officials. I had seen no efficient work nor any achievements, but fuelless trains, unlit streets, ruined factories and starving villages. The scene my memory held was a filthy, sprawling city by the Volga where the world lay dying.

Nor could I claim my own work superlatively useful. I had saved some lives in Samara and increased relief funds by my pamphlets and given a better picture of Soviet Russia in far-away America; but for months I had been a burden. I received a letter from the American Friends' Service reprimanding me for having gone to Russia; in my weakened state it caused me many sleepless nights. It made of all that work, which I had waved as a banner to excuse my illness, the individual adventure of a fool.

Yet not for a moment did it occur to me that I could permanently leave this country, this chaos in which a world was being born. It was the chaos that drew me, and the sight of creators in chaos. I intended to have a share in this creation. The wrecked buildings, the pavements broken to dust, the ruined railroads stirred me to an angry lust of battle. America was no longer the world's pioneer. The World War had degraded her to be chief of imperial nations. It seemed to me—it still seems to me—that Russia was the advancing battle-front of man.

I used the last few days of convalescence in Moscow, when

the doctor allowed me to leave the house for an hour or two each day, to make connections which should bring me back when my agreement with the Quakers expired. I met Carr, then representing the American Communist Party in Moscow, and the first American communist I had ever seen. He agreed to arrange for me room and rations on the prevailing "communist wage" of twenty-five dollars a month if I would remain in Moscow as correspondent for various labor papers, including my own Seattle *Union Record* and some new communist papers which were starting. I agreed to return in three months on this basis.

Two months' work and convalescence in Warsaw and a month in England completed my agreement with the Quakers. Just before I left London for Moscow the International News Service (Hearst's) offered me a half-time job as their correspondent in the Soviet Union. "We have no objection to your writing also for the labor press under the name 'Anise' " they added. I agreed to write for them unless the labor press objected or unless I found the double work too taxing. When I reached Moscow I learned that Carr had gone without making any arrangement for room, ration or salary for me. The comrades to whom he had referred the matter leaped with such joy at the Internews offer which relieved them of the responsibility for me that I smiled to think I had hesitated. I agreed to support myself by the capitalist press and write as I had time for the labor press without pay; on this basis I continued for many years.

In my few short trips into Moscow streets during the previous winter, I had been disturbed by the growing speculation and private trade. I had taken my problem to Krasnoschekoff, the first important communist I had met. We had published his wife's story in the Seattle *Union Record* two years earlier when she fled from the Japanese invasion of Siberia, believing her husband dead. He had survived as leader of guerilla forces, then as president of the Far Eastern Republic; when I met him he was assistant commissar of finance in Moscow.

"Tell me," I asked, "how I am supposed to regard all these shops that are opening? The other correspondents and the men of the ARA rejoice; they measure Moscow's progress by the number of stores and the things you can get. To me each seems a step of defeat. The city is becoming a regular Asiatic market-place, bargaining, cheating. There's a horrible new-rich set growing and the opera audiences have changed from workers to petty traders showing off their women. It's rawer by far than the capitalism of America. Must one be glad of this?"

"Would you be glad," asked Krasnoschekoff, "if you saw a starving man and tried to feed him and all your good food gave out, and the man turned to crusts of bread in a garbage wagon, dirty and infected with disease? You would be glad that he needn't starve, but you couldn't feel very cheerful. This private trading is food in a garbage wagon, filthy with greed, cheating, all the diseases of capitalism. But it is better than letting men starve.

"If our government could say to the workers: 'Here is food for six months,' it could also say: 'Produce for us.' If we could say to the peasants: 'Here are implements and clothes and salt,' we could demand the peasants' harvest. But never yet have we had even the beginnings of a surplus on which alone communism can be built. We began with ruin and were forced into civil war; we encountered blockade and pestilence.

"When by extreme revolutionary spirit, workers managed to produce without first being fed, in the hope of giving goods to the peasant and getting bread, their goods went not to the peasant but to the war. If, under interest or compulsion the peasants gave us food and trusted to later returns, that food went not into production but into the army. Then we had two years of drought ending in famine.

"So now we must say frankly to the people: 'Your government cannot feed all and produce goods for all. We shall run the most necessary industries and feed the workers in those industries. The rest of you must feed yourselves in any way you can. This means we must allow private trade and private workshops; it is well if they succeed enough to feed those people who work in them, since no one else can feed them.

Later, as state industries produce a surplus, these will expand and drive out private trade."

Slowly he added: "It was not only goods of which the intervention robbed us. It robbed us of our comrades. Whenever we Bolsheviks planned the revolution we always thought that we should be there afterwards to run things. But now we know that most of us do not survive the revolution; the communists were first to be slaughtered on every front. Ah, if we had all those good comrades now it would be a different story. Our men and means are exhausted; we must train up new forces and create a new surplus."

His words reassured me for the time. But the Moscow to which I returned as Hearst correspondent in the late spring of 1922 seemed to have changed in my three months' absence from a city of comrades living on rations to a city of profiteers charging fantastic prices. The New Economic Policy had turned Soviet Russia into a battle-ground between two worlds: state-owned enterprises paying scanty wages but holding their staffs through rations, and a furiously expanding world of private trade. The latter world was by far the more conspicuous; the earlier world of comrades creating in chaos had to be looked for and was hard to find. The surface of life was ruthless competition and limitless profit-grabbing.

My contact with this surface life began with my search for a room. A brisk little woman offered me a kitchen made into a bedroom with tea in the morning and dinner at night for twelve dollars a week. It was the cheapest thing I had found in the expensive city of Moscow; I eagerly accepted. She hesitated: "I'll have to see the house committee," she said. During the next week she raised her price so often and worried so about the house committee that I gave it up.

A friend explained: "Unless she has the house committee 'fixed' they'll take her room as soon as she admits she has an extra one."

"Isn't it hers?" I asked.

"It is hard in these days to know what belongs to anyone," he answered.

I found another room to let for the summer. It belonged

to filthy aristocrats; I use both words literally. The lady reclined on a divan and spoke in French. She explained that once she had owned the entire seven-room flat. Then the unspeakable proletariat had moved in and left her one room. She kept the largest and piled into it all her possessions. The spacious chamber had become a junk-shop of wardrobes, beds, desks, dishes, gilt chandeliers and bric-a-brac piled in corners —a horrible mess of luxurious dirt. It could not have been cleaned since the revolution; it was impossible to move all that stuff about. The lady was frankly terrified by the little kerosene stove which she kept on a marble-topped table. She boasted that before the revolution she had never cooked a meal in her life. From the clutter on that marble-topped table she apparently had washed no dishes since. I let her waste four days of my time, so desperate was I for a room. She also was afraid of the house committee.

Then suddenly I broke through the barrier into that other world of comrades. A friend spoke to a friend and Suchanova, a woman with an important job in the State Publishing House, took me in. She had two rooms in the Metropole, and her husband's absence in Germany left a vacant cot; without house committees, without money, without even seeing me, she sent word: "Come round with your things before ten in the morning, when I go to work."

She gave me a bed of boards covered with a thin straw mattress; she gave me a table on which to write; she drove two more nails into the wall (I winced as they bit into the expensive hardwood panels), and told me I could now hang up my clothes. She treated me as a good comrade who needed what she needed, a place to work and to hang my coat and a padded board for sleep. She rushed to her office and came back at midnight; then she turned on her desk lamp and worked till three in the morning.

For two months I shared that flat in the center of Moscow. I could not share her hours of work; I needed sleep after midnight. I learned to go to bed with the door unlatched, and never know how many people would be occupying our rooms next morning. She had frequent committee meetings which lasted after the street cars stopped, so her visitors simply slept on the floor and went directly back to their offices. Anyone who came ate whatever there was in the flat and when there was nothing left we went hungry till the next day. What they ate or wore or where they slept did not matter; they were all absorbed in the job of keeping the country going. Such was the ruling class.

In conversations late at night I could feel the grim will that strove to organize the land—a cool, lean will from which all superfluous flesh of emotion was long worn away and which noted incredible evils cynically as parts of a problem through which it drove relentlessly, retreating here, advancing there, towards an end which lay beyond the generations. Yet whenever I left that flat it seemed as if these comrades who worked so feverishly must be submerged in the great storm of profiteering which rose higher and higher in the streets. These few groups of conscientious people working late—were they growing, or dwindling?

One could see at least that the country was becoming better organized. One by one the railroads opened for general passenger service and the journalists began taking trips. The regions where one could not go without being inoculated against cholera were cleared up and the restrictions were removed. There was a struggling attempt to furnish blankets on the express trains, but not yet sheets. The famous fair in Nizhni Novgorod was opening with a sleeping car running each way and even airplane connections. The Siberian express was reestablished and a dining-car put on.

A fury of repair-work was sweeping over Moscow. On every block I had to turn aside for sidewalk repair or the whitewashing of buildings. My work in the Metropole was accompanied by the rasping of iron on stone as they tore up and repaired hotel corridors which had been injured by gun fire during the civil war. In that first summer, Moscow repaired six broken bridges and let contracts for forty-two others; she doubled the number of street cars and extended street car lines; she repaired a hundred thousand square yards of cobblestone pavements; the later asphalt streets were as yet nonexistent.

Color and life came back in one hundred and twenty thousand square yards of flower-beds in the city's squares and boulevards; children began to play and young men and girls to stroll gayly in the evenings.

The aftermath of famine still gripped the Volga, but elsewhere everyone rejoiced in the new harvest and the increasing food.   In June Suchanova and her friends greeted with shouts of joy the white flour and jam I bought at the American Relief Commissary; they made a party with them; by August these things were tame additions to the food supply, not worth an extra trip.   In June my hostess and her friends borrowed my clothes; we nearly fought over my ancient raincoat which was common protection against storm.   By August they went on vacation trips to Berlin and came back with more new clothes than I had.   Everyone went on vacation; it was the first time they had stopped to breathe since the beginning of the World War.   But "enough to eat" still meant one meal a day, about five o'clock, supplemented by tea and bread at morning and night.   Not for another year did eggs or butter or porridge appear for breakfast and the habit of having luncheon begin.

Outside these charmed circles of comrades there raged a mad hunger for money, madder, more unashamed than anything I had ever seen in America.   American business men came to negotiate for concessions.   They were chiefly of a flashy type, adventuring into the wild lands of Russia in hope of quick gain.   They declared that all the recovery was due to private trade.   Russia had learned her lesson; she was going back to normalcy as fast as possible; normalcy meant capitalism with all its ancient ways.

All the surface of life seemed to approve their words.   Scores of chances for making a fortune were pressed upon these newcomers.   "Autobus monopoly for Moscow" was only one of the chances of which I heard.   The Physical Education Association had been given the monopoly of all sporting goods in Russia; out of the profits of this trade they supported their organization.   They bought one autobus in Germany as a sideline; it earned a hundred rubles a day profit on Moscow streets.

"If someone would only finance us to buy a dozen autobusses,"
they said, "we could get the monopoly of autobus transport for
Moscow. We can't ask for monopoly with only one autobus!"
They sought a foreign capitalist as partner.

A young mechanic who had spent some years in America,
and who was now working in Soviet industry, showed me a die
for making the metal part of electric light bulbs. "There is a
state factory in Leningrad," he explained, "making light bulbs
at the rate of two thousand a day; when they get machinery
they will expand to two hundred thousand. They import the
metal part of the bulb from Germany; I have a group of seven
mechanics who want to make it here. If we had a few thousand
dollars we could organize a little workshop and get contracts
with the state factory to supply the metal parts. Some day
they will want to buy us out, but not immediately; they will
first expand their total production of light bulbs. We shall
expand with them, on a contract for making the metal part."
His eyes glowed; he saw himself a millionaire immediately.

There was even a government office which showed me docu-
ments all ready for a Russo-American Trading Company, of
which the Soviet government should own half the stock and
American capitalists the other half, which should have the
monopoly for all Soviet-American trade. The amount of
foreign capital demanded in 1922 for this was so small that
even I thought I could go to New York and raise it. But
they drew this project back. "Our policy on combinations
like this is not decided," they said. "There is a growing
tendency to push the concessionaires into industry, and keep
for ourselves the quick turnover profits of trade."

Many things, it seems, were not decided. Small state industries or coöperative organizations would dicker with foreign
capitalists, and hold out the gleam of incredible profits; they
would even make tentative agreements. But before these agreements were approved by higher authority, most of them fell
through. Yet the atmosphere was that of a boom town in the
West where anything might become possible. Small fortunes
were being quickly made; men dreamed of big fortunes. No

one knew what were the limits, what would be permitted to private capital.

The communists knew, what nobody else believed, that the life of private capital would be as short and as circumscribed as they could make it. They knew the plan they had for eliminating private capital; but they did not know how rapidly it could work.

Their plan was to hold the "commanding heights" of industry, on which all lesser enterprises depend. They had studied capitalism far better than most capitalists; they knew its sources of power. They retained ownership of land and natural resources, banks and foreign trade, railways, all heavy industries and all large industrial enterprises generally. The state itself operated four thousand large industrial enterprises, employing a million workers; * they were ready to lease to coöperatives or to private capital four thousand small enterprises, employing eighty thousand workers. City lands and buildings were the property of the municipalities, which ran the city budgets from their rents. Retail trade and numberless incidental enterprises fell into the hands of any person who would run them, but the government callously used its licensing power and discriminatory regulations to force the direction of private investment or to crush it altogether.

"We keep the commanding heights." Thus said the communists. To me, and to many of us in 1922, the state seemed to have chosen all the worst enterprises on which nobody could make money. The State Bank's only capital was rapidly depreciating paper rubles; the state railroads were utterly demoralized; the coal mines of the Donetz were ruined by long invasion and the miners fled to the farms for food. Steel production was five percent of normal; the oil of Baku was flooded deep in water. All the commanding heights were ruined hills. But the lighter industries and retail trade could make money rapidly, and these were permitted to capitalists. In part this seemed to me normal; we in Seattle were accustomed to that form of state and municipal ownership which ran without profit,

* Note that by 1934 there were twenty-three million workers in state enterprises.

or even at a loss, as a "public service"; socialism, perhaps, was just an extension of this.

Yet it worried me. The fury of private profit-making was so much louder than the slow improvement of state industry. Old "friends of the revolution" came to Moscow and grew discouraged. "There is nothing left but an Asiatic market place," they said. Foreign traders cheered the thought and stayed to bargain; foreign imperialists waited for greater collapse and better terms. As I look back at those days of swaggering profiteers, it seems hard today to understand by what hypnotic illusion they expected prosperity and ultimate control. It is the same illusion which leads the independents to believe that they may overthrow the octopus, the same illusion which led the Seattle workers to believe that small, flourishing workers' enterprises might peacefully drive out capitalism, till one government order closed the shipyards and wrecked their dreams. I saw the same illusion arise in California in 1934, when the unemployed believed that their small enterprises were building a new society within the shell of the old, though all the commanding heights were in enemy hands. They lived by faith; but the Russian communists lived by the study of economic laws.

Such state industries as were able to do so profiteered shamelessly, even more shamelessly than the private capitalists, since they had less to fear. Were such state trusts, I wondered, really socialistic? Apparently it didn't worry the workers; they not only exulted in each new accumulation of profit in state-owned enterprises but made incredible sacrifices to attain it. They gave their holidays to making street cars or locomotives as presents in a May-Day celebration. I also, though I worried over the "spirit of greed" which arose in state trusts, caught by contagion some of this attitude of the workers. But I judged the struggle in terms of ideals and emotions, rather than of basic economic processes.

It was the president of the State Bank who gave me my first lesson in economics. I went to him to ask by what alchemy he turned ten million dollars' worth of rapidly depreciating paper rubles into twenty million good gold dollars in a single year. I had met him first in January of 1922 when the State Bank had just opened and I wanted to know why it took me an hour to get a check cashed. He had smiled affably and given an answer I shall never forget.

"You see, comrade, I'm not a banker. My chief training was ten years in a tsarist jail. Now it seems we need a state bank to establish a gold reserve. We can take our choice between two kinds of presidents: expert bankers who want to see our state bank fail, or a man like myself who would give his life to make this bank succeed, but who knows nothing about banking. So they put me in charge and give me the expert bankers as assistants, and I have to make them work and keep them from cheating." It was a perfect picture of the whole of Russia's economic life.

Months later I saw him again; he showed me bars of gold and high piles of British and American currency, then the sound values of the world. The ten million dollars' worth of paper with which he had opened his bank had depreciated to one-third of its value in the first three months. Yet he had twenty million dollars in gold. "How did you make this from paper?" I asked in amazement. "As the money-maker of a government which doesn't believe in money, tell me."

"No governments believe in money," he smiled swiftly. "They make their people believe in it. Rulers believe in coal and oil and natural resources—the real wealth of the world."

Then he explained. "We loaned money to the State Timber Trust—paper rubles with which they paid their bills in Russia. They exported timber to England and paid us in English pounds. Not only the loan with interest but also a share in their profits; sometimes we took half they made! The fur industry is also very profitable, making two and three hundred percent in the export trade; on this we demanded a good share. We also charge ten percent in gold on all remittances received from abroad."

"No wonder the state industries call you a robber," I gasped. This callous banker smiled. "The party permits this robber policy," he said, "till we get our gold reserve."

High finance was just as simple as that! After that lesson

in banking I understood quite well in later years where Stinnes got his money, and the British owners of Baltic timber and all the other sudden capitalists of the inflation countries. The State Bank shamelessly showed me that when a currency is dropping in value, those who pay workers and creditors in depreciating paper and sell abroad for sound values can make millions. Thus Stinnes robbed the German middle class to make a private fortune; thus American exporters profited in the days of the New Era; thus the State Bank of Russia was allowed to "rob" the struggling industries to make a gold reserve which later served to build up these same industries.

As the State Bank showed me the secrets of financial power, the Industrial Bank showed me the intimate control of industry by credit. Towards the end of 1922 I attended a conference of the administrators of state industry who were fighting the State Bank's control.

The state industries were called "trusts," a capitalist word which perplexed me. We independents had fought the trusts in America; I was not disposed to welcome them in Soviet Russia. Then I saw that their form was really that of the capitalist trust, but the shares were held by the state. They were made by combining groups of factories under boards of directors, who were partly engineers and partly communists, and who were charged to make the properties self-supporting and self-expanding or face removal after their first report.

They began their struggle under incredibly hampering conditions, with ruined equipment and without money for wages. Coal miners from the Donetz sent delegates to Moscow, saying: "We work waist-deep in water on a scanty diet of black bread. Give food and means to repair the mines." But Moscow answered: "Not yet! Give coal for famine transport, give coal for steel. Here's what bread we can spare for you in a year of famine. Next year, perhaps, you'll get some wages."

The miners gave coal till their food was exhausted and then fled to the farms for bread. The union halls all over the Donetz posted lists of "deserters" who stopped giving coal because they wanted to eat. They posted also lists of "heroes" who collapsed at their work but returned as soon as they could stand. Thus they mined coal on the Donetz through the civil war and the first year of peace. Yet by 1922 the Donetz miners put the railroads and industries back on mineral fuel instead of the wood fuel of the civil war. Only then did they begin to get paid for their coal.

They got it by a drastic method; they attached the funds of the railways in the State Bank. The state railways thereupon protested that their own workers were unpaid for months. "We have a harder task than the mines," they argued, "for they can close the worst mines while we must keep the whole line going. We have no working capital, yet must haul freight and wait for our payment. Give us the right to charge half the prewar freight rates, so we can fix up the railroads." . . . To this modest request Moscow answered: "Don't charge so much or you'll ruin the struggling industries."

Seventy million dollars' worth of products was taken from industry and transport in the first half of 1922 without payment by a hungry state feeding hungry peasants and workers. When the harvest of 1922 gave some means to the peasant, the lighter industries, such as cotton goods, matches, dishes, were able for the first time to charge prices which covered the cost of production. They then revived comparatively rapidly, but heavy industry, iron and steel, remained in a catastrophic condition, producing four to seven percent of the prewar standard.

Under such conditions, the representatives of state industries met in Moscow to fight the State Bank for its power of credit. "You've had a year to start your gold reserve," they said. "You demoralize industry by lending to the less important industries because they can make the quickest returns. We demand the power of credit to build a united program for industry and assist its planned revival." They got the right to organize an "Industrial Bank," whose shares were held by the state industries, the railroads and the Commissariat of Foreign Trade, and which used the autocratic power of credit, not for a gold reserve but to force industries into a joint plan.

"We lend raw cotton to the textile trust," explained the new bank president to me, "and compel the textile trust to advance certain textiles to the clothing trust, which is ordered in its turn to send clothes on credit to Donetz miners. This credit extended to the coal mines permits us to demand coal on credit for certain enamelware factories, and to order these factories to send pots and pans to the Fur Fair in Irbit, Siberia, whereby the fur trust purchases furs for export to London. Our bank demands from the fur trust these foreign credits and uses them again to import raw cotton. Such is the intimate control of credit over industry; we use it to strengthen the plans of the Council of National Industries over the entire network of production, building all our industries into a firm basis for socialism."

To me the most amazing thing was the openness of the discussions. The power of credit, the relations between finance and industry, which elsewhere are the hidden secrets of private interests and which I had been taught to think too complicated for ordinary minds to understand, were the commonplace talk of open congresses and workers' meetings. I saw that they had been deliberately obscured under capitalism, lest the common folk should know how they are ruled by the owners of money. In the Soviet Union all workers were expected to listen to detailed accounts of their common properties, to take part in decisions, and to give heroic effort to reëstablish these properties out of the vast disorganization left by war.

Painfully and slowly, ignoring the wild clamor of speculation that filled the market places, they organized and strengthened the jointly owned "commanding heights" of their economic life.

CHAPTER XIII

THE FRONTIER OF THE NORTH

WHAT was happening in the rest of the country while Moscow fought its narrow path between two worlds? "You must come up to see us in Karelia," said Nuorteva, whom I had met in the press department of the Foreign Office, and who had recently been assigned to some wilderness of the north. "Our government of lumberjacks is managing a billion dollars' worth of timber in trust for the state. We have so many lakes in Karelia that every fisherman has a separate lake of his own."

I laughed. I am used to tall tales from the West. There was a breezy frontier atmosphere in Nuorteva's description that attracted me. How far beyond the borders of Moscow, I wondered, penetrated either the ideas of the communists or the orgy of speculation that marked the New Economic Policy? Which would be the stronger in the backwoods of the north?

Under the midnight sun in summer and the northern lights in autumn, under the winter shadow of Arctic night lies Karelia, a wilderness of primeval forests set with a hundred thousand tangled lakes and jeweled with mountains of marble and mica and iron and copper. It runs for almost a thousand miles north from Leningrad to the polar waters, a long thin strip of country between Finland and the White Sea. It is the backside of Finland to which the revolutionary Finns escaped to entrench themselves when the counter-revolution seized their capital Helsingfors. Through its length runs the Murmansk railway, the Soviet Union's only connection with her ice-free port on the Arctic.

I first met its president, Gühling, in Moscow, where he came to protest against the addition of extra territory to his young state. In a postwar Europe where every government was clutching new lands with unwilling populations, his attitude was so amazing that I inquired the cause. "It is a matter of administrative convenience," he said quite simply. "They want us to take a lot of additional country which can be reached most easily via our waterways. But the people in that territory speak Russian while our Karelians speak Finnish. It would seriously complicate our problems of education and necessitate a double language at all our meetings. So we don't want that area but we may have to take it temporarily till a railroad can be built to reach it more directly from Leningrad."

I laughed. "I wish you could explain this sensible point of view to the Poles," I said. "They are grabbing four different nationalities, each with a different language. Or to the Czechs or the Rumanians or the Jugoslavs. Or to any of these postwar countries of Europe for that matter, every one of which has a crazy yearning for alien populations. How much simpler it would be for the League of Nations if they could all get the point of view of Karelia!"

"Yes, it's simpler under socialism," smiled Gühling. "We have no reason to divide territory otherwise than conveniently. We have no private wealth."

"Now that you mention it, who owns the wealth of Karelia?" I asked. "Is it Moscow or the Karelian government? Don't you have quarrels over that?"

"Why should we have?" said Gühling. "Our Karelian organizations own as much as we have strength to develop. We borrow food and clothing from the south on credits loaned by the central government. Our larger wealth, which is of all-Union importance, will be developed by all-Union organizations. There's no fight over ownership but only some competition between regions as to which shall be developed first. This depends partly on local initiative and partly on central plans which we take part in forming."

"If ownership slides so easily over your borders," I asked, "why do you call yourself a separate nation?"

"Convenience again," smiled Gühling. "We have a separate language and a different historic culture and a certain preference for our own ways and customs. We therefore have a sep-

arate nation to handle education, health, agriculture * and
local laws and courts. But matters which concern the Union,
such as railroads, posts, and resources of timber, minerals
or waterpower must be managed by the Union. A sensible
division—but impossible under private ownership."

I went to Karelia. I learned in the following days why
the people of Karelia love President Gühling; he is still their
president, as I write this book in 1934. He is a man of wide
culture; once an aristocrat in Finland, professor of statistics
in Helsingfors University and a director of the Bank of Finland. Yet he was a leader in the revolution; and when counter-
revolution came in Finland, it was he who stood quietly at his
post in Viborg to organize the flight of the other people's commissars to Sweden. Six weeks thereafter he hid in a sewer
pipe from which he briefly emerged at night into a cellar; every
morning he heard above him the rattle of machine guns which
killed his comrades by hundreds in the prison yards. From this
past he had come to his work in Karelia, where he lived with
his family in two rooms in the government building, with
offices below. Like Suchanova and her friends, his family slept
on mattresses laid on boards or even on the floors. He was a
quiet, hard-working man accessible day and night to the needs
of the simplest folk.

In other rooms of the state house or in the log cabins around
it lived a government of men who never intended to be personally rich. Individually poor, they held in their hands the
forests, mines and quarries of a vast, unpillaged empire; they
talked in terms of millions. . . . They said: "Last year we
got a million dollars' profit from our timber even in the midst
of famine." But this million was profit for the state budget
of Karelia, not for themselves. They personally had just
begun to draw money wages and to hope that the local stores
or their ration cards would soon give them clothes as well as
food. They were too busy exploring, developing and building
to think of personal comfort. They were pioneers—but of a
new type.

---

* Agriculture acquired an All-Union Commissariat in December 1929 when
wide collectivization of farming made it an enterprise of national scope needing national planning. The basic land policy was always union-wide in scope.

There was Veltheim who lived with his British wife next door to President Gühling. I shared their two rooms. He had escaped death more than once in the revolution; now he helped organize Karelia's foreign trade. Saxman, who had charge of Karelia's miscellaneous industries, was an old Finnish trade-unionist who had brought food trains through to Petrograd during the revolution when half the cars were filled with machine guns to fight the way through. Potojeff, once a farmhand, was now chief of Karelian agriculture. The chief of the Economic Council was Shotman, an "old Bolshevik" who had been on the small committee which had fixed the hour of the October Revolution with Lenin.

They were all real men, men with a past, tested by prison and death and achievement under seemingly impossible odds. Now they had turned to the task of rebuilding a war-ruined land. All their advance was still under threat of war. Every year since the revolution war had come when the deep snows made the swamps and lakes of Finland passable—every winter for the past five. The armies of White Finns and Germans from the west, the armies of British and Americans from the north met the armies of Red Russia from the south, and fought on the snows of Karelia. Then the intervention wore itself down to little border wars and bandit raids, the last of which had occurred the winter before my visit. Would the White Finns attack again in the winter of 1922-23 which lay ahead? This was the question all were asking.

"Every winter," said Mrs. Veltheim to me one evening, "we look towards the north and wonder: 'Will it come?' And every winter it comes!"

Yet war did not stop their pioneer drive to the north. "There is less timber to saw this spring in such and such a district," I heard them say, "because last winter the battle-line moved back and forth through those woods." That was their only comment as they got busy sawing the timber.

Worse than war to fight was the backwardness of Karelia. I met a native son of California who had come over the previous year to help the revolution; he had been assigned to the timber industry where he was supposed to increase production by

American methods. How he groaned over Karelian ways.
"Peter the Great built this town and its shipyards," he said to
me, "and they're still building barges as Peter built them.
This year they made four new barges and repaired fifteen old
ones for the timber industry. Not a single sawn timber went
into those barges; the timbers were hand-hewn by axes. These
handicraftsmen have a lifetime skill in hand-hewing; how they
fight the idea of circular saws. Not a single metal pipe was
used in those barges; they make wooden pipes by boring holes
down wooden pillars nine feet long by a special bore which it
takes three men to operate. It's a ghastly job introducing
American methods to proud men who inherited their craft from
Peter."

Among the revolutionists working to rebuild Karelia was a
romantic young Hungarian, who had reached Moscow through
some exchange of prisoners and been sent north to work in
the open air as a cure for his battered heart and nerves. He
was delighted to meet someone with whom he could talk—we
spoke in German—and he poured forth his story. I found it a
vivid contrast to the tersely practical conversations in which
the Russians and Finns indulged. He had been an educated
youth of good family who had sided with the revolution and
been caught and thrown in jail. Four years he had suffered
in cold and hunger and frequent torture which had permanently injured his heart and nerves. His best story was of
the brutal jailor who had knocked him unconscious five times.

"After the fourth time I said: 'You think you're going to
kill me, but you're not. I'm young; some day I'm going to
get out of this hell. Then I'll find me a pretty girl and embrace her the first night as many times as you have knocked
me senseless. That's four embraces you've given me now,' I
jeered, 'do I get any more?'—Then he knocked me down again
and I came to myself days later in a hospital where they
thought I would die. But I didn't; I was going to live to
spite that jailor."

I asked whether he had carried out his boast. He smiled a
satisfied smile. The Russians and Finns were much less thrilled

by this daring youth than I was. Had they no use for fiery temperament at all? No enthusiasm for courage?

Whatever enthusiasm Nuorteva had was for the growing school system of Karelia. He had a double job in two offices. In the morning as chief of education he toiled on the reorganization of the war-ruined schools; in the afternoon as chief of foreign trade he sold Karelian timber. He was a man of brains, speaking nine languages; he bristled with plans. To his offices came the school supervisors who pioneered in the backwoods. The special fight of the past summer had been to repair the buildings. All the schools of Karelia had been destroyed during the civil war; and those which had been rebuilt had been again destroyed during the previous winter's invasion by the White Finns. With heroic ingenuity the educational workers had repaired them once more.

One teacher, for instance, collected ten half-dead horses, abandoned as useless by the White Finns in their retreat. He had the children feed them and lead them to pasture, brought them to good condition and sold them for seven hundred and fifty dollars for the school fund of his district. Other teachers organized the children into farming groups and sold the crops to repair the school. By such energetic humdrum toil, a land that had barely emerged from war and famine was putting its schools in order. Eighteen thousand children were already in school, more than there had been before the war.

"But I'm having a terrible time getting enough teachers who know the Karelian language," complained Nuorteva ruefully. "There were no schools in their language under tsardom."

"It's nice to see the children playing around with clothes on," said the native son of California. "Last summer they hadn't many clothes and not enough energy to play." These were their harsh and simple tests of progress.

"Does the New Economic Policy worry you any in Karelia?" I asked Nuorteva.

"Worry us?" he exclaimed. "It's the New Economic Policy which permits these teachers to feed horses and raise crops for their schools instead of giving everything to the central government for defense."

"But the new speculators and the chance to heap up private income?"

"It bothers us somewhat," admitted Nuorteva, "through its effect on backward people in our own ranks. Some wives even of communists begin to complain: 'We endured hunger when everyone was hungry, but now some people make money and live comfortably and why can't we? What is the use of a high government post unless you get clothes for your children?' Outside speculators are not hard to fight, but tendencies like these have to be watched lest they sap the strength of good comrades."

From Rimpalle of the far north I got the most convincing answer to my question, not by his words but by his life. He was a Finnish-American quarryman who had returned to work for the revolution; he was developing mica mines and feldspar quarries north of the Arctic Circle. Most of the state budget of Karelia came not from taxes but from its state-owned industries; Rimpalle's mines and quarries were among them.

In a little barn behind the state house I saw Veltheim receive the mica—one hundred thouand dollars' worth—on behalf of the Commissariat of Foreign Trade. Two men arrived in miners' shirts with the bronze of the far north on their faces. They had gone north the preceding spring with ten tons of flour and a few blunt axes as working capital. They had had not even a saw with which to build a dock, not even a change of clothes. Worst of all, in Rimpalle's eyes, they had neither pneumatic drills nor gunpowder for blasting; they had to blow mica out by dynamite which broke it wastefully.

They had waded waist-deep in swamps; they had poled their boats over streams and lakes and portaged over hills. They had trained unlettered peasants to work in quarries and mines. They had wrung wealth from the wastes. At summer's end they came south with their haul not to blow it in on one grand spree and not to bank it for some future stake, as had the Alaskan pioneers who came south to Seattle, but to hand it over to the state. Veltheim examined the samples, checked the weight, gave them a receipt and went back to his office in a building of unpainted boards. None of them thought that anything unusual had happened. Yet they had done something which, if repeated often enough, would wreck all the systems of industry in the capitalist world. They had done something which could check that orgy of speculation in Moscow streets— the only thing that could check it.

"What did you get for your summer's work?" I asked Rimpalle.

"I got rations of potatoes and good fat gravy and one re-soling of my boots!" He laughed and patted the shabby but firm leather uppers. "I've swell boots! Brought them from America. They were on me when I ran the Finnish border through lakes and swamps. Everything on me I kept, but nothing else. Some of the men got boots for their work this summer. I didn't need them; my boots only had to be resoled.

"They tell me we're going on money wages now," he added. "But last year—say, who'd have thought a year ago that we'd have good fat gravy so soon!"

I decided to go north with Rimpalle to the mica mines. President Gühling was going part of the distance on the slow train of the Murmansk railroad which then took four days for a trip which now takes two. We were a group of six which left the Karelian capital; I shall never forget my first night out.

Six wooden bunks on which one could stretch at full length without mattress or bedding were reserved for the presidential party. Only two of these were lowers; as a woman guest I had one of them while President Gühling took the other, not only as president but because tuberculosis in his leg-bones, acquired from those weeks in a sewer-pipe, made movement painful. He left an eighteen-hour day of work behind him and was going to similar work in Kem; he was drooping with fatigue. Yet during the long delays at tiny stations he always got out to talk with peasants on the platforms, inquiring into local conditions and needs.

In the middle of the night peasants, finding the other cars on the train full, began to crowd into the "reserved" car. For only a few years had they known a railroad; they ignored the railroad rules. A peasant woman with a baby seated herself on the edge of Gühling's bunk and began to push against his feet. He turned in uneasy slumber and drew up his legs a little; she promptly put the baby into the vacant place. Slowly but persistently she shoved for more space, using the baby's head as battering ram against Gühling's feet. Had she picked him as a kindly man who wouldn't hurt a baby's head even in slumber? Soon Gühling was sitting up. I told the woman that the place was reserved; she stared stolidly, unanswering. I offered to exchange with Gühling or to rouse one of the men in the upper berths. He smiled: "Let them sleep while they can; they also have heavy work." He hunched himself painfully into half a bunk and dropped into uneasy, exhausted slumber while I lay sleepless thinking of the difference between Gühling and other presidents I have known.

Gühling alighted the following day in Kem but I continued with Rimpalle and his fellow-miner a day's journey further north till we crossed the Arctic Circle to a land of lakes, forests, reindeer and northern lights on the shores of the White Sea. I went with them by the rough paths they had made across the swamps from mine to mine and by the open boat in which they rowed the sea to their quarries of feldspar and quartz. I shared their potatoes with good fat gravy; combined with local game-birds, fish and autumn berries it was an excellent diet. The mines were thus far only a half dozen small out-croppings with a dozen men working at each. Rimpalle taught them the trade which he had learned in quarries from Maine to Carolina. He spent his nights organizing them into a trade union, a coöperative store and a night school.

"These peasants of the northern woods live in a very ancient age," he told me. "The railroad came only with the war. Most of them have no metal implements. The large elkskin on which I sleep was gladly given me in return for the blade of a scythe. I found an old blunt saw in one of the villages, a gift from a passing stranger. It was the only saw they had ever seen and they did not know why it had ceased to cut.

When I sharpened it they would almost have given me the village in return for my 'magic.' "

I went with Rimpalle into a peasant hut. The woman was spinning with a distaff. I recognized it from pictures in Andersen's fairy-tales. She wove on a crude hand-loom, lifting the threads by hand. She had not reached the stage of the spinning-wheel and tread-loom. These were the people whom Rimpalle was organizing into a trade union, a coöperative and a night school, so that they might become equal citizens in a socialist republic!

"It's a useful job," he said simply, in reply to my enthusiasm. "I figure that up here so close to the border and so near to the propaganda of the White Finns, where peasants are ignorant and hungry and where the land will never raise enough harvest, we needed to have an industry to give food to the people. . . ." So it was not merely the increased wealth of Karelia's foreign trade of which he thought; it was also the politics of the revolution.

"We need a real boss here now," he added. "I was all right to open it up. I know stone-cutting; I can handle the feldspar and quartz well enough, but I'm not experienced in mica. Mica is going to be the big thing here; we'll have to get a real boss who knows mica."

That was what startled me most. Not only had he pioneered to do this job for nothing but "potatoes and good fat gravy and one resoling of my boots." This I could understand; I also loved this wilderness of the north. But now that he had built with body and brain an industry on which the government looked with favor, and for which next year there would be capital and equipment, he didn't even ask to retain management and credit.

"You are a communist?" I asked of Rimpalle, thinking I knew the answer.

"Yes," he cried, his eyes shining. Then he checked himself, and added: "A candidate still. I've been here only a year. I think they'll let me in this winter." . . . I thought: "If such are the requirements, even for a candidate to join these creators in chaos, how will I ever get in?"

For three days I tramped the woods and swamps and rowed the lakes of that beautiful wild land. It was a gorgeous Indian summer, warm and bright. Three nights I lay on a reindeer skin and watched the northern lights, far brighter than I had ever seen them, wheeling over half the sky. I thought of Rimpalle and Gühling and Veltheim and the "native son of California" and a million like them. These were the cohorts pitted against those speculators in Moscow, those foreign business men "making a killing," against all that froth of private trade. It was an army, not only in Moscow, not even chiefly in Moscow. It held the ends of the land.

Moscow spoke to my brain; I had learned much in Moscow. But Moscow's debates and conflicts often perplexed me. This wilderness of the north spoke to my heart. "Pioneers of a new kind building a new world," I exulted; "it is with them I must be to the end of my days."

When I reached Petrozavodsk on my homeward journey they were celebrating the first of October, as the end of the fiscal year. The chiefs of industry reported at a truly grand banquet with caviar and smoked fish and salad and Caucasian wine. They said they owed it to the reputation of Karelia to show the contrast with last year's daily ration which had been three-quarters of a pound of black bread and one herring!

"We have two million surplus to put into new development," said Gühling. "It must go to expanding the timber industry, which is the quickest way to give work and food to the peasants." Beyond the timber industry he saw more and more state-owned industries, higher wages, more profits to go for schools and roads and public improvements. "We can go very far in the next few years."

"If there is peace," he added, "if there is peace." With these words silence fell, for nobody knew the chances of peace for Karelia. I did not even ask if they desired peace for I knew that in all of them were two conflicting desires. One was the wish to develop the land to wealth under quietly expanding industry and one was the hope for revolution in Finland which would mean renewed war and hunger for this country of lakes and forests. Karelia was the frontier between two worlds which faced along a hostile thousand miles of border; Karelia must be ready for both war and peace.

Not in their fairest dreams could they guess what ten years of peace would bring them: their scanty farm area expanded by fifty per cent; their industry growing from 4,000 handicraftsmen to 35,000 industrial workers and 45,000 engaged in forestry. Across their land within ten years one of the great canals of the world was driven, the Baltic-White Sea Waterway connecting Leningrad with the coal, lumber and minerals of the north. In four years of the Five-Year Plan Karelia invested ninety-four million rubles in industry and culture, of which thirty-one million was for schools. And north of Karelia, beyond those tiny mica mines where Rimpalle pioneered on ten tons of flour and a few blunt axes, arose Khibinogorsk, mining more than a million tons of ore annually from the largest apatite fields in the world. Proudly they planned, at the banquet which ended their famine, the use of two million rubles' surplus for all Karelia. Ten years later one town, Khibinogorsk, would spend in one year six million on workers' housing alone.

Before leaving Petrozavodsk I asked Nuorteva what had become of the romantic Hungarian. Nuorteva cursed. "Damn these individual revolutionists," he said. "We had to send him south in disgrace. He got a peasant girl into trouble. Haven't we problems enough in our rural districts without the private emotions of these fools?"

It was a blow. I had admired the emotion of that young Hungarian. Those unenthusiastic Russians had been justified. Swinging to the other extreme I began for a time to distrust all feelings, even those which had kept me awake under the northern lights of Karelia. I said: "It is work that counts, only work!"

CHAPTER XIV

EARLY AMERICAN IMMIGRANTS IN RUSSIA

THE joy that kept me awake under the northern lights of Karelia was no new emotion. It repeated the joy with which Ruth White and I had once discovered socialism, till we were shut out by that "class struggle" of Dante Barton's. It recalled the new reason for living which, after the loss of "my America," had brought me down from the mountains to the Seattle *Daily Call*, and when the Seattle labor movement crashed into discord, had taken me over the seas to Soviet Russia. For years this joy and desire had grown ever stronger.

Yet I was not always the same person; contradictory emotions swayed me. The sight of some injustice might suddenly make me see in Soviet Russia a new tyranny or an Asiatic market place. I had the journalist's habit—is it only the journalist's?—of seizing isolated events which were pregnant with feeling, and generalizing them into a law. But I had learned not to act on temporary emotions; I waited to see how often they recurred before making them grounds for action. So much stability I had—a majority vote of my emotions.

This majority of emotions voiced an increasing demand, not only for future work in the Soviet Union, but for organized connection with its life. I saw that the building of socialism was no longer a dream, but real. There were greater difficulties than I had expected, but also greater power. This power I saw rather mystically, as a Common Consciousness coming into being to plan the future of mankind. It was a "Will" uniting a million people scattered across one-sixth of earth. That will was strong; one could lose one's individual will * in it forever. It † was strong enough to conquer all the ancient greeds and inequalities of man, all the world's long wars. If

---

* See Chapter XXXI for later view of consciousness and will.
† Note that I said "it" and not "we."

152

it couldn't, there was nothing left for which to live. I wrote often in this vein in that first year.

The practical connection with this organized power was not so simple. My desire to be part of this country had received its first rude check on my day of arrival when the press representative in the Foreign Office advised me to eat Quaker food if I wished to be efficient. I received even ruder checks when I raised the question of joining the communist party. The first communists to whom I mentioned it laughed: "A sentimental bourgeois like you!"

That hurt; I was a woman who offered a life's devotion and had been laughed at. I grew more indirect, and asked like an inquiring journalist about conditions of entrance to this party. I learned that one joined at one's place of work, but I worked in a hotel room. I learned next that capitalist correspondents were barred. Then why had those comrades to whom Carr sent me been so eager for me to work for Hearst? That seemed unfair. When I inquired further, I learned that I could join by going back to America. This was the unkindest cut of all; those creators in chaos told me to join by leaving them! Did I really want to join? Certainly not under such conditions. Besides I had other emotions.

I was working chiefly for *Hearst's International Magazine*. Its editor, Norman Hapgood, liked my articles, and I liked the standards he set. "We want new, exhaustive information on events of historic importance. Then we want it written so simply and vividly that the milk-wagon driver in Kansas City and the drug-store clerk in St. Louis will find it interesting and important." To write for the great middle western masses of America intrigued me. So I dropped the daily grind of Internews cables to devote myself to long, vivid articles on various aspects of Soviet life: "The Fight for Russian Oil," "The War with Booze," "The Church Revolution," and many other topics. It was in Hearst's magazine in April 1924 that I published the first article about Stalin to be printed in America. Occasionally I went to Germany or Poland as the correspondent of *Hearst's International* for Eastern and Central Europe. I enjoyed the work; it was good training for vividness of style. It paid so well that I had ample time to write unpaid articles for the liberal and labor press.

I was sending out a storm of friendly articles about Soviet Russia at a time when America was deeply prejudiced. My communist friends all said that my work was useful. Why then did this job make them treat me as an outsider, as it was very clear they did? The feeling that had haunted my youth revived. I wasn't wanted; there was something the matter with me. As soon as I tried to read communist literature I found that plenty of things were the matter. The congress of the Communist International was approaching at the end of 1922; long preliminary analyses of theory and tactics were published. I could hardly read them; they seemed so dull, so heavy, so angry with the world. There wasn't a single phrase in them that cheered me. I was used to writing that stirred and cheered.

The more I forced myself to read those reports, the less I felt like a communist. The things that I did understand I resented. The one thing plain was that they attacked German socialists, the British Labor Party and even some diverging members of their own party. Why wouldn't they be more "friendly"? It was just as Steffens had said in Seattle, the gulf was growing wider everywhere. It was true the German socialists had made a terrible mess, and British labor was rather slow. They weren't creating a new world as these Russians were. But hadn't they done their best? If one had to attack somebody, why not attack capitalists?

What connection had all this dull theory with the thrill of being a creator in chaos, like Rimpalle or the factory-manager in Samara? I didn't want to quarrel with German socialists; I didn't want even to read about them. I reserved my interest for people who "did things." I wanted to fight the huge disorder of the world. Had Rimpalle had to hate the British labor leaders before they let him dig mica? I didn't believe it. Gühling—yes, probably Gühling knew all that theory—he was a professor. But wasn't there some simpler way?

I thought of a way. I still had a letter from the Seattle Central Labor Council asking me on my trip to Europe to report anything of interest to Seattle workers through the

Union Record. The Red Trade Union International was to meet in Moscow in December 1922; it was trying to get delegates from all sorts of workers' organizations. I wrote to the Seattle Central Labor Council and asked for credentials to this congress where I might "meet workers' representatives from all parts of the world." Let "progressive Seattle" be among the first to have such a delegate. Seattle agreed; they sent me credentials—a letter appointing me to "observe the Congress on our behalf without binding us to any conclusions."

The Russians take credentials more seriously than the Americans who write them. I have known American senators who would give you letters of introduction to all the world on the day they first met you. But even in America that credential was taken seriously enough for the American Federation of Labor to denounce the Seattle Central Labor Council for giving it. The Russians were sufficiently impressed by it to make me "delegate with advisory voice" in the congress of the Red Trade Union International. This included by courtesy a similar standing in the congress of the Communist International, of which I found it so difficult to read the theses.

My heart sank again at the meetings of the Red Trade Union International where they put me on a commission to discuss questions of theory and tactics underlying various forms of trade unions in Anglo-Saxon countries. I decided that I hated all these theoretical discussions which only caused bad feeling among comrades. But I didn't tell them this; I thought it wasn't polite. Besides, I had made up my mind that all this theory didn't really matter; what mattered was work. If theories had to be swallowed, I'd swallow them somehow, as long ago I had "conquered" philosophy. It would be easier, however, to just let them "do my theory," as once I had let Lena Lewis put into my editorials the Marxism that mattered to her but not to me.

One practical benefit my credential gave me: it got me that room in the Lux Hotel which had been denied me when I came to work full time for the labor press. I said to myself: "How these Russians admire little slips of paper! They give me for that one credential what I can't get for a year of hard work." Hard, efficient work was to me my passport to living. I had no conception whatever that what interested the Russians in me, far transcending my individual work, was the fact that I represented a group of organized workers. I did not understand this for many years.

To the Lux Hotel in those days came foreigners of many nations on a hundred errands, and also Russians who had lived for years abroad and who were now returning to what had become for them a new land. Many came from America. The desire that had brought me over the ocean to this new world's life was shared by thousands. I met them in groups and as individuals in Moscow and in my trips to all parts of the country. Rimpalle, the native son of California, the factory manager of Samara, were only a few among many.

By no means all were happy in Russia. The first arrivals expected a workers' paradise and were swiftly disillusioned by the ruined land they found. Even those who were warned of the hard conditions—and the Russians tried to send out warnings—were unable to imagine the form of the difficulties. They assumed that good will and efficiency would speedily carve a place for them. But they were accustomed to American enterprises where there was division of labor and where all equipment was supplied by the boss; their boasted skill was helpless with broken tools and dismantled equipment. Their high hopes were drowned under floods of bureaucracy and smothered by the weight of unskilled workmen. And those Russian workmen who, for all their inefficiency, could produce by sheer strength or handicraft when the Americans could not produce at all, sneered at the ways and the clothes of the newcomers as bourgeois.

Yet Russians wanted American skill and efficiency. Lenin himself had said that it was the one thing needed, when added to workers' power, to build socialism. The Russians tried to fit the Americans into their system, but they could not protect them from the vast disorganization in which everyone was entangled and out of which heroic groups in factory, mine and oil-field were fighting their way. The Americans had to fight, and they did not know the method. Nor could they fight easily on a diet of black bread.

The assimilation of individual foreigners, coming from all lands to help the revolution, proved so difficult that the Russians adopted a policy of admitting only organized groups or "communes" supplied with their own machines, equipment, food and clothing, and prepared to develop land or a productive enterprise. Commune Seattle, Lenin Commune, the Kuzbas Colony, the Astoria fishermen, and many groups of pioneering Americans, some of which failed and some of which succeeded, but all of which contributed to the building of Soviet Russia, date from those days. They had the best conditions which the new land afforded: skilled workers, American machinery, agreements with appropriate government organs. There was good faith on both sides, yet even these groups swiftly encountered the shock of unexpected difficulties.

The little fishing community of Finnish-Americans who came from Astoria, Oregon, to settle in northern Karelia, bringing carloads of equipment for a model fishing and canning industry—how could they imagine that their freight would be lost for months in the chaos of the Murmansk railway and that they would face an Arctic winter with a few hand-saws and hand-axes, with scanty clothes and inadequate food? The valiant Finnish-American farmers and lumberjacks who came from my own state of Washington to organize Seattle Commune as a comradely center of farm technique to enlighten a whole district—could they know that the local authorities would clear off a host of unregistered "squatters" to make room for them, leaving a neighborhood hate which made peasants refuse to sell even a chicken to the Americans for two years? Could they foresee the malaria which for three years so devastated their colony that the few who could stagger to work could barely sow enough for the commune's food?

The most ambitious of all the American projects was the Kuzbas Industrial Colony in Siberia. A vast, rich territory equal to the Pittsburgh Valley and the Mesaba Range combined was offered to a coöperative colony of American workers —if they could develop it. But this stupendous chance for "workers running their own industry" needed thousands of skilled and harmoniously organized workers supplied with complex and well-chosen equipment. Radical enthusiasts came from New York's East Side, crumpled under the touch of Siberia and went home. Other men, more fit and determined, came and fought to the end. They fought the great disorganization of transport, many local engineers who hated both Americans and Soviets, the anti-foreign sentiments of local workmen. They fought their own dissensions and inefficiencies. They fought and starved and sickened and kept on fighting; but there weren't enough of them to develop Kuzbas as fast as it was needed. So the American Industrial Colony was bought out by the Soviet government, which reorganized the valley as a series of state trusts. Yet part of the strength of today's center of steel in Siberia came from that group of hard-bitten fighters, who are scattered today in Soviet industry, fit to rank with the best of her conquerors. Everyone treasures an "old Kuzbasser."

Except for these communes, the Russians discouraged new immigrants. They made it hard to get visas. If would-be immigrants were communists, their own parties kept them away by party discipline. They said: "If a man is a good revolutionist, let him stay at home and make the revolution in his own country; if he isn't a good revolutionist, he would be of no use in Russia."

We Americans did not understand the Russians' attitude; we thought in quite different categories. We said: "Why are they so exclusive? Isn't it a world revolution which belongs to us also? Aren't we efficient? We'd rather work for socialism than for capitalists." There were even people who dropped membership in the American Communist Party in order to come to Russia. They said: "I am more apt at building than destroying. I can be more useful by my efficiency in Russia than by attacking capitalists in America." Thus they phrased their flight from the difficulties of class struggle. Thus had I also phrased my flight from the problems of Seattle's labor movement. If such individuals, against all advice, persisted in going, the Russians accepted and tried to place them. Who knows, after all, where a man is most useful? They respected, as one deciding factor, the man's own will.

Both the men of the communes and individuals, who came in various ways when the blockade was broken, drifted in and out of the Lux Hotel, discussing their problems. We began to analyze ourselves and our troubles. We decided that we Americans are a sentimental people. We came to Russia full of awe, enthusiasm and muddled ideas. We thought that mere expansive sympathy merited room space and interpreters and the time of busy people. We thought our friendly sentiments would interest the Russians. They never did. We ourselves swiftly grew tired of newer arrivals who spoke our national language, that "friendly service" approach of Rotary: "I'm not exactly a communist but I do so sympathize with your revolution." We admired much more the "hard-boiled" Russians, who wanted to know impersonally if newcomers could do enough to be worth the inevitable trouble they caused. But when we tried to be hard-boiled we were merely brutal, which is sentimentality in reverse. We lacked the harsh experience of those Russians which had made them wary of gusts of emotion.

Then we learned that we were accustomed to bosses; we either submitted to orders or ran away. It never occurred to us to analyze and change the orders; we couldn't know how. Harold Ware brought the first American Tractor Unit to Russia towards the end of the famine. His plan was to make tractor-farming self-supporting and self-expanding; he had not only machines but a well-picked group of American farmer boys to teach the Russians. The German chief of International Famine Relief who knew nothing of farming, sent Ware's unit to the scant soils of northern Perm eighty miles from a railroad in a country so raw that he had to repair twenty bridges to get his tractors to the farm and on hills so bleak and with such a short season that self-support was doomed from the start. He told Ware it was "party orders" and Ware, like a dutiful worker, submitted. When his cherished harvester-combine came, the relief society installed it in a Perm shop-window as a "demonstration" while the Americans sought for it at railroad stations, and eighty miles away reaped their harvest with sickles.

"So I learned," said Ware, "that even party orders aren't acts of God but of human beings; you've got to know where to go and whom to see. You've got to learn when to submit and when to fight and how. The will of this country is honest; but you have to learn how to connect with that will. You have to know politics as none of us Americans knows it."

We learned also that there was no "square deal" in the country. No individual ever got what he expected, what he "earned and had a right to." Sometimes he got more and sometimes less. It was disconcerting to us Americans. Some of us said: "These Russians don't keep promises." Others said: "It's Asiatic inefficiency. They would give a square deal, but they don't know how." We saw at last that there was something more in it, something old and something new. Part of it was really inefficiency, but part was a new collective standard. You would join a coöperative and pay in advance for an apartment and get something different from what you had paid for, three years too late. Nobody owed you anything; it was your fault, collectively, that your coöperative was badly managed. Or you would get quite unexpected windfalls, free theater tickets or cheap honey or a half-price vacation in the Crimea because an organization to which you belonged was collectively efficient. We began to see that the concept "square deal" is derived from trading capitalism, and has no connection with anything else in the world: neither with friendship, nor with the family, nor with ancient feudalism nor future socialism.

Instead of "square deal" the new concept was "collective struggle." You were either on one side or the other, either grabbing private gain or strengthening workers' power and building socialism. In the first case, the fighters for socialism tried to thwart you by "fair" or "unfair" methods; in the second case, they helped you when they could, which wasn't often, and as much as they could, which wasn't much. But all of you kept on fighting, and learning what would work and what wouldn't for the things you were building together. On personal matters you weren't supposed to be sentimentally

self-sacrificing, as we idealists tried to be; this only annoyed
the Russians. You were supposed to look out for yourself
without making too much of a fuss.

"It's a harder war than the war we've left," we began to
say after a while. "Harder for us at least because we don't
know the language, the weapons, or the intimate reactions of
the social background. It may be our revolution, since it belongs to the world; but it isn't our country." We began to
understand why the Russians had told us to stay at home and
make our own revolution. It wasn't exclusiveness; it was common sense. We had chosen an environment that handicapped
us. Yet having chosen, some of us had gifts to bring.

In understanding our new fight and its new concepts, we
newcomers were chiefly helped by the "returned Americans,"
those Russian revolutionists who had spent some years in
America and had come back with the revolution. They were
of all gradations; those who had been longest in America were
closest to us, those who had been away the least were closest to
Russia. But together they made a bridge between two worlds.
They knew our ways and wanted to help us, for their own
sakes as well as ours. For they were standard-bearers of
American methods in Russia who hoped that some day we
would help them. They prized our abilities and understood
our shortcomings.

There was Bill Shatoff, brilliant, energetic, who had returned
from anarchist agitation and free speech fights in America to
run Siberia's railways and the Petrograd militia. He had
been since then a bank president, an investigator of mines, a
manager of oil export. He was later to build the first of the
great new railways.

Shatoff bragged of America. "She was my teacher," he said.
"She would not own me now, but none the less she taught me.
When I work in the railways here, they call me a railway expert, when I work in the army, they call me a military expert.
But hell, I'm no kind of expert; I'm just an American. I
got my military training chasing scabs in Colorado, and my
police training evading the police and my railway training
riding the rods. You learn a certain trick of organizing work

in America, a way of doing things without waste motion, that is good for any job, once you get it." We newly arrived Americans thrilled to Shatoff. He knew what efficiency was. He justified us.

Melnichanski, another returned American, was at that time president of the Moscow trade unions. The militiamen learned to take all stray Americans who were lost on the streets to his office. He was trouble-shooter extraordinary for scores of struggling communes; he fixed their contracts, located their freight and helped them on their way.

There were dozens of others in various posts of the state industries. Krasnoschekoff had managed a school in Chicago, returned to be president of the Far Eastern Republic, and was now, as chief of the Industrial Bank, bringing money and workers from the Amalgamated Clothing Workers to Russia. He was planning an "American Industrial University" which should be farm, factory and school combined, to be run on fifteen estates not far from Moscow. Arthur Adams managed the AMO Auto Works which was largely staffed in those early days by "returned Americans." Borodin, formerly of Chicago, was later to win fame in China. Losev, member of the American Society of Engineers, was repairing power plants all over the country. He said to me: "Next only to communism I fight for American engineering methods."

Only years later did we realize that even these "returned Americans," whom we admired as guides and mentors, were also handicapped in fully adjusting themselves to Russia by their years of residence with us. They knew how to organize industry; they were useful in production. But as Ware had said, they didn't "know politics"; in the upper posts they often failed. They were out of touch with the instinctive demands of their fellow-Russians; they had become Americanized. Bill Shatoff to this day remains outside the communist party; Melnichanski rose high in the trade unions but was transferred from them for his opposition to party policies; Krasnoschekoff was arrested and jailed for graft.

Shall I say "graft"? It is the word which carries to American minds the opprobrium which was felt in Russia. But his actions carried to Americans no opprobrium. I heard Russians say that he should be shot for treason. I heard Americans cry: "But what he did was only good banking practice, building up the Industrial Bank." Both were right. What he did was good American banking practice and treason in a communist.

Krasnoschekoff dealt with foreign business men on behalf of Soviet Russia. He gave expensive dinners to prospective buyers, treating them and himself and his secretary to good wines and gypsy concerts at government expense. He loaned state money to his brother, who was a private contractor building houses in Moscow. House-building was a needed service, and private contracting was legal. The security given by the brother was an adequate amount of actual dollars in cash, which was sounder security than many state industries afforded in their ruined plants and unskilled management. But can such a defense be made by a communist, whose bank was created to serve the state?

In those early days of the New Economic Policy, the limits of action were not yet clear. The anger of Soviet workers was rising against the speculators who strode the streets. A clear voice and a clear line of ethics were needed. Krasnoschekoff's case became a signal fire that lit the boundaries of NEP. His sentence said: "Private profit may be legal as a necessary evil, but for a communist to be concerned with it and help it prosper—is crime." The enemy was still the eternal enemy. There might be truce, but no peace.

Years later, long after Krasnoschekoff had been released, returned to responsible work at the head of an industry and even given his party ticket again, he said to me once: "I stayed too long in America. My habits, my impulses, my methods are too American; they never entirely fit. It has cost me very much."

Not by accident did many of those Russians who had spent long years in emigration slip from the posts which they took when the revolution started and which they lost as the Russian masses put forth new leaders. The closer they were to our outside world, the further they were from those masses, who were the source of power.

We Americans noticed, indeed, that our admired friends and mentors were noted more for efficiency in industry than skill in politics. This was to us no lack but rather a virtue; we admired them the more. They were "practical men" of industry who occasionally came to grief when other men "pulled wires." This was the meaning to us of most of the early party discussions and struggles.

Our American past had taught us contempt for "politics." It meant in our lexicon personal wire-pulling, the use of oratory to win votes, and of votes to win office, and of office to win personal wealth and power. It meant the giving of posts to personal adherents to build a political machine which would give its manipulators greater power. We saw some of this in Soviet Russia and assumed that politics meant the same thing here. We thought: of course they have to have politics, but the less of it, the better.

Not for many years did it occur to me that what we Americans called "politics" was but its outer, corrupt technique into which it was constantly pushed by the pressure of personal greeds, and that in essence politics was the study of the deep, instinctive will of masses, the dynamic analysis of social and economic forces, and the continuous adjustment of relations between a thousand groups that together make society.

CHAPTER XV

THE WORKER-RULERS

How are we going to make our steel mills go? And our coal mines? And our oil wells? These questions were on everyone's lips in the Soviet Russia of early 1923. Workers discussed them in union meetings; administrators of industry conferred with trade union representatives in public conferences to work out joint programs. People who had grown used to the terminology of war and beaten the enemy on many fronts, and who recently had fought on the "famine front," now spoke of the "battle-front of industry."

The *Pravda*, one of the two big newspapers of Moscow, ran a contest to determine the "best directors in our enterprises." Imagine an American newspaper holding a contest to decide whether Rockefeller, or Gary, or some factory manager in Pittsburgh, is the best director! Even more amazing than the contest itself, from my American point of view, was the standard set and the way decision was reached.

Letters came to the paper from workers, bragging about their bosses. Other letters came denouncing bosses, some of whom were subsequently fired. The twelve best candidates, set up by their own workers and then checked by investigating committees from other factories, were given a banquet in Moscow and decorated with the order of the Red Banner of Toil, one of the highest honors in the country.

The standards of judgment set by the workers surprised and stirred me. They wrote: "Our factory was working part-time. Then Archangelsk came. With just words he enthused and united us. He introduced order. He rapidly brought production to 120 percent of prewar. Comrade Archangelsk spends all his physical and mental strength for his factory workers. He repaired housing and the workers' dormitories. He arranged courses of technical instruction for factory youth. For ten months we see that every day our life becomes better."

Of a bad director they wrote: "For ten months of his management 2,500 more tons of oil were used than were needed; healthy locomotives decreased twenty-five percent; accidents increased threefold. Workers began to fear him, saying: The union seems unable to protect us from this man. Nothing was done to increase production; nothing was repaired. He took no interest in education. For two and a half years he did nothing to improve the life of his workers."

Such were the standards set by these workers in judging their directors. They were not asking if the manager piled up profits. They were not even discussing hours and wages. Nor did they support him, as the workers of Seattle supported political leaders, because he was "convincing" and they "agreed with his ideas." All these categories seemed to have been sidetracked. They asked: "Can he organize us to conquer chaos, to set our factory in order, to produce a good life for all of us?" It was the sane test of people that are building; beside it all the standards set by the rest of the world seemed suddenly insane.

It was quite clear that these workers spoke as owners. Yet in what sense did they own? I had known public ownership in Seattle—our city-owned power plant, docks and street cars. All the progressives were proud of them; we said we owned them. This meant that every year or two we elected men to sit on their board of directors. But our publicly-owned utilities never aroused such continuous interest and devotion as these publicly-owned industries of Russia. Certainly our street-car workers never thought of giving their holidays to repair cars as part of a celebration. Were the Russians more devoted to the public good? Or was this a different form of "ownership"?

More than a day's journey south of Moscow, in the Ukraine, lies the Donetz valley of coal and steel, the Russian Pittsburgh. Three days further southeast, on the shores of the Caspian, lies Baku, the greatest oil field in the world. These were chief centers of Soviet heavy industry. They had been held in turn by various armies of intervention; they had been ravaged by civil war. On them the attention of the whole country fastened. The Communist Party Congress which was approaching made the revival of industry one of its three main topics. Rakovsky, president of the Ukraine, was going to the Donetz to attend local party congresses and prepare a report on coal and steel. It was arranged that I should go with him.

I anticipated long hours of vivid, interesting discussion. There would be plenty of time, I thought, on a private car. I did not yet understand how these Bolsheviks worked. Rakovsky entered the car at six in the evening and went immediately to sleep; he had worked the two preceding nights till after dawn. At midnight he rose and attacked a pile of foreign newspapers several feet high—the conservative press of England, France, Germany and Italy. He read all these languages easily and rapidly, marking items for his secretary to clip and tossing the papers aside. He worked until he was tired, or until the "comrade porter" brought some food; he ate or slept and worked again, with total disregard of night and day.

"During my week in Moscow I got behind on the foreign press," he said, smiling. "We must know what our enemies think of us."

"Do they take as much pains to know about you?" I inquired.

"They know next to nothing about us," he answered. "I learned that in Lausanne."

While waiting for the trip to the Donetz I visited Kiev, and spoke on March 8th, International Women's Day, to a great throng of women—worn, intent faces under faded shawls. I spoke in very bad French which was probably worse translated. But the band played and the women applauded, thinking me a remarkable person to have come all the way from America. But I knew that every one of those women was more remarkable than I. Every one of them had kept house through sixteen bombardments.

Sixteen times in the civil war the city of Kiev changed hands. The Germans had held it, Petlura, Denikin, various guerilla bands, the Poles. One-fourth of its buildings were ruined by shot and shell. When I asked the women what was the hardest thing to endure, they did not mention the danger. The hardest thing, they said, was cooking meals when the water-works was destroyed and you had to go miles to the river, when the coal mines were held by the enemy and one had no heat. Dangers of war are fleeting and carry the alleviation of excitement; but who has ever sung of the endless drudgery of war these women endured?

Kiev, reviving now, was holding a big fair "to get acquainted with our new industries." In its scores of booths six million rubles' worth of business was done in six weeks. The emerging forms of new government enterprises were clear. There was none of that monotony usually attributed to socialism by capitalist propagandists, no single owner regimenting everything. There were a dozen forms of organization, vertical trusts, horizontal trusts, small municipal trusts for local products, and big all-Union trusts for oil or grain. All were publicly owned but the forms were many and flexible. Textbooks were sold by a trust which belonged to the schools; drugs by a trust organized under the Commissariat of Health. A Cement Trust from the Caucasus, an all-Ukrainian Paper Trust, and a Grain Trust using 17,000 tons of grain to break all private control of grain: these were only a few of the many publicly owned enterprises I saw.

Clearly much local initiative was at work. Even the private speculators, it seemed, could be used if you knew how. Vidensky, chairman of the fair and chief of Kiev's public utilities and housing, told me how he had repaired the broken water-works, the power-plant, the ruined street-car system and hundreds of broken buildings, in a single year without a cent of taxes, by renting shops and market-booths to private traders and charging them, as capitalists do, "all that the traffic would bear." Vidensky was not sentimentally bewailing private trade as I had done; he exploited it to rebuild the city. His dream was the future "Garden City of Kiev" with the winding Dnieper below its noble hill and 25,000 acres of forests planned for a people's joy.

"No city in the world has such a site," he said. They had as yet no specialist on city planning, and no maps of other

garden cities. But they had all Kiev, broken Kiev, in their
hands, all its rents and industries and forests. What was impossible for men who had kept the collective wealth of a city,
seizing it from sixteen bombardments?

Half a day south of Kharkov in Rakovsky's private car we
plunged into the valley of coal and steel, the proletarian heart
of the Ukraine. You could tell you were among workers, and
ruler-workers, by the blasts of criticism that began. "Hallo,
there, Comrade Rakovsky, when are we going to get those
working-clothes they promised? When are we going to get
safety-lamps for the mines?"

Rakovsky was no longer reading the foreign press; he was
buried under local reports; he conferred twenty hours a day
with local party leaders. Newspapers were full of workers'
correspondence, most of it devoted to attacks. "Comrade Ste-
pansky had a big opening celebration for his power station last
December, but the station isn't delivering power yet!" . . .
"The milk from the municipal farm that should go to tuber-
cular workers goes to friends of the administration while the
workers stand in line and find it gone." . . . "Our mine has
fine equipment . . . it's the deepest in Russia, but it's under
the care of 'specialists' for two years with no results but trouble.
Give us honest workers' management; these 'specialists' sabotage!"

One of the mines was proud of its manager, Abakumov.
They had entered him for the *Pravda* competition as one of
the "best of the best" bosses. They wrote of him: "He received
the mine abandoned, condemned to destruction; it had reached
a depth where steam made working conditions impossible. But
Abakumov brought electricity four miles through frozen earth
to restore it; he replaced the horses by an electric railway.
Thanks to him we averted ruin and even increased output, and
thus started the gas and coke ovens and chemical mills." . . .
Could any other land sing such a battle-pæan over a coal
mine?

Down in one of the mines I met some American miners.
They were swinging up the wet, slippery slopes from the lower
level. They heard me talking English and hailed me, and

inspected me by the dim light of miners' lamps. Then we sat
down on a muddy ventilating pipe, crouching in half-darkness
and wet with coal mud, while they told in the twang of Illinois
what they thought of Russia.

"Pretty awful last year. Conditions upset by the famine.
We were sorry we came. But now—well, we figure we live
about as well as we did in the States. The mines aren't well
organized and it takes a week to earn what we made there in
two days, but over there we couldn't count on more than two
days' work a week. So it evens up. And we'd rather have it
regular. It's more peaceful here."

"Peaceful," I exclaimed, remembering the civil war and
famine barely over. But they gave me the workers' idea of
peace.

"Yep. No strikes nor lockouts. You can go to bed at night
feeling sure of work in the morning, which we never could do
in the States. No rows with your boss at all. You've your
union and your mine committee and you're insured against
sickness and accident. Some things are pretty rotten. We
don't get on with the older peasant-workers; they call us bourgeois when we go to town in decent clothes. Those fellows
have got to die out before they'll get coal here. They're so
shiftless that they won't learn reading and writing when the
union organizes classes at the mine entrance after work. This
government gives them every chance but they don't take it.
But we wish this government could afford to buy good machinery. They've good intentions but no machines. But we don't
want to go back. We figure in five or ten years this will be a
first class country for a worker."

It was an attitude I was to meet hundreds of times in ensuing years, the typical attitude of American workers in their
first experience of Soviet industry. They believed in the country's policy; they wanted to do good work; they were annoyed
when backwardness of Russian workers or lack of machines
injured their own efficiency. Not for years did I understand
why the leading Russian workers called the Americans "too
passive." In spite of their energy in production they were
socially passive, waiting for machines to come, waiting for lazy

men to die, waiting for inevitable progress to save them. The Russians said it was because they were accustomed to bosses, whom they had never overthrown by revolution. Certainly they lacked that intimate sense of ownership and responsibility which I found in the more advanced of the Russian workers who had seized these mines by bloody struggle and who knew that under any and all conditions they must somehow bring "their mines" to production.

The eight hundred men, with a sprinkling of women, who met in Red Lugansk for the district congress of the communist party, in preparation for the All-Union Party Congress, knew that they owned the country and must run it. They were men from mines, steel mills and villages, in working clothes as if they had come from their job. Theses on industry and on minor nationalities had been published and were under discussion in congresses throughout the country. Red Lugansk was not deeply concerned with the problem of nationalities; on this they listened to Rakovsky, who explained the new Council of Nationalities which was to be added to the central government. "We communists hold it a point of honor to find a solution to this difficult problem which vexes all Europe," he said.

On industry the delegates broke loose, not waiting for Rakovsky. They, not he, were experts in industry, the men of steel and mines. They said bureaucracy in Moscow and Kharkov was ruining industry; they demanded local authority, decentralization. "We've raised production of locomotives from 13 last year to 34 this year," said the manager of the locomotive works, taking the floor. "But those 34 locomotives still stand in our yards; they've stood there a year! How can I keep urging the workers to produce under hard conditions for the needs of socialism, when somebody in Moscow forgets to tell the railroads to take those locomotives away?"

"What do you charge for your locomotives?" called a voice from the floor. "The railroads are on a money basis now; perhaps they can't pay. Perhaps the price for your locomotives is too high."

"How the hell do I know what I charge?" the manager shot back. "That's more of this damned centralization. I know everything in the plant; I know we've reduced the hours it takes to make a locomotive. But my coal comes from a mine ten kilometers up the valley and neither the mine manager nor I know what I pay for the coal. That is a bookkeeper's secret, lost in some office in the center."

All day the men of industry, mine managers, shop committee secretaries, workers direct from coal face or lathe, piled up complaints and information, giving harsh details, voicing concrete demands. Then they elected the men who most expressed the common viewpoint and who had most information with which to support it, as delegates to the regional congress in Bakhmut, which should consolidate the views of the whole Donetz basin of coal and steel. From Bakhmut would be chosen delegates to Kharkov for a week's session of the All-Ukrainian Party Congress, where the views of all the workers of the Ukraine would be compiled. From Kharkov they would go to Moscow to the All-Union Party Congress, whose final resolutions would embody, not the views of any single authoritative leader, but the combined experience of a thousand factories, mines and villages. The delegates, surging back to the city and village, would explain and champion the program thus arrived at and carry it through in their places of work during the coming year.

This was the intimate mechanism of that common consciousness of which I had seen flashes all across Russia. There were creators in chaos; but they were not isolated in chaos, as they had seemed in the hungry villages of Samara and the newly-opened mines of the Far North. They had a firm base in a million brawny men of forge and foundry, men of coal and oil and steel and railroads, whose determined will they expressed. I understood better now what Rimpalle was organizing when he tried to form those illiterate peasant workers of the north into a trade union, a coöperative and a night-school. Those were no mere social services, donated to ignorant men by the kindness of Rimpalle, as a progressive capitalist in America might do welfare work to educate his labor. They were forms of workers' power which ruled the land. Here in the industrial south the workers had long been organized; they had thrown out the old owners by armed battle; they had seized the means of life and work. Now they put forth from their ranks new Rimpalles by thousands, sending them to Moscow as delegates, sending them to the ends of the land wherever needed, to organize the industries of the nation in ever-expanding power.

On the basis of information collected from a continuous series of such meetings, Rakovsky was writing a report for the All-Union Party Congress. It was unlike any political report I had ever seen. I was accustomed to the parliamentary form of political speeches, in which, with brilliant flow of oratory intended to overpower the minds of the listeners, the party in power brags of all its achievements and the party out of power attacks all the abuses, and neither side seeks anything so uninteresting as truth. Rakovsky was trying to give an accurate picture of the needs and desires of the Donetz. His success as a leader would depend on how far he succeeded in combining the demands of thousands of workers, scores of whom would also sit in the Congress.

He was writing: "Production is only half of prewar. This means that the cost of the product—a product we must use in all our industries—is doubled. The wage of metal workers is only forty percent of prewar in purchasing value, and even this is delayed in payment. Housing is appalling. Before the war the capitalists would spend no money on repairs since their concessions were expiring, and even of these unrepaired houses one-fourth were destroyed by civil war in many localities. However, the food shortage which last year caused tens of thousands of workers to desert to the farms is now over. There are no more indignant protest meetings. Complaints have changed from food to housing and equipment; they go in orderly process through unions, factory committees and press. Production is steadily increasing. Red Lugansk made 13 locomotives in 1921 and 34 in 1922." *

A thousand miles southeast of Red Lugansk were other cen-

---

* In the four years of the Five-Year Plan, 1928-32, the old Lugansk locomotive works produced 845 locomotives: a new locomotive works was opened on November 27, 1933, with capacity of 1,000 locomotives annually.

ters of workers' power: Baku, the oil capital, and Tiflis, where
the burning passions of forty Caucasus nations were being expressed on the problem of nationalities. When Rakovsky
turned north, I went to Baku.

Oil-fields in Baku! The largest field in the world. Forests
of shining black derricks against every horizon, against blue
skies or blue water or in the smoky hollows of the hills. Except
for these derricks—desolation. No green thing lived in Baku.
The mocking blue of the Caspian is salt; Baku brought fresh
water, barely enough for drinking purposes, across a hundred
miles of desert. Baku was never built for happiness; it was
built for the exploitation of illiterate native workers in the
interests of absentee owners. The only trees in all its desert
were in the Villa Petrolla, built for the chief officials of the
Nobel Oil Company, but occupied at the time of my visit by
four children's homes.

Here was modern industrialism on a background of primitive Asia. Workers whose dialects had hardly been reduced
to writing were operating rotary oil-drills fresh from America.
Mohammedan women, drawing their veils across their faces and
balancing heavy water-buckets across their shoulders, toiled
up narrow streets under the ruins of a thousand-year-old
castle; on the plains below them a modern power-plant larger
than any in Europe sent current to operate eight scattered
oil-fields. Under my feet the rumbling of a gusher, expected
hourly in Bibi Eibat field, announced its coming half a mile
below the earth. Not far away was another famous gusher,
delivering oil for seven years, a million barrels a year. From
other derricks sounded the rattle of chains as an oil drill
whirled its way through sand and gravel hundreds of feet
below. Little olive-black streams of oil crept through the
greasy dust of the fields, flowing towards great reservoirs.

All this oil came at last to the city of Baku, and its great
refineries on the bay. Here were pipe-lines leading to docks,
and ships loading and unloading. Here stood the largest re-
finery in Russia, once owned by Nobel, turning out eighty different kinds of oil products, benzines, kerosenes, machine oils,
paraffins. Benzine in twenty different weights poured in con-

tinuous streams of diamond white; the many-toned machine oils gleamed golden to deep brown. There were great vats of milky green "soapy" oil followed by vats of slate-colored "washed oil." Outside were great pools of mazut, black olive in color, waste useful for fuel.

All this wealth had once belonged to more than a hundred private companies who drained the oil from one another's fields in wasteful competition, fought and went bankrupt, in the time-honored capitalist way. The tokens of ownership were scattered in a dozen countries, as tiny slips of paper over which stock markets gambled. The workers of Baku, Russians, Turks, Armenians, Persians, never saw their owners. Not until they rose with the rest of the Russian workers, seized the fields and became owners themselves. Then race and religious wars had been fomented by the intervention; there had been great massacres of Turks by Armenians and Armenians by Turks; Baku had been seized first by German then by British occupation, and taken once again by the oil workers. Under these struggles the fields were damaged till it seemed in 1920 that the oil of Baku might be lost forever under the floods that rose in unworked wells.

Engineers told me that Serebrovsky had saved the oil wells. He led the fight of hungry, half-clad workers and engineers against the rising waters, against fires that burned great gushers, against spying and sabotage of managers, against the attrition of blockade and famine. The lands of the hundred private companies were combined in one state-owned oil trust, Azneft. The wells were organized on a rational plan in eight chief oil-fields, each with its engineering staff. Azneft bought American machinery through London, there being then no way to deal with America. Steadily production climbed; in 1923 it was double its low point of 1920.*

Then Azneft rebuilt the life of Baku's workers. Serebrovsky bought quantities of flour from North Caucasus and sent rep-

---

* In the low month of 1920, September, Baku produced 180,000 tons of oil; in the year 1922-23, it produced three and a half million tons, an average of 300,000 tons per month. But after the Five-Year Plan Baku produced 12,493,000 tons in the first eight months of 1934, an average of a million and a half tons per month, eight times its 1920 production.

resentatives into Persia to exchange oil for rice. Lacking sufficient workers, he went to Turkey and from the demoralized hordes of Wrangel's army brought back eager men who became champion workers in an effort to redeem their past. Financed by the profits of Azneft, sixty-three schools arose by 1923 for the oil-workers' children, and fourteen children's homes for the war orphans. Factory schools and night schools and an engineering university—all on the profits of Azneft.

For the first two days I sought for information through Serebrovsky's office. He was an impossible man to interview. He sat at a desk with four chairs around it, all filled with men waiting to see him. He answered them each in turn, briefly; as one of them rose I took my place in his chair. It is my turn: I say I want to know about refineries. Not a word does Serebrovsky give in information; he scribbles an order on a pad and hands it to me, saying: "The chief of the refineries will send an engineer with you. Tell him what language you speak." That is all; it is the turn of the next chair's occupant.

This Serebrovsky, who had "saved the oil of Baku," lived in two rooms up an iron fire-escape on an inside court. His wife was a beautiful woman with pale transparent skin and flaming cheeks, ill with tuberculosis caused by the hard conditions of Baku life. It was lack of milk and eggs that slowly starved her; it was a climate where sun beat mercilessly and wind whirled dust into the lungs. It was living in one room with a husband who brought men home late at night for discussion. "It is better now," she told me. "We have two rooms and I can always rest in one." She lay all day in the little flat till she heard her husband's step on the iron stairway; then she rose for a brief half-hour at the table till he went back to evening work. I heard him late one evening in his office answer the call from home: "No, not till midnight surely. Probably not till one. Don't wait up for me."

On the third day, as I was writing a hero-story about this new type of oil king and his wife, a worker who spoke English came to me. "We hear you have credentials from Seattle workers. What are you doing, spending all your time with the bosses?"

I stammered: "Why, I thought that Serebrovsky . . ." I had thought in a state-owned oil trust of a socialist state, that Serebrovsky represented the workers. Was I wrong? Was he a boss, like the bosses at home? And didn't the workers like him?

My visitor grinned at my discomfiture. "Serebrovsky's a good enough manager," he said. "But there are some others of us too. Why don't you come round to the union?"

I went. The union wanted me to understand that they had as good an automobile as Serebrovsky, so they took me around to some of the twenty-five libraries and thirty workers' clubs and one hundred and twenty-seven classes that were fighting illiteracy. They showed me hospitals and sanitariums and social insurance. "But I thought," I said, "that these things were financed by Azneft."

"Sure," they said. "Did you think Serebrovsky was Azneft? . . . Azneft, that's us! Serebrovsky runs engineering and production, but we organize the life of the workers. The money comes from the oil-fields, but the unions do the spending."

It was clearly a form of ownership which differed from the "public ownership" of docks and light and street cars in Seattle, which we had thought of as a step towards socialism. That ownership had taxed the "people" to produce cheap public services, which might enable small business men and farmers, "independents," to compete with other cities and keep on competing forever. It had actually played into the hands of the larger capitalists, enabling them to concentrate on the more profitable aspects of business, or to sell out-of-date utilities at high prices to a public eager for "municipal ownership" or to entrench control in the great banks which finance cities.

This Soviet "public ownership" on the other hand, developed great natural resources and monopolies, whose profits not only paid the bills of government, but transformed the Asiatic backwardness of workmen—Tartar, Persian, Tyurk and many other nationalities—and built a developing life under those workers' control.

This ownership was complexly organized. I did not yet

understand all of it. But I saw clearly that there was an economic organization, the oil trust, responsible to the state for efficient management, and a social organization, the trade union, which organized the local workers for their share in the common product, and a political organization, the communist party, which correlated all the demands of the country, deciding which "front" was most important.

It was also clear that the old ownership whereby holders of small bits of paper who had never seen Baku claimed its oil wells—as such men by such paper claim most oil wells of the world—had vanished like a nightmare at dawn. I knew there was another story of Russian oil far away from Baku, a story in Paris and London and San Remo and Genoa and the Hague. I knew that treaties had been made between France and Britain, and joint programs between Shell and Standard on the disposal of Russian oil—when they should get it. Riots of speculation had raged in Paris; widows and orphans and *demi-mondaines* had staked the cost of bread and the price of lust on paper claims to the oil of Baku. All those strange myths of property were still believed beyond the Soviet border.

They were no longer believed in Baku. When I asked a worker if he knew whether Shell or Standard now claimed title in Nobel's Oil Company, he looked bewildered and then grinned in sudden comprehension. "How should we know? We live in Baku. And the wells are in our hands." The oil-workers of Baku—were rulers!

CHAPTER XVI

MY FIRST GREAT FAILURE

MANY kinds of Americans came to Soviet Russia in those first years of her rebuilding. Besides the would-be immigrants there were press correspondents, officials of the Hoover relief, communists arriving legally or illegally, and business promoters seeking concessions. To me they were all of them "Americans"; I didn't divide them into rigid classes, as the Russians always did. My experience in Seattle's labor movement had taught me that class struggle existed, but I saw it as something occasional and specific, occurring in strikes and revolutions. It seemed to me that the Russians saw class struggle everywhere. Why wouldn't they see also individuals, good and bad people in all classes? I myself mixed with all groups of Americans to perhaps a greater extent than anyone in Moscow.

It seemed to me cynicism when a Russian communist said to me early in 1923: "Have you noted the change in the personnel of the American Relief Administration? Army men the first year and business men the second! Their military spies found no way to overthrow us, so now their business spies seek concessions to corrupt us. It is a sign of our advance." I knew of course that Hoover had used his food control to help break the Hungarian revolution, and that American threats of continuing the food blockade had helped bring German workers to terms in the 1919 revolts. But I looked upon the employees of the Relief Administration as individuals, efficient people under a too-conservative leadership, doing a hard job of food distribution in a very inefficient country.

Yet no one could deny that they were looking around for business chances and meantime profiteering on the ruble-exchange. I knew of men among them who bought a diamond a week out of their salaries. Their income in dollars enabled them to buy at famine prices quantities of jewelry, gold ornaments, paintings and art treasures which their diplomatic immunity allowed them to ship out of the country. I disapproved of these acts, but I was unwilling to class the whole Relief Administration by them, even when a well-informed Russian communist said to me: "It is becoming a question whether the millions of loot they are taking out of the country isn't more than their relief."

Among the Russian populace Americans enjoyed a wide, if shallow, popularity because of the relief. It was even common practice for the less sophisticated Russians to allude to all Anglo-Saxon intervention as "British," and to all Anglo-Saxon relief as "American," a credit greater than Americans deserved since both nations took part in varying degrees in both activities. The communists decided to teach their people a lesson. They waited till a Christmas shipment sent out by the American Relief's special courier bulked unusually large in precious gifts. Then they detained the courier at the frontier, brought him back to Moscow and asked the American Relief Administration to open the bags in their presence for smuggled exports. The resultant find in jewelry and art treasures was duly featured in the Soviet press.

A few protests appeared in the American press. "Interfering with our Christmas presents," the Americans called it. Most of them thought it the folly of over-zealous officials; surely American "friendship" was worth that small shipment of loot! It was no folly; it was clear intention, now that relief was almost over, to show the Russian people the wolf of capitalism under the sheepskin of charity. They showed it.

As our hotel became the natural center for American workers and communist sympathizers, the American Relief Administration was, until its liquidation in the summer of 1923, the natural center for Americans coming to do business. It fulfilled the functions of a tourist agency, a mailing address and an unofficial consulate, none of which things existed in those days for Americans in Moscow. Its commissary even became the American grocery store.

Americans of all kinds felt isolated in Russia. It was especially felt by the press correspondents whose job was to make connections in order to get news. They found this difficult. Even short interviews were incredibly hard to get. Those personal acquaintances which obtain in all the world's capitals between important newspapermen and high officials were quite unknown in Moscow. I saw more than one correspondent who had sought his Russian job because of friendly admiration for the Soviets, driven by isolation into eventual opposition. Communists gave them no time; the only society they could attain was that of a few worried, dissatisfied intellectuals and remnants of the old régime who drifted to them for their money and the amusement of their parties. This environment at last destroyed their "sympathy for the revolution."

Even Walter Duranty, whose understanding of Russian events was admired by the Russians, told me he had to go abroad frequently "for a little intelligent conversation without which I cannot live." "Aren't there intelligent people in Moscow?" I asked, and he retorted: "Very—but do they give me any conversation?"

Those Americans who wished to help build socialism were less severely isolated than the correspondents, but even we found ourselves getting our information from the wrong sources, and finding that our guides were being "cleaned out" as oppositionists. We saw more opposition than actually existed, since these were the people who had time to talk to us.

Out of the wish of all sorts of Americans for contact with Russian life was born the idea of a Russian-American Club. I hardly know how it began; it arose from so many needs. I swiftly became its chief promoter since everyone else was busy and I craved something outside my writing, something "to do." As soon as I took it up everyone began adding suggestions, and since my own chief interest was in the new pioneers who wished to apply American efficiency to the building of socialism, the club took form at first as an expression of their needs.

Men in industry said: "Let's have a reading room with American technical literature. Our technical libraries have nothing since 1914." Losev said: "I'll give my two thousand dollar engineering library if we can have a librarian; we'll form an engineering section and teach young Russians from my books." Visiting American musicians, doctors, engineers, educators said: "Can't we meet the Russians of our profession?" I put the suggestions together and promoted them everywhere.

We would get one of the big residences which would soon be vacated by the American Relief; I picked the one on Granatny Street, a spacious house with ten bedrooms, two baths and many fine reception rooms, already remodeled for American living. The American Relief agreed to donate their beds and office furniture; I was ready to advance two thousand dollars which I had saved from my magazine articles, since I thus acquired a permanent room. We would rent rooms to visiting Americans, give them lists of interpreters, typists, art-museums, and the sights of Moscow, keep them on a mailing list and get them to send us technical literature when they went home. We would have receptions for engineers to meet Russian engineers, for teachers to meet Russian teachers; we would publish a monthly bulletin and build up relations between the two countries.

Would they really let me do it? I had already made two or three attempts to enter the life of Soviet Russia and had felt myself rather casually brushed aside. Would I really be permitted to start anything so wonderful as a club which would help bring American efficiency to Russia, and which might grow to tremendous importance in tying together two lands? How did one get properly authorized in Moscow, in order to obtain a building? Everyone seemed vague about this. Where, I wondered, was a "big man" whose word would settle it? I thought of Trotsky and took it to him.

I had met Trotsky through a letter of introduction from a French communist when I was "Seattle delegate," worrying over adjusting my work for the capitalist press to the theories of the Communist International. Like everyone else he had told me to keep on writing for the capitalists and had then asked me to give him lessons in English. I had asked in return for "lessons about the revolution," and had got some twenty English conversations which were mostly anecdotes of his experiences. I was unaware of any lack in these conversations; they merely confirmed my view that theories didn't matter; what mattered was energetic action.

So now I took to him our Russian-American Club with its preamble about building socialism with American technique, and its list of Russian-Americans in responsible jobs of Soviet industry who wanted to organize it. "If you say it's good, I'll do it," I told him. "If you say it isn't, I'll drop it."

He read the list of signers carefully. "They are all our own people," he said. "Can't you get some American business men?"

"I can get any Americans you like," I answered in surprise. "Everyone is crazy to organize something. I kept away from the business men because they don't care about building socialism, and I didn't think they'd be allowed to organize anything here. But I can get them; there are plenty in town this summer."

"Leave out the socialist slogans," he said, "and get all the important business men you can. We'll let in our own people later. I'll take your project to Chicherin."

I got his meaning. England was trying that summer to inflame international hate against the Soviets. An ultimatum from Curzon threatened intervention and on the day when it arrived, there came also the news of the assassination in Lausanne of the Soviet representative Vorovsky. Moscow workers, with minds still fresh from the days of armed invasion, poured into the Red Square in demonstration. The city was still tense; discussions with Britain still went on. Meanwhile there were many American business men in Moscow, and even some American senators, La Follette, Brookhart and others, inquiring into trade relations.

If prominent American business men should now apply to form a Russian-American Club in Moscow! Oh, yes, I saw it! It was the high bluff of international politics to which I was invited. It would make a nice telegram to London. And I could do it. Americans are easy joiners. Even if you told them all about it, they would laugh and do it, if only to bluff the British, so long as it didn't cost them anything or commit them to anything. Well, our club was non-political, "for technical, cultural and social relations between Russians and Americans." They would all of them join. It didn't even occur to me that I was abandoning my earlier project. The rest would join later; it all moved in one direction. Analysis was swamped by the joy of "doing something." My American craving for efficient action was appeased.

In some ten days I had nine-tenths of the Americans in Moscow enrolled as members. Walter Duranty became a charter organizer and drew in other correspondents; Templeton of Sinclair Oil advocated special memberships of $100 and offered to be the first to subscribe. A visiting president of the New York Chamber of Commerce gave his blessing and the American senators put themselves down as "honorary members," i.e., absentees on our mailing list. Our executive committee contained Duranty and Templeton, Hecker, an American Methodist who was active in the Russian "Living Church," a Russian-American communist engineer and myself. It was what we love to call in America "all elements represented." How incredible it sounds in today's Moscow! But it was not so untypical of those days of the New Economic Policy.

Ten days of this and then—there began the most horrible summer of my lifetime! It began with "only formalities." We must get a charter and premises. Trotsky had gone south on vacation; Chicherin had put the affair in the hands of Nuorteva who kept me coming back to him in the Foreign Office day after day. I must rewrite the constitution in conformity with Soviet legal practice; next I must get it translated, next it must be officially stamped as to accuracy of translation. Next I was told to bring three copies. The more I did the more irritated Nuorteva seemed; it almost appeared that he intentionally delayed me.

After two weeks of these "formalities" I said to Nuorteva: "What do I get from you when I satisfy you? A charter or a house?"

"Oh, no," he said, "your charter comes from the Commissariat of the Interior and your house from the Moscow Housing

Department. We merely forward your requests to these organizations as a sign that we have no objection."

"I'll take them over myself and save you the trouble," I said. I browbeat Nuorteva into giving me a note to Moscow Housing, saying that our Russian-American Club was in process of organization and wanted a house of the ARA. With this I invaded the Housing Department and got an order for the premises on Granatny Street "as soon as the ARA shall vacate." In five days more we would enter our building.

I never was sure how the opposition started. It seemed to begin with an unpleasant man in the Committee for Correlating Foreign Relief Organizations. He had promised the Granatny House to the Joint Distribution Committee and was enraged when I got it direct from Moscow Housing. "I'll get it away from you," he threatened. I didn't see how he could.

But now, in place of Nuorteva's "watchful waiting" an active opposition began to spread through channels which I could neither trace nor reach. A worried Housing Department canceled our order for premises, and told me sharply that our organization had no legal existence and got the house on a pretense. Nuorteva became difficult of access; when I fought my way to him he said that he was doing his best. Could he help delays in the Commissariat of the Interior? I asked whom to see in the Commissariat of the Interior; he turned angrily away. I would not yet understand the language of foreign offices; I hunted up the Commissariat of the Interior, found the commission which gives licenses to social clubs, and demanded what they had done with the constitution of the Russian-American Club, sent them by Nuorteva.

"Nuorteva," they said. "Who's Nuorteva?" I explained our club and they said it was a fine idea on which they would act at once. Thereafter they also were inaccessible.

The Joint Distribution Committee moved into the premises on Granatny Street. The man who got it for them received a present of an automobile, properly presented through his organization. But I did not yet despair. An Agricultural Exhibition was opening that summer of 1923 in Moscow. They hoped for foreign visitors. But there was no tourist bureau in

all Russia, no facilities for supplying interpreters, not even a
list of museums, art galleries, consulates, or sights to see.   I
compiled such lists and mimeographed them and listed a group
of qualified interpreters.   If we could get a legal constitution
we could start our club without premises.   I asked the Agricultural Exposition for a corner of any kind to offer these
services to visiting Americans.   They asked—for a request to
that effect from the Foreign Office.

Back and forth again, day after day.   A dozen times I said
to the Foreign Office: "Perhaps you object to our organization
and want it changed."   "Oh, no," they said, "be patient.
You'll get your constitution."   A dozen times they told me at
the Commissariat of the Interior that somebody was on vacation and the commission hadn't met.   Was I really too impatient?   Or was somebody lying?   I couldn't tell.

Then came the farewell reception of the Soviet Government to the American Relief.   Important men whom we Americans seldom saw were there.   Chief of them was Kameneff,*
head of the Moscow City Government and holder of other high
posts.   People were saying to him: "Too bad that Russian-
American Club wasn't started, so that we could have more of
these meetings with Soviet officials."   So I also asked Kameneff
for an appointment to tell him about it. . . . He said: "Yes,
come.   What's this they all want?"

In an hour's interview I told the whole story.   I said: "Tell
me whether or not to continue.   If you say to keep on, I want
your help."

"Keep on," he said.   "It's a good idea.   What do you need,
a house?   I'll speak to the Housing Department."   He telephoned them in my presence.   "A constitution?   I'll tell the
Commissariat of the Interior and you'll get it next week."

"Shall I keep the business men or go back to the first idea?"
I pressed him.   "The business men," he answered.   "I'll tell the
Commissariat to overlook any irregularity in your lists." . . .
We laughed together over the idea of American senators fill-

* The same who was convicted in 1934 as a leader of the counter-revolutionary group which organized the murder of Kirov.

ing out the questionnaire on party membership. "Keep on,"
he said, as he smiled me out.

I kept on for another month on the strength of that smile.
But I never could see Kameneff again, nor the head of Moscow
Housing, nor the commission which grants club permits, nor
anyone in the Foreign Office. I became a pest in Moscow
offices, to be treated rudely by clerks. Everybody I asked for
was "in conference." Yet I still kept trying to carry out what
I thought was authorized by Trotsky and Kameneff, till Mr.
Templeton of Sinclair Oil came back from a three months' trip
to America and said to me: "I tried before I went to leave
that hundred dollars for you at the Foreign Office. They
wouldn't take it. They said: 'That club doesn't exist and never
will.' "

I raised a storm among the Americans in Moscow. Then at
last they sent for me from the Foreign Office. Rothstein administered the *coup de grâce*. "Drop the Russian-American
Club; we do not desire it."

"Thank you for telling me now," I said. "But why not
sooner? Do you know what life and faith I have wasted this
summer? Do you know I no longer believe a single Soviet
official? Why did they all tell me to keep on? Every one of
them lied."

"Nobody dreamed you were working at it so hard," he answered kindly. "They probably thought you would drop it
yourself."

"If they ever give me a chance to do anything in this country," I cried furiously, "they needn't expect me to drop it while
I'm told to keep on." As I left the office I thought bitterly of
all but Rothstein: "Damned Asiatics! Polite and shifty liars
who never tell you frankly what they do." I gave no consideration to the exigencies of foreign offices. I made no analysis
of the incompatible elements I had been thrusting upon them,
or of the delicate complications of refusing a club of senators.
I simply swung to the other extreme from my "creators in
chaos."

I would rather go through typhus again than through that
summer. It was worse than when I lost "my America." Never

before had I failed in a job of organization. This was failure utter and crushing, which left marks of destruction on my soul that will never entirely pass. Never since then have I been able to press blithely into Soviet offices in the cheerful American way, with the clear confidence that friendliness and efficiency entitle me to a hearing.

Something of this I mentioned to Michael Borodin, whom I had met earlier that summer. He soothed me with a two-edged philosophic consolation. "It was a good idea, the way we started it. You pushed it, and it was needed and some of it will come through. Not now—it may be too soon, and perhaps not in the same form. As for you personally, I understand just now you are completely broken. When you have been broken twenty times more, you will be fit to live in Soviet Russia."

"I shall be fit to die," I cried stormily.

   .   .   .   .

There were two sequels to the Russian-American Club. The first occurred a year or so later when the Society for Cultural Relations with Foreign Countries was organized in Moscow. Walter Duranty said to me: "Have you read the statement of their aims? Our Russian-American Club! We all noticed it." Yes, paragraph by paragraph were words from that very statement of purposes I had circulated.

"We'd have done it more efficiently," consoled Duranty, "but they have to have it the way they want it."

I agreed with Duranty. None the less I went to ask what I could do for the new organization. I was going to America soon on a lecture trip; I had many personal connections there and also a long list of people who had been to Soviet Russia and wanted technical and cultural relations. Would they like me to organize an American branch?

One of the assistants looked embarrassed. "You might give me some letters of introduction," he ventured. "I am hoping for a trip to America myself."

I smiled agreement and gave him letters. Inwardly I smiled a more cynical smile, telling myself that not the revolution refused me, but only a man who wanted a trip to America, and that I no longer cared.

But I did care. The second sequel showed it a year later. To a visiting foreign communist—I think he was a German— I told the whole story of the Russian-American Club and of other futile attempts to take part in Soviet life. I told it still with bitterness. I was amazed to see that my story made the German comrade very happy. His eyes were shining with joy.

"I have been so worried," he said, "by all this storm of private trade in the streets, by all these foreign concessionaires who strut through hotels. So many strange forces are around us; one wonders how far they may go. But you have answered my doubts! Oh, completely! You have shown me that nothing can get started here unless our party starts it. Not even with your great talent and energy and Trotsky's backing."

"It's a poor thing to take pride in," I cried, incensed, "the blocking of a good idea. This country is so inefficient it can't let people work for it when they want to." Yet his words re-echoed in my mind for later thought.

"Perhaps it was a good idea," he admitted. "And perhaps it had its dangers. I admit that this country is not very efficient. But it's efficient enough to block outsiders. That's enough for me."

I also had thought, in the intervening years, of some dangers. As I saw the variety of Americans coming to Moscow I had pictured myself presiding over a club where all-night drinking bouts and affairs with women caused scandal, or at a table of cynical conversations about the Soviet Union. I had several times begun to suspect that I was well out of it. But I wouldn't admit it yet.

"They did it anyway," I protested. "If we had done it with all the American enthusiasm, we might have got recognition by now. Was it any responsible decision that stopped me at the last? It was a man who wanted a trip to America!"

"Don't be a child about recognition," answered the German comrade. "It's not done by a few senators as honorary members. No doubt that man was pushing himself for a fine excursion. But—they know of him as a man who carries out orders. Always—not just on a single trip."

Was there any answer to that? No, there was no answer to that. I was a writer for the capitalist press, an outsider. There was for me no door to that charmed circle. . . .

Only eleven years after, recalling for this book that ancient story in the light of my present knowledge of Soviet organization, did I see how I myself had killed the Russian-American Club, child of my own desire and the desire of many good comrades. I took it to a single boss, saying: "Kill it or bid it live." In my blindness to class divisions I had not even noticed the changing of my own purpose from its slight but growing reality to an unreal bluff of international politics entangled with a group of speculators whom Soviet life refused. That earlier idea had life in the needs of men who were working, so it rose again after a year.

CHAPTER XVII

MY CHILDREN OF THE VOLGA

SUDDENLY my chance arrived. Mrs. Fisher said to me: "The
Children's Commission would like you to take a 'sheftsvo' over
a new colony of homeless children on the Volga."

Mrs. Fisher was the wife of an old Bolshevik who had lived
many years in an English exile. She had been go-between for
government organizations and Quaker relief; I had met her
then. Now she worked for the Children's Commission which
correlated on behalf of the central government all work for
homeless children. During her vacation in her old home town
of Khvalinsk on the Volga she had found such dire need that
she had decided to organize a self-supporting farm colony of
the older boys and girls.

"We want you to make it a model by bringing machines from
America. Won't you go down with me to organize it?" My
father was visiting me in Moscow that autumn of 1923. Together we all went.

That was the period when communes were springing up in
all parts of the country, for adults and for waifs of all ages.
Ordinary children's homes could not attract the older vagrants
left by war and famine; they came for winter shelter and ran
away in spring. Why not organize them in working groups on
some of the ruined estates now owned by the government?
With teachers and equipment they might become centers of
good farming, a light to the peasants.

My impression of Khvalinsk was not favorable. There were
plenty of needy children and the local authorities were glad to
give land. But the place they proposed was an old convent
whose grounds were a tangle of ancient orchard, woods and
a pond with a broken mill—admirable for vacation outings.
The farm lands offered were in four scattered fields of which
the furthest was fifteen miles away; such was normal peasant

191

farming on the Volga. They were connected by sloping hill tracks. Even I, though not a farmer, could see that a hillside where our cart slid persistently off the road was not good for tractors. I was supposed "to bring American tractors and make a model farm."

"For exactly what shall I be responsible?" I asked Mrs. Fisher. "What will happen here during my four months' lecture tour in America?" She looked distressed by my definiteness but said that the Children's Commission would organize the colony, pay its teachers and feed its children, but the work of a "shef" was to make technical improvements beyond the state budget. "You are not responsible for the basic organization. Anything you get from America will be clear gain."

To take any responsibility for a colony two days' journey from Moscow, a colony which I could seldom visit, was certainly not the task I might prefer, especially since all nature seemed stacked against me. But it was the first thing I had been asked to do by any Soviet organization, and I was feeling bruised by their total rejection of me in the Russian-American Club. I wasn't going to turn the first chance down. Mrs. Fisher knew it; she counted on it.

I learned from the local land department that other lands were available if we could promise development. When I asked for a large farm in one piece, they proposed Alexeyevka, an old estate some twenty miles down river near a dock which ensured transport. It was now a state farm but we could get it for children if we could develop it better than the present management was doing, which they assured me would not be difficult. State farms had little equipment and few good managers in those days. They estimated that five thousand dollars' worth of machinery and livestock would be more than enough to convince the most exacting branch of the government of our prior rights to that state farm. Such were the principles underlying Soviet public property. Private owners were barred from these government possessions, but any public organization which could show best chance of development might hope to get it. Then they must keep on developing it or lose it later to some newer organization which showed a better case of public good.

It was agreed that our colony should open at once in the Cherumshan Houses, as the hillside convent was named, and plow for the first year the four scattered fields, but that if I could come back from America with adequate machinery to develop, we could count on the Alexeyevka farm. Ten boys at once moved out to the convent, with Yeremeyev, a peasant, and Fedotov, a carpenter. They camped in empty rooms with broken windows; they brought, from the other children's homes from which they came, a dowry of five burlap bags of straw and five thin blankets, two lamps, ten bowls, ten spoons, two iron pots for cooking, some black rye flour and potatoes and oil from sunflower seeds. One horse and cart which brought them from Khvalinsk remained to work their acres. They got permission to tear down two broken shacks for lumber, and began making tables, benches and bunks with the worn set of tools which belonged to Fedotov.

Thus began the John Reed Children's Colony in the Cherumshan Houses while I went off to America for money, machines and people. Already I saw not only a model farm but a Russian-American university arising on the Volga, Soviet in form but American in technical skill, self-supporting from the work of its students. I knew there were hundreds of Americans who wanted "a share in Russia's future." Teachers, farmers, nurses, carpenters were begging to pay their own way over and live on anything to help Russia's children. I would select and bring such people; since few of them could speak Russian, it seemed fortunate that our first volunteer was a teacher of English, Anna Graves, already in Moscow. If she could teach English to a few of the children the first winter, they would be ready to absorb a growing host of American experts. A Russian-American university commune, that would be something to organize for the Soviet Union. It would be better than a Russian-American club which might—I admitted it now—have degenerated into booze and bridge.

Those waifs of the revolution did their part; they were heroic. Though badly educated ragamuffins, many of them thieves and all of them vagabonds, they wore themselves out for the idea of a commune where each should work and contribute to all. They had the will to life; they expanded steadily. Soon they sent a delegation to the town authorities: "We have our organization well in hand and are making dishes, furniture, beds, and repairing shoes. We are short of food; give us the broken mill on the pond and we will repair it." They got the mill, and with it four more children, two boys who wished to be millers and two girls to cook and sew. They sent delegations to advertise their mill in peasant villages, and began to earn their bread. They made more bunks and accepted more children; they got a food shipment from the liquidating Quaker relief and took in others. By the first spring plowing when I was still in America, fifty-seven children began their farming.

How they worked! They had planned it out on winter nights in Cherumshan, talking with Yeremeyev about the new life they should build. Buried on snow-covered hills and barely literate, they somehow reached out and drew in knowledge. Two years later one of the girls recognized Wells's *Outline of History* from its pictures as a story of mankind. She pointed to early Assyrian inscriptions, saying "Beginnings of Civilization." She had learned it from a Young Communist who came once a week from Cherumshan to run their club, teaching "human development and anti-religion." But the education was very sketchy, little bits from everywhere. They had as yet no books. Anna Graves succeeded in saving the life of one of the girls by feeding her when she lay in the hospital with stomach trouble, but not in teaching much English in the primitive life that prevailed.

In the spring of the year Yeremeyev taught them farming in the timeworn peasant way. They camped in the four fields one after the other, building straw shelter for the night. Yeremeyev camped with them, drove them, cursed them, cuffed them as a peasant father with his children. He was a village communist fighting religion, so the colony worked through Easter instead of getting drunk; thereby they proved to the whole township that early work rather than Easter celebration gets good harvest, for they had a record crop.

The boys who went the second autumn to conquer Alexeyevka were already a "responsible brigade" on their own. I found them sleeping in the straw of Alexeyevka barn and steadily plowing into late October. The rains of autumn beat on thin bodies and bare legs; they shook with chill and with malaria which rose from the river. Those who had sheepskins plowed longest, then loaned their coats to the others, and crouched under the straw while the next shift plowed. They asked me only for "fat in the soup, any kind of fat, lard, oil or butter, whichever is cheapest." They felt their calories directly in their thin bodies. They fell with eagerness upon a suitcase full of books which the brother of one of the boys, a Young Communist, sent down from Moscow, collected from editorial offices of newspapers. It contained every kind of book, from stories to Marxism. It was their first real chance to read.

They plowed to make the record which should determine how much land the colony could use. The strongest and oldest boys were fighting for the rest. Thus they plowed that autumn two hundred acres of rich soil, besides another fifty sown to winter rye on the hills of Cherumshan. It was more than any adult manager had got from Alexeyevka since the revolution. They were given more and more acres, more and more buildings. They won their farm. In another year five hundred acres of black plowed land lay on Volga hills at Alexeyevka. They even won the rich alfalfa field far beyond the ridges looking west where they camped at night to be ready for work in the morning. They even won the great four-story mill of the old estate which served the peasants of a township.

You could go by river an eight-hour trip from Volsk to Sizran and nowhere on Volga banks would you see so great a farm as ours. Nowhere would you see a tractor except that Fordson of ours from America. Men came for miles to look; we were a "light to the peasants." Homeless children heard of us up and down the Volga and flocked to join.

It was not to be ours alone but a commune receiving more and more homeless children, expanding always towards the Great Commune of the World. It was thus our sixteen-year-old Morosov, the most educated boy in the colony, explained it.

As son of a servant maid in Astrakhan he had seen the revolution at the age of ten: hungry soldiers robbing stores, hungry Persian workers knifing bosses for food. He saw the meetings where workers voted for Soviet Power. He hung around Red Guards who elected officers and declared "revolutionary order." He saw the taking of the Astrakhan fortress when the Theater Square went up in flames. Then he went to school for the first time and finished three grades. Later in the Hungry Year he was taken in box cars with five hundred others to regions of bread and finished the fifth grade in far-away Kostroma. At the age of sixteen he applied for entrance to our commune, giving his reasons to the assembly of boys who ran everything "like regular communars."

"I like this because it is not a school where they put you out at sixteen but a commune where at sixteen you begin to be more useful. I have no home and cities do not interest me. I want to build the Great Commune; it is as well here as anywhere. Here we shall build and no one shall say: 'This is mine and that is yours,' but of everything we see, land and buildings, mills and shops, we shall say: 'They are ours.' "

I asked Morosov how he planned the future when the commune grew to the limits of what Alexeyevka farm could feed. Could he take in more children forever? If not, then the farm would become a grown-up group of property-owners, two hundred joint owners instead of one. I thought in terms of property; Morosov didn't.

"There are other Soviet farms badly run, and later there is empty land, when we grow strong to build our own houses and barns. When the homeless children are all housed there are peasant children who live badly and who will wish to join. We shall add always more sections to our commune. The land will not be gone and the children will not stop coming in all the days that I shall live. And beyond that time we shall still be part of the growing Commune of the Soviet Republics of the world."

Morosov knew what he wanted; the other children knew. They were waifs of the revolution. But John Reed Colony never became the commune of which they dreamed nor my

Russian-American university. The Volga Valley was not ready for either. Neither its managers, its peasants nor its government officials were ready.

I first discovered that something was wrong with our commune when I returned from my first American trip and went to Cherumshan. For two months I had been sending money from that precious five thousand dollars to buy livestock for Alexeyevka. I found no livestock; the money had gone to feed children, yet the children were pale with sores of malnutrition on their bodies. The colony had never been on any state budget. The local children's homes had donated only children and buildings. The Children's Commission sent all money to provincial organizations, and the provincial town, Saratov, refused to endorse a colony so far up-river.

Mrs. Fisher had persisted. When Saratov proved obdurate, she begged "supplementary rations" from the Quakers and got enough for the hundred and fifty children which the colony was expected to have. Since actually the colony averaged twenty-five children all that winter, it bartered the sugar, condensed milk and cocoa in a hungry peasant market which had not seen sugar for five years and had never seen cocoa. Thus it obtained grain, clothing and a sewing machine. The Quaker products gave out about the time my money reached them and my money barely covered rations.

Teachers' salaries were also on no budget. Yet the Young Communist League, the Teachers' Union and the Women's Section of the Party fought each other for the right to give us teachers, who would thus get rations from our stores. Usually they compromised by all organizations appointing them, giving three times the number needed. Each teacher had "relatives," who were emerging from famine years. They ate more than all the children. Those eager waifs of the revolution were feeding them all. When I tried to fire those teachers I couldn't learn who had hired them. Saratov and Moscow disclaimed responsibility; the local organizations had nominated but not hired. So nobody could fire them; they simply stayed. Nobody would admit that he had organized that colony.

Then local rumor gave me reasons for Mrs. Fisher's persistence against Saratov. During her vacation in Khvalinsk, her oldest son had gone for a walk. He returned, saying: "I have seen the loveliest old convent, just the place for homeless children." Two weeks later he was dead in Moscow, saving a comrade from Moscow River. His mother remembered her hero's last wish for a children's colony in Cherumshan.

So—what I had welcomed as the will of the Children's Commission, even perhaps the will of the party for my participation in Soviet life, had been the will of a desolate mother bending us all to honor her dead son. Not even she, perhaps, could tell how much was the need of Khvalinsk and how much was her personal sorrow. I saw that under socialism, as under capitalism, the varied wills of men survive; that the wish to take part in Soviet life does not of itself bring wisdom; that not even in building socialism—Oh, least of all in building socialism— should one be a credulous fool. I saw with a stab of pain that a brain is needed, even in dealing with comrades.

But the children—they were organized already; they had strength to conquer land. Fed thinly on philanthropy and barter, they dreamed of the commune of the world! What should be done with the children?

I knew nothing of Soviet organization, to whom or what to turn. Mrs. Fisher had left Moscow. It was Yavorskaia of the Children's Commission (she became my closest friend thereafter) who brought the children aid. She had fought for homeless children under tsardom; her life was one long mothering of the motherless; she was tireless, shrewd and wise. Bit by bit she got the teaching staff on the county budget; she got their numbers and rationed relatives cut. But it took two years and the price it cost at last was the abolition of the commune, which was turned into a school. So I am not even now certain that Mrs. Fisher's daring was so unwise. Communes started in those days with little benefit of budget; some of them survived.

I think if any adult had known as well as the children what a commune was, if there had been a single organizer as good as a score of those youngsters already are today, the commune might have lived. Of the hundreds of communes that began in those years in the Soviet Republic, a few are famous now. There is the Labor Commune at Bolshevo which runs expanding industry; there was the Krupskaia Farm Commune that I visited in 1930 in Siberia. As I saw the growing factories, as I roamed the spacious acres, I thought of our scattered boys. But the few successful communes endured great upheavals; they needed a firm, wise hand. There was no wise, firm hand in the John Reed Colony. Yavorskaia came for her month of summer vacation, giving her rest-days to the children; I came for the same period. Even if I had been able to live on the Volga, I knew too little the Russian language and ways.

So the children's communal dream had heavy blows from careless officials, whom they early learned to distrust. When the provincial authorities in Saratov, who had disowned the commune, learned that it had one hundred blankets from the Quakers, and plenty of lumber for beds, they took the right to send fifty additional homeless children—and they sent them without food. Through what dire need or what disorganization they did it, is useless to question now. Our sixteen-year-old communars who had won a good harvest with sores of malnutrition on their bodies, shared that harvest with a double number, and got no fats or sugar, which they might have got by barter for their bread. The county authorities in Volsk, gradually taking the colony on its budget, showed their first authority by sending thirty-five of their worst hooligans who ran away with the approach of springtime, stealing a double share of shoes and blankets. And the youthful communars who had fed those idlers through the winter from their second hard-won harvest, began again the toil of sowing in bare, robbed feet.

Nor were they lucky in the series of managers. The three they had might serve as a picture of the stages through which Soviet rural administration passed. The first was Yeremeyev, a rough and ignorant peasant who rose through civil war to be a Red commander and the Khvalinsk chief of militia. He had to his credit a sincere desire for a commune with himself as boss. In theory a communist, in practice a patriarchal peasant. The supreme good to him was to get more land and then more land again; and next to get more horses and to feed them; and next to feed the boys. Last of all, he thought of feeding the girls who were good for washing and scrubbing. He never gave girls interesting work—farming, tractor-driving, carpentering; nothing but washing dirty underwear without soap. How the girls hated him!

For the larger farm at Alexeyevka he proved totally inefficient. He sold nearly all the second harvest to buy spare parts for the big mill. But through some inefficiency the project failed; and our mill couldn't keep up with the growing flood of peasant grain. So we lost it to a state trust that could repair it; we were left hungry in January facing the winter. It was then the colony threw itself on the mercy of Volsk and got with a little food those thirty-five young thieves. As for education, Yeremeyev never thought of it; he didn't know what it was. He distrusted boys who had a strange vice for pencils and paper. Nor was he honest; he stole cement and lumber from state trusts for our commune; he sent the boys to a distant market to sell a bad horse by trickery; I called him a thief. Yavorskaia and I removed him, using the episode of the mill.

But how we came to long for the honest thieving of Yeremeyev, who stole on behalf of the commune, when we experienced the crookedness of the second manager, Petroff,* who stole against the commune for himself. How we longed for the rough peasant who had slept in the fields with his communars, lousy with lousy boys, beating them in fits of drunkenness or anger, but showing them how to work, instead of the smooth, sly idler who rose at ten in the morning and strolled to the mill and kitchen before spending his afternoons in Alexeyevka village, building his political connections.

It was Petroff, corrupt party member, who smashed the commune. He feared the righteous wrath of the older boys. The climax came with a shipment of clothing from America.

I had found, I thought, ideal connections in America for John Reed Commune. In Cornell Agricultural College a young Russian peasant, Pavel Yashin, was studying agricul-

---

* I have thought best to use here a fictitious name.

ture and supporting himself by work in the experimental station. He had come to America before the war but been unable to return; he had worked on American and Canadian wheat farms. His wife and child were still in the Saratov district and he was studying farming with intent to go back. A party control commission which investigated our colony had told me that my task as "shef" was to hunt a good technical manager. Who could be better than Yashin? The Cornell students went romantic over the return of Yashin to build a "Cornell-on-the-Volga," which should almost at once exchange seeds and experiments and some day students with old Cornell. They raised money for all kinds of equipment; Yashin was going back with several thousand dollars in machinery.

Other students sent clothing, overcoats, shoes. The packages were not addressed to the John Reed Colony, for already I distrusted the manager. They were addressed to the Young Communist League of the colony, which meant the older boys. They could be trusted to make a public division of any goods received. But Petroff, with the local postal clerk, and the head of the coöperative store, conspired against the sacredness of mails. They opened those packages behind locked doors and distributed them, some to the coöperative store, some to their friends, none at all to the young communars.

They were no longer children; they were youths of seventeen and eighteen years who had built a famous farm which was going to pieces under Petroff's rule. They held an indignation meeting of their Young Communist League and worked themselves up to bang on the closed doors. When no answer came back, they held another meeting and banged the doors again. When at last the room was opened and Petroff came out, the packages had been removed. American goods that the young communars longed for appeared in the village coöperative store.

After that it became unsafe for Petroff to go to the dormitories. He complained to the Volsk authorities against the "young hooligans." When these went in turn to Volsk, stealing rides on the boat to get there, they were met by the testimony of Alexeyevka officials, welded into a neat whole by

Petroff. Who would believe "young hooligans" who had come by stealing rides? The ring-leaders who persisted were thrown out of the school, discredited; it was time they were at work. The others were dropped more gradually as overage; for the commune was becoming a school.

When I returned from America with Pavel Yashin, the process was nearly over. Our great rich stretch of five hundred black plowed acres no longer waved as a commune flag on the Volga hills; the acreage had been cut to an experimental school garden, and the state farm was coming back. The younger children remained; the colony was a school with a sixteen-year age limit. Communes were going out of fashion everywhere in Soviet Russia; most of them were smothered under teachers' relatives and "Petroffs." "Farm Schools for Young Peasants" were in mode.

Petroff stayed long enough to dispose of Yashin and to graft a bit on the machinery he brought. "Cornell-on-the-Volga," exchanging seeds and scientific experiments with America— what did Petroff care for Cornell? The garden of prize vegetable seeds was disdainfully placed in the track of the village cows, nor was it allotted a fence. No boys were assigned to do the garden work, and when the children, liking the friendly, despairing Yashin, hung about after other jobs to plant and weed vegetables, Petroff sent them to other tasks. He treated Yashin as a "foreign specialist" come to spy for a "foreign shef"; he even managed to keep him out of the union. So Yashin got a job at last with the Saratov Experimental Farm, and sent what explanations he could to Cornell. Petroff got the machines, even Yashin's sewing-machine which, thinking himself a communar, he had not listed as private property.

When Petroff's sins piled up and threatened exposure, he slipped conveniently into a job in a state trust; everyone was too busy to track him down. The third of our managers arrived; his name I have forgotten: this fact itself is typical as he was typical of the new stage in management in Soviet Russia. Young, just out of teacher-training school, he hid his worried inexperience under spasmodic orders, but he painfully wanted to make good. He was the first who prized education. Others followed; the John Reed School, too far in the wilds to attract good managers, became a place where new graduates got experience.

None the less it survives, a Technical School of Collective Farming, which is the stage today; it has moved inland from Alexeyevka to a populous village. It is still the best equipped of all such schools in a wide region; it still boasts American machinery from Cornell. Even that earliest tractor, on which all communars learned, the first tractor between Volsk and Sizran, plowed on through the days of mass collectivization; at last accounts it was plowing still. Perhaps it will plow clear through to socialism; but not to the Great Commune. It will be worn out by then.

But our young communars of the early commune, those gallantly defeated warriors, where are they? This is no tale of youth in ruins; this is a tale of Soviet Russia; those communars were her worthy sons. Out of the crash and dishonor around them they picked, far better than I could have done, what they needed. They had grown up on war, revolution, famine.

They were no property-owners to be destroyed by the loss of a farm. If the commune crashed, state farms were arising and new state factories. After all, they had learned on tractors; after all, they had run a mill; some of them had worked with an American specialist. They were the Volga's new aristocrats, foot-loose workers, knowing machines. If what they knew was painfully little, it was more than others knew. Measured by all the standards round them, they had been to my "Russian-American University."

If their world had Petroff, it had also Yavorskaia. For a month each summer she gave her vacation to helping them find good jobs and schools. She sorted them out by their capacities; every child was one of her own. Our two worst thieves were also artists; she got them a place in Saratov Art Technicum. The best of our tractorists studied further, becoming an engineer. The girl who understudied the local doctor in our malaria epidemic went to a medical school. All those students got government stipends, as is the way of Soviet schools; the rest got jobs in the new cement mill or new state farms.

More than mine they are Yavorskaia's children; she kept in touch with them by letter, advising them in their youthful problems. Advising also on their marriages and on the coming of their first children. Yet in a sense they are mine also. No longer did I raise money in America; my own surplus from articles gave enough for their lessened needs. But year by year, with Yavorskaia's planning, we gave to them what the poorest Soviet parents give to eke out government stipends. A coat for one, some shoes for another, an extra allowance of milk for a third. They were no longer "homeless" children; John Reed Commune was their home. Because of this personal thought of Yavorskaia, and their fighting strength of peasant youth, the percent of success from John Reed Colony was higher than from Moscow's best run schools. Of two hundred and sixty boys and girls who passed through the colony, Yavorskaia kept track of all but ten till they were adult and settled citizens—workers all!

They are scattered from Leningrad to Baku, in factories and farms and schools. Most of them still write to each other, knowing themselves as the "John Reed crowd." Once in a while they pass through Moscow and stop to talk about old days. They are glad to hear that Yeremeyev studied three winters in special courses and is managing a big state farm. "Yeah, there was lots of good in Yeremeyev," these judges of the future say. They once said they should hunt up Petroff and see that he was cleaned out of the party; but it is ancient history now.

Those who remained within reach of the Volga went often at first on vacations to John Reed School—proud worker-alumni returning to help in the harvest and show the young ones how to work. They digested Yeremeyev and Petroff as their strong stomachs had digested war and famine. And they love those sweeping hills where their roving feet first settled and their labor first made home. They love the dewy dawns and the slow march of Volga seasons and the old camp in the far field of alfalfa and the lost mill. From all of these, and even from Petroff, they took what they needed for work and battle. They write to me of the John Reed Commune as their "pass to life."

CHAPTER XVIII

I MAKE MYSELF AGENT IN WALL STREET

AFTER nearly three years as correspondent for *Hearst's International Magazine* for Russia and Central Europe, I received a cablegram from Norman Hapgood canceling the work on which I was engaged, a study of Jewish settlement on farms in South Ukraine. Mr. Hapgood's efforts to build a popular international journal had raised circulation to a point where it began to cut into the sales of the *Cosmopolitan*, another Hearst publication. The great magnate decided to combine them; two "properties" were made one for greater profit. It was announced to the world as a bigger, better magazine combining all features of both. Hearst told the truth in a blunt telegram to Hapgood: "Your magazine stops with the issue now in press." The organization of *Hearst's International* was abolished.

When I came to America soon afterwards, Hapgood sent me with a glowing letter of recommendation to the editor of the *Cosmopolitan* who had swallowed him. The new editor said: "No, we don't want Russia or Central Europe. We're going in for confessions. They thrill the readers more."

"If you want personal life, there's plenty in Russia," I said. I told of Sonia and others like her, stirring tales of new standards in personal life. His eyes shone gluttonously. Then he shook his head and sighed.

"Wonderful tales! But no! A confession doesn't really grip unless the milkman in Kansas City and the drug-store clerk in St. Louis can feel that it might have happened to them. They couldn't feel that about these tales from Russia."

That Kansas City milkman, that drug-store clerk in St. Louis—where had I heard of them before? I suddenly realized them as a slogan held aloft for the servants of Hearst. Hapgood had used them to me; I had thrilled to think they meant

the great American masses. Now I saw that they meant the
petty tradesmen's world to whose lusts of sex and luxury
Hearst catered. Hapgood, a man of international education,
had sought to stir them with great historic events of our epoch;
but Hearst had decided against it. I felt so sorry for Hapgood, chained to a boss like Hearst.

The *Cosmopolitan* editor was kind to me. "You tell very
good stories," he said. "If you could get us up some good
American confessions. . . ." I smiled. "No," I said, "I have
other plans."

My new plan was to make myself leading specialist on the
Soviet Union for miscellaneous publications. I would come to
America once a year on a lecture trip, renew connections with
editors, and plan with them to what parts of Soviet Russia I
should travel and on what subjects I should write. I should
thus keep my freedom and would use my leisure time for John
Reed Colony or for something else in Russia.

I tried to make these trips to America serve as many purposes as possible. In those days Soviet organizations were
making their first contacts with the outer world; they wanted
books, technical journals, contacts of all kinds. I watched for
expressions of such desire and tried to serve them, hoping to
find a niche into which I might fit. Thus I brought to Russia
manuals of sports and mass games for the Pioneers, suit-cases
of the latest books on education for Krupskaia, widow of Lenin,
who worked in the Commissariat of Education. But these
efforts were amateur handicraft; I sought for some institution where I might use to the full all my American connections.
The chance seemed in two directions: American Educational
Workshops in Moscow and the Chief Concessions Committee.

The American Educational Workshops grew out of my
John Reed Colony. Despite its discouraging chaos, the people in Moscow who worked with waifs and strays had been
impressed by my ability to get machinery from America.
"Why waste it all on the inefficient Volga; we'll give you a place
in Moscow," they said. The educational authorities owned
one hundred and twenty houses in the suburb of Tarasovka,
mostly summer cottages used for children's camps, but some of

them winter villas housing waifs and strays. They offered me six of these as educational workshops, in which I might install American mechanics with tools and machinery, and run self-supporting workshops, giving training to adolescents drawn from the nearby homes. We could expand as fast as we could develop, in Tarasovka or to communities outside it.

A gorgeous idea! It combined everything I had yet tried into something better. Again I saw arising that bridge for American efficiency to the Soviets. We would avoid all the old pitfalls of failure. No red tape with food, housing, teaching; no harsh adjustment to Russian methods. Just choosing American mechanics and letting them teach pliable children who adored American technique. "I can organize any Americans anywhere," I exclaimed gladly. The Moscow educational authorities offered me full control of all the workshops I could organize and affiliation to the Moscow schools through the Tarasovka School Council. It was the greatest autonomy yet given a foreigner in education. I could use my American trips to pick the mechanics; thousands wanted to come, and offered their tools and equipment.

Meantime I acquired another contact in the Committee on Concessions, which had been organized to handle the hundreds of business adventurers who poured into Moscow seeking a chance to get rich. Soviet Russia offered chances on definite terms. Unable to develop all their country immediately, they were ready to give "concessions" to capitalists who would bring in machinery and modern technical methods. But the communists were harsh bargainers; they weren't giving wealth away. They expected that men who took a coal concession should know something about coal mines and should actually produce coal. The men who came were chiefly promoters, wanting to capitalize concessions and sell shares in Wall Street. Some few were ready for business. Still others dealt in international adventures and juggled governments for millions.

Thus the Fall and Sinclair group came on a special train to Moscow to negotiate for oil fields. Fall was at the time still a member of Harding's cabinet and political end of this great oil trust. They bluffed the Russians with their political influence, hinting that oil for Sinclair meant international blessings for Russia, the least of which would be American recognition. The Russians bluffed back; they gave Sinclair Oil Company rich oil fields in Saghalien, conditioned upon definite annual work of exploration and development. Saghalien was at that time held by Japanese occupation, and when this prevented Sinclair's digging, the Russians brutally canceled his concession. The oil man's shrieks in the American press about "Soviet perfidy" did not move the imperturbable Russians.

"He bragged about international influence! He knew what it meant when we signed that concession. Get the Japanese out and we pay you in oil! He's no child in the relation of oil and governments."

I didn't like trade; I didn't like concessions. I didn't like the type of American promoter that came to Russia. But I applied to the Chief Concessions Committee, saying that I went to America every year and might be of use in forming connections if I could first work in their offices and learn their desires. They made me "American referent" immediately, with a Number Seventeen rating, the highest in the civil service. I made lists of American publications on business for which we should subscribe; I read them and made digests of American business conditions. I inquired into the rating of business men who drifted into the office, and helped decide which ones were worth introducing to important Soviet officials. I also compiled lists in English of all available concessions and their terms and made this material available to inquirers. Yet the job seemed very unimportant; it never took more than an hour or two a day.

It was time to go to America; I had a series of lectures for the winter of 1925-26. I had written a book on the John Reed Colony, *Children of Revolution*, which I planned to sell to raise money for the work. I would use the trip to get mechanics and funds for the American Educational Workshops. I asked the Concessions Committee what I should do for them in America.

They said: "Meet the business men of Wall Street and see what they say of us, what kind of concessions they want."

I asked for a credential as their representative in New York; I wanted it to feel myself no longer an outsider.

They said: "It might not be advisable for you to cross the frontier with such a paper. It might embarrass you at the American customs. Amtorg will know who you are."

I was outraged. What did they think I was—a secret agent? I'd like to see the American customs make trouble. I should like the chance to wave that credential in the face of the State Department, crying: "Here's the country that you won't recognize and here am I, a good American citizen whose birth certificate you can't take away, going to Wall Street for a commission of that country. Start something if you dare and give me a chance to call on Borah, Wheeler and La Follette! I've friends in the Senate all ready to break loose." . . . No, we Americans are not conspirators; our technique is not discretion but bluff.

Feeling half-disowned, I thought: "When I get to New York, I'll show them." With an idealistic gesture I refused the salary due me for two or three months of what they considered work. I had been so proud of that Number Seventeen rating; now it seemed to have meant little. "Since you wish me to go as a private person, I prefer to be able to say that I never got any Soviet money. Send the salary to John Reed Colony." They did it without comment; money had not the symbolism to them that it had to me.

It was a mad trip that I made to America that winter. Arriving in Seattle via China by a trip elsewhere described, I had a triple task: to make my living for the coming year by lectures, to talk to Wall Street for the Concessions Committee, and to make the most serious drive yet attempted for funds and technical assistance to John Reed Colony and the American Educational Workshops. Out into Canada as far as Winnipeg, back to Seattle and down the coast, across by Kansas to the eastern cities, I gave that winter eighty-four lectures, sometimes as many as five a day. I turned out articles and "little blue books" for Haldeman-Julius publications on an iron schedule. At times I made my speeches in a feverish daze, hardly knowing what I said, pouring out vitality remorselessly with my eyes on those creators in chaos, Gühling, Rimpalle and others, by whom I felt myself not yet accepted.

Applications of mechanics who wished to go to Soviet Russia poured in upon me. They offered thousands of dollars in tools, if only they might cast off capitalism forever and work for socialism beyond the seas. They agreed to pay their own transportation, to support themselves till the production of their workshops should begin, and to accept thereafter union wages, out of the proceeds of their own production. All income above this should go to their boy helpers and to expand educational workshops for Russia. They would "give all they had" to the promised land. They brought recommendations from labor organizations; district organizers helped me make selection.

Meanwhile I sent frequent letters to the Concessions Committee about my journey, the comments of business men in China, Japan, Canada, and a long account of Canadian wheat pools whereby coöperative organizations of farmers, fighting the grain speculators, had secured in one year control of sixty-eight percent of Canada's wheat export. A small left-wing among them talked of a "world coöperative grain market" and wanted connections with Soviet grain organizations. I sent samples of bookkeeping methods "which might be of interest to Soviet grain-procuring." I don't know what happened to those blanks or the Grain Pool; I haven't heard of either since.

In Detroit I tried to see Henry Ford, but he still believed in Russian monarchists. He sent for me a year or so later, when the Soviets had begun to buy his tractors and he thought of beginning serious business. For a whole hour then he talked in the platitudes of a high school orator. He was interested in my experiences in John Reed Colony; in how life organized itself on the Russian soil. I tried to sell him the idea of mechanizing the vast expanse of Russia by twenty-five self-supporting agricultural universities—great farms based on modern machinery, acting as teachers and service stations for the growing mechanization around them.

"You could 'Fordize' Russia in fifteen years. But you mustn't make profit down in the country; the people won't let you. Make your farm-universities only self-supporting; get your profits from the central government through the sale of your machines."

"It could be done," said Ford. "I'll think it over. But industry is more important than farming. To organize man's food supply is relatively simple; it is man's industry that is both more important and more difficult." It was the only thing he said that was worth remembering. . . . Nor could I dream, as I promoted twenty-five self-supporting universities run by a private capitalist, that within a few years the Soviet Union itself would organize thirty-five hundred such centers of farm-instruction and mechanization, the machine tractor stations, mechanizing agriculture not in fifteen years but in five.

In New York I learned that Amtorg had never heard of any "American referent" to the Concessions Committee. On my insistence they unearthed the rumor that someone had said the journalist Anna Louise Strong might come to see them, and they should use any influence and connections she had. But I had no "influence"; I had skill in writing. I had no Wall Street "connections"; I had an easy American approach, which could talk to any American business man, but could not be transferred. An American promoter of farm machinery said to me: "With you as assistant, I'd guarantee twenty million credits on farm machinery from my acquaintances alone. We'd do it by little dinners with the manufacturers where you'd give them the facts. We'd send an Amtorg agent around later; all of them are crazy for business."

I also believed I could do it. But to enter the Amtorg office in those days was to be engulfed in a vagueness which made even the mention of such a proposition seem indelicate. Part of this was due to inefficiency, but part was an attitude toward business which felt it alternately as a state secret and a criminal offense. Their smaller men had the technique of small eastern European trading towns; where else could the communists find their traders? Their higher men were dignified by a strange shame; they drew back into odd reticencies. And one would wonder: Is it that they wait for a better bar-

gain or are they afraid to be caught in crime? It was as if
they committed prostitution to save their country.

The Americans were lawfully wedded to business; they felt
it as lifelong, dutiful passion. They were jovial and proud as
with a wife. They honored it with talkative banquets, served
by twin lackeys of efficiency and bluff. Its outer form was
flattering frankness, its private parts were veiled seductively
yet decorously, its violences sanctified by law. How could
such different folk do business? Lenin never gave his communists a harsher order than when he bade them "learn to
trade." They learned; eventually it was admitted that they
could sometimes beat the Americans. But not in those early
Amtorg days.

I was American. If I no longer revered this business, I knew
its approach. Amtorg didn't know how to use me, but I had
an assignment to put through. I would go then as a private
journalist, saying: "Four years I have lived in Russia. Last
summer I helped the Concessions Committee compile its lists. I
can say nothing official but I know what life there is in Russia
and can report your desires to important people; I am returning soon."

Thus I made myself Soviet agent in Wall Street, an agent
without salary or credentials. The business men wondered, no
doubt, what I was promoting or whether I looked to them for
a job. That didn't matter; they were used to promoters and
didn't despise them. I made my approach through friends in
social settlements or on newspapers and found the access to
Wall Street easy. Business men gave me luncheons and dinners, invited others and thus it spread. They were so anxious
for Russian business that they would even have talked to
Amtorg, but the head of Amtorg didn't talk English and no
one but the head dared talk at all.

Those are strange days to remember, the winter of 1925-26.
Several small oil companies were trying to get American recognition for the "Republic of Georgia" with headquarters in
Paris; they wanted the oil of Baku. Standard Oil championed
the Soviets, with whom they already had dealings. Ivy Lee,
public relations counsel for Standard Oil, invited me to a din-

ner of jeweled women and capitalists, including Dwight Morrow, whom he was trying to convince that the best way to "kill Bolshevism" was to "do business with Russia and break down her isolation." My function was to be well dressed and happy, as living proof that an American woman could emerge in health and confidence after four years in Soviet Russia.

Considerable talk went on among bankers about old Russian debts. Frank Vanderlip, who had been president of the National City Bank when it handled the tsarist loans, invited me to his home in the country. He said: "The Russians should put somebody on the job of checking those claims while old data are available. I personally know that the claims are grossly exaggerated. They will probably make in the end some political settlement on a percentage basis. It would be better to investigate each one separately, beginning right away."

Important business men were not yet visiting Russia; they feared to lose their conservative standing. Walter Sachs, president of an international bank dealing in tens of millions, decided to "lead the break-away and visit Russia." I gave him letters of introduction to Moscow. He said: "My banking friends all envy me my trip; they call it 'wonderful.' But they don't dare go themselves. The president of the Equitable told me: 'The moment I crossed the border it would be said that Equitable will finance Russia. We don't dare risk that yet.'"

Le Blanc, vice president of Equitable in charge of their foreign business, wanted to risk it. He was a buccaneer among bankers, a French Canadian who fought the British tradition of bowing to London. He was already doing a small amount of Soviet financing and was proud to be a pioneer. "We were the only bank in New York that wasn't caught with those tsarist loans," he boasted. "They wanted us to take five millions. But old Jacob Schiff, our biggest stockholder then, as Rockefeller is now, knew Russia. He said: 'No loans in that country are safe till they've had a revolution; it's long overdue.' We consider Russia safer now." He added jovially: "Borah says that all the anti-Russian notes that come to the Foreign Relations Committee of the Senate, come in an en-

velope of the British Embassy. They have a regular factory
for making them."

Le Blanc even had ambitions to battle Morgan with the
help of the Soviets. He said: "There are a few bankers who
might break away from his domination on a large Russian loan.
A prerequisite is recognition, but that mightn't be so hard. It
would have to be made worth while to the bank that did it."

"What do you call worth while?" I asked him.

"The first loan here would hardly pay," he answered. "The
Russians think a bank just gives the money, but the loan has
to be sold. There's a lot of bad publicity to combat. But if
a bank could get the contract to be Russia's fiscal agent in New
York for a term of years, as Morgan is fiscal agent for Great
Britain, then it would pay to lose money on initial publicity to
sell Russia to the American public. There are sound banks
which consider very seriously that it might become a bigger
thing to be Russia's fiscal agent than even to be Great
Britain's."

Only two organizations blankly refused to discuss Soviet
Russia: the National City Bank and the House of Morgan.
Martin Egan, public relations counselor for the House of
Morgan, said: "Let them stop killing people and give back the
property they stole." His tone stunned me for half an hour
like a hammer blow. I could not doubt the implacable hate of
the House of Morgan.

Amtorg took little interest in all my conversations. Didn't
the Russians really want concessions? Was the force that
always rose to block them just inefficiency or some deep un-
willingness of heart? I think, as I look back, it was partly
both. The workers who had made the revolution resented concessions to foreign capitalists and only grudgingly allowed
them; the growing Soviet life strove constantly to cast off such
entanglements and this reflected itself in the wavering purposes
of its agents. I thought it was the Concessions Committee that
made me feel unwanted, unimportant. I see now that the Concessions Committee itself felt more unwanted and unimportant
than I.

I mailed conscientious reports of my conversations, though

no word ever came to me from Moscow. When I got back I gave them my last report, together with a list of rating services, clipping services and services on general business which made special investigations. Then I washed my hands of concessions; I was sick of being an uncredentialed agent. My lists and reports dropped as into a well, from which no echo returned.

Only once was I able to give to Amtorg my "connections." In two successive years I lunched with Gerard Swope, president of the General Electric. The second time he said: "I understand the Russians offer to repay firms which lost property by giving them new concessions in return for credits. The General Electric might do business on that basis, but I hardly think we should make the first move." I knew that Amtorg ardently desired such business but was equally afraid of moving first. So I made the move, telling each of the other's wishes. Out of it came, in still another year, a twenty-five-million-dollar credit and the writing off of all old claims of the General Electric, the first break-away of the giant firms towards Soviet Russia. But this was later, when the two firms had ripened with the years. Anyone then—a chance— might make the connection.

As I read old reports and letters at which I have not glanced for years, I suddenly see myself as Amtorg must have seen me. That blithe American telephoning the House of Morgan, joking at luncheon with Le Blanc, week-ending with Vanderlip at Scarborough and talking concessions all over Wall Street. Slipping so carelessly over gulfs that had swallowed a million dead, bluffing so gayly the thunderbolts that shatter nations. I thought, and think, they might have found a way to use me. But—how glad they must have been that I had no credentials!

.   .   .   .

With confidence renewed by my easy contacts with Wall Street, I plunged feverishly into the American Educational Workshops. It seemed to me that I could handle any Americans; only with Russians did I fail. I would drop concessions then, and organize Americans in our educational project.

My chosen manager was Kogan,* a Russian-Jewish-American communist. Dental mechanic by trade, he had used a farm commune to reach Soviet Russia, and discovered on arrival that he knew no farming. He gave some excellent help in the first stages of my contract with the Moscow educational authorities and said he could be "more useful" with me than on the farm. So I had left him in Moscow as my representative during my American trip. He convinced me next that our salary restrictions did not apply to him; a general manager could not wait for pay till production began. I gave him party maximum salary, and he found it hard to live on it, since he had an American wife and two children. So I next agreed to supplement his salary by giving him my Moscow room while I was abroad in America. He said: "Mrs. Kogan is afraid of the influence of Tarasovka hooligans on the children; I'll get her used to it gradually by spring."

He had written to me in America that I must raise much more money. "Prousse has arrived with quantities of watch-parts which overrun our budget by hundreds of dollars. I have had to send a hundred dollars to Geneva for his family till they are ready to come. Prousse threatens us with bankruptcy."

I had written angrily to Prousse: "You could be arrested for sending to your family money which isn't yours." I half regretted that I had accepted Prousse.

I had found Prousse the previous year in Geneva making watches in an attic and teaching in the Jean Jacques Rousseau school. Once he had been a Russian Bolshevik; he had known Lenin well. But his wife was Swiss and he drifted out of the party because of the needs of his children. He knew his shame; he tried to solace it by making his little watch-shop contribute to *Iskra*, Lenin's struggling paper of those days. Ever since the revolution he had tried to return to Russia. He had said to me: "Won't you take my workshop and me for the John Reed boys?" . . . "You are a fool," I said, "watches should be made in Moscow." . . . That was what first started me thinking of American workshops in Moscow—Prousse, a

* I have chosen to give here a fictitious name.

Russian-Swiss. His watch-shop was our most expensive venture.

Next came our dental mechanics shop, advocated by Kogan.
He informed me that Moscow was very short of dental supplies and we could make large profit by importing them free
of duty for our school. A friend of his, Wolfson, would bring
in a full equipment and a Dodge car. Kogan himself would
also work in production when the rush of organization was
over. I had found in St. Louis another dental mechanic who
wished to contribute twenty-five hundred dollars' worth of
equipment but Kogan curtly refused. "We don't need three;
Wolfson is a good man." It developed that Wolfson's equipment was not the type needed; so Kogan bought—without telling me—two thousand dollars' worth of new dental equipment
from our funds. Then Wolfson's Dodge had been sold for his
personal expenses. Never mind, I thought, if he starts a
good shop.

Our third venture was a fully mechanized wood-working
shop; the Moscow Department of Education had especially
asked for this, to make furniture for the children's homes.
I had found in California a man claiming to be a skilled cabinet maker, carpenter and general builder, who promised to
bring his Ford car, tools for himself and several helpers, and
some electrically driven tools. I had been somewhat worried
by his lack of recommendations from employers, but he had
several from radical organizations explaining that he had been
thrown out of many jobs for his radical views. When he
reached New York I learned that he had sold most of his tools
and his Ford car to buy clothes and tickets. He had sent his
freight as far as Europe, but not to Russia; he hadn't had
enough money. I had already bought two thousand dollars'
worth of machinery for his workshop; so I paid his freight and
hoped he could start production soon. I regretfully cut out
other shops, which I could not now finance, and concentrated
on watches, dental supplies and wood-working, to which a
small shoe-repair shop and a laundry machine were added.

In Moscow Kogan had lost my room; he had been evicted.
I was not surprised; it was in a house owned by a Soviet organi-

zation for its employees; I had got it by luck and held it by bluff through two eviction scares. I resigned myself to camping out in Tarasovka and in friends' rooms in Moscow; Kogan had got, rather surprisingly, a two-room apartment in a new coöperative house. I had no time to wonder how he got it; he was efficient, it seemed. He always landed right. It was only the people working with him who didn't.

He had discovered that dental mechanics was forbidden by law to our Tarasovka boys; it must be done in a trade school under the Board of Health. There was such a school in Moscow which gladly accepted our equipment and offered jobs to Kogan and Wolfson. The latter went; Kogan was undecided. He told me he could make much more than party maximum salary by piece work in the new dental mechanics shop; he might like to go back to production and be a "proletarian" again. The Moscow trade school had no connection with homeless children, for whom I had raised the money; but Kogan stood high there for his gift of the equipment.

There was friction between Prousse and Kogan. The latter convinced me at first that Prousse's extravagance had begun our downfall, and that his, Kogan's, efficiency was barely saving us. I scolded Prousse; he bent beneath my wrath. He had no business sense at all like Kogan; he explained that it was such a good chance to buy machinery and watch parts which could not be got in Russia. Even I could see that Prousse had a shop worth many times what I had spent. He couldn't tell where it came from; part of it had been his old watch-shop, but now it was "all of it ours." Even that didn't account for the new materials.

Mrs. Prousse explained: "He sent each month a hundred dollars and with it lists of things he needed. We couldn't get them all."

But it was a truly remarkable watch-shop. It had taken careful search and shrewd Swiss buying—and something more. To buy all that from the monthly remittances, Prousse's family must have lived on air. They had no clothes for Russian winters. "Yes, he told us to get clothes, but he seemed to think the watch-parts more important. . . ." Years ago, Prousse had slighted the revolution for his family. Had they felt it? Were they trying to pay it back? For years to come I saw them exhausted with hardship; but I never heard them complain.

Prousse had been buried in Tarasovka all winter, fighting for fuel, for electric connections. He set up his shop on tables, on benches, on anything he could find. He began teaching boys. The educational authorities were staggered; watch-parts worth their weight in gold lay around unguarded among boys who stole doors, window glass, old iron. Such a delicate trade and the only shop in Russia at the mercy of hoodlums! But the hoodlums liked making watches; or perhaps they liked Prousse. Suddenly it was discovered that the skill which makes pickpockets turns readily to delicate trades. Educational commissions visited our workshops; Moscow newspapers had articles about us; the Moscow Soviet gave us an honorable mention because of the watches of Prousse.

Wood-work wasn't succeeding. Machines were late in arriving. Instead of taking hand-tools and organizing boys to repair houses, our carpenter took a temporary job in Moscow, to which he began to transfer not only his tools but ours. He was entitled to draw from us food but no wages until his production started; the expense account for himself and his large family amounted to more than party maximum salary. It wasn't enough for his standard of living, which seemed higher than mine. He joined with Kogan, both being party members, and got the Tarasovka party organization to pass a resolution that "wages must be given at once to the American workers."

They brought the news to my sick-bed. I had rushed from the millionaires of Wall Street to the Volga to try to save Yashin's garden from ruin; I had waited all night on docks till grippe attacked me, and fought through Tarasovka till it became pneumonia. I knew that party resolution ended our commune; our treasury was exhausted and we had borrowed eight thousand rubles from the State Bank on our equipment, and this was nearly gone. The autonomy of our shops gave Kogan power to mortgage Prousse's watch-shop for his own and the carpenter's wages; and the party resolution bade him do it.

I couldn't rise and fight; I had one choice, only one. I wrote a letter to the Moscow Department of Education begging them to revoke our autonomy and confiscate our property. "Take it quickly before our non-productive workers scatter it." I knew the MONO * shops were inefficient, and would divide my wood-working machinery among a dozen children's homes; but I knew they prized the watch-shop for the reputation it had won.

Wolfson and the carpenter went back to America disgruntled, first spreading some slander about me. Kogan strengthened his new job with the trade school by giving them our laundry machine. But Prousse worked on in the watch-shop. He was arrested for having no list of his equipment, and released next morning when they saw that the charge was true; it hurt Prousse badly that "his revolution" arrested him. The new MONO management used the profits of his shop to cover losses of a dozen workshops; they exhausted his irreplaceable parts and machines. He worked for two years for MONO workshops till they profiteered on the lives of his apprentices, refusing to give them wages or discharge them with diplomas since their work was needed. A boy whom Prousse had transformed from a thief to a good workman left the watch-shop for an unskilled job in Suharevka market because he was hungry and homeless.

Then Prousse rose in wrath which neither the long hardship of his family nor his own arrest nor the wasting of his lifelong-assembled watch-shop had aroused. He wrote to *Pravda* and raised a scandal and got a slight improvement. Later he said to me: "I am going in with the new trust which is starting a state watch factory; I am on a commission to buy equipment abroad. We'll have a better school in that factory; the state industries prize their apprentices; they don't drive them into Suharevka." Prousse was right; the new state industries were sounder than MONO workshops, even in their care of boys; they were eventually given charge of all trade training. Prousse today teaches hundreds in the first factory that ever

* MONO—Moscow Department of Education.

made watches in Russia. Prousse, and his pupils, brought "time" to the Soviets!

"I can organize Americans!" I had said it. They gave me every chance. The greatest autonomy ever offered in education—and I hurled that autonomy back. Six houses, a chance to expand, a resolution of praise from the city—this Moscow gave. From a storm of volunteers in America I picked, with the help of district organizers, the ones who seemed the best. But what was I doing, importing to Soviet Russia petty tradesmen who were seeking paradise? What mattered their giving "all to the revolution"; what mattered if they were sincere? The revolution was a fire that burned to the stark frame of a man, disclosing what he himself did not know.

"I can organize Americans!" I did it. What was left of my work? A lost room, a slander spreading through Moscow, some good machines scattered in MONO workshops—and the work of a Russian-Swiss!

CHAPTER XIX

IN REVOLUTIONARY CANTON

A FREE, adventurous and lonely life now began for several years for me. I had lost my room in Moscow, and though Soviet Russia still remained the center of my plans, it was not easy for me to reside there. My connections with John Reed Colony, the American Educational Workshops, the Concessions Committee, had collapsed. I no longer believed that I could organize anything in Soviet Russia; my faith in that personal efficiency which justified my life had at last been hammered to pieces. Even the mad passion of that final winter when I gave eighty-four lectures, raised over ten thousand dollars for technical equipment, selected mechanic-instructors, wrote dozens of articles and investigated concessions from the Saskatchewan wheat pool to the House of Morgan—had brought me no success but only pneumonia. I still intended to live in Moscow so I joined a housing coöperative and paid in advance for an apartment which I was to receive in two years. But I no longer dreamed of becoming a creator in chaos. I was broken; I would organize no more.

Well, I could always write. Everyone told me to do it. The other American correspondents never ceased saying that I was foolish to waste my time on all these projects. "They'll never let foreigners do anything here," they said. This seemed borne out by the similar advice of the Russian communists I met; they were always urging me to continue writing—for that very capitalist press they so denounced.

I was only fit, it seemed, to write for the capitalist press. The capitalist world was more hospitable than I merited. When I went to New York, editors were glad to see me; in all the American cities I was swamped with invitations to dinners. The effortless hospitality of America, based upon well-oiled mechanism and a craving for entertainment, reached out to caress that brightly plumaged bird of passage; to it was added varying depths of real desire to learn of that new world in which they supposed me completely accepted.

Thus I began roving to revolutions, and writing about them for the American press. My job became a game between editors and myself; it amused me to see how much I could "put over" of what I wanted to say. I knew the "high-paying magazines" would not accept me; they paid high for subtle defense of capitalism in a vaudeville of tales and articles. But scores of other publications were accessible; I had learned the technique of my trade. I studied the special interests of editors; to one I sold articles because he wanted "travel" or "women"; to another because he was anti-British in his policy on Asia. Some editors cursed my stuff as propaganda, yet took it because it was so vivid; then they would follow it by other articles which attacked the Soviets. They "gave all sides of the question." Some editors liked my stuff and helped me "put it over" on the owners of the papers; they didn't always last. But if one disappeared, others arose. The editors seemed to have the last word in this game; they changed my copy. Authors weren't supposed to object to being edited; hadn't they been paid? But I could always stop writing for editors who made annoying changes, as long as I could find others who changed me less. And if some day I should cease to find them? Why borrow trouble? For the moment I had the last word; I was "free."

What was this "freedom"? Sometimes in a lonely hotel room I would muse on its meaning. This freedom which everybody called desirable yet nobody defined. Those people who lauded freedom from their tight little nests of compulsion— would they like to be cast forth as I was, to wander across the earth? Free to say: "Shall I go next month to Mexico, Canton or Moscow; there is nobody in all the world who cares!" No confining job, no compelling dream of creation. Only my father's home long since abandoned in Seattle, and in some future Moscow a flat not yet completed; otherwise a suitcase at the last hotel till the next lecture. It seemed to me at times that any bondage would be better than to be thus adrift upon the world.

Freedom?—I mused. It isn't doing what you want to. I wanted to be a creator in chaos, and something—my own inability it seemed—stopped me. Then freedom is being allowed to do whatever you have ability to do? What nonsense! If you really have the ability, you don't have to be allowed; nobody can stop you! Then is freedom the right to act without outside hindrances? No, the whole tang of life is the overcoming of hindrances; without hindrances there would be neither freedom nor life. Is it then absence of tyranny? This was a mere negative, yet it seemed coming nearer. Who were "tyrants"? How did one get their absence; by running away or by overthrowing them? Rather rough on the tyrants who wanted also to be free—to tyrannize! But one couldn't permit that!

I was getting it now. Freedom was to do anything you chose that didn't interfere with others. No, this also was nonsense; for everything you did interfered with somebody. Freedom, I said next, is relative; everybody has his own variety. Factory owners call it freedom to pick their workmen and settle their wages, to open any factory they like even if there are already too many, to beat down competitors without legal interference until they get rich; but then they want "law" to protect their property. Workers call it freedom to change bosses, organized workers want freedom to strike; but they don't see freedom as the right to a job and the right to seize factories to produce the goods they want. That's already not "freedom" but "lawlessness"; is there any difference between the two, except that one is established and the other arriving?

Politicians, intellectuals—I myself as a writer—what was my "freedom"? It was to talk, to write, to express myself as I chose. As I chose? Oh, no, it was the right to hunt new editors who would change me as little as possible, the right to adapt myself to editors and learn what they wanted. My pioneer forebears saw freedom as the leaving of an oppressive human society for the hardship of a new but hopeful land. Of all these many kinds of freedom there seemed to be less and less. The world grew organized and squeezed out freedom. Then was freedom lack of organization? Couldn't one be both organized and free? Not for many painful years was I to discover a freedom that grew not "less and less" but "more and more."

The hardest aspect of this enforced freedom of mine was not its loneliness but its lack of stability. The human mind demands a moving foam of choice on a great sea of habit; my habit was now in turmoil and I lived in a great sea of tossing choices. Any hour of any day a suggestion might impinge upon me that Canton or Samarkand was the next place to visit, or that lectures were more important than articles; or that a month in some friend's home on the seashore would perhaps be pleasanter than either. Having no stern necessity as base from which to stray to freedom, I seemed to have no grounds for preferring one choice to another. I sometimes became so exhausted by this endless choosing that I would seize the idea of my last, most persistent adviser. If any place or person seemed to want me, I would go to it almost across the world.

Especially did I respond to advice from Russian communists. Not from American communists—I almost never took their advice. I saw them as quite fallible human beings who knew less about my life and work than I did. But for Russia I had no background of discrimination; I saw Russia and its communists mystically, as that group of creators in chaos into which all my efforts were unable to break. They could do miracles in a country where I couldn't start one decent workshop, so I accepted them as almost superhuman beings. With that sentimental American inclusiveness which asks moving picture stars their views on politics, and accepts from illiterate politicians advice on science or women, I was ready to take a Russian communist as oracle, not only on revolutions, but on personal plans and details of personal life. Casual comment I often saw as authoritative advice and tried to follow it, till only my sound American practical sense saved me from odd and painful endings. A tennis ball hit through the air by the last racket—such seemed my utter "freedom."

Beneath this emotional anarchy there remained a steady stream of instinctive action, which moved towards its chosen sea. Outwardly I was becoming a writer of increasing fame and authority on Russia and on other revolutions which began to appear. Inwardly, and only half-consciously, I was seeking a successful revolution in which I might be reasonably important without having to endure the distressing preliminaries. Was I alone in this? Is not half America like me today? Any such revolution seemed then too far ahead in America; besides I was not sure that I wanted to take part in America; I had too many friends on the wrong side. Germany, Mexico, China —these were the places where I might become "chronicler of the revolution," in addition to writing about Soviet Russia.

The pains of choice and loneliness were intermittent; the human mind cannot endure them long. Once I was started on a trip new emotions arose to claim me. I thrilled with joy to know what a great and vivid world lay open. Vast peasant populations astir in Asia, new governments rising and falling in Europe, Mexican peons fighting American imperialism—all were accessible at short notice to the writer-lecturer I had become. Lonely? Why lonely? Had I not good comrades now in every land? Comrades I had met in old days in Seattle, comrades who had come and gone briefly through Moscow, were scattered through the world. I had little share in their life, yet across the world I loved them. To launch into this undiscovered, vivid yet beloved world, when once the pain of decision was over; to be going half across the earth by the lonely plains of Siberia to find new friends in revolutionary Canton—what joy!

Thus in autumn of 1925 I took my first trip through China on my way from Moscow to Vancouver. I could give only a month from Mongolian blizzards to the heat of Canton for I had before me the exacting winter described in the last chapter. Yet I found in that month that my four years' struggle in Soviet Russia—the famine, the John Reed Colony—had revealed to me the continent of Asia as an American seldom sees it. Instead of exotic culture of shrines and ancient palaces, amusing laws and quaint religions, I saw peasant populations, essentially similar over the greatest land area of earth. I began to see the Russian revolution not only as a pioneer land emerging from chaos but also as first stage in the awakening and industrialization of Asia.

Day by day on the trans-Siberian train I saw the plains unroll from Moscow over the Urals, across the rich Siberian lands to the great forests, down by the Khingan range to Harbin, Mukden, Peking. Russians, Tartars, Buriats, Chinese succeeded each other—all ancient peasant peoples left behind in the march of the world. The advancing, fighting tribes had poured westward by the black earth lands of Russia and Poland down to Rome and Spain. Breaking across the sea they had reached America—adventurous subduers of wildernesses. With inventive genius awakened by new conditions and rich, undeveloped lands they had built an ever-expanding industrial civilization.

Now this journey of man had come full circle; it was swinging round the world to Asia after three thousand years. It was crashing upon these peoples of earth's mother continent, huddled in villages, bound in a farm and family routine that had endured through centuries unchanged. To them now were coming the railroad, the factory, the industrial civilization of the west. They came in two forms between which was war irreconcilable: naked exploitation in the south by the world's imperialists and the Russian revolution in the north.

I remembered a cynical phrase with which a correspondent had given me his estimate of Soviet power: "Admirable—for Asiatics!" Well, let me see how it fitted Asia; let me for the moment drop the west. Here were great rural areas shaken with famine when primitive methods failed against drought. From them peasant-workers migrated to newly established factories to herd in barracks. Family life was under the rule of the "old man," and tormented by superstitions—holy pictures with many names. All these conditions were repeated across the width of a continent, and all arose from the same cause, the primitive form of production, the isolation and lack of transport. All over Asia this ancient system was crashing. Not only in Moscow; it was crashing also in Canton.

No wonder the Russian revolution stirred these people. Students in Peking were ravenous for Russia; Chinese merchants coquetted with Moscow against the imperialisms of the west. Great mass movements of peasants and workers were rising in south China. The imperialist nations raged at "Russian propaganda"; but those nations had spent billions of dollars and thousands of lives in spreading Christian propaganda for more than a century without stirring China as this revolution did. The Christian propaganda was imposed by alien exploiters; the "Russian propaganda" rose out of their own past to meet their needs.

There was no "government" in the modern sense in China in 1925. There were warlords temporarily supreme in various provinces. All over the country peasant poverty had bred bandits; the stronger of these had risen into generals who systematized the institution of plunder; the strongest of all were chiefs of many provinces, looting with the help of foreign powers. One could see the beginnings of that process in feudalism by which the warring barons of the Middle Ages coalesced into nations. But China would not repeat that history; there were new forces in the world. The forces of the world imperialists; the forces of the world revolution.

The diplomats of earth dealt with Peking in those days. But Peking was no government; it was more like the League of Nations—a place where emissaries of actual powers met and maneuvered through talk. Everybody talked in Peking, in all kinds of assemblies. I also talked on the invitation of half a dozen audiences: American groups, Chinese business men and students. Afterwards I heard that most of them supposed me a "paid Soviet agent." The idea was natural, for everybody who talked in Peking was the paid agent of something: of a general, a tobacco trust or a church. The Chinese were practical; they could not imagine your talking unless you were paid for it. They did not know that we Americans like to talk on ideas.

The warlords of northern China in those days were easily remembered: they were Chang and Feng and Wu. Chang Tso-lin was the gorgeous general backed by Japan. He maintained in Mukden a court of barbaric splendor, and received his interviewers in a throne-room decorated by stuffed tigers, and enriched by a half million dollars' worth of jade. A dozen wives and concubines ornamented his Oriental state and figured in choice bits of scandal spread by foreigners.

I went two days northeast from Peking to the camp of Feng Yu-hsiang on the blizzard-swept plains of Mongolia. Feng was the "simple" general; he made a conscious virtue of a quality which stern necessity decreed. With desert as hinterland, and no foreign port for financial connections, he based his strength on the development of new lands. He kept his soldiers building roads and gave them Mongolian farms as recompense. He suppressed opium, booze and tobacco among his forces. Finding the Y.M.C.A. and the Christian religion useful in this, he became for a time a "Christian" and had Y.M.C.A. men teaching physical culture and puritan morals to his troops. Later he used the nationalist propaganda of the Kuomintang and even of communists for this purpose, till he saw in them a rival power; then he suppressed them.

Feng's surface of modernism made him popular at that time to western liberals, to whom his "Foreign Secretary" spoke with a finished American idiom about roads, schools and irrigation. But the "old China hands" amused themselves with anecdotes about Feng's treason to his allies and his flattering messages to his enemies, which they called typically Chinese, though to me they seemed also the manners of robber barons in the chivalrous Middle Ages. When I visited Feng at his Mongolian camp he was engaged in sending evasively polite telegrams to his chief enemy Chang Tso-lin, offering to turn his soldiers over to the latter "if you need them to run your errands." When I asked him how many provinces he thought he could handle with his present forces, he replied with similar felicity: "Even to administer one province is too much for my inexperience." He was grabbing three or four!

Leaving Feng I traveled south to the center of China, to Hankow on the Yangtze, headquarters of Wu P'ei-fu, the "literary general." (Two years later I was to visit it as "red Hankow.") Wu was backed by the old Chinese merchants,

Ruth Tracy Strong

Sidney Dix Strong

Tracy, Ruth & Anna Louise Strong

Anna Louise about age ten

Anna Louise, college years

Anna Louise, student snapshots

One of the display rooms from the Child Welfare Exhibits

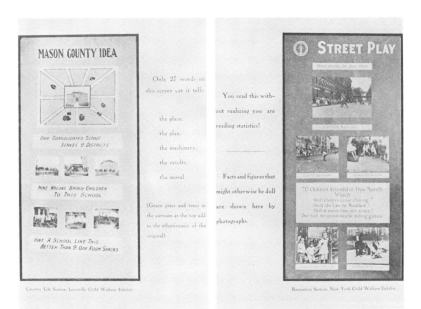

Child Welfare Exhibit display panels;
from Strong's pamphlet "Twelve Good Screens"

A Northwest mountain climbing expedition c. 1916;

Strong in goggles

Strong on snowshoes

The Victims of Everett Bloody Sunday, Nov. 5, 1916

Attention, Workers!

MURDER has been committed by the Lumber Trust in the City of Everett, Washington. Five workers are dead and 31 wounded by the hirelings of the bosses. Over a hundred members of the working class in jail in Everett charged with murder! The right to speak and organize is at stake!

Funds are urgently needed for Defense and Publicity. Let the workers defeat this plot of the murderous tools of the Manufacturers' Association!

Send all funds to Herbert Mahler, Secretary-Treas. Everett Prisoners' Defense Committee, Box 1878, Seattle, Wash.

From a petition in support of the Everett Prisoners' Defense Committee

---

CASE FOR PROSECUTION IN EVERETT I. W. W. TRIALS

GREAT LABOR CAUSE NOW ON IN SEATTLE, WASH.

After a Week, It Is Plain that Armed Lawlessness Masqueraded as Law in City in Which the Troubles Occurred—Ordinance Providing for Free Speech Violated—One Ordinance Enforced Which Had Not Been Passed by City Body.

By ANNA LOUISE STRONG.
(Member of Seattle School Board.)

[Special Correspondence of The Evening Post.]

SEATTLE, March 22.—"It is not alone an individual who is on trial for murder. It is an organization which is on trial, for criminal conspiracy leading to a murder. We, therefore, claim the right to show what that organization is, what its methods are, what it was trying to do when it began its free speech fight in Everett."

In these words, the Assistant Prosecutor, Mr. Veitch, stated what has become increasingly evident during the second week of the great labor trial now on in Seattle, that the case is not one of "the State of Washington vs. Thomas Tracy," but of the Everett Commercial Club and City Authorities against the Industrial Workers of the World. For six days, since the first day of the trial, the name of the defendant has not been mentioned, except in the most casual way. The constitution of the I. W. W., its bulletins, and publications, have been much in evidence, and the members of the jury have received a liberal education in the principles of syndicalism.

"We propose to show," said the prosecution in its opening statement, "that Jefferson Beard was killed as the result of a conspiracy to overthrow the law in the city of Everett; that following a series of labor disturbances lasting for half a year the I. W. W.'s came to Everett on November 5, on the steamer Verona, loaded to violate the city's ordinances; that they hurled defiance at the legal authorities; that in the ensuing fray the first shots came from the boat; that Thomas Tracy was one of the first to fire. Jefferson Beard was killed by an unknown man, a man who, as far as we know, can never be known, but this murderer was aided and abetted by the conspiracy of which Thomas Tracy is a member."

ett, who claims for 1916 "the lowest fire record ever made in the city's history." Obviously something was rotten in the city of Everett. One felt almost sorry for the Mayor. That I. W. W. speakers were arrested repeatedly, thrown into jail, taken next day to the city limits, sometimes beaten, and that this occurred repeatedly during August, September, and October, during which time no member of the organization resisted arrest or violated any city ordinance, or received a trial on the question of street-speaking, is clear from the State's own witnesses.

The I. W. W. secretary in Seattle was called by the State to give information concerning the ramifications of the organization and thus to lay the foundation for a conspiracy charge. He produced a very favorable impression on the large audience. The number of locals, the cities in which they are organized, the secretaries in each city, the official publications, the Free Speech Committee—on nothing was he reticent. It may be that the prosecution can use this information later to show a vast, organized conspiracy, but for the present the cause of the defence has gained materially as the vague, incoherent spectre of an unmentionable organization, which has haunted the minds of average citizens at the words I. W. W., received a local habitation and a name, and was seen to consist of local unions, secretaries, committees, and other commonplace elements.

Nor has the prosecution been much more fortunate in the evidence presented by the six deputies, who were present on the dock during the fight in which two deputies and five workingmen were killed. All of them state that the first shot came from the boat, but their evidence concerning the spot from which it came is widely conflicting. The rear of the freight deck, the front part of the passenger deck, a definite cabin window, and other places, are among the spots designated by men who stood about thirty feet away. Half of the deputies are unable to claim that they actually saw a single gun on the boat; others claim that they saw several guns; no witness yet has been able to describe or indicate a single individual seen with a gun on the boat.

Much must no doubt be allowed for inconsistency due to excitement; much evidence is, no doubt, to come from the State on many points. The fact of gross provocation, even the proof of lawlessness on the part of law-enforcers, cannot legally excuse murder if murder should be proved. Yet, making all these concessions, it seems obvious, at the end of the second week of the trial, that the prosecution will have to bring much stronger evidence than has yet appeared if it is to secure a conviction.

Meantime, while the law-enforcers of Everett are confessing in court their own lawlessness, and to the non-resistance of the I. W. W.'s prior to November 5,

Strong's article on the IWW trial in the New York Evening Post, March 22, 1917

VOTE AGAINST THE RECALL

STATEMENT BY

ANNA LOUISE STRONG

MEMBER OF SEATTLE SCHOOL BOARD

And Report of the **Central Labor Council Investigating Committee**

REGARDING THE PROPOSED RECALL

MISS STRONG'S STATEMENT

THE ISSUES ARE:

Not whether you agree with all my views, but rather:

Whether false charges and twisted rumors can be sheltered successfully behind the waving of our flag;

Whether, in this dark hour of the world's need, citizens can be denied the right to discuss laws pending in Congress;

Whether it is treason to hope that the stand our President has taken may lead to a speedy, democratic peace.

Whether, while making the world safe for democracy, we are going to allow some interests to destroy democracy in our own land.

ON PATRIOTISM

I take patriotism to mean love of country and devotion to its service.

My whole life has been given to the service of my country, in efforts to establish better and more wholesome conditions for its citizens, more equal opportunities for the children who are to build its future, and a steadier maintenance of those ideals for which this nation was founded: freedom of thought and expression, and democratic control.

This I take to be the essence of patriotism.

THE CHARGES

I call your attention to the fact that any group of citizens may charge any official with any crime whatever, and have the charge printed on the ballot. I have no legal redress and no space on the ballot to print a denial.

No attack has been made on my work as a Board member. Hence I need not take space to give my record. I am charged with conspiring against the Select Service Law, by aiding in the distribution of a circular which, it is alleged, urged resistance to the draft.

The charges are **ENTIRELY FALSE.**

The evidence shows, and my accusers know, or ought to know:
(1) That the meeting to which they allude was public and open, and took place nearly three weeks **BEFORE** the draft law passed;
(2) that I had no connection with the circular they describe;
(3) that even that circular was distributed a week before the draft law passed.

ON THE WAR

I was opposed to the war and worked against it until war was declared. But war arises inevitably from conditions existing in the world today, and cannot be waved aside by individual good will or desire for more ideal methods.

Now that we are at war, I wish the best possible fortune for our boys, the hope of our country's future. I hope, at the end of the war, first, that democracy may make signal gains all over the world; and second, that the moment a permanent, democratic peace becomes possible we may be in a position to take advantage of it, without the unnecessary loss of one life.

THE POSITION TAKEN BY OUR PRESIDENT BIDS FAIR TO SECURE THESE ENDS, IF HE IS UPHELD IN IT BY LOYAL CITIZENS. He is being attacked by the same forces that are attacking me—the jingo-autocrat group who believe that war-like enthusiasm is a complete substitute for statesmanlike thinking. I support our President, and any other officials or private citizens, who are sincerely and efficiently trying to gain, out of the present turmoil, the ends above described.

Yours for real democracy and permanent peace,

ANNA LOUISE STRONG.

Strong's leaflet on her own behalf during the Recall Campaign

NIGHT EXTRA -- FINAL EDITION
LABOR TO CARE FOR CHILDREN

PUBLISHED FOR PRINCIPLE AND NOT FOR PROFIT   FULL LEASED WIRE SERVICE OF THE UNITED PRESS ASSOCIATIONS

MONDAY'S PRESS RUN **71,400 Copies**

Seattle Union Record
DAILY EDITION

FINAL EDITION
DAILY EXCEPT SUNDAY

604 Union St. Telephone Elliott 4471.

VOL. L. No. 244.   SEATTLE, WASH, TUESDAY, FEB. 4, 1919   TWO CENTS

Churches Endorse Workers Demands

DRIVERS READY TO SUPPLY ALL MILK NEEDED

BIG BIZ GODS OF OLYMPUS WAKEN ANGER
By JOE SMITH

ON THURSDAY AT 10 A. M.

UPON AMERICA RESTS FATE OF PEACE LEAGUE
By LOWELL MELLETT

WORLD LEAGUE SCHEME NEARS COMPLETION
By ROBERT J. BENDER

STRIKE BACKED BY MINISTERS

LONDON FACES A STRIKE THURSDAY

SENATE REGISTERS ALARM OVER U. S. "BOLSHEVIKI"

POINDEXTER IS OUT IN OPEN

LAWRENCE TEXTILE STRIKERS CHARGED BY MOUNTED POLICE

MAKES CHARGES AGAINST WHITE

BERGER AFTER A NEW TRIAL

SPARTACANS STILL FIGHT

NEWSBOYS

WASHINGTON WILL HAVE AN "OASIS"

WHO PAYS FOR THE PUBLICITY

State Labor Men Called In

Wireless Men Win Demands

Arrest Russian Strike Inciters

CANDYMAKERS' UNION
LOCAL 149

JULIA SMITH, Secretary.

Pre-strike issue of "The Seattle Union Record,"
including Strong's well-known editorial "No One Knows Where"

John Reed Children's Colony on the Volga

RECEPTION FOR ANISE PLANNED

ANNA LOUISE STRONG

Dr. Sydney Strong has just received this photograph of "Anise," former Union Record staff writer, who will lecture at the Y. M. C. A. auditorium here next Thursday and Friday nights on her experiences and observations in Soviet Russia in recent years. The beaded costume and curious hand-embroidered cap are favorite articles of dress among the Russians, Dr. Strong explains.

A reception in honor of Miss Strong will be held at the Olympic hotel cafeteria the evening of the day she returns to Seattle, when "Anise" will renew her many old friendship with her many old friends here.

Tickets are selling rapidly for her two lectures, and capacity

---

Strong returned to the U.S.
several times to garner support
for her projects;

a fund raising letter for
the John Reed Colony

Strong on a return speaking tour
to Seattle from Russia
in the Twenties

A Letter from Anna Louise Strong

THE CHILDREN PUT IT OVER

A YEAR AGO, on the plains of the middle Volga in Russia, *Fifty Children*, with a few instructors, began their fight for a living and an education. Famine orphans fourteen and fifteen years old—they could no longer be supported in the overcrowded children's homes of the little town of Kvalinsk, hardest hit by the famine of all the region near Saratov.

The local government gave them the buildings and land of an old monastery; the Children's Commission of the Central Government gave them its blessing, the name of "*John Reed Children's Colony*" and $500 worth of horses, tools, and teachers' wages; the Quakers gave them blankets and a carload of food; and I was asked to become their official "Guardian" and help them build a model self-supporting farm school "on the American style."

It was the problem of making a SELF-SUPPORT-ING EDUCATION to produce SELF-SUPPORT-ING CITIZENS. If this problem could be solved, it might benefit hundreds of thousands of orphan children in Russia.

I laughed and wept when I saw the place. The land was in four pieces, from three or ten miles from the buildings, in good, old Russian peasant fashion. The houses were charmingly situated in ravines between unproductive forests. And here they talked of a tractor and "American style of farming."

But They Started. *They had to.*

Ten boys moved out to the monastery in November with a few instructors, and began making beds and tables and benches from the wood of a broken house which they had permission to demolish. Old condemned milk cans from the famine-feeding days were hammered in their primitive workshop into cups and bowls and saucers—the only tableware they had for the first year. In December came fifteen more children, including some girls and a matron. They made mattresses filled with straw; they began their task of cooking and sewing and cleaning for the colony. Through the winter one group of boys ran a little mill and secured from it three months' bread for the colony; others made shoes; others few, the tools which I managed to buy for them; others worked in our carpenter shop making beds and tables.

They Had a Right to Call Themselves Self-Supporting.

The school authorities at Saratov took notice and put them on the school budget, paying salaries for eleven instructors and a regular salary. They sent more children and guaranteed their food till next harvest. They gave us the big estate we had had our eyes on from the beginning, but which we were not strong enough to manage the first year. Over a thousand acres of land, with its own village on the Volga, buildings enough for 300 children, a giant mill from which our boys have already proudly lighted their house and stables and their nearby village; big modern brick-kiln—buildings worth two or three hundred thousand dollars.

Here At Last We Can Build That American Style Farm School. Here can be made: a self-supporting agricultural academy, with teachers' wages supplied by the state budget, but everything else raised by the self-governing band of boys and girls. Already we have 150 children; we have our grown bread-keepers, our miller, our carpenters, our shoemakers and dressmakers groups. We have a charming girl of sixteen who dreams of studying to be a doctor, and begins by acting as doctor's helper among the other boys and girls; we have children to pay with the colony summer, whoever can pay to live on with the colony and learn from them and helping him. We have our little theatre and library, inexpensive but developing. We have the luxury of a real English teacher," an American Quaker, Ann Graves, who lives in the colony this winter and will give this connection with the outer world.

The government pays teachers' wages, and food till the first harvest; but it is my job, as "Guardian," to get the tools and equipment and livestock, on the level of which alone there can be produce by letters and articles circulated among personal friends. All the money thus put into the colony was less than $5,000.

A Going Concern.

It is done by $5,000 worth of tools and livestock secured among personal friends in America. (The government, of course, pays teachers' wages and supports the children until the first harvest.)

Our colony already has its Morrow "Izvestia," I received letters of endorsement from the Department of Education and the Central Children's Commission, advising me to

ORGANIZE SOME MORE COLONIES

I investigated two more provinces—Novgorod and Tula. All kinds of estates were gladly offered for purposes of self-supporting colonies. Large lands with thousands of dollars worth of buildings. These estates are disappearing under the expansion of peasant holdings. Some of them, the magnificent old palaces of the nobility, must be saved for the use of the agricultural colleges of Russia. The remedy is to repair roofs and windows and plant farm colonies of adolescent children, and then raise, step by step, the standard of farming and of education.

Since my arrival in America, different groups are already planning to "adopt" a whole colony, or to help in those already started. There is no overhead expense. Contributions may be sent through either the American Friends Service or the International Workers Relief. Or they may be sent to my father,

Dr. Sydney Strong,
508 Garfield St., Seattle, Wash,

who will keep donors personally in touch with the results of their gifts. Make checks payable "Russian Children's Farm Schools."

MOSCOW NEWS
THE FIVE-DAY WEEKLY

May 4, 1931

Second № 34 Year
10 kopeks, 5 cents, 2½ d

EDITORIAL OFFICES
Moscow, Strastnoi Boulevard, 11, "Ogonyok".
Telephone 2-11-48.

Italy Gives Credit to U.S.S.R. While U.S.A. Discourages Trade

ROME, April 29.—Yesterday afternoon at 5 o'clock an agreement was signed between the U.S.S.R. and Italy by which the Italian government guarantees credits up to 350,000,000 lire a year for Italian exports to the Soviet Union.

The treaty was signed in the name of the Soviet Government by the trade representative Levinson, and for the Italian government by Mosconi, minister of finance, and Bottai, minister of corporations. The Soviet ambassador to Italy, Kurski, was also present during the signing, as were a number of Italian officials from departments of foreign affairs, finance and corporations.

WASHINGTON, April 27. — The Anversoise cargo from Soviet Russia will be admitted, Undersecretary of the Treasury Mills announced today.

The importers, he said, have proved that the cargo does not come from the northern regions of the Soviet Union where the Treasury's ruling of February 10 alleged convict labor is employed.

Although Mills' ruling is favorable to the Soviet Union, Tass agency indicates, the decision that each shipment must be dealt with separately will hinder imports from the Soviet Union.

The Baltimore Sun says that the official procedure seeks to discourage even admissible imports.

"If all importers must endure this complicated procedure applied to the import of $85,000 worth of Soviet goods, even our permissible import trade with the Soviet Union may easily be smothered under the bureaucratic procedure."

Spain's Chambers of Commerce "Satisfied" Revolt Against Portugal Wide Spread

MADRID, April 26.—Government of all provinces have been ordered by the Republican Cabinet to refrain from attending religious services.

"Any priest who makes an attack on the government from the pulpit will be summarily dealt with", the order states. The governors are directed to have only courteous civil relations with priests.

The order is regarded as the first move in the separation of Church and State, one of the most delicate problems that the republic faces.

* * *

MADRID, April 25. — The elections for the constituent cortes which will draw up a scheme of government for the new Spanish Republic will be held June 21 next, the cabinet decided today. The voting age, which in recent municipal elections was 26, will be brought down to 23.

* * *

MADRID, April 24 — Complete satisfaction with the preservation of order and the rapid installation of the Republican regime was expressed today to Premier Alcala Zamora by officials of the executive council of Spanish chambers of commerce, while, as a further promise of peace, General Berenguer, former monarchist premier, was among the first to sign the new military oath of allegiance to the republic.

* * *

LONDON, April 21. — The ex-King of Spain arrived here last night as a private citizen for a brief stay.

* * *

TANGIER, April 21. — The Spanish Consul-General has hoisted the Republican flag. The crowd who witnessed the ceremony was quiet. The Re-

publican Committee here is demanding the recall of certain officials whose monarchical tendencies are well known. The situation is normal.

* * *

LONDON, April 28. — The Portuguese punitive expedition has landed at Madeira, attacking a rebel outpost 12 miles from Funchal.

Warships bombarded the rebel fort while troops landed. Rebel guns are silenced by air bombing. Government troops captured 17 prisoners.

The punitive force reembarked after a hasty skirmish. The government has dropped an ultimatum over Funchal, demanding unconditional surrender of the rebels.

* * *

PARIS, April 25.— Several were killed at Oporto, where according to a Havas despatch Portuguese authorities fired on crowds. Reservists have been called to the colors and officers on leave ordered to return to their regiments.

* * *

LISBON, April 23.—The garrison in Portuguese Guinea in northwest Africa has revolted in sympathy with the rebels at Madeira, it was learned today. A censorship has been established in Guinea and a ship is being armed prior to sailing for the colony.

With the outbreak in Guinea, the Portuguese government is faced with the alternative of taking urgent measures to suppress revolt overseas, or standing a chance of losing its colonial empire.

The greatest concern to the government is Madeira where rebels, having dug themselves in well-made trenches, have announced their intention to "fight to a finish."

Catalonian Students Celebrate Change of Government

A Million Moscow Workers Celebrate May Day

IN THE RED SQUARE
Nine Hours, from Nine to Six

By Anna Louise Strong

Sky washed blue by April, streets washed clean over-night, backyards cleaned of lingering snow by sanitary committees—

So Moscow met May Dawn!

Morning air throbbed with bands heard afar going to their place of meeting, throbbed with clatter of horse-hoofs going down Tverskaya to Red Square.

In all the streets rank on rank of children, in blue or khaki with red neckerchiefs proclaiming the Young Pioneer, wait at eight o'clock with shining faces.

•

Nine o'clock by Kremlin chimes! The Red Square filled with the Red Army at attention. Thousands in the tribunes, Moscow workers, workers of the world, foreign diplomats, correspondents. Stalin, Kalenin, Molotov above the Lenin mausoleum.

As the last peal sounds Voroshilov rides to review the army. He addresses them in the name of the world's workers. They repeat the oath of allegiance:

"I, son of a worker"... swear to defend..."

Not any state, but the workers of the world. Thus they declare themselves.

For two hours the army passes the Square, infantry, tanks, cavalry galloping to cheers. Overhead move thirty-seven airplanes.

The military parade is just beginning.

•

A sudden burst of banners, red, uplifted, fills the left end of the Square. They pour forward, flooding like a tidal wave. A sea of red banners above a sea of marchers. Eight Moscow districts send eight long columns, which meet here, forty, fifty, sixty abreast, to form this moving tide of humanity.

Auto workers from Amo in the outer column. Twenty minutes, half an hour, an hour passes, and still the banners proclaim, Amo marches! Amo has 16,000 workers; all are here!

Electrozavod with 10,000 workers, the Sickle and Hammer Rolling Mills with 12,000; the Rubber Factory; the Second Clock Factory displaying a dial on high.

Men march, women, children march! Babies ride above the crowd on their fathers' shoulders! A two-

year-old in bright red suit and cap, sailing forward above the heads of the workers, waves red flags and crows happily at Stalin and Kalenin!

More than a million people, says a commander, are pouring today through the Red Square!

Half a dozen bands play at once, buried under the marchers, harmonized by the immense spaces. Eight hundred bands in all are marching! A hundred thousand banners!

Nowhere in all the world is such a sea of marchers!

Never before have they marched as today; this strong, confident march, this triumph that cannot stop to triumph!

•

Every year the banners have their special character.

This year they review the battlefront of industry! Factory by factory give record.

Moscow Power Station produced 138 per cent of its plan; using 4 per cent less fuel per kilowatt... Banners flame celebrating this victory!

The All-Union Oil Syndicate: "Oil has mdried its Five-Year Plan as Two to and a Half Years! This year we must take from the ground 27,500,000 tons of oil!"

Red flags above 10,000 workers from Electrozavod announce their Five-Year Plan already finished! Hurrahs answer them from the tribune, and echo back from the workers! Cheers again for the Rubber Factory, also with plan completed!

Cartooned above the throng are drunkards, idlers, kulaks, bureaucrats, job-changers, —hit on the head by hammer-blows from workers, strangled around the throat by the tail of a giant FIVE!

"We have 98.8 per cent in shock brigades"... "We have fulfilled our plan for April 100.5 per cent"... "We have abolished illiteracy in our plant"... So report the mills and factories. Models of smoking chimneys, swiftly rising bridges, power-plants, libraries, tower above the sea of faces.

"We mobilize you for a vober life" reads a banner... "For Steel, Bookkeeping Methods", shouts another.

*

War! And what a war! Shock tion, health, banners, a million marching! War for exact book-keeping! War for sobriety and smoking chimneys! War for fuel economy and cost-cutting! War for the Five-Year Plan in Four Years!

On the long white wall above the marchers hang three-cornered banners, repeating in four languages the slogan of this May Day: "The USSR is the shock-brigade of the world's workers!"

Under them a streamer: "Hail to May First,—the military review of the forces of the world proletariat!"

Yes, here they are: Red Army, Red Factories, production programs, Five-Year Plan in Four, good technique and accounting, a million working people! Here they are,—the forces of the world revolution,—passed in this war review!

"Success on the job", say the marchers. "Our success, — shall be our propaganda!"

IN THE MARCHING LINES
Waiting Six Hours on Pavements

By M. M.

I sit on the kerb and watch Tanya dance.

Her feet click on the cobbles of Strastnoi Boulevard. Slender little ankles moving to the tambourin, the plaint of the guitar, the wheezy sweet of the accordion.

Tanya's hair burns about her face, golden red as the little clouds that stand over the sun, just before it drops behind Lenin Hills.

"Dance my girl, dance," runs the cry along the kerb.

We are the workers of the Ogonyok Little Flame. Here is our little flame — Tanya.

(Cont. on page 2)

An early issue of the Moscow News, *May 4, 1931*

Strong about the time I Change Worlds *was published, 1935*

*Strong in China
with the family of Chu-Teh*

Mao, Chou En Lai and Chu-Teh on the Yenan airfield

Strong and her husband, Joel Shurbin

Strong changing worlds

Strong in her later years

the respectable element and literati; he was also subsidized by
any foreign government that wanted anything, as most of
them did. Wu was the center of the choicest lot of well-born
grafters anywhere in China; he was the "honest man" they
could all trust to divide the spoils among his friends. This
was true Confucian ethic, which recognizes friends but not
nations or classes. Wu had more "allies" than any other general, but they were much less stable; they would meet him at
famous temples "to discuss the ancient classics," after which
new lands would be divided.

Wu talked to me at length about foreign influence, which
was, he said in his judicious Confucian' manner, "both good
and bad." It was good in that it set up factories and created
wealth; it was bad in that it undermined the social structure
founded by the sages, the duty to parents, to elders, to husbands, to older brother. Could you do one, I asked, without
doing the other? Wu replied that it might be difficult. Then
he beamed when I asked him to write for me a poem; I had
heard he could improvise verse. He could; he painted verse
with the usual Chinese brush and put my name at the end in
Chinese: "To Miss Strong from Wu P'ei-fu." The best translation I could get for the poem ran:

> The clouds hanging over Europe and Asia
> Have thousands and thousands of changes,
> But the work of a hero is the same now as in the past.
> The flowers blossom in the third moon
> And the fortunate man is found at the peak of Fenglai.

Fenglai, said my translator, was Wu's birthplace; the "third
moon" was held to predict a spring campaign. Such were the
literary forms in which this general of the Chinese merchants
expressed himself, as he balanced the ancient against the modern world.

In Peking I had met Fanny Borodin, an old acquaintance
from Moscow; she and her husband had left that city a year
or two earlier and I had not known where they had gone. Now
I began to hear of them in China; according to all the foreigners, Michael Borodin was the dark force of Russian propa-

ganda, by some revered, by others cursed, behind the Canton strike. I learned from Fanny that he was adviser to the new nationalist government arising in south China: he had come by request of Sun Yat-sen. "You must visit us in Canton," she said. "From the north you cannot know modern China." She told me that communications from Hongkong to Canton were broken. A British boat went from Hongkong to Shameen, a small British-controlled island adjoining Canton. But the Canton strike committee would not let Canton boats meet that British steamer.

"I'll ask the strike committee to break the rule and let me meet you. It is really important that you should see Canton."

They broke the rule for me; I traveled from Hongkong to Canton. As the British steamer with armed guards drew under the lee of Shameen, for which we were all assumed to be bound, one small motor boat put out from the distant mass of Canton shipping, flying a red flag with a blue corner on which was a round white sun. This was my first sight of the emblem of the Kuomintang which was to spread through China. Fanny Borodin sat in the stern. It was the first time for months a Canton boat had met that British steamer. I swiftly stepped into the boat and departed amid the astonished stares of sailors.

Just as suddenly as that I stepped out of ancient Asia into the modern world. All through north China I had grown confused among a dozen disputants, who sighed: "If we could only get rid of militarism," or who blamed lack of tariff autonomy for China's woes. The strange forms of politeness had increased my confusion. I had begun to say, as other foreigners did, "An inscrutable people, whom we never can understand." Even the Peking students with all their modernistic patter were not quite understandable; they did not understand themselves. They talked democracy, socialism, communism, liberty, and begged America or Geneva to do something.

But the Canton strike was hard, ruthless, definite. It was organized labor on strike in Seattle, Hamburg, Pittsburgh, London—anywhere in the world. I felt it the moment I entered the strike headquarters. This was no alien, exotic country; this was home. Here were peasant-workers grown industrialized and feeling their power. I was not even conscious of their yellow color.

Seamen chiefly led them, their oldest "modern union." Sheu Chow-ging was president both of the seamen and of the strike. He said to me: "There are one hundred and forty unions taking part. This is not a racial fight; this is not a Chinese-British fight. Tell the workers of the west from us: We are part of the world revolution!"

The struggle began as a strike of more than a hundred thousand workers against the British port of Hongkong. Homeless and penniless strikers went to their native towns for shelter; forty thousand thus came to Canton, which lay on a river harbor a few hours by steamer from Hongkong. Canton was the center of the new nationalist government, whose aim was to spread itself through China. Borodin was their official "adviser." Foreign advisers have been plentiful in all of China's government, but this was the first revolutionary Russian.

As long ago the smaller business men of Seattle had sympathized at first with workers striking against dictation from New York, so far more did the Chinese business men of Canton, for a generation overshadowed by their British rival, sympathize with men who struck against Hongkong. Under Borodin's advice this sympathy had solidified into coöperation; Canton gave the strikers the empty houses left by a recent clean-up of gambling dens and the great military camps left by half a dozen evicted generals.

From their base in Canton the strikers organized for a hundred miles along the coast a far-flung line of twenty-five hundred pickets who kept goods and strike-breakers out of Hongkong. They confiscated goods which tried to run this blockade and jailed smugglers. Bloody conflicts took place. British consuls protested to the Canton government which answered blandly: "We regret we can no more control our strikers than you can yours in London." The strikers demanded from British-controlled Hongkong "free speech and the right to open union halls; abolition of corporal punishment for workers; equality of Chinese with British before the law; representation in the Hongkong government of the Chinese who form ninety-nine percent of its population." This sufficiently indicates conditions in Hongkong.

Under the impact of this strike, which had continued firmly for six months, Hongkong was dying. Its banks appealed to London for help against bankruptcy; it was losing a million dollars a day. An American in the consulate in Hongkong said to me: "You know those 'dead towns' in the west when a mining rush has passed by. I've been wondering all summer if that can happen to the third port of the British Empire, the greatest port of the east." Such was the power of the striking Chinese workers, with base in Canton.

But the base itself was a strange, unstable alliance. Silk-clad officials felt uneasy at the strength of these workers, yet strove to use them to boycott their ancient enemy and unify a province. Workers resented the presence of silk-clad officials, but used their hospitality as a base against the British exploiters. There was friction in the very air of Canton; could such a combination last?

"For a time," answered Borodin, when I asked him. "These merchants want a stable 'independent' Chinese government, by which they mean one under their own control. They want to clear out bandits, build roads, establish industry, have a stable currency and other things that are good for their trade. This brings them into conflict with the British imperialists, with whom the exploited workers are in irreconcilable conflict."

"But surely everyone wants stable government in China," I protested. "They may have different views on how to get such a government and who should control it. But all the capitalists in Shanghai and Hongkong wish stable government; they complain that China's disorder hurts business."

"So it does," said Borodin, smiling, "but it gives the foreigners control of what business there is. The more disorder reigns in China, the more Hongkong and Shanghai profit from their monopoly of security. Generals keep their funds in foreign settlements; millionaires run there for shelter. Chinese shipping seeks foreign flags and pays tribute to foreigners. China's chaos enables foreigners to loot the country."

I remembered that an American consul had told me how bankers blocked a new government mint which might have given a stable currency to China. He said these bankers profited from unstable currency. But these, I thought, are only a few corrupt banks. It was too preposterous to imagine that the ordinary business man wanted chaos. His very slogan was "law and order." "How many foreign people do you accuse of consciously wishing disorder in China?" I asked.

"Very few," admitted Borodin. "Only a few at the top analyze what they are doing. But plenty are ready to subsidize this or that bandit and let the resultant disorder take care of itself. And most of them are happy when rents go up in the concessions and they can congratulate themselves that they are 'orderly—not like the Chinese.' All such folk, consciously or not, desire at bottom China's chaos." . . . I wasn't convinced; I thought he talked clever paradoxes. I was to remember the conversation a year later in Mexico City.

Meantime I met with Chinese women in Canton, some of whom also had begun to speak the modern language of working-women of the world. I met the widow of Liao Chung-kai. When a Chinese woman loses her husband by death she retires into her house for years. But when Liao Chung-kai was assassinated in the workers' struggle, his widow used his death to stir mass meetings. Her face bore marks of deep conflict; she was a middle-aged Chinese woman, and human beings are not easily made over. But she said to me firmly, through her daughter-interpreter: "Liao Chung-kai stood foremost with the workers. That is why he was assassinated. But his cause still lives." She had hung above her house no traditional signs of woe but a banner marked "Undying Spirit."

Fifteen hundred women in a great mass meeting asked me to tell them about Russia. Where had I seen such faces? Grim faces of struggle? I remembered—the women of Kiev! I talked to them of the conditions out of which Russia made her revolution, the old patriarchal household, the ignorant village, the enslaved women, the factories with their barracks life. Then I told the story of Dunia, a textile-worker near Moscow, of how she had lived before and after the revolution. How the women of the factory took the manager's house for a day nursery, and organized a hospital and factory lunchroom. Those women understood the details of Russian revolution as no American audience of mine ever had. It was their own life I told, as it had been and might be.

After four days in Canton I left for America, using the day and a half which my steamer gave me in Japan for a series of interviews, receptions, speeches arranged by Mr. Saito of the Y.M.C.A. After the rough equality of Soviet Russia and the vigor of Canton, I was startled by the deep obeisance of bowing boys who answered every nod of Baron Shibusawa whom I interviewed in his bank; I was bored by the dull statistics given me by Susuki, president of the Japanese Federation of Labor. But I was really intrigued by Viscount Goto's plan for settling Japanese on Soviet soil near the Amur River, with the agreement of the Soviet, which was willing to have there an "autonomous Japanese Soviet Republic."

"Our government won't do it," said Goto. "They are afraid of the effect of such a Japanese Soviet Republic on Tokio. But I'm backing biology against Marx!" He added: "It might cause Tokio statesmen trouble in this generation, but two hundred years from now all our government and social systems will be the same, while Japanese children would be spreading on the continent of Asia." Goto had a real world view!

The great *Asahi* newspaper arranged a mass meeting for me to speak on Soviet Russia. The editor was quite conscious of his courage; it was the first big meeting on a topic about which everything was rumored and nothing known. He said to me: "We hope you will be calm in your remarks and not inflame your audience. Conditions here are such that audiences easily break into riots. If you give an excuse to people to start cheering Bolsheviks, it might end badly. . . ."

I promised "facts without emotions," and was quite convinced of the need of calm when I saw how thickly dotted that meeting was with armed police. Part of the audience glared at me with hate; others seemed ready to burst into cheers. I didn't want any useless slaughter so I gave them two hours of "facts without emotions" in a quiet tone, with an interpreter alternating on every sentence. The *Asahi* presented me with a modest fee in a beautifully decorated envelop on a silver salver.

Thus I saw the east at the end of 1925, in terms of my past four years in Russia. Backward peasant villages over earth's mightiest continent, beset by floods and famines, by landlords and bandits—all more alike to one another than any of them was to an American farm. Above those villages were rulers and intellectuals, not alike but differentiated into incomprehensible figures of clashing nations and cultures: Chang, Feng, Wu, Peking students, Viscount Goto. . . . But growing out of those peasants, through pressure of foreign ports and modern industries, was an increasing host which talked the common language of the workers of the world!

CHAPTER XX

MEXICO IN CONFUSION

NEVER have I seen such a romantic zeal for revolutions as I found in Mexico. Everybody talked revolution—the peasants, the workers, the government officials, even the American Embassy. Each of them meant a different kind of revolution. The peasants meant "land and liberty," the workers meant "a good life," the Calles' officials meant their own continuance in office, while at the American Embassy revolution meant private armies of oil men preparing to overthrow Calles.

I went to Mexico in February of 1927, six weeks after my illness in the Crimea. I was on my annual lecture tour in America. My father wrote me from Mexico City. He had gone there with one of those voluntary "Goodwill Commissions" that were trying to understand Mexico and thus soothe the tension between the American State Department and the Mexican President Calles which seemed to be leading to war. His letters intrigued me. Calles, it seemed, was fighting both the Roman Catholic Church and American oil imperialists, neither of which were mean enemies. Carleton Beals, the American writer on Mexico, said that Mexican workers were the "strongest revolutionary force on the two American continents." What was really going on? I asked my lecture bureau to give me ten days after some Texas engagements, that I might run down to Mexico City.

I also wanted to meet Alexandra Kollontai who was at that time Soviet ambassador in Mexico. She had been denied the privilege of travel to her destination by the direct route across the United States, and had been forced to go by a round-about route on a miserably slow steamer; this fact had brought her into the American liberal press. I marked her down as someone who could help me organize the vast confusion of emotions that filled my brain. I had never met her but I knew her as a Russian Bolshevik who had lived much in western countries and would therefore understand our west. I had noticed that important Bolsheviks had no time to let me talk with them in Moscow, but that outside Russia they themselves were often lonely and willing to meet persons who had recently come from their country. So I went to Mexico City to get acquainted with Kollontai. It was a wise thought; ever since she has been my friend. I was beginning to analyze how to get the things I needed.

Alexandra Kollontai was often ill in Mexico City; the altitude affected her heart. She had to spend much time in Cuernavaca, a health resort at lower level where many foreigners go. She was very popular with the Mexicans; her personal charm and warm, emotional nature won this warm, emotional people. A Mexican said to me: "A pity they can't send us more like that. We don't like the dried-up type of Bolshevik." The Mexicans didn't like cold logic; they were more aloof from theory than even I was. In Moscow I had felt myself a whirl of conflicting personal feelings; in Mexico City it seemed to me that I was becoming impersonal and able to analyze.

Kollontai was very glad to see me; she said I was her latest news from Moscow. With a shock I realized that what had seemed to me a rather long lecture tour had brought me more quickly than the Russians could travel. What then could Russia and Mexico know of each other, with such difficulty of communication? Yet Secretary of State Kellogg was announcing to the world that the Calles' government was Bolshevik, affiliated with Moscow!

Kellogg was wrong only in his facts; he was right in his class instinct. The Mexican masses were close to Russia; they craved Russia like food. I visited meetings of labor unions in the building belonging to the CROM (Mexican Federation of Labor). In every meeting I was immediately asked to speak. An American who had spent five years in Russia —applause at once! Let all local business wait! We'll hear about Russia! Never in any land had I seen such responsive people; though I spoke through an interpreter they seemed to react to the tones of my voice before the interpreter began.

I remember especially a meeting of women delegates from several unions. Where had I seen such intent, vital faces before? The women delegates in Kiev who had lived through sixteen bombardments, and the women in Canton organizing a Red Cross for the northern march of revolution. Working women on three sides of the world!

In every meeting one felt the vitality of revolutionary feeling. There were none of the doubts that affect the colder peoples of the north. There was none of the evasion of class struggle which had characterized my own youth. These men were ready to die for "land and liberty." They did not even ask if their death was useful or their leaders honest!

That was their trouble. They didn't ask. . . . In one of the rooms of the CROM I found a tablet dedicated to Samuel Gompers; close beside it a picture of Trotsky; in an adjoining room pictures of Tolstoi and Lenin. They had also a memorial statue to the anarchists killed in the Haymarket riots in Chicago. . . . I heard in Mexico City the story of a simple Mexican worker, thrown into jail in the United States, who wrote to the Soviet representative in Mexico asking for help on the ground that he had always followed "the sublime teachings of Lenin, Trotsky, Bakunin, Kropotkin, Gorky and Tolstoi!"

That was the Mexican temperament! Infinitely hospitable to all its friends and ready to accept as friend anybody who said kindly words about workers, anybody who declared that workers, and not capitalists, should enjoy the fruits of toil. The hospitable Mexican would die for his friends; he would die for them all!

I soon learned the historic reasons for this confusion. The first Mexican trade unions had been founded by anarchists from Italy and Spain. By the time these were organized into a federation, socialists were dominant, but not strong enough to adopt the red flag as emblem; the Mexican labor flag is red and black, socialist joined with anarchist. Still later they joined the Pan-American Federation of Labor, organized by Gompers; they reasoned not badly that their chief enemy was the capitalism of the United States which was also the chief

enemy of the American workers. Gompers was an able politician; he trimmed his words to suit the Mexicans. In a congress of the American Federation of Labor held in El Paso,
Texas, he denounced British labor for daring to meddle in
politics, but the next evening, after crossing the Mexican border, he congratulated the Mexican workers on their political
action, and urged them to "seize political power by any force
at their disposal," by which he meant the army. Thus Gompers also became a "friend" of Mexican workers.

Morones, president of CROM, was known as a gangster and
a crook. Even his supporters spoke casually of his use of
private assassins to "bump off" opponents; others alluded to
carousals and stored-away jewels, adding that "Morones is
just the gangster to lead a fascist *coup d'état.*" The CROM
itself, the largest general federation of labor in Mexico, was
engaged during my visit in open strike-breaking in an attempt
to smash the railway unions which competed with its power.
It ruthlessly excluded communists from its affiliated organizations; a CROM official told me, "We'll starve those damned
communists out by keeping them from jobs."

Yet in the halls of CROM the workers of every union
cheered Russia; every letter sent by CROM began "Dear
Comrades" and ended "Health and Social Revolution." I saw
great piles of letters from distant struggling farmhands, who
wrote: "Our only help is in the Union." I waited in the outer
office of Morones, who had become minister of industry, commerce and labor under Calles; I observed that peasant delegates, dusty from all night rides in the provinces, had precedence over American business men who waited for hours. It
was said that any really important oil man who wanted to see
Morones would send a telegram before he arrived in his private
car and would be accepted in Morones' home. But the public
office was chiefly accessible to men in overalls and sandals, who
looked with haughty scorn at waiting lines of small capitalists,
as they went directly to the inner office to call Morones "comrade." Thus strike-breaking gangster Morones also made himself a "friend of labor."

These Mexican workers cheered all "friends"—from Morones to Moscow. The Russian motion pictures which entered their borders had immediate success. Photographs of Russian workers and peasants actually building a new world—schools, reading huts, workers' clubs—were far more readily appreciated than they were in the sophisticated motion picture halls in New York, where Russian workers and peasants seemed quaint figures poorly dressed. To the Mexican these Russians dressed naturally, like workers and peasants, like himself. He saw workers and peasants who had won their fight for "land and liberty" and who were making the kind of world he wished to build. He saw it in pictures; but when it went beyond pictures to logical analysis, he no longer understood. He was cheering everyone without distinction. Just as—I suddenly saw it—just as we had done long ago in Seattle in our general strike.

We were educated Americans, not illiterate emotional peons! But hadn't we cheered everybody, Lenin, the British Labor Party, even Gandhi? Hadn't we published pamphlets from all of them, thinking they all led "in the same general direction"? This characteristic of cheering everybody was evidently not peculiar to peons; perhaps it was not national but a stage of development. Hadn't I myself disliked those reports years ago in the Congress of the Communist International, because they denounced German socialists and British Labor and I thought they should all be "friends." Now I had lost my old admiration for British Labor; they had bungled their general strike as badly as we had. They were not even going ahead gradually; they almost seemed to be going backward. Clearly it wasn't enough just to attack capitalists; you had to have discipline and a clear direction. There was some excuse then for communists attacking socialists, to get their line of battle clear. Lenin had had clear direction and tactics. But where was the great genius who would think it out for the Mexicans, or for those many other nations where all the best minds of the world seemed failing?

Obviously that genius wasn't Calles. He gave a little land to the peasants, and then Secretary Kellogg wrote a stiff note from Washington and the land division stopped. Then the

peasants would revolt again and get a little more from Calles
till Kellogg sent another note.   Calles could not enforce his
own land laws.   The Mexican peasants and workers were so
revolutionary that any Mexican government had to talk revolution; otherwise it couldn't last.   The Mexican Constitution,
adopted in 1917, made all natural resources the property of
the state, and gave land back to Indian villages that had been
robbed by exploiters.   It was so revolutionary that workers in
Central and South America had been arrested for reading it
in public; in all those Spanish-speaking lands the workers
looked to Mexico for inspiration.   But Calles did not dare enforce that constitution, because of the "Colossus of the North."

Was then the great leader Diego Rivera, the artist?   He
was the most famous revolutionist in Mexico.   There seemed
to be in Mexico no discipline, no theory of revolution.   There
was the art of Diego Rivera, which peasants and workers came
on pilgrimages from distant provinces to see.

They take art seriously in Mexico; it is rooted deep in their
ancient communal life.   The hungriest village Indian, the
peon dispossessed four hundred years, has art.   Art is in his
pottery, his dances, his serapi—that blanket which serves also
as coat.   Individual life seemed to be lightly held among them;
a man might throw it away for the sake of a gesture.   But art
was serious; it gave rise to real struggle.   One reactionary candidate for president to succeed Calles was saying: "I want
office so that I can clean those Rivera pictures from the walls
of the Secretaría."

I spent an afternoon looking at those frescoes.   Not since
the days of Michael Angelo has a great artist had such a canvas as those hundreds of feet of high vaulted corridors surrounding the open court of the Secretaría of Education.   Rivera was filling it with simple Mexicans of soil and mine and
forest, the people called peons.   There was brutal impact of
life in them—the earth, the toilers close to it, suffering, emerging, hardly conscious of their power.   The infinite struggling
strength of man, the worker, was seen in the underground
miner with powerful pick, his body bent by seams of earth; the
infinite humiliation of man in that peon with uplifted arms

searched by the mine inspector; the infinite endurance of women, pounding their grain, patient for ages. Here were collective festivals; grotesque traditions of Indian life or celebrations of the triumphant workers' and peasants' May Day with its red banners, red star, red hammer and sickle. The feast of the dead lifted dumb grief of mourners by ceremonial into a solemn harmony. Again and again came peons, toiling, fighting, dying, triumphing in revolution.

No wonder the enemies of the revolution wished to destroy these frescoes! No wonder the peons came on foot for hundreds of miles to see them! Their impact was so great that it was difficult for me to talk to the artist when I first met him; words were feeble beside this expression in paint. Later we talked and often, of art and revolution, which he declared were one and inseparable. "Only a man who is passionately part of the vital urge of his generation and who is able to express it in significant form can be truly an artist," he said.

Rivera was a massively built Mexican Indian, whose face and physique spoke of the peasant village from which he came. "Art has been the great unifier of my people," he said. "Through all these ages it has given us strength to endure. In the old days before the Spaniards my people lived more spaciously than now; little by little their lands have been taken. But they have withdrawn further into themselves, content with the barest food and shelter. They keep alive the spirit of their communities by song and dance. The Anglo-Saxon has not been able to buy us into slavish labor on lands that are not our own. Even today this makes us unconquerable.

"My art also exists to express and strengthen the soul of my people—the peasant Indians and the workers who are just emerging from peasants. I paint them always embracing, the worker and peasant. The bourgeois understand only that the pictures are queer subjects of low people—too many Indians: this they wish to destroy. The visits of foreign artists may save my frescoes; they are talked about in the world. Besides, every Mexican government must pose as revolutionary; the people demand it. But no Mexican government can be really revolutionary; the Americans are too strong. As the leaders slip into compromises they say to the people: See, we spare Rivera's pictures; we are a revolutionary government. They make even my pictures a cover for compromises. But if they really understood how art unites a people and lifts it to action, they would destroy the pictures.

"All our political leaders are unstable. Spanish conqueror blood mixed with Indian, caught between American overlords and the Indian people, and themselves wishing to advance and profit. They are loyal and disloyal together. I have known men who worked for years for the revolution and then did the dirtiest grafts to line their pockets. I have known other men who served the capitalists for years till their souls revolted and they suddenly died for the revolution. Such is the instability of our intellectuals.

"But our peasants are true revolutionists; always forming revolutionary armies, yet always cheated. Twenty-three thousand villages need land and five thousand so far have received it. The biggest estates do not get divided; they are big enough to buy state governors. On these big estates they still flog peons and assassinate the peasant leaders. Yet nothing can be done against them because of the Colossus of the North."

No, Diego Rivera was not the destined leader. He saw the wrongs of capitalism and the beauty of the future world of workers as I had seen it in Seattle, but he did not see a path. He admired peasants who withdrew into smaller and smaller lands, yet maintained through art their independence of soul. Was that anything more than the old retreat of the independents before the triumphant march of the octopus? Was not his art a solace like that of religion, expressing dreams for which he saw no road of realization? Art could unite, art could arouse to struggle; but art could not discover a way.

I went to the American Embassy to the usual Wednesday tea given by Ambassador Sheffield. It was open to all Americans—that is, all Americans who were well dressed. They talked another kind of revolution at the American Embassy; I found them counting the days. Everyone thought Mr. Sheffield might be recalled at any moment, since "the president is not at all pleased with Mexico." The recall of the ambassador and withdrawal of recognition from Calles meant that oil men would be free to arm their private armies. That was what they meant by "revolution," the overthrow of the Mexican government by subsidized forces.

"Calles is a patriotic fanatic who is willing to make Mexico poor in order to make her independent," cried one of the oil men to me, assuming that this was clearly the ultimate insanity.

"Another revolution is needed," said a woman. "You people in the States don't realize that revolution is just the natural Mexican way of changing government. The revolutions are not really very bloody—not in Mexico City." Clearly peons in the country didn't matter and subsidized armies were the "natural Mexican way."

"Why do you leave Mexico just when the excitement is going to begin," said another to me. "A week later you might have to go north by airplane! Well, if you must go by rail, don't leave later than tomorrow night!"

The ambassador himself took no open part in these predictions, which so clearly hailed a government overthrow on territory of a friendly state. He withdrew discreetly to an inner room, emerging occasionally to hail some prominent capitalist, with whom he would withdraw again. One had little doubt that he was discussing more privately the subject which raged through his tea-party.

Due to a letter of introduction I received an invitation to an evening party at the home of one of the most prominent American oil men. Most of the guests were great Mexican landowners, some of whom had lost lands in recent land divisions to peasants, but many of whom still retained their full estates in spite of the law. As the party broke up, my host detained me for conversation. The evening had been a very gay one and he was feeling unusually frank. He wished me to know—he wasn't afraid of my knowing—how strong the American imperialists were.

"That telegram you sent a month ago from New York to your father, advising him to visit Madame Kollontai, was

known by me within fifteen minutes," he began challengingly,
"and by all the newspaper correspondents within thirty minutes. Ordinary private telegrams we don't bother with, but
this was sent to a member of a Goodwill Commission—we call
them the 'damned goodwillers,' enemies of America. It mentioned the name of Kollontai, another enemy of America. All
such telegrams are in our hands within half an hour after they
reach Mexico City, often before the recipient gets them. We
knew you were planning to come a month before you got here.
We knew when you would arrive and what connections you
had. We know all about anyone who comes here with connections with America's enemies." Among America's enemies he
mentioned Dr. Ernest Gruening of the *Nation*, Frank Tan-
nenbaum, Carleton Beals—anyone who had fought the naked
imperialism of oil.

"The worst stirrers-up of trouble in Mexico," he said, "are
these progressive groups in the United States. They don't
understand these people; they corrupt them with ideas of freedom, which only drive peons crazy. You can't make a strong
government out of these Mexicans; in hundreds of years they
couldn't evolve into people capable of governing themselves.
There is as much difference between two-legged animals as
between four-legged ones. You can train a dog to be almost
civilized, but you can't train a cat. Evolution sends off side-
lines like gorillas that will never evolve into men. These Mexicans are not in the direct line of evolution; they will never
evolve into civilization.

"The real difference between the United States and Mexico
is that the Spaniards were few in number, so they only enslaved
and intermarried with the Indians; we Americans killed them
off. That is why we have civilization while they have chaos.
. . . All these Central and South American countries can retain their liberty only as long as the United States gives it
to them and protects them in it. Otherwise, they collapse;
their peasants run right over them or the European countries
seize them. Those men here tonight, the big ranchers, have
enough intelligence to organize a government; but they haven't
the courage. They are afraid of their own peasants!

"But if it were possible to make Mexicans into a strong government, to do so would be the act of an enemy of the United States. We've an enormous border along the Rio Grande, more dangerous than the Franco-German border. It is impossible for two races with such different traditions to be friendly. Whoever makes Mexico orderly and strong dooms the United States to future war."

"Your own actions breed war and make all Latin America hate the United States," I said hotly. He laughed.

"Hate us, yes! But as long as they are weak and chaotic they can't hurt us. These damned goodwillers want to make them orderly and strong. A strong enemy instead of a weak one! That's treason to America!"

He told me that the "best solution all round" would be for the United States to annex the northern provinces of Mexico. "It will give us a land to develop several times the size of France, with very sparse population. I'm not for taking lands with a lot of population; you only degrade your race by mixture. . . . You will think I want those provinces as an oil man. Not at all; I can get better terms from Mexico on oil than any American law would give me; I could till Calles came and he won't last. I speak not as an oil man but as a patriotic American who wants to see his country grow in power, territory and prosperity. Anyone who doesn't want this is America's enemy."

Throughout this conversation his wife moved in and out of the room or sat beside her husband. Once she tried to moderate his words, less, it seemed, because of his indiscretion than because he seemed insolent to a guest. He brushed her aside; he was so strong that he didn't care who knew. "How do you think we know that Calles is slipping? We have gasoline stations in every corner of Mexico; they all send in reports. They are all writing to us now about uprisings against Calles. Little ones, local ones. When Washington withdraws recognition and arms come over the border, they won't be local. Washington is getting tired."

His frankness amazed me so that I wrote down his words before I slept that night; I have the copy still. I gasped to remember how lightly I had tripped through Wall Street, sending reports by ordinary mail to the Chief Concessions Committee. Over what abyss had I been walking? It was just as well that I had been a private person, unable to implicate the Russians. I remembered Borodin had said to me in Canton that orderly, strong government in an exploited country is not wanted by the exploiters, that they profit most from chaos in which they corrupt and loot. Clearly American oil men agreed with him. Small business men and professional men spoke as if "honest, orderly government is good for trade"; they bewailed the banditry and corruption that "hurt business." It did hurt their little businesses. But the big men, leaders of opposing forces, they knew.

The "damned goodwillers," however, proved more persistent than the business men at the American Embassy expected. They poured so many letters of protest on Washington from liberals who resented "intervening for oil men and corrupt priests" that the mail cars clogged the tracks and the posts were more than a day delayed. It was a truly spectacular achievement. So instead of breaking relations, Washington sent as ambassador Dwight Morrow of the House of Morgan, a much abler man than Sheffield. As long ago Leonard Ayres showed me how to preserve my "independence" while exhibits were monopolized, so the shrewd Morrow found formulæ which enabled Mexico to be "independent" while American capitalists took her oil and lands. The "damned goodwillers" ceased complaining; had they not gained their goal?

In Mexico were imperialists from the great Colossus of the North, so strong they thought it didn't matter what they said. In Mexico were revolutionary farmhands and peons, ready to die. Ready to die for Calles, for Rivera's paintings, for Morones, for any "friend" who offered hope. But Calles was a straw upoŋ the blast. And Rivera lived by emotion and analyzed no clear way. Mexico's revolutionary leaders led in a dozen directions. Her peasant-workers needed logic, discipline, a clear direction, expressed through a strong political organization around which the explosive will of the masses might coalesce. Then it might indeed come true as Carleton

Beals had said: "Mexico is the strongest revolutionary force on the two American continents."

Some day in the symphony of human nations, the Indian races of Latin America will have their part. Some day when all the world is "friend" to the peon, he will pour forth his hospitable gifts. The oil man sneered: "We have civilization; they have chaos. . . ." The peon evades capitalist civilization; but he holds high gifts for socialist civilization when it arrives. A people who live in the open air merrily, and make of life's simplest things an art. When man has conquered the earth he must learn to enjoy it. For the gray northern peoples, for his "friends" of many races, the peon has preserved through four centuries of oppression the gift of festival grace and joy!

CHAPTER XXI

RED HANKOW

ALMOST everyone I met in Shanghai advised me to go at once upriver to Hankow if I wished to see the real revolution. Von Salzman, hard-boiled German correspondent of the *Vossische Zeitung*, who had just returned from Hankow, grew lyrical over what he had seen. "Don't waste time on Nanking," he told me. "It does not live, no matter how many years it may drag out existence. It will be compromised by foreign money and the rich Chinese merchants of Shanghai. Hankow will live—if not the men at least the idea that is alive there. If crushed, it will live in history and return. What is that idea? Nothing so definite as communism. But it is that which is behind all revolution—the sudden hope of long-submerged masses."

T. V. Soong, finance minister of a Nationalist Government that had split into two warring camps between which he wavered, sat in an exquisite Chinese robe of dove-blue color in the former home of Sun Yat-sen in Shanghai, and told me: "Nanking is nothing but glittering words over the old inefficiency of China; Hankow is real!" Yet he himself had left Hankow to dicker with the new Nanking government; he could not make up his mind. Twice he had bought a ticket back to Hankow, then found excuses not to go. He told me to assure his sister, Mrs. Sun Yat-sen, who was in Hankow, that he would soon be coming back. But a few moments later when I left, his words slipped out unconsciously: "Good-by till we meet in Peking." He caught himself on that; in his eyes was a look of pain at his own indecision. He had known the power and glory of a great mass movement and it hurt to leave it. But it hurt still more to leave the financiers of Shanghai.

I had returned to China in May 1927 shortly after my trip to Mexico. I was a traveler now, roving to revolutions.

China was on the front pages of the world's news. So I paused in America only long enough to finish a lecture trip through Florida, write the last of seven booklets for the Haldeman-Julius Blue Book series and see editors in New York. Then I sailed from San Francisco for Shanghai where it became clear that my next destination must be Hankow. A semi-official British blockade prohibited travel of women on the Yangtze but I took a German sea-going freighter and passed it. In December I had been convalescing from pneumonia in the Crimea, in February visiting Mexico City, in May I was nearing the "red capital" in the industrial heart of China. So small is now our world.

The nationalist revolution which I had seen a year and a half earlier in Canton had driven northward in a spectacular advance till it reached the Yangtze River; half China was "nationalist." This rapid drive had been effected through the alliance of the Kuomintang, which represented China's upper and middle class patriots, with the communists who organized workers and peasants. The road for the armies had been opened by uprisings of peasants and workers in the name of "people's rule." Then the two contradictory elements which I had seen in the nationalist ranks in Canton—silk-clad merchants and blue-trousered hungry workers—split into two warring governments, one at Nanking near Shanghai and the other three days' journey up the Yangtze River in the Wuhan cities, chief of which was Hankow.

The immediate cause was the slaughter of Shanghai workers by General Chiang Kai-shek. The original plan of the northern expedition, approved by the Kuomintang executive committee since the days of Sun Yat-sen, put first the consolidation of inner China followed by a descent on the coast. They would thus avoid contact with the imperialists until a united China, freed from bandits and war-lords, was solidified behind them. The immediate plan was for the southern armies to drive towards a meeting with Feng's army of the northwest. Chiang Kai-shek, the victorious generalissimo, defied the orders of his party and government and chose his route towards the rich loot of Shanghai where he himself was blood brother to strong underworld gangsters. The revolutionary workers of Shanghai rose at his coming and seized the city for him; he took the power they gave and at once began closing their unions and killing their leaders. He set up his government in Nanking, based on the wealth of Shanghai merchants.

The majority of the central executive committee of the Kuomintang was still three days upriver from Shanghai, in Hankow, the original destination. They proclaimed the "rule of civil power—people's power—over generals," and appointed a new general-in-chief in place of the "deserting" Chiang. Chiang had money and soldiers, but Hankow at the time of my arrival still had the moral prestige of the patriotic movement. They were the "progressives" of China and contained in their ranks famous national revolutionists. They still kept the alliance with communists, through whom the support of peasants and workers had been organized. With them was also Russian adviser Borodin.

The usual rumors came drifting down the Yangtze; one learns to expect them in any struggle of oppressed masses against oppressors. There are always sexual tales designed to arouse powerful aversions. In this case it was alleged that Hankow women had celebrated their new freedom by a naked women's parade. Word also spread that the Hankow government forcibly provided girls over sixteen with husbands. A discredited missionary mimeographed and circulated these stories—also quite typical. The mildest of the tales, and the only ones with any foundation, were of seizures of property by trade unions and peasant organizations.

Copies of actual proclamations also came downriver and were circulated by some of the liberal elements in the Young Women's Christian Association. They breathed a spirit new in the wars of China. When had a victorious army thus placarded a city: "Though we were glad to get the city, we were unhappy to see the pitiful people. . . . The Revolutionary Army must get rid of the sufferings of the people. We and the people are one—in our sorrows, peace and danger, in getting rid of hindrances, in getting a full life, in getting free from imperialism and militarism."

In Hankow I was given residence in rooms above the Central Bank, next to Soong Ching-ling (Mrs. Sun Yat-sen), who was the gentlest and most exquisite creature I have known in any country of the world, yet a woman with the firmness of steel. Trained to the old exacting courtesies of Chinese life, her sensitiveness felt shock from rudenesses which were to me unnoticed, yet she held out against those two ultimate pressures of Chinese custom upon a woman—family influence and the slandering of reputation. Scandalous lies against her were being circulated by Nanking, to destroy her standing among the Chinese masses as Sun Yat-sen's widow, and these were brought to her by relatives who pled with her in the name of her dead husband to come to Shanghai. She held firm to Hankow, and its policy of coöperation with workers, peasants and communists. "The only man in the whole left-wing of the Kuomintang," said Borodin of her later.

Borodin, the Russian adviser, was ill most of the time with tropical fever acquired in Canton; during several critical periods he was confined to his bed, where he received committees and visitors. His importance to the Chinese Revolution lay in his analysis of economic forces, social groups and methods in the light of many past revolutions. The liberals in Shanghai had told me: "Borodin wants to plunge China into chaos, in the hope that communism may ensue." This was mere muddled thinking.

"China is already in chaos, torn by wars between scores of generals," said Borodin to me. "It is the wish of foreign imperialists that this chaos continue, since it gives them control and loot. But we ask ourselves: What social classes have courage, discipline and coherence to bring this country out of chaos, to create a modern independent nation with a stable government?" He found these needed qualities in the workers and peasants, whom the communists were organizing. The opportunity for this organization was given by the alliance with the Kuomintang, which contained the middle classes and intellectuals.

Hankow was infinitely in advance of the Calles' government which I had seen in Mexico; it had logic, some discipline, much power. Yet as oil men hung like a sword over Calles, so in Hankow foreign gunboats lined the waterfront, ready to fire if the revolution went too far. Business had gone downriver, draining the city of jobs and gold. The "workers' center" of China was a city of hungry unemployed, growing desperate for food.

It was not the hungry workers who blenched in the face of the gunboats. They swept in masses over the British concession in Hankow and took it back permanently for control by China. Their Central Bank printed paper money which the peasants in the revolutionary provinces accepted in payment for rice. Cynical German merchants told me how they profiteered on these transactions, buying the paper money cheap and using it at face value—"the only time the Chinese peasants ever took paper for rice" they said, sneering at the men whose sacrificing faith upheld their "people's government."

In a vast hall in Hankow met the fourth congress of the All-China Federation of Labor, 381 delegates of the far-flung masses, duly elected from fourteen of China's eighteen provinces and representing four million organized workers. They had crossed blockades to come to Hankow, that they might strengthen and solidify their country against the combined imperialists of the world. A vast sea of upturned faces, serious faces, smiling faces, faces aglow with youth and faces hardened with life's oppression—in them all was one element in common, a glowing, relentless determination.

Among them I met Yu, a seasoned organizer from Shanghai, who had consolidated many transport unions; Ma, a veteran printer from Canton, who was organizing an All-China Printers Union; and aged Tang, a Hunan miner, who still reckoned time in emperor-dynasties and expected the return of capitalists, but desired a strong union to get rid of sub-contracting foremen. Girls working in Shanghai textile mills had risked death to come upriver, and were utterly unconcerned about danger as they devised means of running the blockade back. The delegates represented all varieties of workers, from backward villagers who were human beasts of burden to advanced metal workers in the Wuhan arsenal. They talked so many different languages that interpreters were constantly needed in the congress; only the written language of China is unified; the spoken language varies from province to province. Most of the unions had been legally organized for less than a year; their forces had grown on the territory seized by the nationalist armies. They were the strongest and most widely representative people's force to be found anywhere in China.

The width and complexity of the revolutionary forces were shown by additional organizations which sent fraternal representatives—the All-China Student Federation, the All-China Peasants Federation, the Nationalist Government, the Kuomintang Party, the Communist Party, and eleven other organizations of national or provincial scope.

The Russian trade unions had sent several fraternal delegates, including metal workers, railway workers, educational workers. The Chinese seized upon them, asking eager, practical questions on the technique of government. "During your revolution what attitude did you take towards sabotage in government industries; did you encourage it, tolerate it or punish it?" . . . "During your revolution, when did the metal workers begin to get benefit, as soon as exploiters were overthrown or only after making long sacrifices to establish the revolution?" The Russians had the prestige of a successful revolution from which they offered knowledge. Meantime the Amsterdam Trade Union International, combining chiefly the trade unions of great imperialist countries, was denying the existence of Chinese trade unions.

Roy, of India, representative from the Communist International, struck the keynote of the meeting when he said: "In the past you have played an important part in the Nationalist revolution: you are now called to play a decisive rôle. The three former congresses of trade unions had tasks of organization and propaganda, but this congress leads the workers of China in the actual revolution. The outcome of the Chinese revolution decides the fate of world revolution in the present epoch of history." These were no idle words; the collapse which came in Hankow led to the present partition of China, and decided the direction of world events for at least a decade.

Sitting in this great congress, I did not feel them as alien, yellow-skinned Chinese; their faces, words and actions were those of fighting, organized workers anywhere in the world. But the city in which the congress met was still full of the old disorganization and feudal militarism of China. On the last day of the congress, some troops of the chief nationalist general seized the buildings of the All-China Federation of Labor and began looting the delegates' baggage. Word spread rapidly through the city that the army had begun to suppress workers in Hankow also, as everywhere else in China. A conference held in Borodin's office stiffened the spine of the "nationalist revolutionary government"; and its leader, Wang Ching-wei "persuaded" the general to withdraw his troops to "save the face" of the government. I met the tired president of the trade union congress, Sheu Chow-ging, as he directed the cleaning up of rubbish left in his headquarters by the looters. "We have it to work in today," he said. "Who knows what we shall have tomorrow?" That night the grand "get-together" of workers and soldiers was held as scheduled. The workers used to the end the breathing-space which Hankow gave them to "educate" the soldiers.

The organized peasants in the nearby provinces were firm and hard like the workers. Long before any Russians came to help them they had formed their own spontaneous organizations under a hundred names—Red Spears, Yellow Bellies— for protection against bandits and generals. Russian advisers, moving northward with the advance of the nationalist revolution, had told these desperate peasants how to make their force effective. "Keep out of your ranks all idlers, bandits, opium-smokers, landlords and money-lenders. (These elements had corrupted all previous peasant organizations.) When you have organized locally, send delegates from your village to meet with other villages. Build up wider and wider over province and country; thus you will have power to withstand bandits and control soldiers and establish 'people's rule.' "

Peasants had flocked to meetings to listen to such counsels and had joined the Peasants Unions by millions. They took action: "People's Food, People's Justice and People's Schools."

They seized rice supplies which the rich were shipping out of the hungry districts, and established food stations which sold at fixed prices to the poor. German missionaries whom I met in rural districts of Hunan told me what scrupulous accounts these peasants kept. They also told me of the "People's Justice," revolutionary tribunals where great meetings tried and condemned landlords who had financed bandits for protection and men who had grafted on famine funds. "People's Schools" arose swiftly by tens of thousands. Every village had its local teacher, who tutored the sons of the rich. The peasants ordered him to open a school for the poor; they commandeered rooms and told pupils to bring stools and writing materials. The art of reading and writing, so prized by all Chinese, was being rapidly mastered by sons of peasants.

Control of food for the hungry, execution of grafters, schools for the poor—these were the harsh simple demands of peasants striving to organize for themselves a decent life. They were accompanied by demands for new land laws, which varied in different places, but which limited rents, gave exemption from rents during famine and provided for uniform systems of land taxation "which shall not be collected in advance." The more advanced peasant unions began to demand control over the renting of land and even redivision of lands. But it was not communism for which they asked and for which they were ready to die; Von Salzman had been right. It was but the first step out of the slavery of the Middle Ages.

The armies of victorious revolution were composed of many incongruous elements. Starting with a disciplined core from the training schools of Canton, they rapidly absorbed workers and peasants in their northward march. The fire of hope which they lit in the suppressed rural districts called forth allies whose willing backs supplied them with transport, whose local knowledge gave into their hands besieged cities. But the armies also absorbed the military adventurers of that part of China who hastened to come over to the revolution when they saw its strength. These armed bands, offered as allies, must either be accepted or left behind to weaken the rear.

To weld these diverse elements into a disciplined and loyal

force a system of political commissars, suggested by the experience of the Red Army in Soviet Russia, was introduced. Instructors, most of whom were communists, rapidly gave lessons in reading, writing and politics to the new troops. This method was responsible for the zeal and discipline which carried the nationalist armies across half China, but as the size and contradictory elements of the armies increased with every victory, political instruction could not keep pace. Moreover, most of the officers in the nationalist armies were sons of merchants and local landlords. As the tension grew between the peasants and their oppressors, these officers began to turn against the revolution. The nationalist armies themselves began to split again into the old militarist groupings. They expelled or killed political commissars, seized provinces by military rule and suppressed peasant and worker organizations.

The civil power for all these warring elements sat in Hankow —the government of the left-wing Kuomintang. Two ministries in this government, labor and agriculture, were given to communists; the rest were held by Chinese intellectuals and small business men—famous as nationalist leaders since the days of Sun Yat-sen. Many of them had studied abroad; they were modern progressive China, aflame with patriotism for "people's rule," demanding freedom from foreign imperialists, and advocating varying degrees of government ownership to develop the country and insure prosperity to its citizens. I could understand them—from Seattle.

A few months earlier, stirred by the enthusiasm of the northern advance, these intellectuals had outdone the peasants and workers by the fierceness of their revolutionary speeches. Sun Foo, son of Sun Yat-sen by his first wife, a Rotary type of business man, had shouted, "Kill the gentry" to peasants who were much more reasonably demanding control of rice supplies and the execution of a few grafters and bandits. Hsu Chien, the elderly minister of justice, had made anarchist speeches of such heat that they worried the communists. Wang Ching-wei, president of the revolutionary government, was the most mellifluous speaker of all, with long-standing reputation as a patriot. He carried the greetings of revolutionary Wuhan to the All-China Congress of Trade Unions, assuring them of undying support from the government in their efforts to organize Chinese workers against exploitation.

At the time I arrived, however, these intellectual politicians had begun to waver. The difficulties which the peasants and workers faced so firmly appalled their less-hardened souls. When Hankow workers overran the British concession and gave it by sheer mass pressure to the Wuhan government, which at once thereby acquired prestige throughout China and the world, it took strong argument by Borodin to induce the timid government to accept the gift. They were cowed by awe of the great powers of earth; they wanted to give it back to the British.

They were cowed also by their own generals. If there was any one thing these progressives believed, it was that the civil power should control the army. They believed this naturally, for they were the civil power; they also believed it by education, for they had seen modern governments abroad. They denounced Chiang Kai-shek for insubordination to party and government, and told me constantly that Wuhan's chief glory was that it was the only government in China where the army was responsible to the "representatives of the people." Yet when their generals began killing peasants, they made no move to stop them.

Such was the "progressive government" of "red Hankow," for whom peasants and workers were dying. Yet the "face" which it presented to the world was so adequate that I said to Borodin: "But if the civil power stands firm, the military will have to yield, won't they?" Such were my American traditions; one had a strong government, and the army obeyed.

Borodin laughed: "Ever see a rabbit before an anaconda, trembling, knowing it will be devoured, yet fascinated? That's our civil power before their military." I thought his illness made him unduly gloomy. I could see that Wang Ching-wei was too polite to the generals and was having a hard time to keep order down in Hunan where unruly soldiers killed peasants. But I still saw Wang Ching-wei as a Chinese patriot and a good progressive, not so roughly vital as those workers

I met in the congress—but the kind of respectable man one has to have at the head of a government. Wasn't it all one government—"red Wuhan"?

Nor did I understand when Borodin introduced me at his bedside to the secretary of the Chinese Communist Party, saying: "Miss Strong is unlucky in her revolutions. She came too late for the Russian revolution and now she has come too soon for China." A clever epigram I thought it; certainly the Chinese revolution was only beginning, but wouldn't it naturally spread through the country? I had no conception of the deep divisions within the revolutionary government which were hastening its downfall. To me, the more elements a government had within it, the better; that made it more "representative"; even the many generals needed only to be tamed a bit by patriotic loyalty to the first real national government. I thought that generals submitted to ideas, not ideas to generals.

I went with Hankow officials to their famous meeting with Marshal Feng Yu-hsiang in Cheng-chow. In a special train, whose dining car was luxurious with iced soda-pop, canned asparagus, Cailler's chocolate and Sunkist oranges—the penetration of America through this Americanized left-wing officialdom—we advanced over a battle-ground strewn with the heroic dead of the "Iron Armies." In one of the first real battles ever carried on by Chinese troops, they had gone against the flower of Chang Tso-lin's regiments and beaten artillery by courage. Their valor had opened an outlet for Feng's northwest army, thus uniting two "People's Armies" which were now to sweep victoriously down upon Shanghai. Such had been the theory of the northern expedition.

Feng was a crafty ally, with an old reputation for betrayals. If the Hankow government expected Feng to help them take Shanghai, he wanted their help to take Peking. Which would dominate the other in the conference, Feng or General Tang from Hunan, who was now the chief of Hankow's armies since the defection of Chiang Kai-shek? Or would the civil power, the revolutionary government of Hankow, dominate both generals and hold them to its bidding? Would it show itself really a "people's power"?

Wang Ching-wei and the Hankow leaders had one strong card in their hand against generals—the might of organized peasants and workers who had given power into their hands and brought the army northward on its victorious march. Relying on that, they might perhaps have prevailed. But they came to Cheng-chow with apologies for the "unruly behavior" of their peasants. Feng saw they were of no importance to him either as friends or enemies. He gave them polite assurance of allegiance and canceled it a week later by similar polite assurance in a conference with Chiang Kai-shek. The forces of the nationalist revolution split forthwith into three separate territories. The blood of tens of thousands of workers and peasants who had carried the flag of the Kuomintang across half of China had bought for three new war lords the chance to bargain over spoils.

Yet under the polite illusion of success our train returned to Hankow. No American progressive, no German social-democrat, no MacDonald, is better at saving face than a Chinese statesman. I was puzzled by an odd atmosphere of indecision; but I was glad that all were united; and all had done their best. They bluffed themselves into merry chat, as their minds adjusted themselves to their new task: no longer the eloquent wording of the hopes of peasants and workers, but the voicing of whatever slogans of law and order might placate the rising generals of Hunan. All generals had been united on this, and the revolutionary civil power had apologized!

They bluffed also their workers as they drew into the Hankow station to a din of fire-crackers and cheers. Delegates greeted them from labor organizations of revolutionary women, students and turbaned Hindus of the Anti-Imperialist League representing many suppressed nations, welcoming back the emissaries whom they had sent to create a new China. The progressive officials of Wuhan raised their heads proudly and walked through the cheers like heroes. They had reasoned themselves into calling their compromise with Feng a victory. . . . A few days later Hankow workers called a general strike in protest at the "betrayal in Cheng-chow."

Not yet was the revolution over. Though the progressives of Wuhan had surrendered to the will of generals, who were now maneuvering for territory in a triangular fight, yet organized peasants on the territory of all these generals were fighting for "people's power." I traveled south into Hunan, whose general Tang would not permit the entrance of a single civilian official from the government he served. He was suppressing all peasants' organizations. Yet in every village peasants advanced with pikes and a few revolvers to meet armed troops, and drove them off again and again. Not easily did they surrender to generals their dream of People's Power, People's Food, People's Justice, People's Schools! When they were overwhelmed by superior equipment they withdrew to the hills, evading, reviving, unconquered. The one hard force today in China which holds out against foreign domination is not the government of Nanking, alternately tool of America and Japan, but the Soviet China which grew from those organized peasants, and which six campaigns by Chiang Kai-shek have been unable to overthrow.

These organized peasants of many provinces had long demanded arms. They had said to their "people's power" in Hankow: "Give us arms against bandits, arms to enforce government decisions, arms against excesses by these half-feudal soldiers who call themselves our own. Our strength is your strength; give arms to defend it!" They were pouring into the "Iron Armies" whose commanders had the most revolutionary reputation; thus friction increased among different armies of Wuhan. The timid politicians wavered, giving a few revolvers and then demanding them back.

When I returned from the open white terror of Hunan to the so-called revolutionary Wuhan of which Hunan was still a "province," I found that Borodin and all the Russians with him were preparing to leave for Moscow. What had happened? The leaders of the Kuomintang bade him a diplomatic farewell at the station; they hung about as if loath to let him go. There was real regret in some of the faces; they said: "When you come back." Was it only that saving of face common to Chinese and to statesmen? Or did they feel their

own power passing, which they had not courage to hold? Like
T. V. Soong who told me "Hankow is real," yet could not go
to Hankow, they also had known the strength and glory of a
great mass movement. It made them leaders until they turned
away to waver from one general to another. After a time they
also slipped downriver to the greater General Chiang, backed
by the riches of Shanghai.

I got permission from Borodin to go with the Russians by
auto across the northwest provinces of China, to Mongolia and
the Trans-Siberian Railway. When Borodin met Feng Yu-
hsiang the latter asked him: "What is the real difference between Wuhan and General Chiang?"

"None," said Borodin, "none. There *was* a difference, but
there is none any longer."

"Then why are they still fighting?" asked Feng.

"Rich Chow," said Borodin wearily. "Rich Chow," alluding
to the loot of Shanghai.

Only years afterward, from books of Chinese memoirs, did I
learn details of what had happened in Hankow. Roy, representative of the Communist International, told Wang Ching-
wei the communists had instructions to arm the workers and
peasants in defense of "people's power." Some hold that Roy
did this as a Hindu nationalist, complaining to a fellow Asiatic
against Moscow; others that he went as to a too lukewarm ally
who must be made to welcome the arming of his worker-peasant
followers. Was not Wang Ching-wei a revolutionist opposed
to imperialists? Did he not cheer the workers in all their
fights against oppressors? Would not this sharp demand from
their communist allies stiffen the whole left-wing of the Kuomintang, and make them accept, even if reluctantly, the arming of the men whose loyal courage gave them rule and who
were being slain by soldiers?

When their wavering souls were held to this harsh decision,
Wang Ching-wei and the Chinese progressives who had cheered
so loudly for revolution, who had shouted "Kill the gentry,"
and made speeches more radical than the communists, knew
suddenly that no humiliation or defeat at the hands of soldiers
was so horrible to them as the arming of their own followers!

Better to make peace with feudal-minded warlords of central China. Or with Chiang Kai-shek and the Shanghai financiers. Or even with the foreign imperialists. Did not Mrs. Wang Ching-wei have her fortune in Sumatra rubber? There was something to be said for foreign powers. If reconciliation with Nanking proved difficult, after all one could live in Paris, but not with rough, armed masses whom one had called "comrades." That was to Wang Ching-wei the ultimate horror!

In a camp in a Shensi orchard by moonlight, sitting on a rough camp-stool, Borodin gave to the vice-governor of Shensi, fleeing south from Feng's suppressions, the first complete exposition of the forces involved in China's revolution that I had heard him give. He had been too ill for discussions in Hankow, nor had there been much time.

"There were three forces in China: the big bourgeoisie and landlords, the small bourgeoisie, and the workers and peasants. The bourgeoisie, landlords and their Kuomintang will never unify China, for they are not really against imperialists; they are allied with them and profit by them. The small bourgeoisie whom Wang Ching-wei represented cannot unify China because they vacillate between the masses and the big bourgeoisie and in the final pressure go over to the latter. Only the workers and peasants can unify China.

"When the nationalists relied on the masses, who took the concessions from foreigners along the Yangtze, the nationalists were 'top-dogs.' While the Chinese bourgeoisie suppresses the Chinese masses, imperialist exploitation will now grow worse. But do not be discouraged. The Chinese revolution is not dead."

Through the moonlit orchard the Shensi comrade turned southward towards no-longer-red Hankow where the Chinese progressives were slipping one by one downriver to make peace with Chiang Kai-shek or flee abroad. Far beyond the Yangtze, a section of the "Iron Armies," led by communists, had begun the famous march to Swatow. Peasants were reassembling shattered forces in Kiangsi and the Hunan hills. Workers in south China were reorganizing for new struggle—the Canton Commune.

But I, the American progressive who had fled from conflict in Seattle and who still got my money from capitalists yet expected Russian workers to trust me, could I even trust myself? Had I ever praised the revolution with more eloquent sincerity than Wang Ching-wei?

CHAPTER XXII

READY FOR NEW WARS

OUT of tumultuous towns of medieval China, whose walls withstood whole centuries of sieges, over the bandit-ridden hills of Shensi, where naked children begged for food, across the desolation of Mongolia—blue-green sagebrush, yellow sands, red cliffs, wide plains of black gravel—we came by deserts of death to new beginnings of human life. Nomad Mongol herdsmen fought the wilderness for pasture; idle Buddhist monks in rags or dirty finery preyed upon the herdsmen; and holy Urga had renamed itself Ulan-Bator, City of Red Giants, for the "reds" were fighting the gods. The radio, telegraph, airplane met us, first signs that this Middle Ages was bordered on the north by civilization. At thirty-mile intervals and then more frequently appeared farms where milk, butter and eggs were at last available. We crossed the borders of Russia and found, with strange shock, soup-plates, forks and newspapers.

Two hotels, a bank and several stores at Verkhne-Udinsk— "meet our party secretary, a woman, a Buriat-Mongol"— hardly prepared us for the hammer-blow of Irkutsk. Twenty newspapers were on sale at the jostling railway station, including four German papers and l'Humanité from France. Across the street from the station a neat little food store announced itself as Number 85 of the United Workers Coöperatives of Irkutsk. Not since the previous April when I left the chain-store groceries of America had I seen such clean shelves with so many spruce little cans. In the nine months of my absence from the Soviet Union, rapid consolidation and strengthening of coöperatives had taken place.

Station by station Siberians entered my compartment. A representative of the "Hunters Association" told of northern huntsmen selling pelts to the State Fur Trust. A lumberman had been procuring lumber from the great forests for the building of a new railroad between Siberia and Turkestan. Organizers of the transport workers union had assisted in a conference whereby the seasonal lay-off of four hundred workers was apportioned to protect the men who most needed jobs. No luxury was seen on the train—and no rags. It was a train of workers building railroads and factories, talking about butter and fur. It might have been a train of the American Pioneer West but with this difference, that no man bragged of the personal fortune he would make. They bragged as loudly about the growth of the country. "You see this crossroads with a little railway station. In five years it will be a big town! That's Siberia!"

Twenty women delegates got on the train at Novo-Sibirsk, bound for a Women's Congress in Moscow which had been called to advise the government. Some of them had never been on a train before; only one had ever traveled out of Siberia. But all were presidents of villages, selected from hundreds of such presidents by superior reputation for energy. "They picked me," said one of the women, "because I know how to tell very strong how rotten things are in our village."

They told of fishermen who traveled thousands of miles every summer down great rivers to the Kara Sea. They discussed the need for more schools, hospitals, coöperatives. They laughed grimly as they told how they had to fight dark peasant men to win their place in government. "They laughed at the first women who got into the soviets, but it's we who are laughing now. It's a new world we women have come into, since the October Revolution." . . . I remembered the shrinking bound-foot women of Shensi, and the girls of south China, dying at the hands of soldiers. Between them and these confident women governing a state there seemed to lie not merely the width of half a continent, but of whole epochs. Yet there was between them only ten years of the revolution.

Leader of the group was Anusia Ustinovna, red-kerchiefed, middle-aged but vital, a member of the All-Union Central Executive Committee—equivalent to senator in America. "You are of course a communist," I said.

"No," she replied without the slightest touch of apology. "I am a representative of the great non-party masses whom Lenin said must be drawn into the tasks of governing." . . . A few years back it had seemed to be only scattered communists who fought so hard to reconstruct their country out of vast chaos of ignorance and darkness. A great host of those who had been most dark and ignorant were fighting now.

"Yes," said a Moscow communist to whom I mentioned my impressions, "we in the center can hardly realize how great is the energy of the masses released by the revolution, how much they can overcome and how valiantly, now that at last they are free." I responded to the first part of his sentence but his last word left me cold. "Free?" Why revive sentimental illusion? Was there anywhere any such thing as freedom? There might be a little left in America, before the old free West was quite divided among the bosses. There might be a half-free choice between masters. But freedom—why prate of it, especially under confessed dictatorship? Were any of us more than whirling foam on a stormy ocean, determined by its winds and tides? Didn't all of us, in spite of high emotions and fine feelings, do in the end what dark unexpected laws of our being demanded? Like—yes, like Wang Ching-wei!

I saw, however, that the country was growing strong and much better organized, full of great confident masses of people valiant to create. They were ready—neither they nor I yet knew for what—ready for another struggle. In the womb of the communist party, fertilized by the vigor of the masses, was growing what should soon be born as the Five-Year Plan.

I had still no room in Moscow; with difficulty I secured a hotel room costing more than four dollars a day. I couldn't keep this up; I must prepare to move on. But the State Publishing House learned that I had material on China; they ordered two books and made advance payments. Soviet newspapers also ordered articles at good prices. I ceased to worry about the cost of hotel rooms. The Soviet Union was growing rich and its masses were spending their first surplus on reading. I had news which they wanted. I no longer needed New York.

Yet I went to New York as soon as my books were finished,* placing a German edition of the books as I passed through Berlin. I lectured again across America and returned again to Moscow. I would travel now in Soviet Russia. There were no very hopeful revolutions in China, Mexico or Germany; the hopeful revolution was in the dark recesses of this sixth of the world's surface, where peasants and workers of more than a hundred tongues and nations were overthrowing the Middle Ages.

I went first to the Volga to see what was left of the John Reed children. Three of them were studying in an art school, ten of our old tractor-drivers were taking machine-shop training; others had jobs in the expanding cement factory in Volsk. One of the girls, Shubina, had had a "red wedding": standing before the teachers and pupils the pair pledged joint lives to the building of socialism. But our valiant Morosov was sick with tuberculosis in a small Volga town. He had a wife and child and they were hungry; his wage in a small coöperative store was not enough. Twenty of our girls still remained disconsolately in a children's home in Saratov; they were long over-age but Saratov had no jobs to give them and the educational authorities hesitated to throw them out.

The Volga was not recovering fast enough. It had repaired the ravages of war, intervention and famine and had reached prewar standards of living; but could tsarist standards suffice for Soviet youth? Everywhere were discontented rumbles. Tens of thousands of unemployed were demanding of the revolution: "Is this all? Are we new dictators in a land of the proletariat? Give us our dictator's right to create!" It was a dull, throbbing pain felt along the Volga, first signal of the coming birth.

From the Volga I took a horseback trip over the ridge of the Caucasus. Soviet tourist organizations, like everything else, were expanding under pressure of new life. Tens of thousands of workers, students, office employees were seeing the country too. Wolstein, head of a new proletarian tourist or-

* The two books were issued in America as one—*China's Millions* (Coward-McCann).

ganization, planned a path-finding trip through Daghestan
and invited me to go. Thus I saw the backward hill villages
of Chechnia, whose women ground grain in a mortar and chat-
tered over the magically efficient properties of a safety-pin
which I showed them. Marriage by capture still took place
among them, and town-bred Russian damsels, venturing near
Chechnia, thrilled to think of its dangers, which were quite
imaginary, as the "capture" was prearranged to avoid the
cost of bride-purchase.

We journey on through Daghestan with its old Arabic culture in more than a dozen tongues. The mountaineers proudly
showed us the fortress-like hamlet where "our Shameel made
the last stand against the Russian conquerors." Visiting Russian workers saw dead Shameel as one of their own heroes; had
not he also, this dark-skinned mountaineer of the Caucasus,
fought their own enemy, the old Russian imperialism? Such
was the ground for the new comradeship of Soviet nations; all
had overthrown the same oppressors.

Tribal feuds in the hill villages dated back to the Arab
conquest or the wars of the Crusades. Village festivals of Mohammedan hillmen hurled stones and imprecations across deep
valleys towards Jewish hillmen who had "backslid" centuries
before. Young communist students came back from newly-
opened colleges to bring roads, canneries and small industries
to these hills, and bitterly debated whether to take part in
these tribal festivals "which embody the lowest superstition
and even religious hatred." Could youth take up cudgels
against the united opinion of centuries? At any rate, the
roads and canneries and schools were growing, paid for by the
wealth of great hillside orchards.

In Tiflis, I spent seven hours seeking a hotel room and secured at last a cot in a room with five women physicians. The
city was jammed with nine hundred medical workers attending
an Anti-Tuberculosis Congress. I saw my hard-won cot refused in a single hour to a line of forty applicants. "Everyone in the Soviet Union is traveling and all of them come to
Tiflis," cursed the distracted hotel clerk. I saw spacious new
workers' clubs and great parks full of joyous youth strolling

late into the evening; I met a delegation of foreign workers, Americans and others, who were heavily loaded with speaking engagements before the Tiflis clubs. But the hotel clerk had warned me that my cot was for one night only, so I left town for Armenia.

Here again were filthy villages, ruined by national wars and intervention, but over them new life already sturdy and green. A power plant and a dozen industries were starting in Erivan, a dozen more small industries in Leninakan. Many nationalities participated; Jews, Turks, Russians held office under Armenians as in Tiflis Turks, Russians and Armenians held office under Georgians. There was not the friction one would expect after centuries of religious wars which had so recently culminated in six years of race massacres. The age-long hates of the Caucasus were dying under the policy of free cultural development combined with economic expansion, while in Europe old hates were reviving, growing towards new war. The Soviet Union had its new war also: war with backwardness, with bureaucracy, the war to organize and build!

Swinging back towards Moscow along the Georgian Military Highway, I was seized with sudden hunger for high peaks. In the early part of my trip every evening had found me utterly exhausted; it was the first horseback trip I ever took. The month had hardened me; my new fitness looked at Mt. Kazbek. "I must climb it," I cried. But I was quite without mountain gear; I had not even bloomers.

I found a guide and borrowed from him an old torn pair of pants which left great gaps when I donned them. I had neither smoked glasses nor grease-paint against sunburn but he gave me a dark veil. For foot-gear he bound straw to my feet with a net of knotted thongs. The knots kept me from slipping on the ice, the straw gave padding, and the netted form allowed glacier water and the drying wind to pass with equal freedom through these "shoes." When the straw wore thin and the sharp ice cut my feet, he gave more straw or added mountain heather. For the steepest slopes he had ice-creepers with stronger thongs that cut through the straw to grip my ankles. He carried a heavy sheepskin to warm my nights.

Thus equipped I went with the guide to the 16,000 feet elevation of Kazbek saddle where we fought two hours with a blizzard, and at last turned down when even ice-creepers would not hold against the blast. We spent the night at 13,000 feet elevation, sheltered by rock and partly buried in snow. Shaking all night with cold, exhaustion and elevation I thrilled with a fiery exaltation. Who said that typhus and pneumonia had finished my strength, that never again would I conquer the mountain peaks of my youth? Without any good American equipment, with just the patched-up resources of a backward village, I had climbed 1500 feet higher than the highest mountain in America, 1500 feet higher than old Rainier! It hadn't finished me either; from Kazbek saddle I had swung lightly down great glaciers almost as well as the seasoned guide. I had renewed my strength like the great land around me. I also was ready for new wars!

.   .   .   .

Two months later found me in Soviet Central Asia where local elections complicated by land confiscations were going on. In Tashkent a conference of communist women was announcing: "Our members in the backward villages are being violated, tortured and murdered. But this year we must finish with the hideous veils for women. This must be the historic year!"

Samarkand, the new capital, was overrun with congresses. I sat up one night in a hotel corridor and thereafter was guest in the house of the president of Uzbekistan, Akhun Babaieff. All the Uzbek peasants who arrived in Samarkand after midnight seemed to walk to his six-room mansion and spend the rest of the night on his rugs. As a foreign guest I was favored with a divan in the office of his secretary, who spoke Russian.

Beneath the magic of age-old beauty, bright with blue-gold November weather, Samarkand throbbed with a hotly modern struggle. Fiercely gesticulating placards stared at me in the chief restaurant, pointing accusing finger and saying, "You, you, YOU are not yet a member of the coöperative!" In the congress of peasant coöperatives a farm laborer was asserting, with a violence which would have fitted Genghiz Khan descending from his charger: "What do we see in our village? The rich peasants get the new machines and we poor ones don't!"

The class struggle was not over, as I had so naïvely supposed when I first came to Soviet Russia. It was as fierce as in rural districts of China, and its problems were much the same. Respectable landholders, entrenched by old religion and new trickeries, throve on usury, rent and exploited labor. Farmhands and poor peasants organized against them, fighting the oppressions of ages. Gangsters allied with landlords terrorized peasants. Veiled women fought for freedom, against religion, against landlords, against their own suppressed husbands who in turn suppressed them. The struggle was as complex and difficult and the ignorance and darkness even greater than they had been in China.

In one thing only had the peasants and farmhands of Soviet Central Asia the advantage—they had state power in their hands—the state power of which the progressives of Wuhan had robbed the Chinese peasants. Yet the holding of state power had not ended the battle. The grasp of the exploiter was strong in rural districts far from the railroad. Young communists penetrated into backward villages, agitating, teaching, telling farmhands their rights. The martyrs among them mounted into the thousands. A girl from a Tashkent school volunteered to agitate during vacation; her body, cut in small pieces, was returned to the school in a cart. A woman refused the attentions of a local landowner and married a communist farmhand; a gang of eighteen men, stirred up by the landlord, violated her in the eighth month of pregnancy and threw her body in the river. Nine murders of women occurred in one locality before any were known to the provincial authorities.

These outrages stirred the oppressed peasants and women to greater action. They fought their way into life. They made heroes of their martyrs; new fighters sprang to combat. When Zulfia Khan, a fighter for women's freedom, was burned alive by the mullahs (Mohammedan priests), the women of her village wrote a lament for her:

O Woman, the world will not forget your fight for freedom!
Your flame—let them not think that in it you were consumed!
The flame in which you burned is a torch in our hands!

How could such outrages continue in the eleventh year of the
revolution? Why didn't the government put them down? But
what was the government? It was the local farmhand and peasant in so far as he had courage to organize and use his power.
The division of landlords' estates among poor peasants and
farmhands had been law for eleven years in the Soviet Union.
It was not yet enforced in Central Asia. Did the local peasants want to take their rights?

The test came in the hearings of Land Commissions, held in
connection with the elections, which informed all peasants of the
law. Landlords whose names and possessions had been listed,
came one by one to deny their holdings. Was the list accurate?
Certainly not. Not since history's dawn had there been a land
survey; no central government ever dared probe these owner-
ships. Village ethic and fear had always resented outsiders
and protected "their own." Thus does every village in Asia.

But whom did the peasants regard as "their own" now?
How far had the local class struggle proceeded? They sat in
the hall, both poor and well-to-do, knowing the truth of local
property. Would a landless one arise and fling in the teeth of
his landlord to whom he owed money: "You lie! You have so
much land! I know, for I farm it. I have paid you rent." If
he dared, he might get land from the state whose law offered
it. He might also get a knife in the back from his landlord.
These village gentry were no Russian nobles skulking behind
foreign armies; they were men who did their own assassinating.
Nor could any government "protect" the farmhand, except as
he organized government, protecting himself.

Akhun Babaieff, on whose secretary's sofa I was passing my
nights, was a former farmhand whose courage, directness and
wisdom had brought him to the post of president. He went on
frequent tours in the villages, where children hailed him as
"Grandpa Akhun" and old men wept with joy to see a man
like themselves grown ruler. He nodded with satisfaction when
I asked how the land reform was going.

"It is going very well," he said. "I am much pleased to see how well the farmhands are organized and what a big part they take in uncovering landlords that are not on any lists of the government." The participation of farmhands in government was to Akhun Babaieff the most important thing in the whole land confiscation; it was the indication of new power.

Akhun Babaieff gave me a glimpse into the new ethics, during a Cotton Day celebration to which I went. A woman begged him for amnesty for her son who had been arrested. He said to me later: "I must look up the boy. If he has not oppressed the poor or been grafting, he can no doubt be amnestied." It was to me a sudden revelation of new standards in crime. Not theft or murder were chief crimes, these might result from need or passion. Men committing such crimes might still become useful citizens. But he who exploited the poor or corrupted their access to government was hopelessly rotten as a social being. He couldn't be used in the new society. . . . Akhun Babaieff was an Asiatic farmhand, but he knew the ethics of that new society better than I knew it, with my doctor's degree in philosophy!

By no means all the Asiatic farmhands knew it. Shocking instances occurred of local excesses, when new power went to their heads, inducing them to arbitrary rule or graft. Sha Muratoff, a farmhand whose energy made him "alternate" delegate in the All-Union Central Executive Committee, began killing his personal enemies. He proudly told the local peasants: "As member of TSIK I have the right to kill ten men at my choice—ten men, no more." A prosecutor thought otherwise and Sha Muratoff was sent away for eight years to be cured of his megalomania. Another official, a communist, in a mountain village, not only sold his daughter in marriage—this was still a very common offense—but profiteered on his party standing as chief local communist to set the girl's price unduly high! His excess greed brought him to the attention of higher authorities, and his "party standing" ceased.

To bridge the terrible gap between the background of Central Asiatic villages and the standards of the new world, state power gave many tools. Radio lectures spread information

about new laws, and also brought "time" to distant villages
which had never seen a clock. Spectacular trials of offenders
educated the masses into the strange belief that a husband
had no right to kill his wife for unveiling. Schools set up all
over the country were feverishly giving education to selected
youth: boys who had fought in the Red army, girls who had
risked life for women's rights. The new workers' power had
for them a great and shining meaning, however little they understood its theories. From dangerous battle-fronts of far
villages, they came to school, and bent their heads over books,
pencils and paper, trying to understand the cause for which
they had been ready to die. Girls who had sat unmoving in
harems learned the strange movements of physical culture;
youth that had never heard of a single law of natural science,
who did not know even the concept of science, fought through
the textbooks of Darwin and Marx, fitting themselves to rule.

The Soviet Union's policy for the rapid advance of minor
nationalities through industrialization gave to farmhands and
peasants a powerful weapon in their struggle for new life.
Capitalists never willingly industrialize a subject people. Imperialist nations suck the raw materials of colonies and de-
pendencies to enrich industries at home. Ireland and India
must fight to industrialize themselves against British opposition. American capitalists own oil wells in Mexico but do not
create industries. But the Soviet Union's principle is to
"equalize the backward regions with the center" that every part
of her vast land may have a ruling proletariat and the wealth
which great industries create.

I visited a new silk mill in Old Bokhara. Its director was
a type I had learned to know, pale, exhausted, driving himself without sleep to create a new industry. He told me the
silk mill was not at all profitable and would not be for a long
time. "We are training village women and making them into
a new staff for the future silk mills of Turkestan," he said.
"Our mill is the consciously applied force which first broke
the veiling of women in Bokhara; we demand that women un-
veil in the mill."

There was far more building going on in Samarkand in proportion to population than there was in Moscow. New cotton gins and great textile mills were arising in Old Fergana valley, new irrigation works and enormous new cotton farms in various parts of Central Asia. Girl textile workers wrote collective songs on the new meaning of their lives.

> When I took the road to the factory
> I found there a new kerchief,
> A red kerchief,
> A silk kerchief
> Bought with my own hand's labor!
> The roar of the factory is in me,
> It gives me rhythm
> It gives me energy! . . .

. . . .

The world outside the Soviet Union first heard of the Five-Year Plan as a wildly extravagant scheme of Moscow. We who traveled the distant parts of the Soviet country saw it take form in villages, factories, cities, provinces. We saw it arise from the need of farmhands to become industrial workers, from the need of unemployed youth to create, from the vast unexplored, unexploited resources of prairies and mountains in the hands of worker-owners eager to use their wealth. We saw it strengthen with the growth of food in the rural districts, and sharpen with the fight between kulaks and farmhands for this food. We saw the country grow strong and rested in a few years' breathing space of reviving farms and factories, yet tens of millions of people were still unslaked in their thirst for life. Then we saw their passion hammered by the brains of the communist party into a mighty plan to industrialize the Soviet Union and make it independent of the great capitalist powers.

Not by accident was it in Soviet Central Asia that I first heard of the Five-Year Plan. The Tashkent newspaper ran a headline across seven columns: "You Won't Know Central Asia in Five Years." There followed a map with plans for new construction, new railroads, new factories and the dates on which it was proposed to begin and complete them. It was the combined project of all the organizations in Central Asia,

which Moscow, the "Center," had yet to approve and corre-
late with similar plans from every part of the Soviet Union.

Twice again in successive years I visited Soviet Central Asia.
The year after my Samarkand trip I rode to the "Roof of the
World" on the Pamirs, a high, wild region inhabited by Kirghiz
tribes. I visited the "traveling government" of the high pastures, a temporary summer administration in its first year. In
a felt tent on worn rugs squatted a native judge; the clerk of
the court lying on the ground beside him was turning over
pages of records. They were carrying the laws against exploitation of farmhands and selling of women to the farthest
wandering hordes.

Several days beyond the end of the railway on the hard-
packed camel trail I stopped to chat with an old Uzbek road-
mender who knew three words of Russian: "Five-Year Plan,"
"road" and "automobile"—the latter so weirdly pronounced
that only his vivid gestures made me get it. With these three
words and many proud motions he informed me that the camel
track would become a road for automobiles as far as Irkestan
on the frontier, then ten days by horse. The Five-Year Plan
would do it!

A year later still, I went on May Day, 1930, to the opening
of the Turkestan-Siberian Railway, of which I had heard three
years before from the man who was purchasing its lumber.
My old friend Bill Shatoff, veteran of a hundred free-speech
fights in America, veteran also of the Russian civil war, was its
director and builder. He had driven a thousand miles of railroad line north and south across plains and deserts of Asia,
to connect Siberian wheat with Turkestan cotton and thus develop both regions.

"First of the Giants of the Five-Year Plan to Open"—thus
the new railway celebrated itself on banners and in the press.
In all the land from Leningrad to Vladivostok, from the Arctic
oceans to the semi-tropic valleys of the Caucasus and Pamirs,
arose already a mighty hum of building. The farms of one-
sixth of earth had been shaken the previous winter by the
earthquake of mass collectivization,* and were now in chaos

* See next chapter.

and conflict driving through the "first Bolshevik sowing." Day by day we advanced over a great expanse of this country, till cities and farms fell back and we emerged on rolling prairies dotted with camels and sheep and felted tents of nomads, and deserts where all life died out.

Our train ran by no schedule. There was no schedule yet created; we were the first train. On new-laid rails our locomotive swayed drunkenly, a festival locomotive painted green. It was a present from the railway-repair shops at Aulie-Ata, repaired by volunteer workers in spare time without wages—their present to a great celebration. It flamed with banners and inscriptions. A shining steel star replaced the headlight, and over the star the words: "Daesh Sibir"—"Give us Siberia"—a battle-slang from the civil war. An engine crew selected from the volunteer repair gang had the honor of riding night and day on their engine. This was their new war, their victory— the opening of Turk-Sib!

"Nothing I ever did in all my life will hurt capitalism as much as this Turk-Sib railway," said Shatoff to me. Not the old, valiant free-speech fights, not the battles of civil war, not the organization of metal import and oil export. This railway united wheat and cotton, industrialized the farms of Central Asia and the nomad tribes of the great prairies, sent Soviet trade beyond her borders to Asia's backward peoples, and bound the far southeast frontier of the Soviet Union with a thin steel line of defense.

The workers on our special train knew it; they were delegates from half a hundred factories, chosen "champions" rewarded for good work by a trip to Turk-Sib. The foreign journalists on the train also knew it; thirty of them came from America, Germany, England, Italy. They knew this railway changed the history of Asia, joining two streams of life that had moved separately for ages: the life which flows along the forest rivers of the north and the caravan life across the plains of the south. They knew it fixed the grip of the Soviet power in the heart of Asia. They noted this and sent it in cables, cursing because for a thousand miles no telegraph operators could be found who even knew the Latin alphabet!

Along the line new towns were springing up already, rough settlements of pioneer men and dauntless women. Young Pioneers bore banners to greet the train. They had built this railroad in record time, a year and a half earlier than the first calculation and half a year sooner than Shatoff's revised estimates. Shatoff spoke to them at meetings in all the stations, recalling tersely the details of their heroic struggle: hunger and thirst in the desert, blinding sandstorms in summer and blizzards in winter through which they worked, though bureaucrats from the "Center" failed to send warm clothes. He noted babies held in the arms of mothers—yet "older than this town." He spoke of the new world their labor was creating, a better world for workers of all nations. I heard a gaunt woman mutter with a smile on her lips and tears in her eyes: "Swell guy, our boss!" Two years on these deserts had burned away all her youth, but given her unconquerable life!

Under hot sun at Aina-Bulak a Russian-Kazak festival went on. Encampments of nomad Kazaks had traveled hundreds of miles to view the arrival of the great "Iron Horse." They raced the train as it approached the new junction where the north and south lines should be joined. Young men danced on the rails and sang new songs about the "black steed, swifter than a hundred horses," which should bring them victory over tribal chieftains.

Under the eyes of ten thousand people who had journeyed to this empty wilderness, the north and south rail-laying crews put the last steel in place. The last spike was driven by Risku-loff, vice-president of the Russian Soviet Republic, Isaieff, president of Kazakstan, Shatoff, and seventy-year-old Kata-yama, leader of Japanese Communists and delegate from the Communist International for this occasion.

Katayama? Why Katayama? The meaning of his blow on the joining spike was clear. This railway was not only a link between wheat and cotton. It was not only the opening of new lands to pioneers. It was not only the weapon of young herdsmen against tribal oppressors. This railway was world revolution marching down through Asia!

The workers along the line, who felt the great importance

of their achievement, asked eagerly of our train who had come to open it. Not Stalin? Not Kalinin? No? Then they resigned themselves to the lesser dignitaries, and to their own great celebration, knowing that from Moscow and return it was still a two weeks' journey, and that all across the land were equal enterprises yet unfinished. Far to the west the world's greatest power dam was rushing to completion on the Dnieper. Far to the north the new steel town of Kuznetsk was struggling into life. At Stalingrad the largest tractor plant in the world was almost ready to open; in Sverdlovsk the world's largest plant for heavy machine-building was being built.

"First of the Giants to Open"—the Turk-Sib claimed the honor. But only one of several score such giants in the thundering Five-Year Plan!

CHAPTER XXIII

THE FIRST BOLSHEVIK SPRING

In a single year, with a single harvest, the Soviet Union leaped into place as a great power in the world. In 1929 still widely regarded as a backward inefficient land trying a visionary experiment, she became with the harvest of 1930 a factor to be feared in world markets. The legend of her incredible chaos changed to the legend of her incredible power to conquer the world.

A revolution in farming lay behind this amazing change. From autumn of 1929 to harvest of 1930 one-sixth of earth's surface was shaken as by an earthquake. I had heard the low rumble of discontented farmhands along the Volga; I had seen the harsh and bloody struggle whereby the once suppressed peoples of Soviet Central Asia established their new rights. Now I saw these merged in an infinitely vaster conflict: the whirlwind of farm collectivization.

In autumn of 1929 I went again to the Volga. With me on the train, bound for Saratov, were a score of young men of the "Grain Center" who were assigned to tour the rural districts taking orders for tractors for which they received advance payments in grain. "All the peasants are joining collective farms," they told me, "and they all want new machines."

Three years earlier I had known a few scattered communes like our John Reed Colony, most of which sickened and died. Some survived, the strongest, to be a light to the peasants. I had also noticed scattered "artels" in the villages—a dozen or more peasants putting their lands, horses and implements together for greater strength in farming. Both these forms of joint farming had been favored by government credits. They had received the first machines; they had expanded. But none of this prepared me for the whirlwind I now saw in the rural districts.

The president of the Collective Farms Union of Atkarsk County—there had not even been the name of such an organization before—waved in my face a pile of telegrams, saying: "On November 20th our county was fifty percent collectivized; on December 1st it was sixty-five percent. Today, December 5th, telegrams still come in. By December 10th, no doubt it will be eighty percent."

Great enthusiasms and great apprehensions shook the country. In Balanda township a thousand horses took the field together, and plowed in a long advancing column. An aged peasant rushed up to a press photographer. "Photograph me too with these horses. Now I can die! I never thought to see such a day." One day a village decided to form one united farm; a week later it combined with five villages; the following day, with thirteen.

A year earlier they had talked of collective farms doubtingly and shrewdly, weighing the gain in sown area and harvest yield per acre, and discussing the possibility of state credits for tractors. But now it was as if the countryside had gone crazy. Men talked like soldiers in war: "If one goes hungry, let all go hungry. If one has felt boots, let all have them. Let us build one great farm over the whole Volga from Volsk to Astrakhan." *

Into these discussions penetrated organizers from the city, sometimes workers ignorant of farming but with knowledge of organization, sometimes cool farm experts overwhelmed by this storm but striving to direct it with advice. What is the correct size for a farm? Are not a thousand horses in one field too many? Later there was to come from Moscow sharp reproof for the "disease of giantism." But just now the hot enthusiasts were calling the more cautious ones old fogies; they were lucky if they were not called counter-revolutionists. The farmhands and the younger peasants followed the young enthusiasts; the women shrank back, frightened over the possible fate of the family cow. Older stable peasants, with families and some fair amount of farm equipment, stood wavering

---

* Volsk to Astrakhan is a three days' journey by river steamer, the whole lower section of the Volga River.

between hope and doubt. They had been getting ahead a little; they had planned by hard work to advance beyond their neighbors. But the whirlwind of collectivization caught them too.

Still stronger peasants—kulaks—who had been renting "land rights" from poor peasants, or exploiting the ownership of creameries, threshers and other machines, finding always some way to evade the land laws of the revolution, were fighting with sudden fierceness against this movement. They did not shrink from arson and murder. A trial of such kulaks was closing in Orkina village, where twelve men had conspired to murder the local party secretary. Tears came into the eyes of witnesses as they spoke of Comrade Kudraseff . . . "How hard he worked to organize new life for us!" For the first time, perhaps, they truly appreciated him! Resolutions poured in from surrounding villages, demanding death for his murderers. Hundreds of peasants joined collective farms in Kudraseff's honor. The storm of collectivization rose higher.

One of the five churches at Atkarsk had recently been remodeled as a school. Now it was needed as a jail for kulaks; the older jail could not hold all the men arrested in the villages. . . . An old woman rose in a peasant meeting saying: "Once we had in our land witches, house-goblins and many other devils. Now the Soviet Power has driven them all to hell. Now there are no witches or goblins, and not even God himself any more. So I have taken down my ikons and put up a picture of Lenin."

Through all this storm of collectivization the communists were moving, organizing it, giving it form. The Five-Year Plan with its rapid industrialization was beginning to produce farm machinery. They had determined by organization backed with machinery to swing one hundred and fifty millions of earth's most backward peasants rapidly into farming more modern even than that of America. They planned an agriculture in which old bounds of ownership were abolished, where the organization of land might follow the most efficient use of the machine.

The peasant himself was to be forever abolished. To replace his dark, illiterate village there must arise great farms based on division of labor and machines. This change must not be made as industrialization of farming comes in capitalist countries, by the slowly painful conversion of farmhands into the unemployed of cities, while the lands fall to the strong and shrewd. It must come through joint ownership of the new farm enterprises, and joint planning for a richer life based on increased production, thus bringing the advantages of cities to the farms. It must abolish in the end the age-long antagonism between city and rural district—the "agrarian problem" of history.

It had to be done quickly now. The medieval farm methods of Russia were already holding back the cities. The first year of the Five-Year Plan had absorbed millions of farmhands into big construction jobs, and the demand for farm products had increased. The kulaks tried to corner the local supplies of grain. Their own farming, while often better equipped than that of their neighbors, was planned for profit, which they got less by increased yield than by buying up the harvest of others. At best, their rigid division of land into uneconomic private holdings made rapid mechanization impossible; at worst, they actively disorganized farming by arousing local peasants not to efficient production but to charging high prices for grain.

The small collective farms of poor peasants and farmhands were loyal to the state, which gave them machines and credits. The "middle peasant," owning his own means of production but yet not exploiting others, wavered for several years. He wanted to get ahead. Could he do it best by slowly becoming a kulak, grinding the poor and accumulating property, or by joining the new collective farms which were backed by state credits and machines?

But now the new factories of the Five-Year Plan were giving the state more machinery, and at last the middle peasant saw his way. Allured by hope of tractors and by successes of subsidized farmhands, and worried by the tax discriminations that faced the kulaks, the great mass of peasantry, immobile for generations, moved like an avalanche by villages, townships, counties, whole regions, into the collective farms. This created an elemental conflict, scarcely less tempestuous than that

October Revolution of 1917 of which it was the ripened result.

As the earthquake of collectivization shook the economic base of the ancient Asiatic village, so it shook also the old forms of patriarchal life. I went on a tour of villages with Burmina, a former peasant wife who had left her husband because of the oppression of his parents. She was an able organizer now; in a few years' time she had risen to the third highest post in Atkarsk County. We visited a backward village where a collective farm formed by a group of young men had been destroyed by the opposition of the village fathers. Burmina began to talk in the village meeting about the rights of daughters-in-law. What had daughters-in-law to do with efficient farming? When I saw how they gathered around Burmina I knew. The sons of patriarchal families felt through their wives the bitter domination of the "old ones." The new kind of farming set them free. Burmina built on this, and showed them how to organize.

In villages at a later stage of development men were talking about efficiency, saying: "The small artel of poor men kept us from starving, but we never had enough implements. But when the whole village pooled its implements we were able to throw away all the wooden stick-plows, and harness three horses to each of our best plows, thus plowing deeper and faster. We stopped for no boundaries but drove straight to the horizon; never was such farming before!"

The kulaks and priests tried to cloud the issue with emotions —using sexual passion and fear. In every village there arose in various forms the tale of the one great blanket under which all the men and women of the new collective farm would be forced to sleep. There arose also the rumors that babies as well as horses and plows would be "socialized"; it worried the women. I heard a husky youth jeer at a group of these women: "Are babies means of production? Who wants your kids?"

A woman defended herself against him. "I cannot read; how can I know whether the priest speaks truth? My father was a literate man; he feared neither priest nor devil. So also will my children be. But we, who are dark, how should we not believe in God and all these rumors?" Another woman was saying: "Two months ago I couldn't tell letters from figures. But now I've learned letters and figures. We can learn more. We have learned little collective farms; we can learn big ones. They say in other lands they even put hundreds of cows in one big barn, yet they do not lack for milk."

A few collective farms had already reached an even later stage. In Balanda, where the class division was sharp between a few kulak families which had formerly possessed several hundred acres and the poor peasants who had worked on the landlords' estates, mass meetings were being held to "clean out" such kulaks as had entered the collective farms. There was even talk of cleaning them out of the village. "What use have we for exploiters any more? They spread rumors; they burn our barns and haystacks."

When I left the farms I asked an organizer in Saratov: "What does Moscow say about this—about that?" He answered hurriedly but proudly: "We cannot wait to hear from Moscow. Moscow makes its plans from what we do." But back in Moscow the foreign correspondents called it the "orders from Moscow," and "Stalin's war against the peasants."

Moscow was making its plans, swiftly, feverishly, correlating the news that poured from the Lower Volga, the Middle Volga, the Caucasus and the Ukraine. Moscow was shifting its mighty Five-Year Plan to meet these new activities of the peasants. The plan had called for twenty percent collectivization by 1933 and prepared for farm machinery accordingly; this autumn storm was giving sixty percent collectivization in a single winter, and though these first paper figures sank to thirty percent in the actual sowing, it was still a number for which no adequate base of equipment had been prepared.

Moscow cut to the bone the imports of raw cotton, and doomed the Russian people to a few more years of rags; Moscow canceled orders for Brazil coffee offered at bargain prices, and made an enemy of Brazil; Moscow increased the import of farm machinery and tractors, and made a friend of Henry Ford. The city of Kharkov decided to build a giant tractor plant "outside the plan," thus facing colossal difficulties in raw materials, funds and labor, all of which were already assigned. Kharkov stirred its entire population to give their holidays to voluntary work on that tractor plant.

Stalin also was making plans from this great storm of the peasants, as the man in Saratov so proudly said. The great Party Line by which the whole land knows its policy, and which is above government and trade unions, was shifting to include this new will of the masses. On December 27, 1929, Stalin issued his famous statement to the conference of Marxist Agrarians that the time had come not merely to "limit" kulaks but to "abolish the kulak as a class." Collective farming, backed by state machines and credits, could feed the land without individualist exploiters.* The world's press carried the story that Stalin ordered the extermination of kulaks. Stalin had merely analyzed and authorized what farmhands were already instinctively doing.

Like Moscow, like Stalin, like other persons of great or small importance, like twenty-five thousand workers who poured from the factories at party call to help in farm organization, I also began to make my plans from what the peasants were doing. Even the mighty *Pravda* wanted articles on what I had seen on the Lower Volga. The storm of collectivization had found them unprepared with adequate reporters. The State Publishing House asked me for a pamphlet and printed two hundred and fifty thousand copies of what I had seen. I judged the new farming from the standpoint of efficiency, and also gave the distinctions whereby Balanda peasants cleaned "alien elements" from their farms. These pamphlets were sold from Odessa to Kamchatka; I found them in a railway book-stall on the newly-opened Turkestan-Siberian Railway. Beside this new work all my past work paled. Why publish books for two thousand American readers who changed their minds with every new book, when I could give to two hundred and fifty thousand peasants information which they used to reorganize their lives?

I went next to Odessa district to see Shevchenko Tractor

---

* In 1929 the state got ten million tons from the peasants, 86 percent of it being from individual farms; in 1934 the state got twenty-five million tons, of which 92 percent was from state and collective farms which had thus proved adequate to feed the country.

Station, which had emerged from a dozen similar attempts as the best way to rationalize peasants' farming. It comprised a central machine shop with two hundred tractors and a complement of all necessary machinery, servicing the surrounding peasants on one hundred and fifty thousand acres. It maintained a training school for village tractor-drivers; it rented machines for a percentage of the crop, and required peasants who wished them to adopt crop rotation in consultation with the station's experts. The peasants still lived in the ancient village they had always known. Yet their fields were knit with other fields beyond the horizon into one great factory system, producing not cloth or iron but grain. Credits, traveling libraries, health exhibits, grapevines, cattle, pigs, orchards were entering the medieval farms through Shevchenko Tractor Station. In December, 1929, there was in the whole U.S.S.R. only one such station; by 1934 they came to be three and a half thousand, servicing two-thirds of all Soviet farming.

The State Publishing House wanted a pamphlet about this station also, so I began to write more for Soviet publishers. A certain episode had disillusioned me with my American editors. For a year or more Moscow had seemed to regard me with vague suspicion. Then Tivil, who read English newspapers for his economic research, told me frankly that I was considered a Trotskyist. I thought a moment before I answered: "No, I hardly think you can call me one. I've rather forgotten Trotsky. I never quite saw why he was thrown out; I couldn't see so much difference between those theories. Everybody wanted to build this country, didn't they? And all of them want world revolution. It seemed to me just a question of emphasis. But I've too much experience in the labor movement of Seattle to go against a workers' movement because it throws out a candidate I liked."

Tivil looked dissatisfied. "How about that article of yours in the ——?" he asked, bluntly.

I was puzzled. He reminded me of a comparison between Stalin and Trotsky which I had written for a New York paper in early 1927 when Trotsky was still a member of the Central Committee of the Communist Party, but under heavy attack.

I had gone to China after writing it and had never seen it in print; my memory of it had been buried under the thunders of the Chinese Revolution.

"But there can't be anything wrong with that article," I said as I recalled it. "It wasn't a discussion of views, but of personalities. Some communists saw it and thought it was rather good."

"Impossible," said Tivil. Then my bewilderment convinced him and his firmness convinced me. "Let's see what's in that article," I said.

Together we unearthed it—a paper two years old. There, above my signature, had been added two paragraphs of contemptuous allusion to Russian communists. Another paragraph in which I spoke of the organizing work of Stalin, "under which the day-by-day efficiency of the country improves" had been removed from the article. These changes made it a sneer at the Soviet Union and a praise of Trotsky.

I recalled that I had especially written the editor: "You ask me to handle a very delicate subject on which my reputation for political accuracy and balanced judgment is at stake. I therefore insist that, if you must edit, you at least add nothing; and if you must cut, do not cut one side of a comparison."

When I told Tivil, he grew indignant. "The man has destroyed your reputation," he said. "Cannot you write and demand a retraction?" I smiled bitterly; I knew the capitalist press better than he did. "They wouldn't even understand my demand," I said. "A reputation for political accuracy is to them only a means for making money. And my reputation among Bolsheviks—is even less to them than that."

The conversation with Tivil gave me an idea. I said: "You know those lessons in English I once gave Trotsky in return for political instruction. I seem to have got mostly anecdotes, but the idea wasn't bad. Even after eight years in the country I don't always understand things. Nobody has time to explain; everyone who knows anything is busy. Can't you find some well-informed person who wants English lessons and will answer questions that occur to me?" It was thus that I met Perchik, an economist recently arrived from the Ukraine, who found some time for English lessons before his new Moscow duties quite engulfed him. He helped me understand the rural districts through the difficult first months of 1930.

Swiftly the autumn storm of collectivization I had seen on the Volga deepened into a January blizzard. Rumors poured into Moscow as wild as those which were flooding the villages. One favorite tale was of the kulak's wife who, when her husband was jailed, spent her last ruble on rat poison for herself and seven, ten or thirteen children. Authenticated stories came of the unroofing of kulaks' houses, the chaotic exiling of victims. It seemed needlessly disorderly and cruel. This was lynch law! Had a kulak no human rights?

"I think what worries you most," said Perchik, when I had rather incoherently expressed my feelings, "is not so much the cruelty as the anarchy. . . ." He was right; how quickly he had analyzed what I myself hadn't known. "There is really too much anarchy," he added, "for which we communists must hold ourselves to blame. It comes from division within the party. Stalin has stated the party policy—abolition of kulaks as a class—but the right-wing elements in the party and in parts of the government apparatus sabotage its execution, thus delaying its exact formulation in law. Having no guidance in law, the left-wing elements among our local comrades do what is right in their own eyes and the eyes of farmhands, which is anarchy. We expect government decrees soon; then there will be more order." But how clever of Perchik! I had been instinctively sympathizing with the right-wing in its wish to go slowly, which seemed to me more orderly. Now I saw that their refusal to respond to the revolutionary will arising from oppressed masses, actually created anarchy. I saw also for the first time why communists insist on rigid unity within the party—without "fractions." Disunity at the top means chaos in the country.

The first decrees appeared on February 5, making plain that deportation of kulaks could be done only in districts where "solid collectivization" took place, and only on signed petition from mass meetings of local peasants, ratified by the provincial authorities. The larger abuses at once diminished. But there were still plenty of local excesses. Organizers were forcing peasants into collective farms by threats; they were "communizing" chickens, goats, underwear and dishes. These actual excesses were being magnified by local kulaks who incited peasants to kill and eat their livestock and so come "naked into the collective farm" where all should henceforth be equal. Why didn't Stalin act? The foreigners in Moscow saw in the situation a weird Bolshevik love for disorder.

"We cannot attack our local comrades till collective seed is in collective barns and the sowing safe," said Perchik. "Otherwise there might be widespread famine." . . . I did not understand this at all. Wasn't the seed in the villages anyway? What did it matter in whose hands it was? Wouldn't it be planted either by individuals or collectives? Yet my knowledge of even the American attitude towards public property might have taught me that peasants fresh from the Middle Ages would steal and sell their own seed grain, "now that it belongs to the collective," and then expect the state to care for them, not realizing that they were themselves the state. Except for firm control of the seed in that chaotic spring of 1930, starvation would have devastated the land and the Soviet power itself might have gone down in famine.

When the seed was in collective barns at the end of February, Stalin issued his famous statement: "Dizziness from Success." He declared that the speed of collectivization had made "some comrades dizzy." He reminded the communists and the peasants that collectivization must be entirely voluntary and that the "artel" form of collective farm, which was advocated for the present stage of development, socialized horses, lands, and other means of production but left untouched such household animals as cows, chickens and sheep.

Millions of copies of this statement sold at once as a pamphlet. Peasants rode to town and paid as high as fifteen rubles for the last copy, that they might wave it in the face of local organizers as their charter of freedom. For a few weeks Stalin became a personal hero to millions of peasants—a hero who championed them against the local communists. Stalin promptly checked this hero-worship. He published "answers to collective peasants," in which he said: "Some people speak as if Stalin alone made that statement of policy. The Central Committee does not exist to permit such action by any individual. The statement was a reconnaissance undertaken by the Central Committee."

Through weeks of sowing the Central Committee continued to organize the storm which had arisen out of the hunger of farmhands and poor peasants for swift access to a good life. It was an elemental whirlwind which would have strained any government in the world. In all the foreign embassies in Moscow and in all the lands along the border, they watched like hawks this farm revolution, guessing how it might end. I went in spring to the American consulate in Riga to renew my passport and found men giving their full time to studying the details of Soviet collectivization in a dozen Soviet papers. They were sending thousands of pages of reports to Washington. Collapse and famine were widely predicted by foreigners; it was said that more than one country along the Soviet border was getting its armies ready to march.

Towards the end of March I went south to meet the spring. Twenty-four hours from Moscow I found it, on the line to Stalingrad. I was appalled by the tales I heard at the station of Alexikovo where my train set me down at midnight to wait till three in the morning. Twenty peasants surrounded me and poured forth bitter words. "A former bandit got into the party and bossed our village." . . . "Stalin says that collective farms are voluntary but they won't give back our oxen." Next morning I sat in a township office in the town of Filonovo and heard similar complaints poured upon a weary secretary from morning till long past dark. "The president is not here," he told me. "He went to a village where kulaks last night burned a barn containing twenty-seven horses on which the collective farm relied for the spring plowing."

Farms were going to pieces under a dozen pressures—the attack by priests, the violence of kulaks, the stupidity of local officials, the ignorance and inefficiency of medieval Russia. Peasants were joining and leaving so rapidly that no one knew what land or horses the collective farm might have tomorrow.

When I mentioned to Perchik the difficulties I had seen, he told me I had not yet discovered half the troubles: half-baked organizers uselessly violating village feelings, bandits getting into office and using the new laws to wreak personal vengeance, plenty of anarchy everywhere.

"We are like a man on skis on a swift slope," he said. "Our acceleration is terrific and grows ever greater. We cannot stop nor control speed nor distance. We can only guide our jumps and endeavor to land properly. . . . We *must* succeed, for if we do not, then everything is finished. . . ." Then he added slowly: "But for that—are we communists." . . . I suddenly remembered Sonia, years before, facing civil war and famine and saying: "There is nothing impossible."

As soon as I went inland from the railroad the sense of chaotic struggle vanished. Then I realized why all the journalists who travel along the railroad must needs judge wrongly. All the troubles of the land flowed together at the railroad; all complaints sought the township center for adjustment. Beyond the railroad had remained the men who were succeeding; they were plowing desperately to establish themselves on land, as once had plowed the boys of John Reed Colony. They had no time to go to the railroad, no time even to talk. Confusion gave place to a great organized sowing. I saw for the first time spring on the collective farms.

Miles of rich black earth in a single field—the land of a dozen hamlets worked as one. One crop rotation planned by an expert for the whole, with field brigades at regular intervals, horses, oxen, tractors, the factory system of division of labor. At night the fields were dotted with collective encampments whence music of balalaikas arose. A white-haired professor of astronomy from Leningrad was touring the brigades with a lantern-slide lecture. Opera singers came down from Moscow to help with the festival processions with which collective farmers "took the field." Brigades of mechanics arrived from factories to repair farm implements. Millions of peasants, helped and organized by city workers, teachers, farm experts, artists, journalists, were building in a single spring the agricultural basis of socialism. It was the most dramatic sowing in human history.

. . . .

Three figures stand out for me from that great mass sowing: Ustina the farmhand, Melnikov the reporter, and Kovalev, the party secretary of a township. Ustina was chicken-woman of the "Fortress of Communism," a large collective farm not far from Filonovo. She had been a servant maid from the age of eight. After the revolution she was one of the first members of a small struggling commune, so destitute that she wrapped her new-born children in sacks and newspapers, having neither blankets nor clothes. Step by step with incredibly heroic labor, the early communars built a sound farm. They had tractors and an incubator which Ustina won as a prize from Moscow in recognition of her excellent work. After two years of relative comfort, their farm had recently expanded to many times its original size, under influx of hundreds of penniless farmhands whom they must feed till harvest time. The communars again were hungry. Ustina said: "It is our second war. The great war was a murdering war; this war is not murdering but it is war all the same. So we must struggle again and help all who are with us."

Working out of Stalingrad went the *Traveling Struggle*, a newspaper published in three railway cars. In late winter and throughout the spring it journeyed from township to township, spending two weeks in each and issuing a newspaper based on investigation of local abuses. In a single season this paper was effective in arresting more than two hundred local officials for offenses ranging from graft to banditry. Melnikov, its most energetic reporter, could digest ten shocking cases of corruption daily and find in them no discouragement, but a call to battle. He told me with gusto of the bandit Zotev, who elected himself president in a village and listed as a kulak for deportation a Red army man who tried to expose him. He told of the over-zealous organizer who made a sweeping tour through seven Kalmyk villages, and collectivized the whole lot in seven days by the simple device of listing their property and telling them they were now one farm. Not in all the tsarist news-sheets in

Europe can an editor invent more "Bolshevik atrocities" than Melnikov triumphantly recorded in his routine of helping the "self-criticism."

But when I asked Melnikov whether the harvest would be much less than previously as a result of all the turmoil of new organization, the graft and corruption, the slaying of livestock, he stared in amazement. . . . "Less! But it must be much greater! Have you not seen Tractor Stations doubling the area? Have you not seen, even without tractors, how farm-hands and poor peasants use the kulaks' horses to increase sown area seventy per cent? The kulak sabotaged the harvest, for he hated the Soviet Power and feared taxes. These new owners drive forward like mad men."

The hunger of farmhands and poor peasants for new life— that was the great power released in what came to be called the "first Bolshevik spring." This power was organized and led by the communists who in spite of inexperience and excesses, in spite of sudden shocks when Moscow checked Saratov, were a firm, disciplined and tireless group. I learned to look for them in every farm; I could pick them out in a field brigade by their tense concern that everything go well. I learned to know and admire the best type of party secretary of a town-ship—sleepless, poised and always driving, driving. I saw no middle-aged men among them; only youth could stand their pace.

It is thus I remember Kovalev, secretary of a district south of Stalingrad. He gave to an audience of ten shiftless, desert-ing peasants the best and simplest analysis of the need for col-lectivization that I had heard. These peasants had decided to leave the collective farm. One said: "I have no warm coat, and they make me pasture livestock at night in the rain." An-other: "They work my camel hungry and he dies before my eyes." A third: "My wife won't live with me since I joined the Kolkhoz." (Most of them actually were influenced by their women and by the opportunities to get well-paid jobs hauling materials for construction on the near-by tractor works.)

Their reasons seemed adequate to me, but not to Kovalev. "You give no serious grounds," he said. "These conditions you always had. Nobody offered you a golden dish in the collective farm. There seem to be some faults of management which can be corrected; certainly peasants working at night must get warm clothes. The question of hay is difficult because of last year's drought; but it will be no better in individual fields. Those who seek to profit on construction jobs, let them know that as soon as the sowing is over, the collective farm will get those hauling contracts. For the whole Soviet Power is behind the collective farm. Who leaves will not better himself!

"I also was a peasant and in the spring never saw meat. A peasant is not, even if he wishes, an independent person. His farming depends on the whole nation and the whole nation depends on his farming. Our land is surrounded by capitalist lands. We must swiftly build great industry and modern farming or we perish. That giant factory in Stalingrad will this summer pour tractors into our farms. That giant power station, Stalgres, will this autumn give light to your homes. While these great works are unfinished we need food; there must be great increase in bread. Can this be done if every peasant sits at home deciding when to plow? The task of the Soviet Power and of every citizen this year is to strengthen the collective farms. This year is like 1917 when we went with rifles to take power. Now we must take the front of husbandry."

After two hours of Kovalev's patient, persuasive argument, the wives of the men called shrilly from outside. Kovalev invited them in; they refused. They had made up their minds and their sheepish men obeyed. Swiftly, without wasting a word in regret, Kovalev turned to the five communists left in the room. "Kulak agitation is going on in the field brigades. You, and you, and you into the fields tomorrow to work on harrows." He thus assigned three young teachers and a librarian to field work where their chief task was to keep up morale. He telephoned Stalingrad for a Tartar woman organizer to work among the wives, and for an emergency supply of hay. He ordered the librarian to send traveling libraries into the fields.

Thus swiftly he marshaled his forces for attack. It was able

generalship, worthy a large sphere.   Yet this was one backward Tartar village on poor soil.   Into every such village the
organizers of the party penetrated, fighting in spring of 1930
the war for Soviet wheat.

Melnikov guessed right.   Though the seed was sown in the
midst of violent class war, by men who were storming their way
out of the Middle Ages in a single year, yet such was the force
of their newly-awakened will that when crop returns at last
came in, the workers of the world and the representatives of
foreign powers who watched like hawks knew that the Soviet
Union had achieved the widest sown area and the greatest harvest it had ever known.

That harvest changed the history of farming for the world.

CHAPTER XXIV

WE ORGANIZE THE *MOSCOW NEWS*

THOUSANDS of Americans were flooding into Soviet Russia in 1929 and the years thereafter—new Americans of the Five-Year Plan. Some fled from a world crisis to a Soviet refuge, others had wished to come for years and found their opportunity in the expanding industry. Others were brought, with varying amounts of intelligence, by Soviet state trusts needing specialists whom they were willing to pay in dollars. These last were known as "valuta specialists."

Most of these Americans had one urge in common—the will of the pioneer to create something new in a wilderness. This lured them on. Whether they fought to build a great steel mill in Kuznetsk or to make one machine work better in Stalingrad, whether they loved socialism or dollars or were just normal Americans to whom efficient work is God's own permit to exist—the motives were oddly mixed in most of them—the many men wished to make something that would live and expand in this new country. I saw them going through my own past experiences, fighting to organize under new conditions. Out of my own past I wanted to help them; like them I wanted efficiency in Soviet industries and farms. But I had given up hope that I could do anything; I had resigned myself to being a writer.

Shortly after my return from the opening of the Turkestan-Siberian Railway—on the same trip I had also visited the vast mudhole of Kuznetsk where first foundations of a projected steel plant were being dug with primitive spades—I dropped into the office of Michael Borodin, at that time president of the Paper Trust.

"Didn't you once have an idea of starting an American newspaper in Moscow?" he asked me. "If you tried now, I think you would find support."

"I've had the idea for years," I told him. "If you want to start it, I'll take the job of getting a staff and issuing the sheet. But I won't do any organizing in this country. I know my limitations."

"So," smiled Borodin, and left it. Two days later I was back in his office. "I know I'm going to curse you for this," I said. "But—who is thinking of starting that paper?"

"Some comrades are handling complaints of Americans and think an organ is needed to help them." He gave me names, chief of which was Rutgers of the old Kuzbas Autonomous Industrial Colony; he was in charge of a new bureau for handling foreigners' complaints.

I sought out Rutgers. The small group interested in a newspaper didn't seem to be getting ahead very fast. Somebody was going to report; somebody else was on vacation. I grew impatient. Didn't I know anybody really important, some big man who could put this over fast? Suddenly I thought of Valery Meshlauk, vice-chairman of all Soviet industries, who had several times praised my books. I took him a plan worked out in detail. A board of directors on which all main economic organizations employing Americans should be represented— industry, trade, transport, farming—financing a paper by large blocks of subscriptions taken for the Americans in their employ.

"But I don't know how you organize in this country," I admitted. "Tell me three things. Do you like the idea? Then how does one organize it? And is it possible that I, a foreigner and not a party member, would be allowed to do this job?"

"The fact that you are not a party member is even an advantage to the paper," answered Meshlauk.

I saw that too. But his words didn't entirely please me. They seemed to put me too definitely outside. I wanted to be in and out at the same moment. At least I wanted them to want me, to help me make up my mind. . . . "I can't join the party while I write for capitalist newspapers," I justified myself, "but after I get on a paper like this I could, couldn't I?"

"You would find it hard," said Meshlauk kindly. "And it's not at all necessary. You'll do very well as you are."

So! They didn't want me. Not as a comrade-creator. They wanted me only as a skilled employee. Just as the capitalists wanted me. Well, I would rather slave for them than for capitalists. At least they were building something for the future of the world. From the dark past of my youth sprang up the old defiance: "They don't want me; then let them see how I can work."

"The idea is very good. I shall take it up at once," said Meshlauk. Later he mentioned names of men who approved. Yakovlev, People's Commissar of Agriculture, Kuibisheff, chief of the industries and other important men in railways and trade unions. There was talk of men like this on a board of directors. My heart sang! Was I at last to meet with people who did things?

I began promoting the idea all over Moscow. Prominent American engineers were enthusiastic—Hugh Cooper, Calder, Freyn. Bill Shatoff sent "best wishes for American efficiency in Soviet industry." Walter Duranty and Eugene Lyons, the chief American correspondents then in Moscow, promised to write for it "if it comes out the way you plan." I urged the idea on the press department of the Foreign Office, and they also showed interest, intimating that they might like it as "their paper." I stayed away from them after that; I was off Foreign Offices since that Russian American Club. Better leave it all to Meshlauk, a word of his would put it over, more than any great effort of mine. I took a vacation at his suggestion, and when I came back I heard of three different English newspapers all of which were soon to start. This was the result of my widespread promotion.

"So many people want to run papers," I said to Meshlauk. "Don't fight for my candidacy. I've other things to do."

"I haven't even heard those rumors," he answered. "Our paper is settled. The delay was due to difficulty in finding the right editor. We have him now, Vasutin, head of the planning department of our industries. The Central Committee asks me to see what you are willing to do."

"What do they want me to do?" I asked, rather nonplused by what seemed to me a change of plan.

"They want you to organize it, put it over," he said.

"Then what's Vasutin for?" I asked bluntly.

"He's your connection with industry," answered Meshlauk. "He has no time to run a paper; you won't see him more than twice a week. You hire the staff and run it, getting advice from him. Ogonek Publishing House has orders to give you an office and money within the budget you drew up." I sighed to see disappearing all those representatives of farming, trade and transport whom I had hoped to meet. But Meshlauk said: "We'll get them later; they are slow in agreeing."

It worked. Ogonek Publishing House actually handed out money on my first order. Only then did I believe a paper was going to be. So many times I had tried to organize and nothing had come of it. This really seemed assured. I collected a staff from Americans residing in Moscow. We were on the streets with our first number on October 5, 1930, fifteen days after Meshlauk told me to proceed. Americans telegraphed greetings from all parts of the Soviet Union. Correspondents volunteered in Kharkov, Stalingrad, Leningrad, Irkutsk, even Alma Ata on the far Turk-Sib. Wives of engineers in Moscow's best hotels offered to type mailing lists. Nobody asked for pay; they were lonely. Starting a newspaper was good fun for them all.

We began as a "five-day weekly" to celebrate the five-day week which at that time was being tried in industry. The first staff included Maxwell Stewart, formerly editor of the *China Outlook* and today one of the editors of the New York *Nation*, who handled world news and serious articles; Ed Falkowski, well known in the American labor press, who took charge of local news and correspondence from workers and specialists in industry; and Herbert Marshall, secretary of the London Film Guild, who managed photographs and art. Part time contributors were Jack Chen, a young cartoonist; Lem Harris, a brilliant youth who was working at jobs all over the country in order to see the Soviet Union; Joshua Kunitz of the *New Masses* who was in Moscow doing theaters. When Walter Duranty saw that our chief editor was Russian, he cannily decided to wait till he saw our policy, but Eugene Lyons took

a chance and contributed some travel articles for which he
asked no pay. Louis Fischer also promised to write regularly.

A spirit of energetic devotion pervaded our early staff.
When Ogonek offered me six hundred rubles' salary with extra
pay for every article, I scornfully turned it down. "You can't
start a self-supporting paper on salaries like that. Make mine
party maximum, three hundred and seventy-five rubles; that
covers everything I write." Led by me, the entire staff made
the same decision and put it down in a "shock-brigade pledge"
—never to take more than party maximum. We were sick of
the way Russians thought Americans only wanted dollars; we
were going to be a noble bunch. We would show these communists who treated us as bought-and-paid-for outsiders that
we were as good as they!

I set the policy of those first numbers. Jack Chen's first
cartoon showed steel mills arising out of a Five-Year Plan,
portrayed as a blue-print. "Soviet power plus American
technique will build socialism," the caption ran. We left out
world revolution; our readers included some very respectable
business firms. But anyone who wasn't for "Soviet power plus
American technique building socialism" needn't take our paper
and had no business in Soviet Russia.

It all seemed to come true as Meshlauk promised. Vasutin
didn't interfere. He liked our gay young crowd. Our enthusiasm overbore all difficulties. I personally typed most of
the first issue; I made up and wrote heads; we all read proof.
We even sat next to the linotype men against all rules of
printing shops, pointing out keys to men not yet used to the
Latin alphabet, and cajoling them with American cigarettes
and "historic copies" of our first number. The story of that
first issue, when we carried our type-face at midnight across
a slippery construction job to a distant press-room, was told
in newspaper offices in many parts of the world.

My confidence that first night even stunned the Glav-Lit *
man. He went in routine through our eight pages; then suddenly he grew angry and seized a blue pencil. "It is a slan-

---

* "Chief of Literature." A Department in the Commissariat of Education,
known as "political editor," which gives final reading to all publications.

der," he cried, pointing to a humorous skit by Falkowski on "Moscow Nomads," describing our wanderings in search of a room. I hotly protested that it was humor. As we argued I became aware that our American sense of humor is based on an exaggeration which is difficult to explain to a man with a different sense of humor. Ed had said terrible things about Moscow, so exaggerated that they were funny. If you took them seriously, they were incredible slander.

I grabbed the telephone furiously and tried at midnight to reach everyone I knew. I got Vasutin out of bed and was advised to "submit tonight but write out your complaint for tomorrow." But I had impressed that censor. "Do you really mean that Americans will take this as funny and not as attacking our Moscow workers?" "I do," I said. He weakened and we agreed to cut out two short paragraphs which even I admitted might be misunderstood. We parted with no hard feelings. After all, I thought, he is only an extra editor.

Five weeks like this—seven issues. We all worked in one small room, writing, typing, interviewing under the feet of a throng of eager visitors. We were all over the printing shop teaching English to printers. We heard: "That English newspaper will succeed; it's the only Ogonek publication that has the printers with it." We were really the only one that had any regard for printers' deadlines; we got that from America. I worked flushed with fever or shaking with exhaustion, but my brain worked clear, doing everything that nobody else had time for. At last, at long last, I was efficient in this country. I heard a secretary of Ogonek say: "What's Strong killing herself for? She's no communist." I laughed in triumphant defiance. Let them produce a communist who could drive himself harder than I!

Then I went on lecture tour to America. Meshlauk encouraged it, saying: "You can build circulation." The moment I left Moscow the paper dropped out of my existence. I sent articles; they weren't published. I sent cables; they weren't answered. I saw from copies that reached America that Vasutin had been replaced by Axelrod, whom I didn't know. Articles grew dull and full of revolutionary theory, clearly

translations from Russian. Amtorg, the Soviet trading office
in New York, refused to have it on the premises: "It insults
our clients, the American business men," they said. Amkniga,
which sells Soviet books and periodicals in America, told me
they hated to handle it. "It is becoming so dull that nobody
wants it. Go back and fix it up."

"Go back!" Was there anything to go back to? Was I still
on a paper that didn't answer my cables? I broke down from
exhaustion and spent a month in a health resort where I wrote
the first draft of my book *The Soviets Conquer Wheat*. Then
Meshlauk came to America; I met him at Dr. Susan Kingsbury's house in Bryn Mawr.

"You have deserted long enough," he said. "Go back and
fix the paper."

"What authority have I on that paper?" I asked.

"Full authority," he replied. "You were appointed to that
post to make it a good paper." Dr. Kingsbury smiled: "Now
you have what you wanted. We witness your authority," she
said.

I caught the morning train to New York and sailed that
same evening, using my last day to interview several people
and to write letters to American authors whom I knew—Sinclair
Lewis, Upton Sinclair, Theodore Dreiser, Lewis Gannett—asking them for articles. I wrote inviting two American news-
writers to come to Moscow—Bill Prohme and Milly Mitchell,
known to me from the days of "red Hankow" where they organized the *People's Tribune*. Milly Mitchell came to Moscow, entered the battle and survived. Bill Prohme came from
Arizona to New York, but I cabled him there to stop. I had
found in Moscow that I could guarantee nothing at all.

Far out at sea a radiogram from Meshlauk cheered me. I
had left him a letter in New York telling all I had done that
last day. "Foresee great future for *Moscow News*," he ra-
dioed. So what I had done was right; Meshlauk approved.

I cabled *Moscow News* that I was coming. Nobody met me.
I went to the office; nobody knew me. In my four months'
absence a new staff had arisen, a large, expensive staff of translators and typists. In a second room I found the American

members, waiting for me to save them. Their shock-brigade pledge had won no credit; it never reached trade union or party organizations, for Ogonek gave them neither political nor social attention. But it reached the Ogonek business office which noted and complied with the strange desire of Americans for low salaries. My cherished staff, who had responsible jobs in their own countries, were getting about one-third the pay of translators. Some of them were spending their American savings. To this my idealism had betrayed them. But that pledge and the mutual help they gave to raise the qualifications of the lowest, had united them into firm devotion. They meant to fight for a good paper if I would tell them how.

Worse than low salary was their low status. Axelrod, the new editor, who held half a dozen editorial posts simultaneously, and was well known among Russians, had been building the paper on articles translated from Russian and then polished by our Americans. They found these articles long, dull and expensive, and felt that they could write much better ones. Having sacrificed their salaries to make a paper self-supporting, they resented the time and money spent on stuff they thought beneath contempt.

I began with Axelrod as a good comrade and he began with a friendly attitude to me. He had a sincere, ascetic face, framed in tangled locks beneath a battered sombrero. Day and night he plodded from one editorial office to another in multitudinous tasks. Tuberculosis of long standing predisposed him to frequent illnesses; he was clearly one of those honest revolutionists who work themselves to death. He expected my style to improve the paper, and I expected the same. Axelrod doesn't know how to get good stuff from Americans. I thought, "Nobody could possibly print those long theoretical translations if he could get a good story in English."

I soon found that our ideas of good stuff differed fundamentally. He would accept most of my articles, only correcting them a little—always toning down vivid, flashing statements in favor of "the exact line." It seemed to me he always made them duller, till I feared to lose all reputation for style. What chiefly worried me, however, was his attitude towards my cherished staff, whom he considered fit only for trivial work. In vain I argued about their style, their standing in America. "No foreigners know enough about our country to write about it," he finally said. My world collapsed. Henceforth I saw in Axelrod the enemy.

It never occurred to either of us to analyze our different views of a paper, views which we drew from our different pasts and took for granted. To me the first law was to be interesting and to meet our printer's deadline. Accuracy was important; I didn't intend to misrepresent anybody, certainly not an important Soviet official. I respected them all. But there was no denying that their speeches were long and would stand editing—playing up the important points and anecdotes and condensing the theory. But whatever we did we must make the printer's deadline and the requirements of column space.

Axelrod cared nothing about deadlines, column space or anecdotes. To condense theory and play up anecdotes in a speech destroyed its "exact line," which to him was all-important. He would hold up a whole printing shop of fuming workers while he analyzed, telephoned and consulted to get the exact line in some dull sentence which seemed to me no different after he finished. "If he must be politically exact," I raged, as if yielding to a vice of Axelrod's, "let him be it in time for the deadline. These communists who will let workers walk home after the last car so that they can 'think'!"

His attitude towards scoops enraged me. I personally attended the opening of a big congress and rushed back with my summary of the first speech. We would rush it into print and beat even _Pravda_. Axelrod wouldn't use it; we must wait for the Tass report which the maker of the speech edited. He suspected me then of mis-quoting a speaker? No, but we must wait even five days till our next issue to be utterly accurate on that speech. Could any American editor understand it? Yet the Russians were equally puzzled by me.

Our conflict was intensified by what seemed chaotic organization. When Axelrod was ill he worked through Chumak, a so-called "secretary of the staff." Chumak tried to boss everything; he took articles I had sent to the printing shop and sent them outside the office for further approval. This worked havoc with our schedule. What was he anyway, only a secretary? My name on the paper was Managing Editor. He should be fired for insubordination!

I went hotly to Axelrod. "Is Chumak my boss?"

"Certainly not," he said.

"Then is Chumak under me?"

"Not exactly; he is staff secretary."

"But who gives orders when you are out of the office?" Axelrod evaded this; he said he would speak to Chumak and we must get on together. We Americans decided that Chumak must be a G.P.U. agent "whom Axelrod can't fire or control." We had no conception of the form of Soviet organization which works by consultation rather than orders. We couldn't see where Chumak got his authority.

After a long time I discovered that "secretary of the staff" has on Russian papers the function which Americans give to managing editor. Chumak had been managing editor in Russian and I had been managing editor in English and neither had known the other's function! Where was this Central Committee which was said to have appointed me? Let them tell me what I was supposed to do! I spent hours on the telephone but never could reach them. I couldn't get into their building; it required a party card.

I wasn't beaten yet. I took the underpaid Americans into my apartment, sometimes as many as six in two small rooms. It didn't matter; I only went there to sleep and then I was tired enough to sleep in a battle-trench. All waking hours were spent at office and printing shop; the latter was my chief fighting-post. One by one I got American articles approved by Axelrod; I smuggled them past Chumak; I chaperoned them into type. Then I ruthlessly used my knowledge of make-up to bury Axelrod's long, pet translations on back pages; I gave headlines and position to my American stuff. I had no conscience at all towards him.

I was actually winning a little. Axelrod was often ill and Chumak kept routine hours while I was doing the work of ten. We began to look like a real paper. I had one triumphant day.

President Stuart of Stuart, James and Cook made a report to the Supreme Economic Council on the coal industry in the Donetz Basin, one of the sore spots of national industry. It was the first time an American had reported to that high body and Meshlauk gave me the stuff with permission to spread it. I compiled the material myself, featured the high lights and put it all over the first pages in first-class style. Stuart asked for fifty copies to send to his home office. "I'm proud of that report," he said. American correspondents of capitalist papers noticed us for the first time in months; we had made them run to Stuart; we had thoroughly scooped them all. I breathed more easily. Perhaps I should get back my reputation as a newspaper-man.

Then Axelrod was through. My long, typewritten prayers sent frequently to Meshlauk had got a new editor from behind those inaccessible scenes. Axelrod seemed really ill when he went on vacation; I certainly had not made his life easy. He left behind not only *Moscow News*, but *Workers' News*, a still smaller sheet which we all attributed to Axelrod's passion for many papers. It had still longer, duller articles and seemed to me the last insanity. We all thought the two papers would combine now that Axelrod had left us. Then we might become a daily. The same staff produced them both.

The new editor Vacsov sent me my first "orders" through Chumak; he did not even ask me to come to the telephone but merely to be sent over to his office—"like a package," I thought. Clearly he had arrived with firm intent to rule. But I went smilingly into Vacsov's office and listened to his new plan of organization, a departmental scheme which seemed to me fitted to a paper the size of the New York *Times*, but not to our modest sheet. It would triple requirements in translators. I explained our simpler American form of organization, based on sources of news and adapted to shooting material rapidly to the printing shop. . . . "That wouldn't do at all," he said. "May I introduce my new department heads?"

He brought them in. He had had them also sent over to his office half an hour after me. He had everything settled, it seemed. I thought of the four or five Americans still on the

staff. Drowned under an ocean of translators they were fighting hard for a good paper. Were new chiefs coming on top
of the translators to drive them lower still? I mentioned their
qualifications; Vacsov wasn't interested. But that staff trusted
me. So I smiled at the new department heads—three nice
English and American boys—and said: "All come to tea at
my house tonight to celebrate our new paper. I'll invite the
English-speaking members of the staff and we'll all get acquainted. We'll do our organizing there."

In joy our evening's celebration opened. We were drunk
—on tea, candy, cakes and hope. It was the first time the
staff had been together talking English since the old, glad days
with Vasutin nine months before. They weren't worried over
new departments; they didn't care who ran them. A real
paper with English talked in the office was enough for joy.
No more long Russian articles; that silly second paper of Axelrod's would die now. The road seemed clear to a daily.

Vacsov made a speech and asked for questions. I said: "This
staff expects me to give orders because I am called managing
editor. But I find the secretary of the staff has the same function. Please tell the staff and me what is my job. Who gives
orders when you are away?"

He grew embarrassed. He said my function was "very important," second only to his own. But he wouldn't tell me
that I could give orders. "I see," said I, "honorable but in-
definite. Let's drop the name 'managing editor' and call me
'associate editor' till we see whether I am any kind of editor
at all. That's clearer."

Vacsov looked unhappy; he wasn't sure he had authority to
change my title. "I've authority enough for that myself," I
said.

Let my job be what he liked if my work was clear. I wasn't
going to quarrel with Vacsov; he was my desperate last chance.
He was Meshlauk's choice, so I could not easily complain to
Meshlauk. If I failed with him I could never organize in the
Soviet Union. I would be an outsider always.

Vacsov didn't want to quarrel either. He wished to rule a
smooth and jovial world. He made a sharp contrast to Axel-

rod's revolutionist appearance; he was typical Rotary Club in manner. He even had a synthetic foreign look, due to the number of articles of apparel which he induced foreign friends to bring from abroad. He got on excellently with new Americans who were trying to bluff the Soviets into giving them dollar salaries. He had a hunger to be liked as a good fellow. To make people like him, he gave parties, sometimes cozy ones to friends, sometimes grand ones for the paper. He invited his new upper staff, not my "early Americans," and the latter exulted vengefully when most of the prominent Russians he invited didn't come.

The style of the paper improved under Vacsov. He was rather good at getting writers. He found some in Moscow and imported some from London, British communists who were old friends of his and whom he entertained at frequent parties. They at once got rooms and foreign food-books, which our older staff waited for in vain. My Milly Mitchell, whom I had induced to leave a high paid job to work for the revolution she had loved in Hankow, shared a bedroom with half a dozen Russians and earned hardly enough for food. Vacsov's appointees lived in hotel rooms, worked when it suited them and traveled the country with interpreters in first-class sleeping cars. Their pleasures of life were much less serious than we had come to expect from communists. "Axelrod at least was sincere," we said. If style improved, belief diminished. Under Axelrod one fought and hoped; under Vacsov, one resigned.

The best thing Vacsov did for the paper was his appointment of Max as secretary of the staff. Young, inexperienced and not super-efficient, no better comrade than Max ever worked in any office. His work laid him open to hate from our best-hating people. He had to cut copy of temperamental reporters, keeping it to the party line; he intervened between Vacsov and those who hated Vacsov. Yet everyone loved and respected Max. He was intelligent, honest, considerate, always ready to explain his actions. He would toil all night to befriend some reporter whom he had had to oppose on a matter of principle. Nothing was too big or too small for him to do if it helped him weld a united office. Working with Max one believed in communists and thought that even without great personal efficiency they might organize the world.

Then Max was removed by party orders and I, though acting editor in Vacsov's absence, was not even informed. If any responsible person had said to me: "We're taking Max and you mustn't ask why," I would have sadly but firmly surrendered this one good communist from our office. But I was allowed to think that Max was going on vacation; from typist gossip I learned the truth. That stung! I deliberately embarrassed Max's last days by holding frequent conversations on the work he would do when he returned. I didn't admit that I knew he was going and I honored Max when he didn't tell me; but I hated that vagueness "behind the scenes" that gave me instructions through typist gossip.

With Max all comradeship went out of the office. Our new chiefs sat in an inner room and used the intelligent office staff whom we had been training into writers to run personal errands. Acrimony over wages developed. Incited by the high pay of the new people, our older "wage-slaves" protested and eventually got some trips around the country and some extra pay for articles at a lower rate than the others. I was offered a desk in that inner office; I wouldn't sit there; I wrote at home. Why go at all when none of my suggestions seemed wanted? I wrote again and again to Meshlauk; he gave no answer. Not for nine months had I been able to reach him; he had given me Vacsov and that was the end of it. I no longer had the slightest desire to join the party. It seemed to me that everyone had cynically exploited all my aspirations to betray me into this chaos, to chain me to failure and keep me chained.

For the worst was that it was really failure. We weren't absorbing *Workers' News* and expanding to a daily. Axelrod had reorganized the other paper with a new staff. And *Moscow News* seemed stationary while *Workers' News* was growing. In spite of its long articles in atrocious English, it grew because it was a friend to workers. It maintained a large "mass department" of very green people to investigate complaints, and nothing much came of their investigations. But it had at least convinced American workers that somewhere was a listen-

ing friend. That friend wasn't myself; it wasn't *Moscow News*.
When workers came to us with troubles, we had instructions
to send them to the other paper. We did some high-brow organizing in the engineers' club, but *Workers' News* was getting the crowds.

The *Workers' News* kept calling us bourgeois; our writers
called them back illiterate. The two staffs hardly spoke.
Well, we were bourgeois; no denying it. Look at that inner
office of ours. I looked at the anarchy of *Workers' News* office,
with hordes of people underfoot. We had been like that when
we started, full of enthusiasm and young. In spite of their
long articles in impossible English, in spite of the fact that
they called me bourgeois, it was over there that I wanted to be.
Most Americans read both papers and blamed the staffs for
our constant fight. Why have two papers instead of one
good one? As if we could help it. All of it seemed a row between two Russians, Vacsov and Axelrod. We were just foot-
balls kicked between them.

"A rotten sheet on which you've lost your reputation," was
what the foreign correspondents said. And I, who twice had
helped organize a daily, couldn't change even this miserable
weekly. It was clear they hadn't really "wanted me," neither
my energy nor my efficiency; they had only wanted my "bourgeois reputation" to take—and throw away. And now they
wouldn't be honest with other Americans. They kept pretending that I had something to do with this paper, when they
wouldn't let me do a thing. . . . That was how I rationalized
the storming emotions that arose whenever I thought of *Moscow News*, the culmination of ten years' struggle and defeat.

Several times I resigned from the paper. Vacsov "had no
authority to accept the resignation."

"Who has?" I demanded.

"The Press Department of the Central Committee appointed
you."

"Appointed me," I jeered. "I never got into their building." Then he told me my resignation was a political act, an
"anti-Soviet act." . . . By God! I would get off this paper
somehow. I stayed out of the office for two months and worked

with Borodin in the Commissariat of Labor handling a sudden influx of American immigrants. Surely that took me off the paper! It kept my name on, paid me a salary, and wrote up my work for the immigrants. I see it now as normal work for a Soviet editor, but I saw it then as the last deceit. I wired Mrs. Sun Yat-sen and got an invitation to come to China where the struggle had begun between the Nineteenth Route Army and the Japanese. If I left Moscow for two years, they would have to take me off that paper. . . . Yes, I was really becoming hysterical.

Yet I always knew there was one way out for me—one way, if I chose to take it. The American correspondents had observed the changes in our paper. If I went to one of them and said: "I long ago resigned from this paper but they won't take my name off. I release the story," he would send it. Duranty, for instance, would do it in a dignified way, no sensation. And I would be off that paper forever! I would find eternal rest from torment. Not only *Moscow News* would be over but all my struggles in Soviet Russia, all my hopes of ten years. Ten years? Oh, more, much more! Something much older would be finished. It was some deep self within myself that I would be betraying, not Vacsov, not *Moscow News*. . . . Yet I played with that thought as a desperate man plays with suicide, when all of his deep instincts cry for life.

CHAPTER XXV

AMERICANS OF THE FIVE-YEAR PLAN

"TAKE a trip," they said to me on *Moscow News* when I kept on resigning. "Take a trip to write up Americans in our new industry. You'll come back feeling better."

I saw the trip as a bribe, but I would take it. Let them keep my name and pay expense accounts all over the Soviet Union. I would resign when I came back.

I went by way of the Volga down to Stalingrad to see the giant Tractor Works, across to Rostov to the new Agricultural Machinery Plant and the giant farms, over to Dnieprostroy where the great dam was almost completed, back to Kharkov where the second tractor plant was getting ready to open— one trip. I went to Novo-Sibirsk and the giant steel works growing in Kuznetsk, back to the third tractor works which was being constructed in Chelyabinsk, on to Magnitogorsk where a steel town rose around the Iron Mountain—a second trip. Both in summer and autumn of 1931. The tourists take these now.

I was writing up the problems of Americans employed in Soviet industry; that was my assignment. I gave a second assignment to myself. "I want to find out whether I am personally crazy or whether there is something crazy in the whole relation between this country and Americans. Is there anywhere in the Soviet Union an American who is really satisfied with his work? If there is, how does he do it?"

As I passed down the Volga I looked for our old John Reed colonists. The twenty girls who had hung on so long in a children's home in Saratov had disappeared; the Five-Year Plan had snapped them up into jobs. Those of our boys who had learned machines were rapidly climbing into good posts in new mills or on state farms. There was labor shortage all over the Volga.

316

Stalingrad Plant was not a tractor works; it was a war! A war for the first Soviet conveyor. In America the conveyor system in industry took a generation to grow; here it must be won at once by battle. Stalingrad Tractor Works was costing youth and life. Young communists from all the land came to work here, drawn in quotas from every province and district, that all the rural areas might learn of tractors. I had met them a year and a half earlier, when I explored collective farms near Stalingrad and the plant was under construction. They had said to me: "Tell the American workers that we give our youth to this struggle; we do not spend it as they do in dancing and flirting. We throw from our ranks all doubters. We shall not stop till we have built the Socialist City of Stalingrad!"

On this second visit I found American workers in Stalingrad. They had been there more than a year. Some of them also gave lives. Several had died the previous summer of typhoid, when there was as yet no decent water supply. Strong men fainted on hot summer days to drive the Stalingrad forge to production; Americans were among them. Three Americans—Zivkovich, Covert and Ninchuk, call those names American?—worked sixty hours on end to repair machine No. 7 which held back the line. The plant was singing their prowess when I got there. They had staggered from work more dead than alive.

Work? That's not work! That's war!

Three hundred Young Communists devoted a long, hot "free day" to discussing how to finish the 11,000th tractor by Youth Day, September 5th. They planned the relaxation of a boat ride in the cool of evening; but the boat arrived too late. At eleven o'clock its lights appeared in the distance; young voices turned it down. "Got to go home; it's late. Got to be fresh for the line tomorrow."

Strong men sobbed and wiped away grimy tears when the camel went up on their shop. The laughing camel—sign of spoilage and disorder—was put up on the shop that lagged behind. Strong men who had done their utmost but whose shop had not done its utmost, turned back to struggle again. It wasn't enough for one man or a hundred men to do their utmost. Stalingrad Tractor Works needed both devotion and organization. They concentrated on one detail and another slipped up to stop them. They must learn to concentrate on a thousand details at once. That was something that had never yet been done in Russia. Could Americans show them how?

Below the plant in a dozen or more brick apartment houses along the Volga, lived one hundred and seventy Americans with their families. The first group had come in May 1930, but when I arrived in August 1931 only five of that lot remained. The others had come later. Holmes was one of the first; he had been general foreman of the melting department of Ford Motor Works. He was working on foundry cupolas in Stalingrad.

"There were bad eggs in that first lot," said Holmes. "The Russians got stung with gangsters who had to skip Detroit. The administration here was also to blame. For a month we got no work and no attention from either the administration or the union. We got plenty of attention from prostitutes, old-time girls in Stalingrad who had never seen such a bunch of free spenders, not even in the days of the tsar! Drunken Americans smashed street-car windows to climb aboard; you know those waiting lines! They bashed the watchman in the face when he tried to keep them from dragging light-o'-loves at night across the works. The decent Americans elected a vigilance committee and asked the Russians to deport those toughs. But it took a long time for the Russians to act; and meantime all Americans got bad names."

With pride Holmes showed me his "udarnik" * book, which rated him "champion." He got it when one of the cupolas burst and he was hauled from his dinner to fix it. He stripped off part of his clothes and led the workers in a fight with a broken cupola near a floor of red-hot iron.

Holmes didn't think he was efficient. "I once could do good work in America," he said. "I thought I was something—general foreman of Ford's melting department. But God, how

* Udarnik—shock-worker or champion, one who is a model worker in production and social activities, formally given a card or book.

slowly it goes here! They pay us big wages to come, why can't they use us properly? For the whole first year nobody took our suggestions. I wrote out lots of lists of instructions for my department, but they always lost them."

McLane was an able foundryman; he was working ten to fourteen hours a day making records. There was a time when McLane had been very sore. That was when Verjinsky came as new superintendent of the foundry. Verjinsky openly stated that there were no good Americans in the plant. He told McLane to his face: "You know nothing and do nothing." Now McLane had been general foreman of the molding division in the Oakland Plant in Pontiac and this upstart Verjinsky made him mad. For two days McLane was going back to the States; he was "through with Russia."

Then somebody persuaded Verjinsky to put McLane on the fly-wheel which was holding up the line. The fly-wheel had sixty-five to seventy-five percent of scrap; McLane cut it to ten percent and got four hundred fly-wheels ahead of the line. McLane said to me: "I have no control of the metal as I had in America. But if I'm there myself when poor metal comes, I can stop it. I sometimes have to get between the red-hot iron and the molds to stop it. So I've got to spend a lot of time there. Verjinsky's a good boss; he supports me when I stop bad iron. But scrap is still too high; we're not efficient."

Ball had worked twenty years in drop forgings; he was in the forge of Stalingrad. "When I first came here," he told me, "there were two gangs in this plant. One gang was making tractors, the other gang was preventing them. Think I don't know sabotage when I see it? I've seen it in the States when companies were at war. I didn't know where to go to complain; you might talk to the wrong person. But I saw what they did to those machines. I wanted to resign before I got that big crank-shaft hammer going. Once they broke the water-pipes; once they plugged the drain with rags; next they burned out the motor by throwing on the full charge at once. 'I give up,' I said to Sokoloff, head of the department. 'They break it on me all the time.' Sokoloff put a special guard on that machine and we got her going. Little by little they seemed to catch those guys. At first the shop was loaded with them but oh, boy! they took them out of here!

"It wasn't only wreckers. The green guys were almost worse. One of them wrecked a hammer that was turning out an important detail; the line was going to be held up. I got her fixed just in time and started a fairly good man on her when the head of the shop committee appeared with a new green guy from Kharkov who wanted to learn on that machine.

"I wouldn't let that Kharkov fellow on. But my man didn't dare work either against the shop committee. So I took that hammer myself. In a couple of hours' hot work I got enough details to keep the line supplied for a day. Then the shop committee man came back with reënforcements and I gave him the machine for the Kharkov guy. 'Take the damn thing and bust it,' I cursed. They took it! They busted it! Next day we had it repaired.

"After a long time I found out where you go. There's a Communist Committee or something up on the third floor. Those folks care what happens to this plant. Every time you yell for the Communist Committee, the guys that are blocking you look sick. But even they told me we've got to 'train up workers for Kharkov,' so I guess we've got to. It's sure hard on Stalingrad!"

The man who had done the most for the Americans in Stalingrad was not a mechanic. He was a "political worker," Geller, a slight, thin man who never made a casting and couldn't have handled a hammer in the forge. But he knew his way about the Soviet world, and began to show the Americans "how to work." He got the Americans into the trade union; the union had paid them no attention but they had been union men in the States. He got "production meetings" of Americans in each shop to make suggestions on efficient operation. Geller didn't know a good suggestion when he heard one. But he knew that if a suggestion was backed not by one American but by all the Americans in a shop, he could go to the BRIZ (Bureau for Realizing Workers' Suggestions) and demand that it be followed. "Since Geller came, they begin to take our suggestions," said the Americans.

Not one of the Americans thought that he was "really efficient"; all complained that they "couldn't function" as they did in the States. None of them saw how "this country" could ever get ahead "in all this mess." . . . "We have forces to call on that they do not know," said Tregubenko, party secretary of the works, as he lay in bed burning with fever but organizing by telephone and conference the prosaic details of piece work and strict accounting, and also giving an interview to me.

"Why don't they take a trip?" I said to Geller. "I'm going to the giant farms. I'll take a delegation along and interpret. Let them see where their tractors go." The Americans said they hadn't the time and couldn't afford it. "It will do you good," said Geller. "The trade union pays your way." . . . "Well, I guess perhaps they owe us something," grumbled the Americans—and went.

Most of them became enthusiastic over the giant farms. "Gee, they're doing something in this country in spite of our mess in Stalingrad." . . . But the Americans on the farms felt as inefficient and inadequately used as the men in the tractor works. They told me that nobody took their suggestions. They said that pig-headed bosses wouldn't buy wrenches but let expensive tractors shake to pieces for want of a few cheap tools. "Better take a trip and see the country," said one of the Stalingrad workers. "You can get them to pay your way!" Not even then did it occur to me that the same thing had been said to me.

I came to Dnieprostroy. The water was beginning to rise behind the giant dam, and the people were moving out of the old condemned houses of Kichkas village, soon to be covered forever by the river. The constant roar that had filled my ears on a previous visit in January, 1930, when the drills were eating into the rock of the river-bed, was over now. The great white piers of the largest power dam in the world (1,100,000 cubic meters of concrete) swung in an arc from shore to shore, thirty-four meters above the waters. Across this arc puffed locomotives pulling trainloads of concrete to fill in the gaps between piers far below.

I remembered an eager workman in the foundry whom I had seen on my previous visit. I had asked him how he liked his job, and he had burst out with fiery will: "You know, we're going to finish her in 1932," as if that were an answer. I had smiled at that, and he misinterpreted my smile and added: "All the Americans think we can't; they say 1933. But I tell you, we'll finish in 1932." A simple workman in a foundry had challenged Hugh L. Cooper's engineers!

Yes, they were finishing; they would start five turbines in 1932; this was clear already. Hadn't Tregubenko told me in Stalingrad: "We have forces that these foreigners do not know"?

The four Americans from Newport News who were installing turbines knew something of these forces. They were enthusiastic over the Russian "udarniks" and especially over the girls. "Say, we never knew there could be girls like that!" They themselves had become "udarniks" by installing the nine scroll cases on the turbine two months ahead of time. A banquet had been given in their honor. But they grumbled about the way the work went. "As soon as you get a bright bunch trained in as helpers, they take them all away to be foremen, and you have to start over again with green hands." The men from General Electric were annoyed because the roof of the power-plant was still unfinished, and they had to wait to install the generators which could easily be injured by rain.

High on the bank was the American colony of consultants, the last of the Hugh L. Cooper group. They were responsible for quality and design—a job of inspection and checking. But they were, in their own words, "not directly under anyone in Dnieprostroy," hence aloof from the details of struggle. They felt isolated. Mrs. Puls, with whom I stopped, had told me a year and a half earlier that she wanted to get acquainted. "We gave a party for the Russian engineers," she said, "and we called on them all around once, but they never come to see us. I get my only contacts through my house-maid, who knows workers; she showed me an interesting day-nursery." Mrs. Puls wished painfully to know the life around her; she wanted to see schools, but was afraid of intruding. I had mentioned her desires to the party secretary of Dnieprostroy, who also wished very much to "connect the Americans with our work and help them understand it." . . . A year and a half had gone by; they were still unacquainted. Mrs. Puls was going back to America full of admiration for the heroic creative work of Soviet Russia, yet feeling that she had been very lonely there. What was the matter with all of us?

I came to Kharkov and found the Americans in its tractor plant much happier than they had been in Stalingrad. Most of them had had a year in Stalingrad already; they were somewhat accustomed now to the Soviet Union. But the Soviet Union was also becoming, quite consciously, accustomed to them. The head of Kharkov Plant told me: "We learned from Stalingrad how to use Americans. We don't give them jobs of general administration, for they don't know their way about our institutions. Nor do we give them jobs as 'consultant,' which meant in practice that nobody consulted them and they wandered unhappily over the plant looking for something to do. Here we give them definite technical tasks, and tell them where to go for help; then we hold them responsible. We're getting good work from them that way."

One of the Americans confirmed this statement. "The Soviet Government is sure getting its money's worth out of me in Kharkov," he laughed. "It didn't in Stalingrad." He was pleased to be giving a "square deal" at last.

E. C. Wood, whom I met in the Spartak Hotel in Kharkov, seemed to be a happy American. He didn't have to produce; he investigated causes of breakdowns in steel rolling mills. There were plenty of breakdowns and plenty of causes, so Wood was happy with work. He laughed: "I'm picking out saboteurs for them. Not directly; I don't know the actual people. But when I open the gear-box of a cranky machine down under a steel table that takes half a day's work with a crane to take off, and find those gears clogged with nine pailfuls of dirt and steel shavings, then I just show it to the red director and say: 'This thing couldn't happen by accident.' He's a good guy who doesn't know his way about in a steel mill, but his eyes light up when I tell him, and he knows whom to grab. Wherever I go, somebody gets into trouble."

Yet even Wood hardly knew his way about in the Soviet Union. He lost forty pounds in a series of hot investigations and came down with pneumonia. He was given a day and night nurse and an extra interpreter-nurse and during the height of the crisis he had a doctor night and day. Wood worried so much over what all this was going to cost him that he got up before he was well and had a relapse. He went to the offices of the Steel Trust and said: "You've got to take this out of my salary gradually; I can't stand it all at once." He was thunderstruck to find that the treatment was free. He had actually supposed that a man who was saving hundreds of thousands of dollars for the Soviet Union would have to pay for illness caused by overwork. Wood had been used to that under capitalism.

My second trip took me eastwards to the Urals and Siberia, where I saw the Kuznetsk steel mill emerging from chaos. Two years ago it had been a sleepy village of 1,500 souls; one year ago, on my first visit, it was a giant mud-hole in which excavation was beginning. Now the coming steel works stretched four kilometers along the valley, great towering structures waist-deep in dirt and débris. Eight spectacular "stoves" of the first two blast furnaces cut the sky with cylindrical blackness; around them lay the seven-story power-house, the many-peaked roof of a great foundry, the structures of the open hearth building—"built on the largest scale of any open hearth in the world," said the Americans—and the beginnings of the rolling mills. More than a mile to the right stood a two and a half million dollar fire-brick plant, merely to make replacement brick for Kuznetsk. Such was the scale of the new city.

American engineers of the Freyn Company were working in Kuznetsk—for which their company had drawn the basic design. Glenn, senior engineer in charge of construction, climbed miles daily over mud, steel, and lumber mountains, constantly fighting to introduce American methods. He fought the tendency of Russian engineers and new-made foremen to sit in offices; he spent his days on scaffolds and in pits. "When there is a dangerous job for which I'm responsible," he told me, "I don't ask men to go where I won't lead them. And I've learned that it isn't enough in this country to give orders to a foreman; you've got to explain things to all the workers. They were throwing ice and frozen gravel into concrete in winter to save a little extra work. No orders stopped it. So I called a meeting and said: 'I can't watch this twenty-four hours, but you are on the job all the time. That ice and frozen gravel may hurt my reputation but it's hurting a steel mill that belongs to you. It's the first time your country has laid concrete in such winters; you've got to be careful on this job.' Say, you know there was no more trouble. I'm getting to be a regular communist propagandist!"

Many of the other engineers were mixing with Russian workers, showing them how to do their jobs. Zimmerman was preparing a series of technical booklets, of which three had been translated and published in Kuznetsk. Others were volunteering to help in technical courses; they wanted to take part in the life around them. They did it as well as any Americans I had seen. Yet there still remained an odd aloofness between them and Russians. The Russians said the Americans were "too passive." What! When they tramped over mountains of construction eighteen hours a day. . . . "But they don't complain about abuses to the paper or to the trade union or the party. They just tell them to the administration. They don't really 'take part.' "

I began to test out this passivity. I said to an American who related some technical abuse he had seen: "Did you ever think of writing about it to the Kuznetsk paper?" He looked shocked. "Why, that wouldn't be proper. You see, we work for Freyn and he's hired by the Steel Trust here. The Steel Trust pays for our information, and we give it to the administration as much as they will take. But it wouldn't do for us to go over the heads of Mr. Freyn and the Steel Trust to make a scandal in the newspaper."

"That's the way they work here," I answered. "The men who are popular and effective do just that."

"That seems to me just chaos and demagogy," he answered.

His standards of professional ethics were just the reverse of the Soviet standards.

"Do you suppose," said the Americans one evening, after a round table discussion in which they had quizzed me about Soviet Russia and I had confessed myself "no authority on communism"—"do you suppose we could get one of these communists to come round regularly for a while and tell us what it is all about, and answer some questions? We don't want them to think that we're butting into their politics; but some of us would like to know what it is that we are building. It's different from steel mills we have known." . . . I told them the local party organization would be delighted to send them someone. They were. They hadn't thought it possible that "dollar engineers" could be interested. Neither had known how to approach the other.

Six hours by rail through the Kuzbas Valley, I came to the coal mines of Leninsk, where more than a hundred American miners were settled with their families. They came "to build socialism and live as Russian miners do." They were given much better food and rooms than Russian miners, yet a third of them had left in the first few months. They didn't complain much about food or housing; they complained about chaos. They had a right to complain.

Leninsk had grown in one year from 30,000 to 100,000 population, and was feverishly putting down mines, and putting up standard houses, some of which developed cracks before the roofs were on. There was one interpreter for more than a hundred Americans; and he couldn't understand all their dialects, which ranged from Jugo-Slav to Welsh. Their first trouble was with passports, which had been rather carelessly collected from them, some in Novo-Sibirsk as they passed that Siberian capital, and some in Leninsk. A few passports had come back but most of them hadn't. This didn't worry the Americans; they were used to living without passports. Then somebody told them they had to have passports. Wives of kulak exiles told their wives in the market (some of them spoke Russian) : "Your husbands deceive you. You are exiles here without passports!" The Americans began inquiries and every Russian official, hospitably wishing to answer and really knowing nothing, gave a different reply.

One said: "But it is impossible for you to be without passports; you must have them somewhere." Another said: "They keep passports of men who are on contract so that they won't run away." Panic arose in the camp; the cry began: "Forced labor!" One nervous man went about nights in terror, crying: "I'll never get out of Siberia!" I buttonholed an official of the Coal Trust who had just arrived from Novo-Sibirsk and asked the reason for this "outrage." "Why," he said, "I've most of the passports in my bag. They were in a clerk's desk in our office. Most of the Americans didn't give photographs for registration and he was too lazy to send for them."

The official had come to investigate men who were demanding to leave. He said disgustedly that they were "not miners at all but men who can stick to nothing; they have worked at everything from mines to Ford Motor Works—even petty trade." I said: "Most miners in America have. I don't dispute your judgment about the men who are leaving. But you don't get out of this town without meeting the rest of the men who are getting ready to leave. There's nobody here to explain things."

We had the meeting. Miners had worked for a month and got no wages; the foremen didn't know their names and forgot to list them. With jeers they were exhibiting their undecipherable pay-books. The official explained that this abuse was already understood at Novo-Sibirsk, which had decided to give all the Americans a flat wage for the first three months till they could organize proper checking of the piece work. The worst complaint was that the mines were so badly equipped and organized that brute strength rather than skill got out the coal; the Americans couldn't use "these sticks that they call shovels, and of which there aren't enough to go round anyway." Their pride as efficient miners was dying in torment; they had come to teach Siberians American ways. But in that Leninsk chaos the Siberian peasants got out more coal than they could.

I spoke of the conditions in Leninsk to an old Kuzbasser

whom I met in Sverdlovsk where the biggest plant in the world for heavy machine-building was under construction. He laughed: "It sounds just like old days. We had the same trouble in that valley in 1923. But it won't last as long as it did with us; the U.S.S.R. has moved. Leninsk is building twenty-six new mines in the next six years; so they'll have a bit of a mess. One good political organizer for those Americans to captain their fight under Soviet conditions is all they really need. They themselves will produce all the first lieutenants. They're miners; they'll know how to organize and fight." He added reminiscently: "I'd like to go back and show them, but I'm pretty busy here."

In Magnitogorsk, the greatest job of them all, a new steel city of 180,000 people had sprung in a year and a half from Ural wilderness five hundred miles away from any other town. The autumn evening air was like wine; lights on encircling hills made fairyland. I piled into an autotruck with a crowd of German workers who had come from Berlin and were going to "stay forever." The woman next me balanced painfully on a tilted suitcase and let out sharp cries of pain when the worst jolts impaled her yet more firmly on sharp edges. She couldn't resist the jolts; her arms were round a baby. Between the shrieks her eyes roved over the encircling lights in rapture: "How idyllic," she cried. "A job for always!" . . . An average of three hundred people a day had been thus arriving, Russians, Germans, Tartars, even gypsies, thirty-five different nationalities. For a year and a half this steady stream had been coming; it would keep on for yet more years.

Eleven newspapers, four of them dailies, two technical journals, a literary fortnightly were being produced in Magnitogorsk. Thirteen schools, two technical universities, a big city theater, a "circus better than Sverdlovsk" and half a dozen movies were already running. A wood-working plant turned out four standard barracks daily, each housing two hundred people; a concrete works had already made two million building blocks. A fibrolite factory was making flooring. A limestone quarry sent trains of limestone by a new railroad down the valley. The largest iron deposit in the world had been shipping ore since May all over the Urals. A dam three-fourths of a mile long had made a lake in a once barren valley. A brick works and a fire-brick works turned out their products by the million.

Yet Magnitogorsk was "not yet open"! Not open? No! Pig-iron had not yet begun to appear! All these many plants worked breathlessly towards it.

Forty Americans were on the job in Magnitogorsk, from the McKee Company and the Koppers Company. Many of them were making themselves popular by showing methods to the Russian workers. Yet none of them seemed quite adjusted; those who were most popular with the workers seemed to develop friction with their firms. Calder, working alone on special contract, was the most admired by the Russian youth around him. He handled them without mercy. He told their Young Communist organizations that they were a lot of braggarts; he dared them to put their words into deeds. They took his dares hotly; they would show this American. They stole cranes which were forcibly taken back. Calder made and broke many youthful reputations by keeping account of their work. He talked English so hard that they had to understand him.

It was clear from all my trips to the new giants, that few Americans felt themselves to be making good. Something had happened to their personal efficiency; it didn't work. This made them discontented. Most of the Russians had a simple, cynical cure. "Let them go if we don't need them. If we need them, offer more dollars."

This attitude outraged the Americans. "These guys say they're building socialism, but all they can think of is dollars! They could get a lot of good men cheaper, if they'd give them a chance to work. But God, how they squander the dollars. They'll save on a few men's salary and blow in millions on wrong equipment. I could have saved them a million on that machinery but their engineers were like drunken sailors. . . ." The American's deepest religion was outraged; waste was to him the devil, as it had been in the schools of my youth.

I protested often to Russians. "These men aren't just 'bought-and-paid-for.' They want to do good work."

"They're not interested in socialism," came the ready answer. "And we notice they take the dollars."

Yes, they did. What American refuses dollars? Dollars were to the American a token of worth. He came from a capitalism which standardizes men as "five-thousand-dollar men." His will to create, his craving to know himself efficient and his wish for dollars were so mixed in him that he didn't even try to tell them apart. Dollars made him feel successful, individually significant, personally worthy; the offer of more dollars reassured him when he worried that his work seemed bad. Didn't even I think in dollars, in an odd reversed way? My symbol of freedom had been the refusal of salary from the Concessions Committee; my flag of idealism had been the cutting of salary on *Moscow News;* my belief in my authority began when Ogonek gave out money. Was this all twisted? Didn't money really mean something?

To the Russians, dollars were not standards of worth, but bribes. In their swift leap from the ethics of the Asiatic market to those of socialism, they had not acquired that instinctive standardization of things and men in terms of money which a long period of efficient capitalism gave the Americans. Some of this standardization by money the Russians soon found it necessary to acquire; hordes of workers, recently peasants, needed the stimulus of differentiation in rewards based on standardized piece work. But basically the Russians classified men into those who worked from the will to socialism and those who had to be coerced or bribed. The Americans weren't coerced, nor did they care about socialism. Clearly, reasoned the Russians, give them bribes!

It worked; bribes often got the results they wanted, so the Russians were justified. But I felt the bewildered pain of many of those Americans wanting so hard to make good. I would argue with the Russians: "Why can't you give more explanation, more time, better organization of their work, something to make it possible for them to feel themselves efficient? You would get more from them for less money." . . . Yes, that was true. Later the Russians began to explain things better.

But looking back I can answer my own past self and those other Americans, who are scattered now in jobs and out of jobs all over the earth: "You did your share in this new world —more or less blindly. I also did my share and was more or less blind. But explanation, time and organization were 'too expensive'; they cost the lives of the very best comrades. Didn't Mihailoff die to conquer Stalingrad's first conveyor? Could Mihailoff * give more time for our instruction? It was cheaper to bribe with dollars." And to those Americans scattered in Soviet enterprises, workers who will never go back, I would say, did I need to say it: "You fought your way through. This country needed your fighting, more even than your technique."

The Five-Year Plan was Soviet Russia's "War for Independence" from the exploiting imperialist world. Men died in that war, but they won it. They changed their country from a land of backward industry and medieval farming, defended only by grim will, to a land of modern industry, farming and defense. From an agrarian country of small peasant holdings farmed in the manner of the Middle Ages, the Soviet Union became a predominantly industrial country. Twenty million tiny farms became two hundred thousand large farms, collectively owned and partly mechanized. A country once illiterate became a land of compulsory education covered by a net-work of schools and universities. New branches of industry arose: machine tools, automotive, tractor, chemical, aviation, highgrade steel, powerful turbines, nitrates, synthetic rubber, artificial fibers. Thousands of new industrial plants were built; thousands of old ones remodeled. The Soviet Union emerged from the Five-Year Plan a powerful, modern nation, whose word has weight in the councils of the world. To this end millions of men fought and endured as in battle.

* After a series of directors had proved unable to bring Stalingrad Tractor Works up to its program of production, Mihailoff, one of the upper chiefs of the automotive industry of the country, personally took charge, succeeded at last in reaching program, and almost immediately died of a disease which was admittedly made fatal by his exhaustion. . . . There were many similar instances among less conspicuous men.

In Novo-Sibirsk I ran across Bill Shatoff, building in a single year more railroads than the whole Turk-Sib. He was sick; the nervous strain had affected his eyes. I asked why he didn't bring his wife out, have a home, comfortable routine, healthy living. Bill stared as if I had gone mad.

"The greatest thing in life," he said, "is work! No, not just work! Creation! In this particular bit of time in which we live, there is the chance to create without end or limit. Do you think I could turn aside from an hour of creation to be nice to a wife or to come to dinner on time?"

Unforgettable words! They echoed over the naked steppe and reëchoed into the roar of railroads, steel mills! Out of nothingness—socialist cities! Out of chaos—a world in making! No, not just work! Creation!

Bill Shatoff's words thrilled me with joy, yet at times they shook me with loneliness and longing. What was the matter with me, what was the matter with all of us Americans, that we couldn't quite connect with this creation? All of us could see, from the chaos in which we worked, from *Moscow News*, from Stalingrad, from Kuznetsk, that somebody, somehow, all round us—only not quite where we were—was making a world.

CHAPTER XXVI

AN APPEAL TO STALIN

STEADILY the situation on *Moscow News* grew worse. Vacsov monotonously ignored my resignations; Meshlauk was inaccessible. I suddenly thought of that Central Committee which was said to have appointed me, but which I had never been able to see. Perhaps I should resign to them. I sent them a letter and was eventually received by Gusev, head of the press department. I didn't know whether he was my boss or just an adviser, but he seemed to think he had some authority. He wanted to know of what I complained and what I wanted. By this time I hardly knew of what I complained; it was everything. What I wanted was just to get off. He seemed puzzled but friendly, said he would see what could be done and advised me to talk it over with Vacsov. Nothing more happened and I couldn't reach him again, so I decided that Gusev had been a kindly soul who had really no connection with the question.

I found a Russian communist who was especially sensitive about the use of his own name on certain pamphlets, so I told him my troubles. He was properly indignant, and said: "They are exploiting your ignorance of our ways. They have no right to use your name unless you approve every article in the paper; we are much more serious with names than you are. If you can't get satisfaction, write to Stalin."

"About a personal injustice?" I exclaimed. "I had thought of writing to him about the poor style of everything the communists publish for Americans." . . . "Do both," he said. I did.

Three days later came a telephone call from Stalin's secretariat saying that they were investigating my complaint and would notify me in a few days. The next afternoon Vacsov told me my request for the removal of my name was granted.

"I hope you'll continue to write for us," he said. Relieved by the ending of many months' tension I promised not only to write but to come to staff meetings and give them the benefit of my advice—"as long as at last we are honest."

My letter to Stalin, I thought, had already acted, exerting magic pressure behind the scenes. I was the more surprised when Stalin's secretariat telephoned the following evening, that they were now ready to take up my complaint by a conference between Vacsov, myself and "some responsible comrades." . . . "Why bother anybody?" I told them. "The matter is already settled." . . . "Completely settled? Haven't you anything else to talk about?" . . . Oh, well, I thought, I'll go. . . . My fear of intruding on responsible comrades nearly lost me the most important half hour of my existence.

Vacsov telephoned importantly: "I'm coming to take you to Stalin." . . . Some more of Vascov's bluff! It was some secretary of course to whom we were going. His Ford turned to the right at the foot of Tverskaia.

"But aren't we going to the Central Committee?"

"No," said Vacsov, "we go to the Kremlin."

"We sped along by the Alexander sunken gardens under high dark walls in the early evening, where the old Neglinka River which guarded the Kremlin gates in the Middle Ages runs underground now to Moscow River. We turned at the White Gate and crossed where the drawbridge has become an auto road, and the gardens sank beneath us as we passed by rows of street lamps towards a pale moon of a clock looking down from the ancient archway.

A sentry stopped us at the portal.

"You will have my name from Stalin's secretariat," said my companion proudly. "I am Vacsov." . . .

The sentry checked a list and then glanced questioningly at me.

"Strong," I answered.

"Correct," he said, drawing back to let us pass. Then we rose by the curving driveway which turns right to the larger palaces and left towards the government buildings and the former homes of the Kremlin guard.

We turned left; we stopped in the middle of a cluster of buildings, went in an unimposing entrance and by a small elevator rose a couple of flights. I found myself in a large, well-lit office where half a dozen secretaries worked at desks. One of them near the entrance informally waved me towards Meshlauk and Gusev who also were there. So these were the "responsible comrades" with whom I should talk it over. I didn't care to talk to Meshlauk, who for nine months deserted me to Vacsov. Towards Gusev I felt friendly. He had asked once of what I complained and had seemed puzzled. Then for two months he had been inaccessible. But what's two months in Soviet Russia? Anyway, I was off that paper; they couldn't put me back.

Then a door opened to a long conference room with several green baize tables at the nearest of which I saw Stalin, Kaganovich and Voroshiloff rising to meet us. Were these the "responsible comrades"? I was ashamed to be taking their time. Somehow we should have settled that miserable paper without bothering people who decided the fate of one-sixth of the world. I had never expected this from that informal telephone call, so informal that I had answered: "You needn't bother." This was taking me pretty seriously. I would just explain and get it over.

I walked quickly forward and shook hands with them. It didn't occur to me to wait for an introduction. There must be no delay. They knew who I was, since they had sent for me; and I of course knew who they were from Red Square demonstrations and their pictures in the papers. Stalin was stocky and strong, with bronzed face and graying hair above his khaki-colored "party tunic"; he seemed like a man who is neither tired nor rested but who has worked very long and can go on working much longer, because he knows how to use strength—quiet, with no waste motion. Voroshiloff was more vivaciously wasteful of energy; Kaganovich was tall, handsome and dark.

Stalin asked whether I could follow discussion in Russian. His eyes were kind yet grave, giving rest and assurance. Then we all sat down at the green baize table, Voroshiloff at the head and Stalin next to him on the far side where he could see all our faces. Our side of the table began with Kaganovich, then myself almost across from Stalin, then Meshlauk, Gusev and Vacsov. Some lamp on the table seemed to obstruct Vacsov's view; he often walked up to stand behind me, resting his hand on my chair. Thus began an utterly informal conversation with no obvious chairman or notes.

Stalin turned at once to Vacsov. "How does it happen that the comrade here complains that you give her no authority on the paper, yet insist on retaining her name, and call it an anti-Soviet act if she takes it off? Why is it necessary to use such violence?" . . . Direct like that! I even felt sorry for Vacsov.

Then I smiled to see how equal Vacsov was to the occasion; he always was. He said he had referred the matter to the Central Committee, and must wait for them to act. Stalin turned to Gusev to investigate the delay. I thought: "Why bother Gusev—a decent fellow—now it's all over?" I interrupted to tell Stalin that it was agreed last night that I might take my name off. Vacsov, to emphasize our utter harmony, pulled out for display the letter in which I agreed to keep on writing for the paper.

Voroshiloff was chuckling: "When was this agreed? Last night? After we began to investigate!" Kaganovich added a witty remark. Gusev protested: "It was done without you; we didn't know you were investigating." . . . Yes, that was quite possible. But Stalin turned to me.

"Did you write this of your own will or under any pressure?"

"I wanted to write it, now that they've let me off . . ."

"But you intend to continue writing for the paper?"

"Why, yes."

"Do you intend to sign your articles?"

"Yes, I suppose so. . . ."

"Only not sign the newspaper?" * persisted Stalin. Why did he want to know these trivial details? It was all over anyway.

Vacsov rose, contented with victory, and opened a copy of

---

* The editor's name, on a Russian paper, is signed at the end of the last page, and attests his full responsibility for the contents.

Moscow News to show the inside editorial pages. It flashed into my mind that Stalin had never seen it, and Vacsov was showing off. "Her name comes off the list of editors on this page. That's all," he said.

There was brief pause as if they tried to understand this. Then Stalin asked in quiet, analyzing tones: "Isn't that something of a demotion for her?" . . . What! Then he saw clear through to the bottom! My heart leaped and I smiled. He saw that if a useful worker was willing to keep on working yet fought to avoid all credit there was something twisted and wrong. That mutual agreement hadn't deceived him; he saw I had given up hope. He wanted to know what my hope had been before it died; I could tell it from his tones.

"There is nothing more that you want then? Nothing more?" It was Stalin speaking to me. Two or three times he had made occasion to say it in different ways, with searching yet reassuring tones. In tones that said: "Have you then quite finished with life?" Here was a man to whom you could say anything; he knew almost before you spoke; he wished to know more clearly and to help. Never had I found anyone so utterly easy to talk to.

Suddenly the will that had been dead within me was alive, flaming and free. I knew now what I wanted; I had known these two years long. Two years? Oh, longer, longer! It came from a deep past. It had been buried under distorted routine; it had been twisted beyond hope. Now again I wanted to bring American efficiency to Russia; I wanted a newspaper to help our Soviet-Americans in their difficult fight. Had there ever been a time when I hadn't wanted it?

I was speaking swiftly; this was something they must know. I was telling about the two papers, one for engineers and one for workers. They fought each other, organized competing activities and muddled the Americans. "Neither paper can be strong, neither can be good."

"Of course there is some difference between workers and engineers," I admitted. . . . Stalin said in a deep, firm voice: "There is." . . . It threw me off for a moment, the only time I found it hard to talk. What did he mean? That I didn't see that difference? He was right; I had given no weight to it even when I spoke. But he mustn't mean that we wouldn't get that one, united paper.

"American workers and American engineers—all of them in Soviet Russia—are not different enough to need two papers," I rushed on. "The American engineers rose mostly from workers; the workers' chief problem is the proper use of their technical skill. I don't count some valuta specialists who won't read a Soviet paper anyway. All the rest want to be efficient in this country, and don't know anything about its life. They all need stories and facts, not long arguments and theories; they need problems of daily life and struggle, showing them how to be useful in Soviet industry. They need one paper to unite them, not two to separate them. They themselves don't like two papers; they go to our excursions and then to *Workers' News* excursions and always ask why we have two little fighting weeklies, instead of one good daily?"

Vacsov was supporting me; he spoke for "one strong daily." I thought: "He intends to swallow Axelrod, but that's not fair." . . . I might have known by this how events were moving. Vacsov always could pick the winning side.

Gusev next was explaining the theory behind two papers. Had there really been a theory then? I had thought it Axelrod's desire to keep something going. No, Axelrod was a good communist; he would be sure to have some sort of theory.

Gusev said: "It was the idea that for engineers and circulation abroad we need more or less a liberal paper. . . ."

"What do you mean by 'liberal'?" asked Stalin.

Did it check Gusev, I wondered, as "there is" had checked me. But Stalin wasn't asking for an answer; he threw it in as a guide to thought.

Gusev went on: "But for the increasing number of American workers coming into our industries we needed something more serious—more of a party organ."

There was a pause. Stalin seemed to consider. "No, not even for them," he said.

Kaganovich added: "Facts, sharp facts are good for them also."

"If they stay long enough with us," said Stalin, "they will learn Russian and get their theory from our Russian papers which are—very full of it." . . . What! He knew the weariness of theory for people just learning to analyze? He knew the dullness of long arguments?

Meshlauk next was telling how *Moscow News* had been started as an engineers' journal. It was Meshlauk then who had betrayed me, intending it only for engineers from the first. But now, he said, conditions might be changing. The chief trouble had been Axelrod—an impossible editor for Americans. He had been replaced by Vacsov, a man "easy to get on with."

"You think Vacsov easy to get on with," remarked Stalin. "Possibly Comrade Strong has a different idea. How is it?" he turned to me, smiling. "Is Vacsov easy to get on with?"

Here was my chance to annihilate my enemy. I couldn't take it. Vacsov didn't matter. Now that I knew there was real theory against the union, I was afraid it would not go through. Somewhere deep down, below all conscious thinking, I knew if that one paper could be settled, Vacsov would be settled too.

I paused; I grew embarrassed. I didn't want to speak of Vacsov, not even to answer Stalin. "I don't think Vacsov's character is the point at issue," I blurted out. Then I rushed on. "This is the first I knew it was ever supposed to be an engineers' journal. It was supposed to be for all Americans, and to grow to a daily."

"Who supposed this?" asked Voroshiloff.

"Why, all of us did," I said. "We didn't know how there came to be two papers." . . . I was still talking, but suddenly I knew it was all settled. Everybody seemed to know it.

"One paper?" . . . asked someone. "One paper," said another. . . . "Not a party paper?" . . . "No, not a party paper." . . . "But a Soviet paper?" . . . "At least," said Kaganovich, "not an anti-Soviet paper." Everyone laughed. The decision seemed to come from everyone.

"If we are going to have that kind of paper," said Vacsov to Stalin, "you'll have to tell the Glav-Lit not to interfere with us. They censor even our workers' letters. We got a good letter from an American sailor who spent four days in the port of Odessa, which we know isn't a very good town. He was impressed by the hope he found there. He wrote: "I saw misery in Odessa as I had seen it in all ports of the world. But . . ." Vacsov got no further.

"And they took out the 'misery' from Odessa," said Stalin in tones of perfect comprehension. Comprehension, not only of us and of the fallibility of censors, but of Odessa and its hardship and of how good it would be if "misery" could be so easily "taken out." And suddenly I understood even the censor—no final autocrat, but a very limited human being trying to protect his country in a world of enemies; one must know how to coöperate with him, when to argue, when to fight and when to yield.

We rose, and Stalin nodded to Kaganovich, who must call us later with Axelrod and others added to work out the detail of reorganization. . . . Where were all those twisted emotions that had hurt me to madness? All pain was gone.

Vacsov was saying exultantly as we went down the stairway: "You won't leave us now. It means a big expansion. We must press this chance to get a good technical base for our paper and enough valuta for correspondents abroad." . . . Was it possible he thought he could be the head of a big daily which included also the workers? But it was so clear, so clear!

I must break it to him gently. Why should one hurt him? All fights were over now. "You can't think of it as just a *Moscow News* expansion," I warned him. "Axelrod has built another newspaper, whose staff is larger than ours."

"Yes," said Gusev firmly. "It means a whole reorganization on a new base." I was glad to know that Gusev would be protecting Axelrod—Axelrod, my old enemy, who had built a living paper while ours was going dead.

.   .   .   .

I have tried to make clear the essence of that small meeting, but I do not think that any words can give it. Everything was so unemphatic; it dealt with such prosaic things. The effect of personality and tone went far beyond the words. When I left I was hardly aware that Stalin had done anything. It seemed we had all done it. I remembered the decisive nods of Voroshiloff, the cheerful wit of Kaganovich. Stalin seemed to stand out less than any, less even than the minor people. "Not very imposing for such an important man," I thought. "But how wonderfully easy to talk to!" It seemed that work might be forever clear and joyous, if only sometimes one might go to him with questions, and watch one's tangled skein of thought untangle through knowledge deeper than one's own.

How swiftly everything had happened! How suddenly it had all come clear! So swiftly and suddenly that I could hardly catch it. That night and all next day and for many nights thereafter, the memory of that half hour began to grow. Day after day I understood more of it. It began to explain my work; then it began to explain the Soviet Union. It solved new problems as they arose; it gave me a method. Other hours in my life that were marked by great emotion—when I have adored great men—have all died out; I cannot recapture their feeling. But that half hour grows with years. Even today I can feel the atmosphere of that meeting—its sympathetic but unemotional analysis, seeking fundamental lines and relations and acting to set them right.

I began first by thinking of the people; how clearly they had all been revealed. Vacsov, that cheerful bluffer! If a liberal journal for engineers had been intended, Vacsov was not a bad choice. He was good at making the dollar specialists feel at home; with them he was really "easy to get on with." He ran our paper as he might have run the "Boosters Journal of Kankakee," with a bluff, free-spending bunch on top and a hard-worked staff below. It had torn us to pieces in Moscow. Those dollar specialists also were torn to pieces by Moscow. They were going home; that was why our paper went dead.

Axelrod grew clear. How I had fought him over those long translations from Russian; I wanted American writers and vivid style. But if Axelrod was told to make a paper instructing workers in communism, he was right to get those Russian articles. Certainly none of our Americans could instruct them with our breezy style.

Meshlauk—I saw him also. Not as the god who was to give me a big paper, and not as the devil who for nine months refused to speak, but as a very busy man, vice-chairman of all the Soviet industries, on whom I had pushed the idea of a paper. He had seen at once that it helped solve one of his problems—discontented engineers. Then I had thrust god-ship upon him with long typewritten prayers, asking him to settle all my troubles. He had given me Vacsov—to cheer the engineers—and then had turned to his own job, refusing to be my god any longer. Hadn't he a big enough job—all the state industries? Why did I expect him to solve everybody's job—the American workers, my job, the job of trade unions?

Why were these people all so clear, and yet no longer pain-ful? Because I saw them no longer through unanalyzed but powerful emotions, but in relation to a new clear "line" of common purpose. They were elements to take account of in doing a certain job in a certain direction. The most important thing in the world then was the finding of a clear line and direction. When you found it, people also became clear.

For the first time in years I remembered that little group around Rutgers who had investigated complaints from Ameri-cans in Soviet industry, and had talked about starting a paper. They had seemed so inefficient that I had looked around for a "big man" to put it over. It was I, in my passion for gods, who had rushed from their need, to serve Meshlauk. I recalled now their baffled looks when I told them that Meshlauk and I had started "their paper"; they had been barely polite but I had expected them to be pleased. Had they wanted to start their own? They had done it—the rottenly-written *Workers' News* that was a "friend to workers." My rush to Meshlauk created the paper for engineers. I even rushed to the Foreign Office and almost got them to start a paper in my desire for "wide support" instead of a "clear line." It was I who had muddled it all!

Well, it was I who had suffered, so that wasn't so bad. Two papers had not been entirely evil. There had really been a difference in the tastes of workers and specialists, more than there was now with most of the dollar contracts over. I had twisted myself into a lot of painful emotions; but now we would combine the papers. Our "line" was clear.

But wasn't it amusing? They were organizing by putting us all together—Axelrod, Vacsov and I, who had so bitterly fought each other—with Borodin, for whom I had asked, as "responsible editor." That certainly wasn't the way they reorganized in the capitalist world; the winner cleared out the old chiefs. That meant that none of us was winner; we all had something to give the paper and were supposed to get on with each other and give it. Well, we could. Now that we knew our line. The line, it seemed, and not the people were important.

But wait! The line itself was created and carried out by the people. Stalin hadn't handed it to us. We had all made it. We had analyzed the past and out of this had come the future. After all, we all wanted the same thing—American efficiency brought into Soviet industry through American workers. That was why we could unite.

But what had united us, when we had all been fighting? Now at last I saw what Stalin had done. I remembered his different approach to the four people he questioned. That frontal attack on Vacsov that had startled me; how exactly it had suited Vacsov! Those subtle tones of teasing comradeship to Meshlauk, which implied that Meshlauk was a very big man but perhaps he didn't quite know Vacsov. To me he had been very gentle, asking many times what I wanted. He had known that my hope was dead; he had wished to find what was left of it. How deftly and swiftly he had brought out every person, till we all saw our common purpose. It was Stalin's analysis that had united us. What an expert, I marveled, what an expert! Is this how he does it, across the whole Soviet Union?

I recalled the strength of my will as it flamed up hopeful and free, and thought: "For ten years I have seen this happen across one-sixth of the world, wherever they use this method. I have seen it from outside, now I see it from inside. It is not a will imposed, but a will residing in men, a will to create— which these communists know how to uncover."

I recalled the words of Tregubenko: "We have forces to call

on that the foreigners do not know." I recalled remarks of cynical American observers: "How do these communists 'put it over'? How can they make one hundred and sixty million people starve themselves and work like demons? It would be a secret worth knowing! How do they make them stand for that Five-Year Plan—and like it?" . . . No, they didn't "put it over"; they found it deep inside.

Foreigners said they weren't "democratic"; they did not ballot on the "will of the people." What was this "will"? My will had been dead; I had wanted to escape my job with its torturing complexities; I had begged and threatened. But deep beneath that craven wish to evade, far deeper, was the will I had forgotten—the will to create. It had sickened of failure when the line was twisted. But when clear analysis had shown a path for it, how it had flamed anew!

So had the will of the masses arisen, defying the craven wish for rest from struggle. No orators had stirred them in the way my youth had known. The communists had analyzed the world situation and the need of making the U.S.S.R. self-sufficient; they had shown the socialist goal and the hard road to its achievement. I remembered speeches of Stalin at party congresses, to leaders of industry or to peasant champions; they never appealed to emotion; they analyzed difficulties and direction. Then out of submerged people, entangled in ignorance and inefficiency, arose a will they didn't know they had. I had seen it arise like a whirlwind over the Lower Volga in the days of mass collectivization, needing no longer to be stirred, needing only control. Had they all felt set free as I had, when they saw the clear direction of a line?

Stalin, then, did this for everybody. No, not for everybody. That little group of us that met in Stalin's office—we could combine because we had at bottom the same will. So clear analysis united us. But when you analyzed humanity through to the bottom, you found, under a thousand tossing desires and emotions, two wills which could never unite. The will of exploiters to hold power and the will of exploited masses for freedom could not be reconciled. The will of the masses was hottest in those who were most exploited; it exploded strongly for instance in Mexican peons and Chinese farmhands. But it was confused in them, striving partly against property and partly to gain property. The will of the masses grew clearer in workers organized around machines of modern industry who could never individually possess their tools of production. In them the will for joint possession, for socialism, could become conscious, could find a path and a line. This was why they became leaders and the other exploited masses coalesced around them.

The will of the working-class that beats its way through the crashing débris of centuries with the tools of new production in its hands! That was the deep will that Stalin analyzed and thus released to action.

Not only Stalin did this. It was the job of all communists to do it. Each in his own sphere analyzed the will of the masses near him. Burmina, ex-farmwife, became expert organizer of villages because she saw through her own wrongs as daughter-in-law the need of collectivization. Kovalev, near Stalingrad, knew the needs of poor peasants because he had also been "a peasant who never saw meat in the spring." Men who rose from mines could analyze miners. I recalled that party congress at Red Lugansk, which had sharpened the will of the Donetz Basin on coal mines and sent it down to Kharkov and at last to Moscow, to mix with the wills of all other worker-groups of the country. Each of these groups developed a line of direction as we had done on our paper, and all of these lines together, each of them growing yet all of them fused by analysis, made the general line of the party.

I saw in a flash why I had never been able to organize in the Soviet Union. Long ago in Kansas City I had been an able organizer. All these years I had thought that organizing ability could be moved to another place. Organizing was done not by personal efficiency but by expressing the life from which one grew. I had been flesh of the flesh and soul of the soul of that western democracy, strangled by the monopolies of New York. That was why I fought New York's control as outrage. I had given an honest analyzing brain to release from routine the will of scores of people towards Kansas City children. The will in those cities had flamed up hotly enough to frighten the local politicians.

I had lost that old democracy of Kansas City; it had died even while I watched it; it had been buried deep by the war. For a time I had been an expression for workers in Seattle; they still remembered me so kindly that whenever I went to Seattle they would travel all day across mountains to hear me. I no longer knew their intimate will; I could only mislead them in their daily problems. I had thrown all that away. Yet again, after long loneliness, I had "my people." Thousands of Americans adjusting themselves to Soviet Russia; hundreds of thousands beyond the ocean asking: What does that new world mean? I could interpret from one world to another as no dweller in either world could ever do. Not by efficiency or genius but because I had lived and struggled with them—thirteen years between two worlds.

Why, that was how I had done it! That was why Stalin had sent for me. A foreign correspondent said: "Stalin intervenes even in personal injustices." How silly! Even I had thought it was rather a sign of my importance. Well, it was, but not because of my personal cleverness, but because I had mixed with Americans in Soviet enterprises, had learned and could express their desires. So when I said that American workers and engineers all wanted one paper, the great "party line" by which one-sixth of the world operates had shifted itself a bit on the subject of workers and engineers to fit the needs of our Soviet-Americans. It had seemed so clear to us Americans that we thought the two papers an accident created by Axelrod. But it hadn't been clear to Gusev or Meshlauk, who were very able men. It was clear to me because I was close to the Americans. Thus even I, non-party member and foreigner, had actually made a bit of that famous party line.

Others could express groups that were much larger. A factory director had told me: "It depends on how widely you can think. I can think for a single factory for two years; others can think for a whole industry for five years. Stalin thinks wider than any of us. We have people who can think for all of industry, or for all the trade unions. But no one so matchlessly as Stalin can analyze the place of the U.S.S.R. in the changing scheme of world revolution, and give due weight to each aspect of our daily struggle. That is Stalin's function, the highest function in our country." . . . Yes, that was clear; men never asked for Stalin's "will" or Stalin's "orders," as they did with personal dictators. They asked: "What is Stalin's analysis?" The Soviet Union was the only country where this function of analyst ranked highest. Why? Because it was the only country that really sought to release a great mass will.

Who were the great men of this country? Kaganovich, Voroshiloff, Kalinin, Ordzhonikidze, Zhdanov—all the "big figures"? Foreign correspondents called them "Stalin's puppets," saying: "They can't even speak foreign languages; we never heard of them before." Well, why should they hear of them? Was fame in foreign countries the test for understanding Russia? They were the able men who had lived in the heart of the Russian masses all their days!

Those Russian revolutionists who had lived abroad had found it harder, though they brought back useful gifts. Often they went against the will of the masses. Suddenly I remembered Trotsky, and the men around him who had fallen when he fell. When those men first came back to Russia, and the workers of the whole world seemed flaming to revolt behind them, was it strange that Russian workers, conscious of their own industrial backwardness, should hope for help from foreign workers and see in these returning revolutionists the promise? But when the world revolts of 1919 died down and the German workers failed in 1923 to make a revolution, while the strength of the Russian masses steadily grew, then the Russian workers turned for allies to their peasants, crying out: "Let us build!" . . . But Trotsky refused to listen; he was so determined to impress his own ideas on people that he never tried to know what they really wanted.

Well, what had they really wanted? What had he wanted for them? It was so clear looking backward towards the place where streams divide. I had thought those differences so minute. They were like drops of water side by side on different slopes of a mountain, bound in different directions, each gathering to itself new waters, to empty into seas a world apart. The Russian workers had made the peasants their allies, but Trotsky had thought the peasants a counter-revolutionary force.

Into what valley would Trotsky's stream have descended? Seeking alliances with foreign workers, alienating the peasants close at hand? It led to adventurous escapades among the nations whose workers were not ready to revolt. It led to conspiracy in uncertain upheavals; and such adventures bring either capitulation or war. In such a war a non-industrialized Russian proletariat, already bled white, betrayed by a battle-exhausted peasantry, would have gone to doom. Dying for their friends, like the Mexican peons, dying for all their confused, conflicting friends. But what great genius had avoided this line from the first? Stalin—yet not alone Stalin. A method Stalin used!

One must not make a god of Stalin; he was too valuable for that. He analyzed the mechanical and human forces out of which gods arose and died. Not Stalin, but the will of the working class which Stalin analyzed, had thrown out Trotsky. Trotsky had thrown himself out when he went against it. Had I not seen that will arising—in struggling waifs of John Reed Colony; in farmhands hungry for machinery; in women presidents of villages, fighting down the past; in workers of small factories unable to create. I had seen the brains of communists give at last a line and a name to it, till the Five-Year Plan burst forth from the loins of a hundred and sixty million people, who were tortured by a thousand compromises, clamorous for the pains of birth.

People wonder abroad—I had heard them wonder—how do they keep it up for seventeen years? Professor Laski of the British Independent Labor Party had said: "This energy of the Russian revolution has not yet died down; it lasts longer than any revolution before." Why did they think it must die down; was that a law of revolutions? You could see quite well that it wasn't dying. It was growing stronger and surer of direction. I thought again of the flame that had been Trotsky —the hot emotions he had stirred. I thought of other flames in Europe—personal leaders flaring, dying! People grow tired of personal allegiances; their will is tangled in disillusion. But if you steadily analyze their will and release it, why should they ever grow tired?

This was no transient flame, no hot emotion in which a man might die. This was firm ground beneath my feet forever— and beneath the feet of the world!

CHAPTER XXVII

THE WEB OF DAILY LIFE

FIRM ground beneath my feet—it never entirely left me. That half-hour experience of Stalin's method proved a turning-point both in my work and in my personal life. Yet for some time new perception warred with old habits and emotions. The chain of thought described in the previous chapter developed through two years. Accompanying it the daily tasks went on.

The first big job was the welding of one paper. The formal decision came; we were ordered to combine for May Day and forthwith became a daily. It was two days after the limit set by the printing shop. We told them our troubles; it was a political matter, we said, for a united paper to appear on the first of May. They took it up with the trade union and agreed to work overtime and give the first day of their holiday. We tore galleys apart; we wrote and reset articles, and battled with "city delivery" to accept us later than our turn. *Moscow Daily News* appeared on the streets for the May Day festival. Our joint staff marched in procession holding copies of it aloft on sticks!

Then came the work of reorganization. Two staffs had been hating each other, flinging the words "bourgeois" and "illiterate" back and forth for months. With Borodin as chief there were three associate editors, Vacsov, Axelrod and myself. I was the only one on full time. I needed all my old technique of organization; how were both sides to be satisfied and kept working? *Moscow Daily News* had put over the one paper and given a name to it; *Workers' News* then must get first choice of jobs. I sought out the strongest minds on *Workers' News*—Rose Cohen and Schwartzstein—to learn what the members of their staff could do. There followed conferences, new departments, some people side-tracking themselves by apathy, others by energy shooting ahead.

There was one mad scramble when the Ogonek Publishing House, which gave us offices, took advantage of the amalgamation to move us out of the *Moscow News* rooms in favor of a new magazine. Typewriters, desks, papers and office seal vanished without notice over the May-Day holidays; we found a new magazine in our place when we returned. Borodin threatened by telephone: "You saboteurs, keep your paws off our offices or we'll charge you with wrecking." I was prying the locks off the French windows, mobilizing the staff to carry desks and tables through them, and moving in what we needed to go on typing. Some of our copy we never found. I think it was eight days later when we found the office seal. This flurry occurred on our third day of organization; yet the daily still came out.

Hour by hour and day by day, as long ago in Kansas City, I felt collective life take form in chaos. I could feel it into its farthest tentacles as I called it into being. The blood flowed badly through the typist tentacle; I got them together, tried new assignments, put the most energetic one in charge. Tomorrow the sore spot was translators. Everywhere the life began to flow more freely; I was exultant now. Then someone said: "Strong's making it a personal organ; she decides everything herself." That hurt. Wasn't I making it everybody's organ without the slightest thought of myself?

Borodin said: "I shouldn't have taken this paper if I had known you would do so little writing." How could I write when I spent eighteen hours a day organizing? Perhaps he didn't want my organizing then? Bit by bit decisions I was making were taken from me. I watched them go; I was too proud to protest. "All right," I said. "They don't want me. They just want my facile writing. Very well, I can easily do that."

I saw them drift into bad organization; I saw them slip into bad style. I drew back and made no suggestions. They didn't want me, then let them do without! But in spite of the bad style and organization it never again occurred to me to remove my name. After a long time I understood that that fury about my name had been a disease in my pride of efficiency, which was almost the deepest thing in my soul. I hadn't really cared so much about reputation; I had been infuriated partly by seeing a paper with which I was connected go to pieces in ways I couldn't understand, and partly by the feeling that I had been cheated with a promise of full authority when apparently they didn't want me at all. I had rationalized it, saying: "They bought my reputation." Now I knew they at least wanted my writing, and that was a big part of me. But not yet did I understand what full authority means on a Soviet paper; and how little it has to do with the giving of "orders."

After a time I saw how out of the bad style and bad organization they slowly created a paper in the Soviet way. Borodin held meetings, the trade union held meetings, "production conferences" took sometimes hours daily; it seemed a terrible waste of time. They took up the paper page by page, article by article, and everybody criticized. There were not many competent to criticize, yet after those meetings headlines, articles, style began to get better. On the occasions when I went to meetings I saw that my suggestions were usually taken; they seemed even pleased that I should make them. Even then I didn't see that my knowledge and experience were my "authority." I said a bit cynically (I have heard other Americans say it): "It's a funny country; the less you do, the more they prize you. The less you worry, the more they take your advice." . . . Slowly I began to realize that I had been trying to make a paper "for everybody," but "everybody" had wanted to make a paper themselves.

Meanwhile I traveled again and wrote for the paper; it was a regular daily now. Americans everywhere in the industries were changing, even as I. Kuznetsk was already a flourishing steel town; the dollar specialists were beginning to go home. Half the American miners were gone from Leninsk; the others still complained but without panic. The older residents were telling the new ones: "I used to talk like you about damned inefficient Russians. But you can't just rely on yourself: you'll get nothing done that way. You've got first to learn the whole collective life around you." Everywhere the "old Kuzbassers" were especially helpful. Men said: "They're not afraid to buck any combination of men or devils; they've been here twelve years and know their way about."

.   .   .   .

Before going to Kuznetsk I was married. I met an old acquaintance whom I had not seen for several years. I told him my impression of Stalin, and ended enthusiastically: "I'd like to take orders from those men anywhere in the world. I feel they wouldn't give an order until I knew myself it was the thing I must do." I still thought in terms of "orders."

"I think," he smiled, "you must be getting ready to join our party." I nodded, but at once panic seized me, as it always did when I approached ultimate decision. I should like Stalin for a boss, but they wouldn't give me Stalin. I should have to obey some bureaucrat in an office. No, I couldn't! But here was the first responsible communist in ten years who had had such faith in me. I badly felt the need of such a comrade. Friendship resumed and deepened swiftly into marriage. The trip to Kuznetsk was made together.

Thus began to end for me that loneliness in the Soviet Union which had been for ten years more stormily painful than the quest for work which I have described in this book. After some months my husband gave me a clew to it. "You always attracted me," he said, "but in former years I never felt sure that we were on the same side of the barricades."

Barricades? Was that what those others had seen, both men and women, for whose comradeship I had hungered so long in vain. The many American idealists who wish to pioneer in this new land, to give their services, always tell me they are not afraid of hardship, by which they mean some trivial lack of housing or food. How can I tell them of the loneliness—they who expect their facile gesture of friendship to win great hosts of comrades, who think the land they deign to "love" will love them also. Let them look at the first generation of immigrants in America and tell themselves that the gulf they seek to cross is greater.

In ten years I attained in the Soviet Union two friends who had time to talk with me; they were non-party women of my own temperament, idealists working hard.* Of the many communists whom I admired and from whom I hoped for friendship, some simply exploited me in passing while some took time to toss an encouraging word. Some men sought from me the adventure of the alluring stranger, never companionship and home.

I learned to snatch enlightenment from brief contacts, to study in isolation fleeting words. From one I gained some understanding of the peasant, from another the need of careful analysis, while another suggested my letter to Stalin, which more than any one event changed my life. I learned to say, as each new hope for friends gave place to a new despair of isolation, "In all this land of comrades there seems to be for me no comrade, but the knowledge here is worth whatever I have to pay for it." Yet at times it seemed the price exacted would be ruined health, broken nerves, and emotional storms which shook the bounds of sanity.

I learned at last to understand my loneliness though never quite to endure it. We whose souls were formed by an old social system cannot pass to a new one without the change of every nerve-reaction, every habit, every "ideal." No single generation in all history has crossed so deep a gulf as our generation is crossing. It is crossed only in mortal combat and those who win across find on the far shore ruins to rebuild. Workers, fighting in compact ranks for life, cross most easily; their conflicts are outer ones. Capitalists never cross; they die when the old world dies. We intellectual idealists cross only when everything that the past has built is broken in us—everything that we ever called truth, virtue, friendship, freedom, and that made up our highly cherished "souls." Only then do we reach new truth, virtue, comradeship and freedom upon the barricades.

This crossing, painful and difficult for all who make it, is easier when we go forward with an army of marching workers in the scenes of our youth at the speed and with the thought-forms that we know. I challenged that crossing in a strange land whose habits, thought-forms, rate of movement derived

* See Chapter XXX, "Death of a Saint," for these two women.

from a different past. I gained a swifter but more shattering knowledge.

To a country where every person had been long tested and classified by conflict I came as stranger; not for many years does such a country accept strangers. I derived my concept of "friendship" from a land where we shared ideals and emotions by hours of vivid talk; I came to a land where even close comrades found one hour a year for talk. In the vast disorganization they rebuilt they had scarce time to snatch scant food and sleep; they shared not emotions but labor, danger and victory. In such a land I continued the divided purpose of a writer for American capitalist newspapers; what sharing of labor and danger arose from that?

One man, a worker from the Donetz coal-fields, sought of his own desire to cross the gulf between us. I met him in a workers' sanitarium where I never became for him a well-known foreign writer but just "a good-looking woman who wrote." He said: "I've left my first wife because she persisted in remaining a dark peasant, weeping every night when I went to party meetings. I've responsible tasks for the party and I want an intelligent wife who has work of her own. I don't know whether you could stand it on the Donetz but it wouldn't hurt you to try. At least you'd learn a lot about our workers while I'd learn culture and American efficiency." His realism shocked my American sentiment; I decided that I couldn't feel "in love" with him at all. I look back at it now as an honest, workmanlike proposal.

In choosing the Soviet Union for my residence I added to the perilous gulf another chasm, those early thought-forms which harden into the lifelong symbols of reality and desire. To the difficult analysis of class struggle, I added the difficulties of alien forms of expression. Our deep, unanalyzed feelings derive from a different past. Most intelligent Russian men of my generation feel life in terms of the 1905 barricades. That worker of the Donetz felt deepest desire as the old peasant hunger for culture. My husband's daughter and the Soviet youth of today find the deepest symbols of reality in steel mills and construction jobs. I have met a few people whose symbol of ultimate reality is some great festival in color, some harmony of the spheres in music. One old Bolshevik told me: "My deepest reality is still the developing human soul, but we shall have no time for that for many years."

These ultimate symbols of theirs are for me embroideries, which I note, analyze but do not deeply feel. My symbol of reality remains—whenever I feel most deeply—the unexplored trail in the untamed wilderness, the hiking into the West to undiscovered ranges, the glad adventure of man to conquer the stars! So feel the men from Chicago west to the Pacific; with them I might more easily have "held the barricades" or "dared the crossing."

Though our youth gives us lifelong symbols, their content is steadily changed by blows of environment. Our minds react with pain to new surroundings, reshaping themselves and helping to reshape their surroundings. Thus do we build our future. It was thus I chose the Soviet Union as environment that it might make of me what I wished to be. It was thus I chose my husband, not from any of those emotional flurries which American romanticists call love but from a need far deeper—the deep, instinctive need of my own future. American youth which wastes so much of life in bewildering emotion needs to be told what I took years to know. To fall in love is very easy, even to remain in it is not difficult; our human loneliness is cause enough. But it is a hard quest worth making to find a comrade through whose presence one becomes steadily the person one desires to be. This I have found and hold.

We are multitudinous types of minds, yet in our present epoch all of us have one choice. Whether to join the men who have hands on the levers, or the men who own machines. Whether to seize all means of work for all workers and collectively build socialism, or grab for ourselves our bits of private property, the small one grabbing posts or fame or houses, while the big ones grab banks and mills. This is the great decision of our epoch for all these many minds of men. In all the clashes that invade our lifetime, we choose our side of "barricades."

CHAPTER XXVIII

THE FIGHT FOR BREAD

In the early winter of 1932, after we returned from Kuznetsk, disquieting news began to come from the southern harvest. I had lost touch with the rural districts during my work on *Moscow News;* I had thought that splendid harvest of 1930 had conquered wheat. Others more important than I had had the same delusion and had lost sight of the farms in the exacting problems of a state industry which was doubling production in five years. The harvest of 1930 had been put over by a great drive, as once our John Reed communars, hungry, barefoot and ill-equipped, had stormed the Alexeyevka farm by force of desire. Even as they had receded under difficulties of organization, so the harvests of 1931 and 1932 receded in the whole Soviet Union.

In three years the U.S.S.R. had completely reorganized eighty-five percent of its farm area, combining fourteen million small private holdings into two hundred thousand large farms owned collectively by the peasants in them. Primitive implements were being rapidly replaced by machines with division of labor. Where were good managers to be found for so many great new enterprises? The difficulty was increased by the fact that new construction jobs and new industries were absorbing in four years eleven million workers, often taking the most energetic elements from the farms. The new expansion of industrial crops also lessened the proportion sown to grain.

A drought in five basic grain districts in 1931 showed two chief defects in the country's farming: a grain area which in the existing quality of tillage was insufficient for the growing needs of the population, and a serious lack of managing ability in the big new farms. The harvest of 1932 was still more serious; the actual crop was better, but less was gathered.

Hopeful farm presidents, unwilling to admit inefficiency, claimed they were getting it in. Hopeful district secretaries, inspired by optimism rather than knowledge, sent these reports to Moscow. When Moscow awoke to the actual condition, a large amount of grain lay under the snow.

Everyone at once interpreted the situation according to the pattern of his mind. Foreign capitalists nodded: "Collectivization has failed; it gives the individual no incentive." . . . But I had seen the incentive which fired those farmhands. Local peasants groaned: "The government takes all anyway," and correspondents addicted to human interest tales sent reports of the not infrequent official excesses. . . . But the trouble wasn't with grain which the state had collected; it was grain that was under the snow. Local communists cried: "It is sabotage by kulaks who mold the dark peasant to their will." . . . But that didn't explain why, despite considerable exiling of kulaks, the farming had grown worse.

I, with my concept of efficiency, explained the matter thus: "It is one of the inevitable costs of progress; you can't get good management in a backward peasant country for two hundred thousand big farms. The peasants couldn't get organized, so lots of them got discouraged and ran away to construction jobs leaving their harvest in the field. Such folks' families will die for their inefficiency. It's probably no worse than the way we industrialized farming in America, pushing surplus farmhands for a hundred years into the ranks of the unemployed. Anyway I don't blame the government for taking some grain when it put up the machines.* Why should efficient workers who made good tractors die for inefficient peasants who couldn't get in the grain?"

This view seemed to explain things to Americans. It was held by other Americans who worked on farms. Some old Kuz-

---

* In the four years of collectivization, the state made food and seed loans to the farmers of 157,000,000 bushels of grain, gave money credits of 1,168,000,000 rubles (not depreciated but so-called "hard" rubles, of which 435,000,000 of the earlier loans were later written off without payment), and invested in farm machinery through tractor stations 4,800,000,000 rubles. The state's donation to farming in these years was thus very much greater than the sum total of all means of production previously possessed by the peasants. (From Molotov's report to Seventh All-Union Congress, January 1935.)

bassers had been given the management of a big state farm in
North Caucasus whose ex-director was in jail. One of them
came up to Moscow. "Old women are picking up grains of
wheat under the state elevator," he said to me grimly. "But
I've no sympathy for them. Their whole village sabotaged the
harvest. My sympathy goes to the workers on our farm who
are hungry all this year because of the drunken thief they had
for director. I've lost thirty pounds myself because of him."

When I mentioned my view to my husband, he shook his head.
"You are harsher on the peasant than we are. We communists
take the blame. Haven't you understood the report of Stalin?"

Yes, Stalin saw wider than any, as long ago a factory director had told me. He surveyed all these other views but took
a dynamic attitude, instead of the fatalistic one that I had
taken. At the plenum of the Central Committee of the party
in January 1933 he analyzed all the difficulties—the activities
of kulaks, the stupidities of officials, the backwardness of peasants—but stated: "Communists usually throw the responsibility on the peasants; they declare that the peasants are to
blame. But this is absolutely untrue and certainly unjust.
The peasants are not to blame at all. If we are to speak of
responsibility and blame, then that responsibility falls wholly
and entirely on the communists; we, the communists alone, are
to blame for all this.

"There is not, nor has there ever been, such a powerful and
authoritative government in the world as our Soviet government, . . . nor party, such as our Communist Party. And if
we are not always able to manage the affairs of the collective
farms in a way that Leninism calls for, if, not infrequently, we
commit crude, unpardonable errors, in grain collections, say,
then we and we alone, are to blame."

Out of Stalin's analysis of difficulties there came at once
a plan of action: a new law on grain collections, the organization of politodels (political sections) in the tractor stations,
and the congress of farm udarniks.

The earlier grain collections (which are not taxes but compulsory sale of about one-fourth the total normal crop to the
state at fixed prices, in return for which state stores give goods

also at fixed prices) had been based on estimates of harvest when the grain was already in the fields. Such a law favored the weaker farms. But the efficient farms increasingly resented the need to make up for inefficient or disloyal farms which delivered little or nothing. The new law stimulated efficiency by fixing in advance a definite quota of grain expected by the state from every acre, varying with soil and climate but independent of actual yield. This favored the efficient and prodded the backward.*

This prod, which might have ruined weak farms in their early stages, was justified now by the three thousand five hundred tractor stations, which had grown in four years from the single Shevchenko Station elsewhere described. They were centers of machine power for the new farming, and already serviced in varying proportions two-thirds of all collective farms. Attached to them there were now organized politodels, centers of leadership, organization and knowledge, made up of men and women of a caliber never before seen in rural Russia. Directors of factories, chiefs of production, army commanders, university professors—to the number of twenty thousand—were poured into these politodels. They had to learn farms, but they knew organization. Their task was to investigate the character of administrative and accounting personnel on the farms, remove and sometimes prosecute inefficient and corrupt farm managers, organize education in farm methods, and make the farms more efficient and more responsive to the plans of the state.

To arouse peasant enthusiasm for the coming struggle for a good harvest, there was held in Moscow in early February a Congress of Farm Udarniks, chosen champions from the best farms. Their selection in January was used to stimulate farms to collect seed, repair implements, get draft animals into condition. Then the local heroes descended on Moscow, girl tractor-drivers who got the best acreage, brigade leaders whose

---

* In practice the law is not quite so rigid. Hail, drought or natural calamity, if properly attested, are grounds for partial or total remission of grain collections; even inefficient farms, which show intention to improve, may postpone their debt to the following year. But the burden of proof lies on the farm.

gangs made records. They came, the farmers who last year succeeded, to organize leaders for the whole land's success.

They were the center of the whole land's attention. The delegates had right of way on all railroads; they were sped on their journey by bands. Moscow sent delegations down the line to meet them. The Agricultural Publishing House got out an "udarnik's library" in thirty volumes. Museums, factories, planetarium put on excursions for their benefit. In no less than a hundred meetings in Moscow factories peasants and workers got together. Every newspaper in the country devoted at least a page daily to the detailed tales of their success and their detailed explanations how others could do it.

Stalin addressed the delegates, the first time he had appeared at a non-party congress. He compared their difficulties with those of the industrial workers in the October revolution, saying: "Compare your difficulties and privations with the difficulties and privations of the workers and you will see that they are not worth talking about seriously. . . . The best lands have been transferred to the collective farms and have been firmly attached to them. . . . Our tractor works and agricultural machinery works are working primarily for the collective farms. The government . . . stands solidly for the workers and collective farmers, for all the toilers of town and country. Hence you possess everything in order to be able to develop collective farm construction and achieve emancipation from the old path. From you only one thing is demanded—to work honestly, to distribute collective farm incomes according to the amount of work done, to take good care of the tractors and machines, to organize proper care of the horses, to fulfill the task set by the workers' and peasants' state, to consolidate the collective farms. . . . You are now working not for the rich and not for the exploiters, but for yourselves."

The congress noted many achievements of three years of collectivization: extension of sown area by seventy-five million acres, the supplying of the farms with one hundred and fifty thousand tractors, the billions of rubles advanced in state credits, the thousands of trained agronomists in the countryside. It appealed to all farmers to enforce collective discipline and rally around the new politodels in the fight for higher harvest yield.

The Congress of Farm Udarniks was locked in Moscow blizzards. It looked beyond them to the south where spring began. Into the blizzards poured the first political workers bound for the southern districts to form the first politodels. The tractor industry reported its plan for spare parts accomplished to schedule; thousands of workers' brigades went from factories to help in farm repairs. On melting snows near Rostov, airplanes were preparing to sow the "Gigant" and the "Verblud" farms; two hundred airplanes in all had been mobilized for the "extra-early" sowing of the Soviet Union. The weather bureau announced that this year's data would be compiled from a thousand points and sent by radio to all collective farms. . . . The delegates from Turkmenia hastened homeward; their wheat sowing had already begun. But the delegates of the Northern Urals had still to travel five hundred miles by sledge across the snow.

. . . .

I visited the sowing campaign in Molvitino, a township overnight from Moscow in northern swamps and wooded hills. Its population of fifty-five thousand peasants on poor soil fifty miles from a railroad were being stirred, organized and prodded by three hundred and seventeen local communists to fight for the "red banner" of Ivanovo Province. That banner was the gift of the German communist newspaper *Rote Fahne;* Molvitino had won it the previous year. Since they now ran fifth in the province (among some fifty townships) the party secretary Krotov wired to Moscow for a delegation of German and Bulgarian communists to stir up enthusiasm for sowing. I went with this delegation and saw bearded men and kerchiefed women listen with staring eyes to tales of white terror in Europe.

The local communists made the application (the visiting delegates knew nothing whatever of sowing) : "Our foreign comrades are tortured and killed for the revolution. Our job for the revolution is to plant more grain. We must fight like devils to do it." The three days' drive covered the ten worst villages to pull them up with the rest. News was sent out each dawn by the new township newspaper, a two page sheet devoted entirely to the sowing.

This backward township had under tsardom been more than ninety percent illiterate, with drink and brawling as only recreations, with tuberculosis and syphilis rotting its hamlets. Now it was being rapidly jerked into modernity by the local communists. Five thousand adult peasants had taken special courses the previous winter in arithmetic, geometry, field measurement, organization of farm labor, rotation of crops, tillage. With thousands more in political courses and seven thousand children in school, nearly one-third of the total population had been studying.

The results were seen in the organized sowing, led by the communists under Krotov and Feodoroff, chief of the new politodel. Worried peasants had for the first time planted not by the ancient festival of "Helena the Flaxen" * but by the principles of new farm experts. The extra-early shoots were coming up already; the land was flushed with green. There remained the days of ordinary sowing. School children reported tons of wood ashes and bird droppings with which they had fertilized the soil. For the first time in a century Molvitino, whose men had always supplemented their scanty soil by winter work in cities, was raising all its own bread. Unorganized peasants were flocking into collective farms saying: "Bolshevik seeds are strong. Those folks are full of food."

Krotov told me the secret of success in Molvitino. "First we keep up the quality of our party members; if a communist isn't known by his work, we clean him out quickly. The second help is our organizational plan, keeping day and night in touch with sowing. The mass believes us, believes us without limit. See how they went with us against century-old tradition and religion in the matter of extra-early sowing. They threw down the Holy Helena. And they were worried. But already they see the shoots!"

I saw a sample of that "organizational plan" of Krotov's

* Old festival days of the Orthodox Church are now thirteen days too late by the slow shifting of the church calendar through the centuries.

when I went with the head of the local branch of the State Bank at two in the morning to his party assignment in a small collective farm of twenty families. We trudged three miles by hills and swamps and reached the village as dawn was graying. The banker walked in the field beside them, stopped in the president's home, noted their sowing record, made suggestions on their book-keeping, gave them news from the rest of the township and discussed minor problems of organization. He was back in town by six in the morning, worked at the branch of the State Bank from nine till three and went again on party assignment in the evening to a different farm. Every communist in Molvitino either had similar tasks or else a full-time assignment to the fields for the period of sowing.

Chief of my memories of Molvitino was not the remarkable success in sowing, nor the excellent organization of school children, nor the new hospitals which had had no fresh case of venereal disease for a year. It was the mad night ride in a swaying auto-truck whereby the five "big chiefs" of Molvitino, with a score of other passengers, came on time to the provincial conference in Ivanovo. It was forced upon them by the backwardness of others and by certain minor inefficiencies in their own ranks. But the ride itself rises out of its erring environment like an epic, testifying to human flaws even in Molvitinians, but flaunting superhuman will that none the less drove through.

Molvitino had not even one automobile; it depended for transport on Kostroma, a rival township on the railroad which sent on demand, sometimes, an auto-truck. On the night when party delegates from Molvitino should have taken the one evening train from Kostroma to Ivanovo for a conference, the truck came to their dark, rain-drenched township after the far-off train had gone. I was going with them to take that train to Moscow.

"We shall go through Kostroma to Nerekhta junction where the Ivanovo car waits till five in the morning," said Krotov. "If that forty miles of new mud road is passable we'll make it."

The chauffeur grumbled in his cabin. He said he had had no decent sleep for ten months and had driven since six that morning. He said nobody knew the road to Nerekhta and Feodoroff had been stingy with gasoline. He said it was raining and the road would be impassable and robbers had been seen in the woods. He dozed in exhausted snatches and woke when the auto hit a bump while Feodoroff at his side watched to see that he didn't doze too dangerously deep.

Above in the tonneau the rain poured down at intervals, driving us to retreat under a canvas which normally lay on the floor. Four Young Pioneer girls bound for camp near Ivanovo warmed themselves with songs till they fell asleep. They cuddled near Krotov, lucky chosen ones, chaperoned to camp by the adored young party secretary. A swarthy man grinned at them and began to troll a ribald ditty from Odessa about "all the girls fall for me. I get 'em without a red cent because I am so nice." It didn't worry Krotov; he knew the girls adored him. The fight for sowing had thinned his cheeks but his smile flashed undimmed. Even I, comfortably married and in my middle forties, adored that unconquerable youth.

The ferry over the Volga at Kostroma had closed at one o'clock but we roused the workers and got them to open it up and take us through. They offered to let me off at Kostroma and find me a bed. What! Leave this conquering auto-truck? Not till they threw me off. This was America as I had loved her, "my" America before the war. Where local bankers mixed with farmers, where ribald ditties cheered our battles, where men drove on through night and rain. My America of the old frontier days, long lost to the profiteers! This was no semi-Asiatic country, sleepy and slow. This was a land of fighting settlements and still unconquered hills. These were the men who drove on sleepless, grimy with sweat and soil—but winning!

Krotov slept like a log on the floor of the truck, skull pillowed on an iron bar. They walked on him, sat on him, fell on him without affecting his sleep. He was grabbing in two hours for the lack of six hard weeks. I had not his cause for sleeping; I sat on a cross-board swaying and watched the slow gray dawn break through the rain. As we climbed the hill beyond the Volga, a line of red morn showed briefly, and we struck the unknown road! I wrung the wet from my head-scarf and snapped it above the truck like a banner in the drying wind of dawn. I sang and shouted; all of us sang and shouted. Singing was not loud enough!

Krotov woke. With a teasing smile he roused to action, and began to quiz the Young Pioneers. "Now, kid, what is a nation? What is the difference between capitalist nations and the U.S.S.R.? What is the international significance of our Five-Year Plan?" So began the political lesson at four in the morning in the wind-blown, shaking truck. "Now, look here, kid," Krotov was shaking his finger, "after the party cleaning and the Komsomol cleaning we are going to clean you Pioneers. And you are just going to get cleaned out for not knowing the Pioneers' laws."

America? No, not America. Where were the real estate signs? Where was the advertisement that shouted somebody's soap? Where was the giant octopus which the young independent beat in all romances, but never on the actual earthly scene? "How fine," I had said so many years ago to Leonard Ayres, "to have a Center which collects our best ideas and speaks with the authority of us all." Then his slow smile had revealed to me the octopus. But Molvitinians had a "Center"; that was the name they gave to Moscow, to which some of these triumphant men would go, after Ivanovo, sent by their approving fellow-workers to spread abroad their best ideas in sowing. "My" America, yet not America. A newer "new world."

Now the truck bounced downward over the ruts and rocks. Feodoroff sat by the chauffeur feeding the last gasoline direct into the carburetor from a bottle. With motor stalling and starting and stalling and starting we reached white-towered Nerekhta after the only passenger train had pulled out. The chauffeur dropped like a shot in the truck, asleep before he hit the floor. The Molvitinians tackled the station-master.

"Let us on that freight train."

"Impossible! Against rules."

"Who's higher than you?"

"Nobody in this station."

"Got to get to Ivanovo, party orders."

"Can't help it, comrade. Safety rules of the railroad."

"But if we get on?"

"Won't sell you tickets."

"But if we get on without tickets?"

The station master turned his back and walked to the end of the station. The Molvitinians got on. Some on flat cars under farm machinery, some on narrow platforms at the end of box-cars. The five big chiefs drove the rest of us from a flat car and held their preliminary conference, for which there had been in Molvitino no time. Rained upon, blown upon, pulling each other awake to keep from falling, then singing as the sun rode high, we drove towards Ivanovo. Twice at stations the officials tried to dislodge us; we argued and stayed. We were dumped at last in Ivanovo freight yard, three miles from town. We shouldered baggage and marched on foot through fields and cobbled lanes. Panting, foot-sore, red with the heat we turned the last corner into the tall, new building of the Provincial Committee.

It was just five minutes to noon when a bunch of grimy tramps, carrying canvas raincoats wet with rain and black with coal, said to the neat, spruce secretary in the outer office: "Delegation from Molvitino. Whcn's the conference?" She didn't show surprise; she was used to these madmen. "Twelve o'clock," she answered. "Here're your room reservations."

Shortly after twelve the Molvitinians, washed and shaved and sleepless, but looking no worse than others, entered the conference room. They had left behind a stranded truck exhausted of gasoline, a chauffeur outraged and dead asleep, a station master bewildered and broken railway rules. But they got to the conference as ordered.

Such were the men who were putting through the sowing in the spring of 1933.

.   .   .   .

While men in the rural districts, like those of Molvitino, fought for the coming harvest, the insufficient grain from the previous harvest was firmly organized in such a way as to disrupt as little as possible the essential production of the country. A ration system feeding workers in basic industries at low, fixed prices had been in force since 1928; on it the planning of wages and industrial costs for the Five-Year Plan was based. This system strengthened now into an iron law, cutting the bread supply in almost every family.

Besides the rationed bread there was bread in the "free market," but its price was forced ruinously upward by the grain shortage till it was many times that of the rationed supply. The size of rations and the quality of factory dining-rooms became more important than money wages and were ruthlessly used in the interest of production. The best workers, udarniks, got extra rations and special meals in factories. Idlers got worse meals; workers who drifted from job to job—there had been a serious amount of labor turnover—were dropped from rations the day they quit work.

One had to show cause to stay on rations; they were cut or entirely removed from groups which were not essential. Unproductive members even of workers' families lost food cards, and were either forced into industry themselves, where workers were urgently needed, or were fed more thinly from the card of the bread-winner. Housemaids lost cards in families where there were also housewives doing no outside work. Our Dasha kept hers because she served four people who were working; but she worried herself sick getting the papers to prove this. Foreign specialists found their contracts unrenewed or canceled for slight causes; the U.S.S.R. thus saved both the food of foreigners and their dollar salaries which necessitated export of grain to get foreign money. Northern farm areas were told: "Eat potatoes, and produce your own grain this summer." That was what Molvitino had been doing.

Slowly as the spring of 1933 deepened into summer, the tension over the country grew. Rumors spread; foreign correspondents cried famine. Communists were silent or remarked: "A hard struggle with a difficult food shortage. We are concentrating now on the coming harvest." Ukrainian boys from districts where crops had been ungathered came to Moscow begging food; peasant families from these districts sought city markets to trade off everything they had. Typhus appeared in many places; people were dying of it in Moscow. The situation was worst in the Ukraine, North Caucasus and Kazakstan where the harvest organization had been worst. Into these regions the government sent grain from other districts, as reserves in the hands of politodels to feed the men who must plow and sow and reap. This was done even on farms that had failed or sabotaged the previous year. What was over, was over. One must organize harvest now.

One of the spectacular campaigns which gained way that summer was the war against the age-old recurrent drought of the Volga valley, to which this central Eurasian plain seemed doomed by the slow retreat of earth's glacial age.* Individual peasants of tsardom found no answer to this stern decree of nature but prayers and religious processions for rain followed by resignation to famine. Collectivized farmers found a way. Under the Five-Year Plan a billion rubles had been spent by the Soviet government for irrigation, and the total of irrigated lands increased to fourteen million acres, four million more than had existed in tsarist Russia; a new decree in 1932 authorized great dams on the Volga to reclaim ten million acres more. The collective farmers did not wait for this, but organized also local irrigation, declaring: "Dam every ravine, retain all snow water, use all small streams." The collective farmers of the Middle Volga alone thus irrigated by their own labor within two years a hundred thousand acres in a historic fight with nature. It was only one of a hundred campaigns of that summer.

Stirred by returning udarniks from the congress, stimulated by the new grain law and led by the politodels, the organized farmers moved into the battle for grain. Slowly at first, then more and more effectively as organization and hope increased. What the foreign press featured as "Stalin's War Against the Peasants," the Soviet press featured as "Our War for Harvest Yield." They analyzed good collective farms with their methods of success, and bad farms with the reasons for downfall. They pushed campaigns against the great weeds of the south, waist high, that invaded neglected fields. Eighty-five million acres of grain lands were weeded by hand that summer,

* See page 97, "My Utopia in Ruins."

by school children, old people, Young Communists and train-loads of city volunteers. One hundred and forty million loads of manure were carted to fields, inherited from the old strip-system of the Middle Ages, which had never been properly fertilized in all their history.

These were only a few of the many measures which achieved that summer the conquest of bread, snatching victory from a great disaster. When the harvest of 1933 was finally gathered, it surpassed the harvest of 1930 which till then had held the all-time record for the Russian land. It had been achieved this time not by a great burst of half-organized enthusiasm, but by permanent organization which was steadily strengthening, ready to go forward to other victories.*

---

* Gross harvest for 1933 was 89,000,000 tons, almost 10,000,000 tons more than in 1913, an exceptionally good prewar harvest year. But the following year, 1934, in spite of adverse weather conditions, the improved organization of farmers fought the drought by irrigation, improved tillage, replanted drought-killed areas and so avoided losses in reaping that they actually harvested from 4,000,000 to 5,000,000 tons more than in 1933. (Molotov's Report to All-Union Congress, January 1935. Author's Note. Attempts to reckon from this comparative food supply of population must take account of: a, grain export lessened from 10,000,000 tons in 1913 to 1,000,000 in 1934; b, population increased 20 percent; c, livestock consumption decreased due to lessened livestock.)

CHAPTER XXIX

CALIFORNIA EXPLAINS MOSCOW

THE PROBLEM OF TRUTH

To me as a journalist the hardest aspect of that difficult struggle of 1933 which achieved the conquest of bread, was what I called suppression of truth. I raged against this, yet when driven to analyze, I found it not very easy to say just what I meant.

One could hardly claim that the Soviet press kept silence, when they gave columns daily to campaigns against weeds, the need for fertilizer, the characteristics of good and bad farms. Nor did they ignore difficulties; they fought them with all their strength. But they treated them in a way which didn't seem to me journalism; they weren't telling what I called the whole story. Why wouldn't they admit facts and tell the extent of the trouble?

Even my own husband wouldn't do it. He had been one of thousands of communists who saw the "new front" before politodels were organized. By strenuous effort he had succeeded in changing his comfortable city job to the work of journalist sent to bad spots in rural districts.

"Are many people dying?" I once demanded.

"I have no general figures from which to judge," he answered. "Two villages which I recently visited had been reported 'all dying' and the 'worst in the township.' I found that the crop of their collective farm had been fair but had not been fully gathered due to disorganization and sabotage caused by kulaks who had crept into the management. The farmers have now expelled the kulaks, the government sent in seed and food and this year promises well. The rumors of 'all dying' had been spread by the kulaks who had been expelled from the village."

During the harvest I myself visited two large farms in the bad regions of North Caucasus. I would have visited others, but I saw that my need of transport worried the grain truckers, and that farm presidents working twenty hours a day gave up their beds to me, while even to talk to me took strength from men who were haggard with fatigue. Spectacular tales were rife, but they were always just beyond the horizon and modified by later checking.

At Berezanovka State Farm a group of Soviet-Americans were fighting to get a harvest from fifty thousand acres of weeds inherited from a drunken director who had been imprisoned for looting everything from crops to building materials. The new directors and their workers had survived the winter chiefly on state loans of musty grain which the authorities had found buried in the earth in kulak's trenches. An apparently well-informed farm official told me that "Berezanovka village seems to be dying out. We're buying up the empty houses."

When I checked this with the tractor station which served the village, they told me: "We know sown areas, not death rates, but we doubt that statement, for the village sown area has this year very greatly increased. Last year Berezanovka village sabotaged its harvest, then some of them ran off to construction jobs, selling their houses."

Commune Seattle, one of the best-managed farms in the Soviet Union, showed the point of view of the well-run farms. Their good crop of the previous year had been six times drained by grain collections to make up the township quota. "Compel us?" said the president, in answer to my sympathetic question. "Nobody had the power to compel us. We ourselves voted in general meeting for each of those extra collections. It took a lot of arguing, for it meant sacrificing a year's litter of pigs and putting prize dairy cattle on a grainless diet. But when the state gives you credits and the workers give you tractors you can't shirk a common emergency. The ones we were annoyed at were those slackers who left it to us to do their share; and especially those Ukrainian beet-growers who left us without sugar for two years. But we have bee-hives, and life can be very sweet without sugar." I wrote a hero story on Commune Seattle, but even this material was very guardedly handled by *Moscow Daily News*.

I protested to Borodin. "Why does everybody keep this deadly silence? Every communist to whom you mention the hunger glares as if you talked treason. Even my husband won't tell me how many people are dying. He says he doesn't know."

"No more does he know," said Borodin. "It isn't his business. What makes it your business?"

I gasped at that. Wasn't a story like that the business of every journalist? "Why aren't we allowed," I said, "to tell the facts?"

"Your story of Molvitino was a fact, wasn't it?" he queried mildly. "An important fact and very well told."

"Yes, but it's so one-sided. We tell good facts and ignore the worst ones. Do you call that giving a clear picture?"

"I think we give a clear picture to anyone who has intelligence to read," said Borodin. "Our readers know of the food shortage from their own food cards and from Stalin's report. They know that the party takes the situation seriously enough to mobilize twenty thousand of our best men to meet it. We tell them that the problem is one of organization and management, and they understand this very well from the difficulties they themselves have in industry. We tell all the measures taken, the organization of politodels and the new grain quotas. Whom would it help to know sensational stories of hunger, or the details of our difficulties? Would it get additional food for anybody? Aren't we doing all that we can?"

My journalist passion to tell things struggled against him. "We aren't telling the real truth at all," I cried.

"What would you like to tell?" asked Borodin. "Can you analyze it?"

"I don't think I want just to tell horrible stories," I said slowly. "I'm not a Hearst correspondent yelling 'Show me blood!' They're all running off to Vladivostok now looking for a 'good war.' But this is the most heroic fight under the most ruthless discipline I ever saw. You minimize the heroism when you won't tell the difficulties. Inefficient peasants, sabotaging kulaks, stupid officials were starving this country; yet you are organizing to pull it through. I never saw such organization for spreading the weight of a great calamity on all alike. Men have died in the north woods from scurvy and in Central Asia from typhus because of peasants who didn't collect their harvest. Yet they write abroad as if you attacked Ukrainians; they stir up Ukrainian demonstrations in Chicago. Trotskyists say: 'Stalin won't admit the failure of his Five-Year Plan.' Your silence gives them the chance to say it. But I know social workers dying to save homeless children, and workers dying of typhus caught trying to organize peasants, and an American specialist from Cheliabinsk who says a gang from the steppe killed a man in his street to loot his body for clothes."

"Yes," said Borodin, "the Ukraine is a natural weapon for capitalists to use; it is territory that both Poland and Germany covet. Trotsky's attack was to be expected; workers abroad must learn to analyze him as workers learned here. These aren't serious. But you wish to tell them about Cheliabinsk?"

No, that might be going too far. Not Cheliabinsk where they made—caterpillar tractors! "Don't our enemies know already?" I returned to the attack. "Haven't they reports of secret agents? It is our friends from whom we conceal it. Professor Laski says: 'Propaganda is a means of deceiving one's friends without quite deceiving one's enemies.' "

"Laski's clever but inexact," Borodin said, smiling. "Our friends know the essentials of our struggle; they can wait for details. Our enemies suspect, but they do not really know. They suspect also, and we take pains to tell them, that in spite of difficulty our industries still forge ahead and our railroads operate and we are going to have a harvest. Isn't that the essential fact? Why should you wish to hand them a guaranteed list of our troubles, all the way from lumber camps to Cheliabinsk?"

I recalled the international situation: Japanese were advancing ever further into Manchuria, but yet uncertain whether to go north towards Russia or south towards China for their next extension of empire. European powers were trying to push Japan northward while they themselves seized China. No recognition for the Soviets had come from America. "So we're not strong enough yet," I said, "to tell the truth?"

Borodin considered for a moment. "To tell the truth, yes—meaning by truth a clear description of the general line of our struggle, the fact that it is a serious one, and the type of its problems. But not to give away sensational unanalyzed 'facts' from which no good can come."

There was a long pause while I thought this over. Then Borodin said: "We Bolsheviks think that in spite of the technical backwardness of Russia, it may devolve on this country to save world civilization. We do not share the pacifist illusion that peace can be made by expecting it. Nor that other pacifist blindness which forgets how horrible modern war may be. Half of the capitalist world of the west is turning back towards the Middle Ages.

"No god insures to man progress. Civilizations have risen and fallen before. To drift blindly as most of the world is drifting is to drift to doom. We build within firm borders forms of life which are fit for a civilized world. We plan, organize, struggle for peace in every possible way. But we cannot tell what combination of nations may be launched against us, or when the attack may fall. Man's offensive powers grow fast; we might see much of the world, many of our own cities, go up in flames. But even if the worst comes to the very worst, the world need not sink back to dark ages as it has sunk before. We build the organization that can save it."

He paused, and I remembered those great new cities, steel towns of Kuznetsk, Sverdlovsk, Magnitogorsk with the rich grain lands of western Siberia between. Protected by great distances from even the collapse of nations. If the worst came to the worst life could again rise as I saw it rise from the ruined plains of the Volga, from wandering waifs of the revolution, starving themselves to build. And with those steel socialist cities to help them. . . . Was any price too great for such a building?

Borodin said: "You are looking too long at Ukrainians.

They aren't the only people in the world. You have a lecture tour to America. Take a look at fascism as you pass through Germany, and a look at the New Deal in Washington. It will do you good."

"You are just putting me off," I answered. "The Russian harvest is the most important thing in the world just now."

He nodded. "But nothing you can do will help our harvest. We're getting that done without your aid."

"I may fall for this 'New Deal,'" I warned him. "These measures of Roosevelt are very exciting."

Borodin smiled. "Great people, the Americans! They always interest me! They think they can break every known economic law. But you've lived here twelve years; I'll bank on your intelligence." I was still protesting our policy on rural news as I left for America. But Borodin was saying: "Well, we've won our harvest. Now you can tell anything you like."

In Berlin I went to Nazi propaganda headquarters where a clever German-American from New Orleans received the English-speaking press. "The world is telling atrocity stories about you," I said. "I'm not interested in atrocities. Every régime puts down its enemies as roughly as it has to. I want to know what you are doing to pull Germany out of chaos."

It seemed to upset him. His technique was all prepared to deny atrocities. But he furnished a few details and got me some interviews. They claimed to be making a great attack on unemployment. How? Well, there were labor camps for youth who could not be absorbed in industry. They were fed and sheltered in tents; some of them might be given clothing if they were ragged, but this seemed rather uncertain. I gathered that they were expected to wear out the clothing given by their parents. Of course they got no pay. They were going to build great thoroughfares across the country, independent of the ordinary highways. . . .

"I see," I thought. "Great military highways built by slave labor. Well, that's one thing. What next?"

Next they were absorbing unemployed in East Prussia by shutting the borders against Polish and Lithuanian farm-hands who came for seasonal work on big estates. "We demand that the landowners employ good Germans; let them make a sacrifice for their country. We urge them to feed these farmhands through the winter, not of course on full wages. To make this possible we turn over to the landlord the unemployed dole which the man has been receiving. This has lessened our unemployed by many tens of thousands."

"It has lessened your lists," I said, "which of course is good propaganda. But has it lessened your outlay for unemployment doles?"

"Well, no," he admitted. "It costs as much as before. We're saving costs by taking women and Jews off the rolls. But the scheme in East Prussia is good in another way. It keeps these men from congregating in the cities where they only stir up trouble." . . . "Yes," I thought, "they use state funds to make farmhands slaves of landlords. That's another way."

They mentioned one or two lesser ways that were similar. I wanted to get this clear. "What is your plan," I asked, "for your whole unemployment? What proportion do you hope to relieve by labor camps and what by paying landlords; how much can you reduce the whole number and how soon?" They all looked dazed when I put this question. "Why, we don't plan that way. We just push all these methods. How can we tell which will do the most?" I had been so used to definite plans fulfilled in percentages that it took me some time to understand that they really hadn't any. I never saw such a planless bunch. An American in Berlin told me: "Even the claimed decrease in unemployment is hardly more than the usual seasonal change." Some women in shacks outside Berlin said sourly: "We haven't seen our unemployed rolls cut by a single name." Their husbands had been beaten up and dragged to jail the previous evening for having a communist leaflet in their possession.

One thing all Nazis agreed on, when they could not tell me any plan. "At least we saved Germany from Bolshevism. We saved all Europe; let them be grateful to us for that." . . . Did Europe have so much for which to be grateful? Saving the means of production for private capitalists—that was all that it meant. Even revolution might be better than this sliding backward into serfdom, cloaked by a panic fury of medieval hate.

How did Germany get that way? It had been "socialist Germany." But the socialists had talked and talked and never acted. They had explained all their strength and weakness, yet remained passive—just worried the capitalists into action. Just as we had done long years before in Seattle, in our general strike that failed.

But couldn't America do better? I shrank from revolution. What had Borodin said: "Americans think they can break every economic law!" . . . Well, maybe we could. We were an energetic people with a big country. What were economic laws? Were they the property of Bolsheviks? With all our unemployment we still fed people better than they did. America had muddled through so far; couldn't she keep on?

In Washington it appeared that we might. There was feverish activity and plenty of planning. And what a relief! You could see the very highest officials immediately. I saw President Roosevelt, General Johnson, Secretary Wallace, Secretary Perkins, Harry Hopkins, chief of Civil Works, Ambassador Troyanovsky and Ambassador Bullitt all in three days, less time than it takes me in Moscow to see one small official. Moscow made me feel insignificant; Washington made me feel happily important.

I didn't of course see all these high officials individually; I saw them in press conferences. I stood three feet from Roosevelt while a hundred reporters were let loose upon him, like hunters on some great lion behind a rail. They asked impertinent questions for which any European official would throw them out; he laughed and tossed back clever answers as a tennis player returns a ball. Their eyes shone with adoration for his expertness in the great American game of interview. I watched his face and wondered what he was thinking. Was he really thinking at all, or just fencing? The reporters didn't care what he thought; they wanted headlines! He made their Washington job profitable and easy. He was always good for two columns on the front page.

We left; they had the flattering sense that they had been close to the heart of government. Had they not pried into everything? Whether General Johnson had been to dinner? What he intended to do about the dollar? It was the Roosevelt technique of publicity. It soothed my soul to find great men frank and accessible. I wished they had a little of this technique in Moscow, where officials seldom saw reporters and never gave snappy answers. And yet—a simple worker in a far city could tell you the whole policy of the Five-Year Plan.

Could anyone tell me Roosevelt's policy? His closest advisers said: "We do not yet know the mind of the President." Workers in Stalingrad or Kuznetsk could tell you the mind of Stalin. It was outlined in long reports and they studied it in conferences. It was called the party line. They couldn't tell exactly how Stalin would analyze some new emergency; he could see further than they. But certainly the whole Soviet Union knew his general line in detail, better than anyone in Washington knew Roosevelt's. What is this thing, I thought, that I call "truth" and "frankness," when in Washington they tell you personal details while in Moscow they discuss a nation's plan.

Did Roosevelt himself know his mind, I wondered. He was one of our old progressives. If I knew anything of progressives—Wang Ching-wei, myself and others—we were always going forward but we never knew quite where. We shifted from side to side without knowing why we shifted, till suddenly we flopped—usually on the side of the big bosses. We didn't intend to side with the bosses; we maneuvered for independence as long as we could. Was Roosevelt the world's best maneuverer? Did that explain the sporting and yet rather desperate gleam in his eye—a lion at bay holding back a hundred hunters? But didn't he himself say this in radio talks to "My friends"? "I am following the best ideas I can find; if these don't work, we'll try something else. I have faith in the great American people." . . . How clever if this were only good politics! How tragic if it were true—the leader of a great people acting by faith, not analysis. Confessing in the greatest crisis of his country's history that he saw no clear way.

And all the people trusting him just because of this and following into the dark!

Roosevelt's "left-wing" I saw individually. They were my old progressive crowd. I felt at home with their minds, their jokes. They were delightful to talk to; they wanted to know about Russia. The Soviet Union was just then in the limelight. Litvinoff had been in Washington and diplomatic relations were just resumed. The left-wing jested about Russia: "We need not so much a Soviet ambassador as a Soviet adviser."

For the first time Washington had men with some knowledge of economics, men with brains and plans. Secretary Wallace explained to me his plan for cutting farm production "which was over-expanded for foreign markets and has to be cut to fit internal needs." He was delightfully frank in admitting that opposition came from everywhere. "The processing industries oppose the tax; the railroads object to lessened freight, the commission houses to lessened profits, the city people to higher food prices and the farmer just naturally objects because it's against human instinct to cut production."

I laughed: "They used to say that Bolsheviks went against human nature. It seems to me you go against it more."

"I think we do," said Secretary Wallace, smiling. Then as I turned to leave, he added: "This is a funny kind of government, isn't it, for making a plan?"

Yet he made plans, energetically and ably. Everybody in Washington did. Hundreds of the best brains in the country had gone there, and all were making plans. Subsistence homesteads, civil works, civilian conservation—anything that might relieve some desperate group of people for a moment. But all these plans contradicted each other. The farm plans raised the price of food products, the city plans raised the cost of city goods. There was no general plan behind it. Or was there? Where did it all come from? Out of everyone's dollar. Out of everyone's working-time and wages. But not out of big business. "We are making the poor support the starving to save the rich," said one clever man in Washington. . . . Over in Russia the poor were supporting the starving to build the jointly owned riches of a country.

How long could they keep on maneuvering? I heard of a dinner at which two cabinet officers were present. A guest said: "I don't think our Kerensky epoch can last much longer." Another replied: "Well, choose your wall!" . . . To be shot by one side or the other—that seemed to be the doom of progressives. Which side would they choose? But wasn't it apparent? In whose hands were the "commanding heights" of the country—banks, lands, productive means? Didn't the New Dealers themselves proclaim that all these vast expenditures which must impoverish the people were intended to start the wheels of industry so that business men, who held commanding heights, might again make profit? For state enterprise to pile up profit and increase collectively owned factories—that was un-American. The state only spent—for unemployed, for farmers, for cheap power to industry. State funds for handouts, but all profits for private business. People talked a lot about government moved to Washington from Wall Street, and Wall Street had been worried awhile by its own collapse, and willing to accept some regulation which stabilized it, or perhaps only squeezed out a few small intruders. What could Roosevelt really do unless he was ready for a real assault to capture the commanding heights for the people?

In Chicago I found that my best-remembered professor, whose influence had most survived my student days, was seriously incapacitated by amebic dysentery. This disease had raged like a plague through the city—all mention being suppressed lest it frighten visitors from the World's Fair. Robert Morss Lovett was only one of thousands of victims to a policy of silence in which even medical men concurred—not for the sake of peace along two borders but for the private gain of Chicago's merchants. At least, I thought, no one can claim that the Soviet Union's silence added a single case of death or disease. In the world crisis prevailing, sensational tales might have shaken a nation's credit and even encouraged invasion, but could hardly have brought relief.

In California I found amazing mass movements. The greatest farm strike in American history moved in a running battle along the San Joaquin and Imperial valleys, following the nomad agricultural workers who in turn followed the seasonal crops. It was led by communists. From peas to cherries, peaches, pears, grapes, cotton it traveled north through the California "paradise" and then resumed again in January in the lettuce fields of the far south. Forty-five thousand workers in all had been involved.

Tear gas and rifles came into the conflict; unarmed striking farmhands were shot by vigilantes, babies died in strikers' tent-camps. Government commissions established "order." I recalled the rural struggles in China, in Central Asia, in Russia. On which side was the state power in California, the "neutral state power" of America? Yes, it was clear. State power in China had killed poor peasants, in Soviet Russia it had deported kulaks, in California it deported farmhand pickets.

In Los Angeles I found a movement which at first sight intrigued me more than the farm strike. Half a million people had fed themselves for over a year by barter, through more than a hundred coöperative relief associations which sprang spontaneously from the unemployed. They traded surplus labor for surplus products, working for farm produce which lay rotting in the fields or for stale bread from bakeries or for skimmed milk, cottage cheese, soup bones left in markets, discarded costumes from motion pictures, broken leather belting from dismantled factories. They showed amazing ingenuity in thus creating for themselves small industries and a fair supply of food and clothing. They organized sewing shops where women made over discarded costumes into children's clothes; they resoled shoes with leather belting; they even acquired small garages, auto repair shops, auto-trucks whereby the unemployed of Los Angeles exchanged surplus oranges for surplus potatoes with the unemployed of Fresno.

These people attracted me amazingly. They were my own type—the pioneers. They were not degraded into horrible New York bread lines and Chicago flop-houses, where human souls rotted with drink and despair. They still hoped and organized; they developed a philosophy. Some of them would work eighteen hours a day for their "communes," bragging: "The capitalists can't organize; we workers can! Look at the mess the capitalists got this whole country into! See what we have done, starting from nothing!" Some of them were talking the old I.W.W. slogans, about "building a new society within the shell of the old."

Couldn't something come of it? Their emotions stirred me. They recalled, far back, my Seattle emotions—our workers' enterprises, our dreams of workers' power from the inevitable march of progress, without fighting, without guns. One order from Washington had closed our shipyards, and the dreams of fifty thousand men had vanished. These hopeful workers of Los Angeles fighting so bravely, why did the capitalists still tolerate them? Ah, they made it cheap and safe for capitalism! They supported themselves on a slowly lessening standard of living, yet hopefully and without riot, on the garbage heaps of California! They even kept their souls alive, eager workers, ready when the capitalists should wish to use them!

But where were the communists? Some workers said: "They fight our organizations." My emotions rose in revolt. American communists had always seemed to me inefficient, unable to connect with American workers. What was that handful of communists with a mandate from Moscow, to dictate to a movement of half a million Americans?

Then I stopped. Those communists knew at least that this movement was getting nowhere. They knew that the commanding heights were in the hands of the enemy, who could make or break it as he chose. Fifteen years ago in Seattle nobody had known it; we had all been like sheep. It was good that someone knew it now, even if only a few. But how did they know it? It had taken me fourteen years and experience of revolution in three countries to know it. They knew it just from California, and from a book by Marx.

They knew it from "theory," that I had despised and couldn't read. I had learned to read Stalin; one had to read him to know what went on every day in Russia. But Lenin and Marx were dead. I had always thought that Marx was just a propagandist who based his ideas on Germany and England of sixty years ago. This was the view my education gave me. This view had survived even the Russian reverence for Marx, which I saw as a sort of religion. Marx was dogma, wasn't he? I now saw for the first time that Marx was science. They understood these California movements—by Marx. One doesn't reject Galileo because he was Italian, or Darwin because he lived sixty years ago. One may perhaps expand, improve or interpret Galileo or Darwin to fit new life and new discoveries.

I began to think of Marx. I had avoided reading him because he always aroused my desire to look on all sides of the question, and I could admire the Russian communists better when I didn't read their theories. "The working class and the employing class have nothing in common," he began. And I always said: "That's a lie to start with; they have their common humanity. All of them suffer from disease, floods, depressions, and all of them love wives and children." Well, that was a clever answer if you took Marx as dogma. But suppose you took him as scientific theory, intended to guide your action.

Suppose a teacher of painting said: "Red, blue and yellow are primary colors; they have nothing in common," and I retorted: "Oh, yes, they have color in common. They are all mixed by a brush in oil or water and put on a canvas." That might be a very snappy answer, but it wouldn't help me learn to paint. To learn to paint you must analyze colors and know which ones go together and what is the effect of red on blue.

So when I said: "Capitalists and workers are all human beings"—of course they were. But that didn't tell me how to act with capitalists and workers or how they would act to each other. It gave me no weapon at all for transforming human society. Marx's analysis gave a weapon, a useful scientific analysis which helped predict how different groups in society would act. I had lost all that by being afraid of a book; so it had taken me fourteen years of revolutions to understand my own California.

These American communists then, if they really used Marxism not as dogma but as a means of analysis, were not just following a Moscow mandate to boss American workers, but were trying to analyze their own hot struggle in the light of theories supplied by Marx, Lenin, Stalin and other economists as well. No wonder they found it hard! I suddenly saw them also as creators in chaos, a chaos more complex than Russia ever knew. A chaos where day and night were not yet divided, a chaos without clear plan. A chaos not of primitive Russian villages, opposing the new society chiefly by force of old habit, but of earth's mightiest industries and most aggressive capitalism, only beginning to totter to the abyss. In any kind of chaos wasn't it more important to find the right direction than to waste life and energy in one movement after another, movements which were bound to crash? If they found the correct line, they would learn to explain it.

Oh, but they must get over to each other somehow, the communists and these men of the coast, my old pioneers. My men of the Far West, so daring, so full of optimism, so ingenious to organize, so ready to risk life, so blind. It was a pain in my own soul to see them drifting, drifting to disillusion after disillusion. Was there no bridge to be found over which they could pass to each other in great masses? They must be on one side of the barricades!

And I had left them. I had fled from their complexities to build in an alien country. No wonder I felt insignificant in Moscow. What could Moscow workers use but my ability to write? Well, I had specialized that for them; I was a writer now. But American workers could have used all of me—my writing, my ability to organize, my instinctive reaction to the American background, my analyzing brain which at twenty-three had "conquered" philosophy and thrown it aside as alien to life.

Not all of this I thought at once; some of it came later. A chain of thought develops with the years. But some of it I said to Lincoln Steffens whom I visited in Carmel. The great reporter of my youth received me on his sickbed; I wondered if it might be his last illness.

"The most important thing you can do just now," he said

suddenly, "is to write your autobiography. Tell what you have learned from life. You start where I left off. You never had my old illusion that putting honest men in office would save the world. You began with later illusions. Your Seattle was our most progressive city; it stood in 1920 where America stands today. You began with municipal ownership of public utilities, and workers' organizations and coöperatives and a sort of vague drift to socialism. You saw these smash and went to Moscow. What did you find there? I don't know the story you have to tell; I haven't lived it. But I know it is the next story that must be told in America."

"It might help in building a bridge," I said. And Steffens answered: "It would add a very good stone to the bridge."

After a pause I said: "I've had a contract for a book like that for several years, but there's one trouble. I don't get on as well as you think in Moscow. I'm fighting lots of the time on *Moscow Daily News*."

"What seems to be the trouble?" asked Steffens.

"Well, I'm not so naïve as to say that we don't tell the truth on that paper. I'm reporter enough to know that there is no absolute truth. Truth is for each of us our picture of the world. When I say I want to tell the truth, I mean I want to paint my picture. *Moscow News* isn't exactly my picture; it's different. I've a right to paint my own picture."

"Have you?" asked Steffens with a smile.

"Oh, I know it's difficult. Editors always insist on their pictures. But what else have I to give the world? Doesn't collective truth come when each of us paints the clearest picture he can see? I have a very good picture I want to paint of the Soviet Union. It's a giant workman fighting his way through a swamp. He has to get across or he'll die, and then the people behind will miss the road. He gets into mud to his waist; the rocks roll down the cliff and hit him on the head. He gets bloody; he's no 'pleasant guy.' He's dirty and rough and strong, but he holds the road and makes a path for all the world to follow.

"I think that picture would arouse heroic allies all over the world. I think it's a true picture. Part of the time we paint it on *Moscow News*—our workers' correspondence and our fights with bureaucrats. Then just when I'm feeling happy and the whole picture is coming out with a big smash, I find it checked by another picture that I don't like at all. A sort of miraculous virgin on a white horse in white robes, surrounded by the ravening wolves of the world. The wolves all want to eat her, but she rides right along from glory to glory and never gets a spot of mud on her white robe, and never wishes harm to anyone, not even to the wolves.

"I don't say that picture is a lie. Capitalist nations are really wolves. It really is a sort of a miracle how the Soviet Union gets through. She really does do it because she is so essentially right as well as pretty strong and clever too. But that spotless angel bores me. I see now where she comes from; I never saw it before. It's Litvinoff's Soviet Union, so self-controlled and polite, making peace all over the world. Well, she's true also, just as true as my giant. But I'm no diplomat. It's my picture I must paint and not Litvinoff's."

I paused. Lincoln Steffens was speaking. "You lucky, lucky person," he said. I waited breathlessly to hear. Our talk was nearly over; were these perhaps the last words he would ever say to me?

"You incredibly lucky person to have the chance to help Litvinoff keep the Soviet Union out of war. It's the most important job in the whole world!"

So—that was what the great reporter who had "covered" America so keenly for fifty years thought of my work. I looked down into my soul, amazed at the depths I saw. I still had in me the remains of a regular Hearst correspondent. I had held "my picture" higher than the peace of the world.

CHAPTER XXX

DEATH OF A SAINT

THE PROBLEM OF EQUALITY

THE Moscow to which I returned was building a subway. It had an American Embassy and many other improvements. More jazz for the foreigners at the Metropole on the one hand; more torn up streets on the other. The American Ambassador Bullitt said to me: "One month I can't get out of my house towards the Arbat; next month they block my way to Vorovsky Street. They always leave me one little loophole, and the new embassy will have a fine view of the Kremlin when that whole block of houses is down. But when will they get this town built? Didn't they start way back in the Middle Ages?"

Old churches collapsed in débris in the middle of market-places, asphalt swept over the vacant expanse, and a few days later natty policemen waved white-gloved hands to guide bewildered autos as traffic thundered over another square. My own apartment was blocked by subway construction in one direction, and the Palace of Soviets in another. My windows which once had looked on gold domes of Moscow Cathedral, a gaudy monster commemorating the retreat of Napoleon, now looked on a mud-hole as bad as Kuznetsk. If I stayed at home for five days running, I could hardly find my way uptown. Streets were blocked and streets were opened and signs were shifted while you waited.

Over the land in a thousand forms thundered the slogan: "Quality and surplus are the next battle!" The standard of living must be doubled or tripled, said the Second Five-Year Plan. The past year's harvest fight had achieved the highest grain crop in history; but quality for the farms demanded livestock. Pigs, pigs, pigs! * "A cow for every farming fam-

---

* Pigs increased 118 percent (more than doubled) between January 1, 1934, and the same date 1935; long horned cattle increased 21 percent (calves 94 percent). Commodity circulation tripled from 1930 to 1934. (Molotov's report to All-Union Congress January 1935.)

ily!" Great collective chicken ranches rose on the grain surplus. Department stores increased in all cities and in them workers angrily demanded better coats. Trainloads of perfume were going to Siberia. Universities threw out poorly qualified students. Moscow expressed thus the slogan of quality: "Our proletarian capital must be the finest city in the world!"

Perchik came to see me: "I'm chief now of Moscow city planning. Get me any books you can from America. We have to double the width of seventeen main arteries; if the frontage is too good to destroy we drive parallels half a block back through smaller houses. We are connecting Moscow River with the Upper Volga to get more water. The southern part of town will be our port for industries, and we'll shoot surplus water through pleasure canals in the rest of the city. Stalin says: 'Keep your eyes on Moscow River.' It will be our thoroughfare of beauty, bordered by great workers' apartments.

"Kaganovich is our chief planner. We call him: 'Chief Architect of future Moscow.' He gives points even to academicians: here lines which lift instead of bind to earth; there balconies for workers. The old estates around the city will make an outer ring of parks united by green spokes with the center. Your big apartment house comes down; we give you eight years yet. Then you'll go farther out with better traffic."

"I'm living in a construction camp already," I said. "I hate to lose some of these fascinating old churches. That picturesque Chinese Wall, is it really going? It gives the whole tone to the center of Moscow."

"You wait till you see the new tone," laughed Perchik. "We'll rail off the best bits of the Middle Ages as museums. But we can't keep Moscow as a museum. Wide boulevards, great vistas, open spaces—that's future Moscow. We're going to double the width of the Red Square by taking out the Arcade building. Voroshiloff won't have to go way back into alleys to review the Moscow garrison on May Days. A twenty-story Palace of State Industry will stand across the Square from the Kremlin."

"But the Red Square is already one of the largest squares in the world, with such beautiful proportions. That three-story columned Arcade always seemed to me a lovely background for demonstrations," I protested.

"Just trading booths of the nineteenth century," said Perchik. "You study the Square in the next celebration."

I stood in the tribune on May Day and watched a million Moscow workers storm the Red Square. Down Nikolskaia and up by both sides of the Historical Museum they flowed together, ten columns from the city's ten districts, entering as a great advancing wall of marchers, sixty abreast. They surged over the Square like an irresistible tidal ocean, under a tossing foam of red banners. Out of them rose the rhythmic beat of a thousand factory bands, buried under their marching. They flooded the Square from end to end, then split on the many-cupolaed church of Ivan the Terrible which rose like a cliff from the red tidal wave as it ebbed to the Moscow River.

What had these Kremlin walls beheld in the long march of centuries through this Square! They had looked down on ancient battles with Tartars, on holy Patriarchs riding asses to solemnize Palm Sundays, on a forest of gallows in the seventeenth century when a sadist tsar with his own hand beheaded men. Down that Nikolskaia had come Far Eastern caravans to trade at this central mart with men from the "Golden Horde" of southern Tartars, and with bearded men of the north from Novgorod and Tver. Those walls had seen the victory and retreat of Napoleon, and the blatant luxuries of modern monarchs, and the drab recruits of the World War. Last of all, they had seen the October Revolution when red guards swept in from workers' suburbs to storm the Kremlin.

For thirteen years now I had watched those workers storm the Square twice yearly from the growing industrial districts of Moscow, showing in mighty popular pageantry each new stage of world revolution. I remembered the early years when ragged workers bore banners shouting defiance to Poincaré and Curzon and calling on the workers of the world for aid—days when intervention seemed always imminent. There followed the Five-Year Plan with its emphasis on construction,

and a year later on production, when the Square was a forest
of placards showing percentage of fulfillment in factory plans.
Then these had merged into the fight for individual responsibility and quality; the marchers celebrated not only their factory but the shop within the factory and carried pictures of
their "champions" who made records. Collective farmers from
Moscow district had then appeared in increasing numbers.
Foreigners said: "They've dropped world revolution." Yet
every factory knew itself a post of the revolution, and every
collective farm was urged: "Your task for the world revolution
is to plant more grain."

This year, May Day 1934, the pageant shouted surplus!
Abundance, quality, variety of color and form! Hundreds of
airplanes thundered above the marchers. Out of the tossing
sea of red banners rose great models of inflated rubber: locomotives, houses, dirigibles. A dozen men staggered under a
model of the Palace of Soviets; thousands bore emblems
of ball bearings, cotton spindles, new machines. Instead
of one red fist, a forest of red fists shot *"rot front"* into
the air. Thousands of balloons carried pictures and inscriptions sky-wards, millions of colored streamers were hurled
above the masses and fell to be buried under the marching feet.
An undertone appeared of capitalist world crisis, threat of
war and fascism. "Free Thælmann." "Hail to the Chinese
Soviets!"

On all this great demonstration of the masses, the fifteenth
century Kremlin walls looked down. Under the walls were the
brotherhood graves of the revolution, and the mausoleum of
Lenin. American communists lay there also: John Reed, Hay-
wood and Ruthenburg. Along the walls the tribunes held ten
thousand spectators, workers' champions, diplomats and correspondents—the eyes of all the world. And across the Square
that solid Arcade building built by a millionaire for Moscow's
most luxurious trade. No, take it away! It had no place here.
Double the width of the Square, let it stretch from the fifteenth century ramparts to twenty stories of socialist industry,
Moscow's past and future, with nothing between but the men

who made that future—Lenin and his comrades in brotherhood graves.

.   .   .   .

A month later I got a letter from Valentina; she was one of
my best friends. A brilliant girl, she had been in her middle
twenties chief of English courses in the Second Moscow University, with a score of teachers and a couple of thousand students under her. She had shared my apartment for two years.
Sitting on my divan we had discussed at length and repeatedly
our souls, our views of men and our attitude to the party. As
I remembered, we were always adoring the past performances
of the party, but worried about its present state. We had no
use for any men who were not "responsible party members,
doing things." We ourselves were intending to join the party
some day, but always at the last minute we found some flaw
in our souls or in the party to cause another delay.

For always as we reacted to life around us, we generalized
facts, not by logic, but by emotion. We would see some worker
evicted, some person unjustly jailed or hear of some peasant
starving, and swiftly that fact would recall every injustice
we had seen in the past ten years. Soon we would be saying:
"This country is worse than capitalism. It evicts workers,
starves peasants and jails innocent citizens." And we would
feel this very emotionally till we saw a good worker getting
rewards or a collective farm succeeding or men guilty of excesses being punished and then we would swing to the other
extreme.

Eventually I had found a partial antidote by reading
Pravda, not so much the glowing reports of achievements as
the columns of shocking abuses. These were so much worse
than anything I could imagine that they seemed to blot out
my own complaints. *Pravda* met them all, not with emotional
complaint but with grim defiance which would thus infect me
also. They seemed to think they could conquer anything, even
the ancient bases of human nature. . . . "Let's hope they
can," I said. "Humanity needs it." . . . Even in my most
ardent hopes I was saying "they," not "we."

Was Valentina yet in the party? I was sure she would beat

me in. I had said to her: "Get in! It's humanity's last chance. If these Russian communists fail there's nothing left but the dark ages. As for myself, I've some excuse. They would probably send me to join that inefficient American party, and I couldn't stand that." My attitude was changing towards the American party but I had other good excuses now. But Valentina had actually begun to qualify for the party by social work in the Putiloff Plant where she taught Marxism to workers. Anyone who could do that for two years was getting pretty far. Probably she had joined already.

Valentina began her letter by denouncing me for not writing. I recognized the beginning of a soul-storm. She continued: "Have you become one of our 'great ladies' or are you still 'left-wing.' . . . The atmosphere here is getting very heavy-clouded with ranks, privileges and insolences. One must either be a party saint like your husband, who gets restless when anyone starts to criticize, or else just one of the greedy crowd pursuing position—not to see how things are going. Party saints are growing more rare and less in favor, while the greedy lot grow more usual and acceptable. . . . Anyway I shall soon be in Moscow and then we shall talk quite freely as only two non-party members can talk."

What! I didn't like her reference to my husband. When a man has spent forty-four days in an airplane covering the harvest and lost thirty pounds of weight in saving thousands of bushels of grain, he has a right to get restless under Valentina's emotions. Or even under mine. And what was this about non-party members—"as only they can talk." It was true the party members evaded soul-discussions; they offered you a book by Marx. But did Valentina think I was going to wail over sins of the party in the second year of the Second Five-Year Plan?

Nevertheless the letter affected me. For three years the country had been fighting for Stalin's "six conditions" of efficiency, which included increase of engineers in management, organized recruiting of labor and lessened turnover, improved living conditions and differential rewards. Wasn't this inequality increasing dangerously? There really were people who grew snobbish with increasing goods, and acquired privileges, bigger apartments, summer villas. "Must one worry one year about famine," I sighed, "and the next about surplus?" But didn't surplus really present its problems?

I worried enough to take the question to Kollontai, who was in Moscow for her vacation from Stockholm where she was Soviet ambassador. "It's not yet as bad as NEP was," I said. "But isn't it more subtle? It seems to be even inside the party."

"We have absorbed eleven million peasants into our industrial working-class and very large numbers into our party," said Kollontai. "They bring their habits of individual property, and their judgment of life in terms of goods. They are our new strength but they are not at once made over."

So—that was it! Not a new weakness but a new strength! The great masses were coming now, whose wills must be expressed. They needed still that extra prodding—discrimination in rewards. But was it only these new masses? "Those peasants are simple in their tastes," I answered bluntly. "It's bureaucrats who grab the villas."

"Yes," smiled Kollontai unworried. "It gets into rather unexpected places. A man in the Kremlin health resort bureau actually asked me why I didn't have a summer villa. I cried: 'What! When I live in Stockholm!' . . . 'Well, you might live in Moscow some day and might want a villa.' . . . 'If the party calls me back,' I told them, 'the party will know how to house me.' . . . Imagine living in Stockholm and being burdened with property in Moscow. . . . But these bureaucrats only go as far as the masses let them. I think we are really developing a few abuses. If they go too far, be sure we shall fight them. But they are certainly not the problem next in line. And meantime the peasant himself is being made over."

"What is the problem next in line?" I asked her.

"You know it yourself. You read the party congresses. Quality, surplus, to master our technical processes and triple the standard of living. And the struggle for peace."

Her words reassured me until Yavorskaia died, raving of inequality. Yavorskaia, not Valentina, was my closest woman

friend. Valentina and I shared our souls and an apartment
but Yavorskaia and I had shared the fight for John Reed
Colony and the care of its many children. I had thought her
a bit sentimental. But how she had helped those scattered
communars; they were all Yavorskaia's girls and boys, consulting her about jobs and marriages.

Yavorskaia was a real saint from the Middle Ages, too unselfish for this world. Even in tsarist days when husbands
were bosses, she divorced a wealthy husband when he refused
to let her adopt a homeless waif. After that her life was devoted to homeless ones. She lived in a wretched room and took
waifs into it. She went about in all weathers without adequate
coat or rubbers; she had always given her last coat to someone
who needed it more. She had no time to see any achievements
of the Five-Year Plan, or anything happy. She was on the
most discouraging "front." Day and night she worked in
Danilovski Receiving Station for waifs; she always took duty
when others wanted to go to parades. During the long summer fight in 1933 to handle Ukrainian children, organize them
into farm colonies and set them up on the land, she had denied
herself the pleasure of visiting me for she knew she was full
of lice. Once when she dropped in utter exhaustion on my
divan it took us a day to be sure of the blankets.

I saw her the week before she died; she was unhappy. "They
have made our station into a 'model.' Do you realize what that
means? We must refuse children unless we have beds for them;
we must let them lie in the streets! Then people come to see
how well we run the station; how well we classify and instruct.
Other towns copy us.

"I thought last year was worst, when we were buried under
those Ukrainians. So disconcerting ten years after we had
conquered famine to get that unexpected flood. I said: 'I can
never live through such a year again.' We have no Ukrainians
now. They are all home again, on their parents' farms. This
year we have the western province and part of Moscow district where the rain killed crops. There isn't even a fraction
as many; there's been no typhus at all. I really think it's the
last time we'll have them. But I'd rather die of typhus smoth-

ered under lousy children and know that I took them all than
run this horrible 'model' station while children are outside.

"Our director Chervontzeff is so hard-hearted, though he
himself was a homeless boy. He says: 'Don't worry so, Yavorskaia. This isn't a long pull like last summer; it's only a July
flurry before harvest. In a month they'll all go home. What's
a month in Moscow parks when the city is full of food? Only
a good camping trip; I was a homeless kid! But our station
builds quality and others copy us.'

"The worst is the inequality. They've closed our special
staff restaurant; they said it was too small to organize control.
A few directors get special meals in their offices but I refused.
Not when my fine staff walks a half hour to the general restaurant. . . . But I never have time to go." Knowing Yavorskaia, I knew she must be starving; she had time only for tea
and bread at home.

Yavorskaia always refused "privileges." She refused what
to her was the great privilege of party membership. She told
me once: "My life began with the Soviet Power; it alone gave
me the chance to fight for children." But when the workers
of her receiving station voted her their best champion, "worthy
of being a communist," she answered: "I care more for the
party's success than for anything in life, but I cannot honestly
join while their speed of change makes children homeless. For
me they go too fast."

Yavorskaia was many years older than I; she was like a
mother. Yet she clung to my hand that last time when I left
her; she was sick in bed. "You are one of the few I can talk
to. One can't tell troubles to outsiders. Nor often to party
members. My best co-worker was a communist and they gave
her other work. She won't listen now to my troubles. She
says: 'I worked ten years for children and if I hear about them,
it hurts my new work.' That I can understand, but it leaves
me lonely."

Eight days later Yavorskaia was dead of typhus. It was
this that made her yellow and gaunt when I saw her. She had
worked through the first five days of typhus, an incredible
thing. "We cannot understand it," they said at the station.

"Last year we had many cases. But this year we are clean. She is the only one." Yavorskaia had her wish; she died of typhus, smothered under the needs of children.

In the red corner at the receiving station lay the body, smothered now under flowers. In a polished red coffin with red flags draped in black. On the wall was her enlarged photograph, far more like her than the yellow, waxen body; its face showed the madonna of long centuries, the eternal mother of the motherless.

A guard of honor, six people changed often, stood at head and foot of the bier. Her waifs and strays and the co-workers of the station came thus in turn for a few moments, holding in silence the banners draped above her head. From outside rose the strains of the revolutionary funeral march, played by the boys' band of the station, as the smaller children formed in line with awed faces to bid Yavorskaia good-by. "We are naming after her the receiving station that she organized," they told me, "and also a new colony for children. Her picture will remain in the red corner. The Children's Commission is giving university scholarships in her honor to boys and girls from children's homes." . . . No, she had not remained a madonna of old centuries; she had become a mother in the revolution.

Yet she went to her grave broken. Her adopted daughter, once a homeless girl, choked with tears to tell of Yavorskaia's last moments. "Do you know what she said: 'There is no equality! There will never be equality! Some will always have special meals while others hunger.' Then just before she became unconscious she said: 'Do not regret if I die. I am so worn out and so disappointed by people that I want some place in the country where there are only trees.' "

Those people who had worn her out and disappointed her gathered about her now. The "hard-hearted" director who had been a homeless boy and fought for quality had the grime of a tear on his cheek. The old party co-worker with whom she "could no longer talk freely," was sobbing by the bier. The staff was there—the inefficient Young Communist girls for whom she gave up "special meals." The hordes of disorderly children were quiet now for an hour. They had all worn her out and all loved her.

We marched behind the great red bier to the crematorium. We heard the chairman of the Children's Commission pay her tribute, announcing new scholarships in her name. We heard the Young Pioneers' representative tell of children to whom she showed the "path to life." We saw the flame leap up to consume the yellow, waxen body under its heavy robe of fiery flowers. They set aside, to go in the red corner, the great set pieces of artificial roses and chrysanthemums from the hundreds of simple folk who loved her—the tawdriness dignified by pain.

It was hard to face that death of Yavorskaia, the ending of a saint in such despair. I spoke of her last words to others. One old intellectual said: "After all, it is only in our country that men care enough for ideals to die of them." . . . There was something rotten in that answer; it insulted Yavorskaia. But I couldn't analyze how.

Ten days after her death a voice came over the telephone. "Do you remember Morosov?" . . .

"Morosov," I exclaimed, "of John Reed Colony." . . .

"I'm coming over," he said. "I'm here for the night in Moscow."

Waiting I wondered how I would meet, without Yavorskaia, Morosov's new need. I had seen him last on the Volga, sick with a sick wife and two small children. In the months of unemployment after Petroff threw him out of the colony he had acquired tuberculosis. No doubt he came to me now because Yavorskaia was gone.

Morosov came quiet, smiling, confident. We talked about old communars scattered in many jobs. "Most are doing quite well," he said. "We learned how to fight in that commune." He added that he was "doing potato purchases in Voronesh"; I assumed some small clerk's job. He had been detained in Moscow on business.

"How do you like the present state of the country?" I asked, remembering Yavorskaia's last cry for equality. What did

Morosov, who dreamed in youth of the Great Commune, think of today?

"I don't like it at all," said Morosov. "Our 'quality' is poor. I can't get a decent coat anywhere. Yet we Russians can make good quality. Years ago I got a good coat on the Volga. But now we're using up all the odds and ends of materials and people; and quality's poor."

"I'm told it's much better than last year," I said in bewilderment. Had Morosov, who dreamed of the Great Commune, descended to coats? "They say last year you grabbed anything the stores would give you, but now the workers throw them back and write in complaint books."

"We do better than write in complaint books," grinned Morosov. "We arrest men for bad coats. Sure it's better than a year ago!" (The scorn of those words showed a year ago as very ancient history.) "But it's taking far too long to master our new factories. We're much too slow!"

Too slow! With a Five-Year Plan that had more than doubled a nation's production, and that seemed to Yavorskaia too painfully fast! "Have you heard about Yavorskaia?" I asked him.

"I am going to run around to Yavorskaia's later," he said easily. "You can get her best around midnight." . . .

"Yavorskaia's dead," I told him.

He was grieved but not overwhelmed. He had wanted only a friendly talk; she no longer meant a need. Then I told how Yavorskaia died, battling to take everybody, grieving over special meals, raving of equality. Morosov grew concerned.

"Just as some comrades died at the beginning of NEP," he said sadly. "Poor Yavorskaia! We should have looked after her better. She could never look after herself. She lived too long under tsardom. She felt too much."

Was this Morosov speaking? A John Reed Colony boy whom Yavorskaia always looked after. Her comment on equality had touched him only to pity. His lack of tragedy annoyed me.

"She was the best woman I ever knew," I said with emphasis. I meant—the most unselfish.

Morosov nodded. "A worker in a million," he said with enthusiasm, thinking he was repeating my words. "She gave us boys the path to life, when we were downed by Petroff. We should look after these old workers better. I told you our quality's bad. If that station had been properly run they would have forced her on vacation two months earlier, with an extra month sick leave. When she got back the Western province would have its harvest and the kids would all be home. Floods of kids won't happen again. She could have spent the rest of her life happily cleaning up odds and ends of waifs and strays."

It was Yavorskaia's great work that made her great to Morosov. Her high sentiments were weakness excused because of exhaustion. Hadn't Yavorskaia also laid it to exhaustion, saying: "I am tired of people; I want green trees?"

"What about equality?" I pursued him, unwilling to let him off.

"Equality is not so soon," smiled Morosov. "We must get a lot of surplus first." . . . He didn't even connect my words with Yavorskaia; he thought I teased his early dream of the Great Commune.

"But which way is equality going? Are people more equal or less? The closing of that dining room and the meals for directors only, is that a general tendency now?"

"Why, yes," said Morosov unworried. "Most places had to have special meals last year for all their staff but now only for a few whose time is especially important. In another year there probably won't be any; we're getting more surplus. Soon the ordinary coöperatives will feed us all."

He still missed the point. It was to him a mere matter of technique, not of ethics. He didn't see new privileges that worried Yavorskaia; he saw a stage in the abolition of privilege. Was there no way to make him see my question? What was my question then? "Is inequality leading the Soviet Union towards capitalism or some similar system of ranks, privileges, insolences?" Was that what I wanted to ask?

I could never ask that question of Morosov; so much was clear. He wouldn't at first be able to understand that I could

ask it. But if once I drove that question past his unconscious
defenses into his brain, and he thought I asked it seriously,
I could guess his answer. "It's counter-revolution you're talking. That's idealistic stuff." Morosov would never see me as
comrade again.

I must ask myself then, not Morosov. What did one mean
by "equality"? What did Yavorskaia mean? "Some must
not be full-fed while others hunger." Morosov meant that too.
He called it "surplus" and "quality"; his words were better;
they were true. He thought in clear stages: five years the
fight for grain and iron; five years for quality, surplus, butter and coats. Then one might begin to talk equality.

What did Morosov mean by "equality"? "From each according to his ability, to each according to his needs." Morosov thought that far. But was that "equality" either? How
horrible if everyone's needs and abilities were equal! A socialist ant-heap! I suddenly saw that the formula of the Great
Commune was itself a statement of the tremendous inequalities
of man: poet, scientist, explorer, engineer, mechanic, endlessly
diverse and unequal—all free at last to flower into fullest individuality without exploitation, equal only in comradeship.

"Equality" then was a word to make men vague. Like
"God," like "truth," like "freedom," like all those words of
ideals. Like the bluffing words of my youth that covered
smoothly a dozen conflicting meanings. One of its meanings
was the deep need of mankind that no man go hungry and
needy; other meanings were poison mixed with the food. Clear
analysis was needed, not emotion for "equality."

I saw now why I hated that man who said of Yavorskaia:
"Only in our country do men die of their ideals." Such a man
was a viper to be crushed! Yavorskaia die of "ideals," of the
poison in the word "equality"? Never! Yavorskaia was a
"worker in a million." She had a decenter excuse for dying.
She died of typhus, of exhaustion; she died in battle. Morosov, not I, had honored her memory rightly. I had tried to
cherish her holy feelings. Morosov softened her weakness and
celebrated her strength.

"What should Yavorskaia have done about those special dinners?" I asked Morosov.

"She should of course have taken them," he answered casually. "Her strength was valuable; her staff was young. Any time you can convince the party that your time rates special meals, you take them. I took mine in Saratov, but I can't get them now in Voronesh till after harvest, when all special meals may end."

What! Was Morosov one of those "special meal" directors? What was he doing? I asked his exact work. "I thought I told you. I'm in charge of potato purchases in the Black Earth Region. I collect nearly a million tons of potatoes and ship them to Leningrad, Moscow and elsewhere."

"Why, Morosov, how amazing! For one of our John Reed boys!"

"It's not so much," said Morosov. "I told you most of our old communars are doing pretty well. After harvest they're giving me general vegetables too. The Central Committee called me to Moscow for conference; we're reorganizing the vegetable shipments of the country. I left John Reed eight years ago; I ought to know something now."

This was the boy I thought was coming to me for assistance, now that Yavorskaia was dead. I began to ask him not about John Reed communars but about potatoes as I would ask any other responsible person from whom I wished to learn.

"Yes, our vegetable handling was one of the sore spots of the whole national economy," he said. "Two years ago potatoes rotted in our storage, and on railroads and after arrival in the factory coöperatives. They rotted everywhere. Last year we conquered our warehouses, but we got a special order that the consumers weren't ready and we had to store a lot of extra potatoes for them. We dug deep trenches, according to a special theory, but we did it badly. Most of our trenches of potatoes spoiled. 'Quality' was better than the year before, but still rather bad. This year the consuming coöperatives are ready; we can ship more potatoes at once. We shall repeat only a few trenches in an experimental way. The railroads lack refrigerating cars; there'll still be trouble in transport. But warehousing at both ends of the line is conquered."

He talked on about potatoes, the region where they grew best, the quality of Black Earth soils, the quotas from each district. This was Morosov, orphan son of a servant maid of Astrakhan, who had seen the revolution at the age of ten, the theater square in flames and the famine years. This was the boy who, coming at sixteen to John Reed Colony to build the Great Commune, had battered on locked doors behind which Petroff looted the children's mail, and been in Petroff's vengeful fear thrown out to starve.

What had happened to the tuberculosis? "Twice in a sanitarium and the diet got better in general," he casually said. Then I asked: "Ever seen Petroff?"

"Yeah, I saw Petroff a couple of months ago in Saratov. We're working for the same trust. He sort of avoids me and I don't care to see him either. He's still in the party but they gave him a rough time at the last two cleanings. Not about John Reed; that's ancient history. He's a clever guy; he sneaks from place to place just before they get him. But a man like that is incorrigible; they'll get him yet!"

Morosov hadn't time to worry even about Petroff, proved villain and personal foe who threw him out to starve. He trusted the party to get rid of its villains when their sins were ripe. But I took time to worry about men I had never seen who wanted good clothes, prestige, summer houses and who by these human desires might some day grow into villains. Kollontai was right; it certainly wasn't the problem next in line. Around us lay the terrific tasks of organizing, expressing, satisfying one hundred and sixty million people.

. . . .

Valentina came to my divan in Moscow and settled herself for a "good, long talk." I said: "Discussion of souls is out! We've settled our souls for a decade and they bore me now. What job are you on: coats, potatoes, English text-books or the war against fascism?"

She responded beautifully: "I'm here for the Writers' Congress. It's a most remarkable event. We are organizing a world front of intellectuals against the war danger. And we're planning to remake the human mind."

I stared at her. And I had let myself be worried for weeks by an emotion of Valentina's. After a moment she apologized. "You know, I was in a rather bad mood when I wrote that letter." . . . How many bad moods of mine, I wondered, had I passed on during the last thirteen years to struggling comrades?

· · · · · · ·

In the center of Moscow clouds of white dust were rising, obscuring the autumn sky. The great "Chinese Wall" from the sixteenth century was coming down. A week later everyone was saying: "Have you seen those boulevards? Have you seen that stretch that rises towards Lubianka? And the sweep down hill past the Central Committee to Nogin Square? Has any city vistas better than Moscow? But—wait till you see us next year!"

A *Moscow Daily News* correspondent returned from a special tour of Siberia. "You'll never guess the news from Kuznetsk. They're competing with Magnitogorsk—on flowerbeds!"

The office broke into a gale of laughter. Kuznetsk, that mud-hole where men had carted earth in baskets in the ancient Asiatic way! That huddle of barracks and dugouts a year later, where they lived in lice and typhoid to build a city of steel! Blast furnaces they might compete in. But flowerbeds, no!

"It's fact," said the correspondent. "I'll show you the terms of the competition. It includes boulevards, parks and workers' clubs. Magnitogorsk has some lawns and trees and the best auto-busses, but Kuznetsk has a street car line and a theatrical troupe from Moscow. The Meyerhold company was playing there."

"Any Americans left in Leninsk?"

"Sure, and they're going to stay. Tomlianovich's brigade took first place in the big Emelyanov mine in the all-Union competition. The mine itself took second prize in Kuzbas.

Five of the Americans are listed as 'mine notables' but they still complain that nobody takes their suggestions."

"We've got you beat," said the correspondent from Karelia, who handled the affairs of six thousand Finnish-Americans, working out from Petrozavodsk. "They are opening a Miners' Palace of Culture for the November holidays at Khibinogorsk north of the Arctic circle, with sound films and their own radio sender. They have three recreation parks for the miners, a big technical library and a mineralogical museum that is the pride of the north. Their University of Mining and Chemistry opens next year."

Flower-beds in Kuznetsk! A university and sound films on the tundra beyond those trackless woods where Rimpalle ten years ago had taught illiterate natives how to mine. . . . This chaos was really becoming too organized. Where was another good fight?

I smiled to remember the wail of a small boy at the Chelyushkin celebration in Moscow: "Lenin has made the October Revolution and our aviators have saved the Chelyushkinites, and what is there left for me?" . . . No, he was premature! There were plenty of fights left for this country. The conquest of the Arctic was only in its first stages. The writers had begun to remake the human mind; that would hold them awhile! Vavilov, chief scientific adviser to the Commissariat of Agriculture, had said to me: "We scientists used to feel rather unregarded, but now that collective farmers demand our science, we see our work for several thousand years."

There would always be something to conquer. When they got round to it, they would have to abolish death, wouldn't they? Would that be fast enough for Morosov? Or would death remain our most convenient method to get rid of worn-out bodies and brains in order to go ahead faster in new ones?

CHAPTER XXXI

PRELUDE TO FREEDOM

THE PROBLEM OF WILL

"I hear you're writing a book," said Borodin. "All the things you've learned from life. What have you learned from *Moscow Daily News?* It interests me."

"I've chiefly learned," I said teasingly, "that after all my struggles the editor isn't as important as I thought."

Borodin looked concerned. "You have learned a bad lesson," he said. "And after I came on this paper to help you."

What did he mean—help me? Wasn't he the boss of the paper? And how did he "choose" to come? Didn't the party make him? But I relented. "Of course it's pleasanter to work with you than with the others. And you're making a better paper. But I think that just happens because the whole country's getting better. Something besides you really runs us. Once you agreed with me that we needed snappy American articles, and now you are drifting back to translations from the Russian. I don't know what makes you do it: I don't know who really bosses us."

"Do you really need a boss so much?" asked Borodin.

"An outsider might even call me boss," I continued, "when my struggles threw out two editors and got the editor-in-chief I asked for. But I never run anything at all. I just drift in with articles on subjects that interest me, and perhaps you say: 'Can you help us on agriculture?' or Van Zandt remarks that I ought to do more for the weekly. I used to think they meant to side-track me when nobody either took my orders or gave me any. But now I see it's just the style of the country. I don't see how it runs."

"Oh, yes, you do," said Borodin. "You've seen for many years and written well about it."

"Of course I know that the communist party runs things. But there's something I still don't get. Take ourselves as example. I know the press department of the party has something to say about us, but I can't make out whether they are really our boss or a sort of adviser. I know the Corporation of Magazines is our publisher, but they don't even read us. They only fight us for floor space and steal our coated paper, and we're getting strong enough to fight them back. Now one of these new correspondents calls us a government organ and that seems to me inaccurate. But I don't know how to disprove it."

"Ask him," smiled Borodin, "if he knows any government department that would care to feel responsible for what we say." Even I laughed at the absurdity of that!

"You'd be surprised," I said, "if you knew how many ideas I've had in the past four years as to who runs us. I thought at first it was going to be a board of various industries that employed Americans. But they only took blocks of subscriptions and complained when these weren't delivered. I've not seen such complaints for a year so I judge the post-office works better.

"There was even a time when I thought the G.P.U. took a hand in running us, because I couldn't see where the secretary of the staff got his 'authority.' Then there was a time when I thought everybody ran us. The linotype man changed my copy: and Jack Chen's Young Communist conscience wouldn't pass my editorial, so he fixed it when I wasn't looking. . . . That's anarchy: it doesn't happen now."

"It was more than anarchy: it was real interest. But of course we had to get out of that disorganization."

"Who really runs us?" I demanded.

"We do," said Borodin. "You and I. I do it very conscientiously, giving lots of time and thought. Haven't you seen my conferences with reporters? You could be helpful there if you had the time; you know more journalism than I do. But I know better than you what our readers want: I've been visiting more factories. Would it surprise you to be told that our real trouble is that we are still too uncontrolled, too 'free.' "

"The word 'freedom' has no meaning," I said impatiently. "Certainly not as applied to the Soviet press. Why, the head of the Ukrainian State Publishing House told Sherwood Eddy that the Soviet press is the only free press in the world. I'm ready to slave for this country because it's making a decenter world than the capitalists, but to speak of 'freedom' seems to me just juggling words. Sometimes it seems to me that even your socialism will be just like an ant-heap: that gives me a horrible feeling. But I suppose the young ants will be conditioned to it from the beginning: they will never know what it felt like on the western prairies when we had our illusions of freedom."

Borodin seemed to give me up: he began to talk about our readers. "Our real trouble," he said, "is that we don't know them well enough. It is harder for us than for any other paper in the country. I think it is largely this that causes your difficulty. Our readers themselves are a mixed lot and inexpressive: they give us no clear policy."

Policy? Our readers give us policy? I knew that every Soviet paper maintained a large department of correspondence from its readers and that out of such correspondence came ideas which were widely applied in the policies of the whole country, which even became new law, new institutions. But I had never really applied this to *Moscow News'* readers. I cherished their letters as live stuff, but not as "our policy." Our readers, in fact, were almost the only people in the country whom I hadn't imagined as our bosses. Weren't we rather bossing them, instructing them in the things they ought to know?

"Our readers," Borodin mused. "Do you know them? I've been seeing them at factory meetings of 'Readers of *Moscow Daily News.*' I ask what language I shall use and they tell me Russian! Why then do they read an English paper?

"By birth they are neither Russian nor American: they are Pole, Jugo-Slav, Hungarian, Finn, the nomad workers of the world. They went in youth to the new world in America: now they seek the new world here. They are American to us because they learned to read in America and acquired there the technical skill for which we prize them. They understand Russian because it is spoken around them. But few can write a clear letter in English, and many cannot write clearly in any language. They have worked in too many tongues to write in any.

"What do they want? They cannot easily tell us. We maintain a big 'mass department,' two-thirds of all our reporters, to unearth their needs. It is the more difficult because capitalism has made them passive: they know how to complain but not to desire. By hard work we get from them enough letters on local oppressions, bureaucrats, technical troubles, to fill daily our whole third page. But with twenty thousand circulation in the Soviet Union we should get six times our present correspondence, enough to base the whole policy of our paper on their needs. How much foreign news do they want? How much on strikes in America? Do they want football news? What do they want to know about the Soviet Union to understand their own jobs and lives?

"Our readers change, and we change ourselves to fit them. The valuta specialists go and we drop the fluffy stuff that amused them. The summer tourists come and we have some simpler articles. The American Embassy arrives and we strengthen our foreign political news. Our most important readers remain the English-speaking workers in Soviet enterprises. Since their control is lax, I pay special attention to comments by Russians who handle their complaints. If we got expression from our readers, *Moscow Daily News* would be directing those Russians. Then we should really be an organ: we have not become one yet."

An organ of what? Yes, it was clear. Of the English-speaking workers in Soviet industries, just as I had wanted from the beginning. Why did I always keep slipping away from it and rediscovering it as if I hadn't known it?

"As for you writers," Borodin was saying, "haven't you been trying to make it an organ of young and clever reporters giving their feelings to the world?"

He was right: that had been my long struggle. Always I had fought to put more Americans on the staff and play up their breezy articles. Vivid features, style, the ideal of the artist had been my ideal. All the correspondents in Moscow and the American writers who came from abroad had justified me.

"Of course they justify you," said Borodin. "Their aim is clever writing: our aim is to help Americans function efficiently in Soviet enterprises. Did you think our country in its paper shortage could find paper for sentiments of all these newly arrived reporters? They want to pour out their souls, but their souls are not yet useful. Their heavenly love for all things in the Soviet Union, without analysis or discrimination! Do you remember how I said to the reporters: 'Just stir those articles in your coffee and you won't need sugar.'

"Then they rush to the other extreme, long columns of statistics, or unconvincing generalizations based on two or three facts. How many of these new reporters can give a clear, continuing picture either in industry, transport, political life or farming? They give clever accounts of unrelated happenings, sweet stuff or sob stuff, the vaudeville art of the capitalist press. Give me good stuff in English and I always take it before the Russian. But our shifting staff of Americans hasn't kept up with the growing sophistication of our readers who want more thorough stuff. That's why I take some Russian articles. The function of writers is to learn to express what our twenty thousand readers need and to give them guidance."

Hadn't we been doing it? "Free press" to me had meant a press that expressed the writers. But how about a press that expressed the readers? Yet our writers meant to express the readers. Then we bluffed ourselves into thinking we were doing it. We never really inquired or knew.

"They read me more than anyone," I defended myself.

"Yes, you have vivid style and knowledge of the country. But they move fast and all of us have to keep moving. Just because you interest people or thrill them doesn't mean that you have satisfied their needs. If you persist in thrilling without satisfying, some day they will find out and hate you." . . .

Yes, I thought, that is the trick of the intellectual, the parliamentarian, to thrill without even pretending to satisfy, and call those thrills the people's will!

"But surely," I said, "we are responsible to somebody beside our readers. Who pays our deficit?"

"Chiefly the fund for educating minority nationalities, who aren't yet supposed to pay their own way. But responsible? Don't you feel responsible? Why don't you resign any more?"

"When Stalin and Kaganovich showed an interest in this paper, I couldn't feel like getting off," I said. "But they don't run us. Even the press department is almost as hard to reach as ever."

"Why bother them? You and I are supposed to have intelligence. We're supposed to read the decisions of party congresses and know our general line. We're supposed to know how to apply this to our readers and get out of them their desires to add to the desires of all Soviet workers. An appointment by the press department means that they recognize this intelligence; we aren't supposed to keep bothering them for orders. If we make mistakes there are various means of checking us—journals which criticize newspapers, columns of press review in *Pravda*. We're supposed to read these things and keep up."

"I've another reason for not resigning," I declared. "I've decided to drop idealism and be quite practical. I've figured out that this paper will inevitably get better till some day it will be world famous, and I'll be proud to have started it. Everything in this country grows. I need a steady post: I'm growing old!"

Borodin looked amused. "That god of inevitable progress?" he queried. "Many things grow in this country: some things die. If more American immigrants come, our paper will grow more important. If not, our present readers will learn Russian, and the need for *Moscow Daily News* will vanish."

Then *Moscow Daily News* itself might vanish! I needed several days to think this over. If it collapsed just when its fame should justify my work! Would I drift back to free-lancing, seeking editors through the capitalist world? It was amusing enough as relaxation: how ghastly it would be as a life!

A few days later I dropped into Borodin's office. "When I finish my book," I said, "I want to do some traveling around the industries. Or perhaps I'd better have some permanent assignment to keep me in touch with our big Auto Works for instance. I always like this country best when I'm knocking about the farms and factories."

Borodin looked at me oddly. I remembered that this was the kind of assignment they always gave communists to keep them in touch with some section of the working masses. I had always thought it a sort of extra party duty: now I saw that under Soviet conditions it was a prerequisite of good work.

．　　　．　　　．　　　．　　　．　　　．　　　．

Thus I began thinking about "bossing." Was anyone in the U.S.S.R. ever "ordered" in the good, old proper way? We always "consulted" and out of consultation came assignments. We went to the editor and said: "I've an idea for a tour of the country." If several people agreed we went to the secretary and got a little paper which entitled us to expense account and consideration on our journey. We called it getting ordered. What an odd word! When I first heard that word years earlier I thought: "Doesn't anyone in this country ever travel freely? Do they have to get 'orders' and 'permits' even on vacations?" But those papers were no sign of bosses; you wanted them, consulted, and got them.

Why, even our six typists had organized their own work, dividing their shifts to give each a chance at variety. The editors and copy-desk grew desperate, saying: "As soon as we get used to the mistakes of one typist, you give us a new one." But the typists said: "We like variety and a change from day to evening work." Then a new typist came who wanted efficiency. And an editor said: "Stalin himself says people must be attached to special machines and assignments; that's party line." So the typists reorganized themselves in a rather complicated arrangement which seemed to suit everyone. Had Stalin himself "bossed" our typists? What a dictator he was, I laughed. That new typist was now head typist, but when I congratulated her on her promotion, she said: "It's no promotion; I'm just the goat who has to get a substitute when anyone is ill. Since I usually can't find one, I have to do it myself. They call it an honor."

How were the other jobs? I thought of brigades on collective farms. Village officials got fired for too much bossing; they called it administrative action. A good brigade leader was supposed to say: "Boys, we've got to beat that record! How shall we divide the work? Peter here is best plowman." When Peter heard he was the best plowman, he usually decided to plow; if he didn't like plowing he asked for other work and often got it. But if he wouldn't do anything they wanted, they chucked him out and Peter could go home and starve.

Those peasants had had a terrible time learning this new way of working. But they were learning now. The way they fought the drought of 1934 by consulting and combining and declaring organized war on nature under the leadership of science, was proof. It seemed to take us Americans as long as it took the peasants. Why, they even treated us like a minor nationality; that was really good!

The Soviet elections came in late November of 1934. The foreign correspondents said as usual: "Why do they have elections? It's all a rubber stamp." But I went to a village election in Gulin and heard an election commissioner, himself a communist, brag of an election where the collective farmers turned down the party nominee. The farmers had said: "We've nothing against Borisov except that he takes his duties too much like routine. We think Lubov would carry out our instructions with more energy. We want a public bath, a stringed orchestra, a reading hut and some organized study courses not just in the central village but at our hamlet. Borisov is too slow on them."

"Now that's what I call a good election," exulted the commissioner. "Good for all concerned! Let Borisov and the party organization know that they have to keep moving if they want to lead these masses. Let those farmers now work hard to help Lubov justify their choice. Lubov won't go to sleep either!"

What amazing people! An election that was "good for all concerned"! I could never explain that in America. A communist who took an election which threw out his own party's candidate, as a triumph instead of a party defeat. I said as much to a prominent Moscow communist who answered: "What we build cannot be built by passive people. When will is awakened, give it way!"

But of course! Hadn't I known for eleven years, since I saw Baku and the Donetz, that this was a workers' dictatorship? Didn't dictators need will? Why did I always take that word as thinking that I must be dictated to, and never that I might dictate? Why did I call democracy "the right to choose my ruler"? When these men said "Soviet democracy" they meant the issuing of instructions to deputies whom they expected to back up by their own work. Everyone bragged that this year's elections showed great increase of popular activity. Was it because these men had held for years joint ownership of the means of production that they now began increasingly to look on the world as dictators, saying: "What shall we want and make?" Dictating jointly to nature and to their own future, imposing new will on remnants of old habits, riding roughly over all who got in the way. Hadn't a cousin of mine said to me in Chicago: "The group photographs I see of Soviet Russia impress me chiefly as faces of will." We others, in a world where our means of production was owned by bosses, felt even our freedom as the right to choose a boss.

Yet still I saw it from outside, not from inside, till it chanced that Tivil came to see me. During our conversation I said: "When my book is finished, I think I shall apply for party membership." The work on my book had shown me the direction in which my life was tending and party membership had begun to seem inevitable.

A light flamed into Tivil's eyes and was veiled swiftly, as if he had drawn a curtain across bright windows. He talked in a friendly impersonal manner about my book. After he left I thought: "Why should that man be so happy yet refuse to let me know it? He would not influence my thought and will by the slightest flicker of his emotion!"

But these were really new people, getting newer all the time! I couldn't recall a communist who had ever used a personal emotion to sway me towards a political decision. Even my own husband wouldn't do it when I tried to goad him towards it in my wish that somebody should control my emotions. And when I wanted him to tell me whether I should join the party, "What is it *you* want?" he always said.

Yet for me to say "I want" always seemed something indelicate, a sort of intruding. I expected them to want me first. Why wouldn't they tell you if they wanted you? I knew that in spite of that flash in Tivil's eyes, he would never say that he did. Then suddenly I saw why I found it so hard to make ultimate choices. Decision had been trained out of me long ago.

I had been trained as a woman to "want to be wanted." I had been trained by one professor after another to "allow myself to be stirred." I had been trained by my religion to wait adoringly for a will that was "higher." Even as a child I had been trained to be "good"—interesting yet never obtrusive—in the hope that everybody would like me. To be liked, desired, wanted by parents, playmates, sororities, men, editors, had been the goal of life. To desire, to want—food, sex or an evening's uninvited conversation—had been improper. I had been trained to expect a god and then serve him. And what a good little slave they had made of me! My earliest compliment had been that I could invent good excuses for mean girls and persuade myself that they meant to be kind. Able to justify petty tyrants!

It went further back, even before childhood. Wasn't that the function we all had, we intellectuals, makers of laws, art, ideals, governments, education? Didn't we spend our time inventing "excuses for mean girls," and "explaining how they meant to be kind"? We never were masters; we justified masters. We had our preference of course as to who should boss us. Those preferences we called "ideals"; tossing between them was "freedom." We prized ideals, for they distinguished us one from the other and made our value. When capitalism began to decline some of us had an instinct towards the rising power, the workers. That became our "ideal"—our clever instinct towards the coming bosses! Yet still we tended to remain servile, offering our services, wanting to be wanted, wanting to make good. We had been trained to be efficient servants, getting our ultimate will from masters!

I began to think quickly as memory after memory confirmed me. Years ago someone—was it Steffens?—had asked me what I most deeply desired of life. After some pondering I had answered: "I want to be completely used." . . . He had shrunk, crying: "A horrible word! Say you don't mean it." . . . Still wishing to please, I had tried to explain it. But I had meant it; I had felt quite pious when I said it. He was right; it was horrible! Deep and unconscious within me had been the mind of a slave. How had I thought of marriage? "I will give myself up only when I find someone worth obeying." I would be free till I got an important boss!

I had even thought to offer a slave mind to the party. For years I had seen it as a lifelong boss alternately adored and feared. There had been times when I had said: "I care much more for this party than most of its members do. They take it so practically as jobs and organization, but for me it combines and reconciles all the early gods of my youth. It is greatness that blots out my failures, yet the comrade that needs my aid. It is consciousness like mine yet wider than mine that plans and builds a world. Even that absurd *Romance of Two Worlds* is in it—soul-mates in past and future, soul-mates on Sirius. Even that weird wish to be a thousand persons and live a thousand lives. Even the bridging of that impassable gulf that opened a lifetime ago by lilac trees in a garden."

Yet just when I would think that I was coming closest, I would find myself furthest away. I would suddenly think: "No, it's not gods at all: it's an ant-heap where everybody gets bossed."

A year ago I had sought out a communist who specialized in history of religions and had said to him: "I suppose this Russian party wouldn't let me in if I said I often feel about

them the way I did about my childhood gods." He had shrunk,
saying: "Don't! The thought sickens us." I had sadly decided that they never would understand those early gods of
mine whom it was so pleasant to adore. They had understood
only too well: they had hated my thought of submission. Their
very constitution cleaned out passive people.

I saw it now: it was not those human hungers of my youth
that they hated, but the tangle of faiths and emotions which
drugged me into acquiescence. They satisfied those hungers
not by emotion, but by analysis leading to action. The party
was no god to which one's life must be submitted: it was a living mechanism through which a man attained his own deep
will. Not all-powerful, it cherished and guided the great,
advancing power of worker-creators; not all-good, it set new
standards to goodness and forever warred with the slaveries of
the past: not all-wise, it learned from mistakes of a million
members and out of the brains and will of them all moved forward. Forward through a thousand wars with hosts of darkness to a humanity which can plan and build its future, caring
for each man's life and place.

How childish seemed that flight from man to the woods and
mountains when all together we can conquer the Arctic and
drive wheat into the north. Ours is the stratosphere and its
ultimate secrets: ours shall be the inter-planet spaces when
first we have unified the earth. Despite the breeders of war who
make of man's advance a race with ruin, yet all about in factory and village, had I not seen the human wills that should
achieve these wonders? An uncouth man on the sun-struck
plains of Samara building a little factory out of the wreck of
war: a bobbed-haired girl in a Central China village dying
bravely under the soldiers' torture: a group of men in a tossing
rain-drenched auto-truck driving the Molvitino sowing-plan to
triumph: strikers in California valleys fighting for their right
to life—everywhere and knit together more and more consciously throughout the world! Not gods, not some mystic
"Common Consciousness." Men! Out of the dark past of their
own natures, learning to achieve their own awakening will!

The analysis of my own passivity next illumined my view of the American party. I had seen it as an inefficient boss to be avoided. The Russian party one could adore for its tremendous achievements: but the American party—no! If I must have a lifelong boss, let it be a big one. Like ancient Jewish tribes wanting their Jehovah to be all-powerful, like a woman wanting an important husband. If the party were not a boss, but the organizing of one's own will with that of comrades, then didn't one choose to work where there was most work to be done? As my husband sought so eagerly "our most important front—agriculture."

But what became of all that famous "party discipline"? "Iron discipline" they called it: you couldn't get round that! Yes, but "conscious discipline" also. In practice the communists I knew didn't seem to suffer from that iron; they seemed to work on jobs they liked to do. Conscious discipline meant that you chose a joint goal with such firmness that you didn't wait for others to boss you: with your own will and hand you cut off any lesser desires that conflicted. The harshest order you ever faced was when they said: "Here's a joint emergency where you are needed. Either do it or get out of the party!" But that wasn't being bossed: it was a high and strenuous choosing, an act of will!

It was as if I had worked for years on the wrong side of a tapestry, learning accurately all its lines and figures, yet always missing its color and sheen. I remembered how correspondents sneered at party members who actually thanked the comrades who had beaten them for pointing out their mistakes. "Kissing the hand that smites! That's Asiatic despotism for you!" So it looked from one side. But from the other? If you wanted your common goal badly enough of course you were glad when comrades showed the things in yourself that hindered. You didn't keep forever insisting that you were right, any more than you kept forever yielding. You learned when to insist and when to yield, and how to build a joint will and program. Oh, this was harder than adoring gods, but it gave a new color to the world!

Yes, I had always alternately craved and fled from bosses, a boss for actions, emotions, thinking; in work, marriage, politics. Like the nomad workers of the American West seeking always an easier master. Like thousands of idealists indulging emotions of freedom and then flopping into the Catholic Church or into fascism because of the rest it gave their thinking faculties. These communists gave you no rest, no final assurance. They made you keep actively studying, applying science in continuous coöperation. If you stopped for even a little while or couldn't keep up they threw you out as "passive" or "opposition" no matter what great work you had done before.

But I, trained all my life to evade decision, was I capable of will? Could I choose a current into which to throw myself forever, knowing that I must hold myself by constant choosing? If not, then my life would be chosen for me, out of daily impacts and small emotions, transient desires and the last friend's advice, selected by an inner stream of habit of which I had not courage to be conscious. Let me live thus if I must; it is the life of most men. But let me never dare to speak of "freedom"!

What then was I? An eddy of whirling foam on a great ocean, from whose storms I drew both foam and form? No, something more. An inner force that whirled that eddy into wider currents which together made the storm. The older current formed me as pliant water, whirling where the wind might list. But these new men were making a new current; they needed will. It was that inner force they cherished!

As soon as I began to look for will I found it. It wasn't so bad as I thought. I really had quite a lot of it. I had stuck to that John Reed Colony through plenty of discomfort, simply through my will to be part of this country. When *Moscow News* before its reorganization drove me almost insane with emotion, something very deep in me had refused to break with the Soviet Union. I had driven myself through several illnesses to hold to tasks which nobody made me do. What made me? I got the clew in that old "creators in chaos." The slave mind might be deep but there was something deeper. It was my will to create.

That was what held through all my shrinking from their "theory," my torture over their inefficiency, my lonely inability to share their life—a deep allegiance to the builders of the future, deeper than any personal desires. I saw in a flash that this held millions to them, millions like myself in all stages of understanding. They came naïvely and with odd evasions and strange worries; they did not know themselves what drew them. It was man's will to build, buried under a thousand slaveries and distortions yet felt in all men, save those who killed it by the opposing will to rob.

How could this will grow stronger till one could trust it to conquer all opposing emotions? That wasn't so hard to see. My will had been weakest when I sat alone in a hotel room trying to choose; then it even became painful to decide between two similar railway trains to the same place. My will grew strongest when I saw a clear direction growing from consultations with people with whom I worked. It had been strong in Kansas City when we analyzed the city's will towards children; it had been strong in Seattle, when my mind was made by news and complaints from the shipyards; it had been strong when I spoke in Stalin's office out of the needs of our Soviet-Americans. Then it had the impact of many wills behind it; it seemed deeper than I was, for it came from those social forces from which I drew myself and all my thinking. Yet it did not confine me; everything I could think and imagine only helped to expand it, when once I was aware that it was my will too. Certainly the communists I knew didn't lack individuality. They had much more than other people; they were tremendously vivid individuals, yet they stuck to a given line and you couldn't budge them. Their own individuality illumined, expanded that line in a thousand ways.

If then I kept consulting and acting with people who had the same kind of will as I had, my own will would steadily grow stronger. But hadn't I done this for more than a decade, ever since I came down from the mountains to join the Seattle *Daily Call?* In recent years I had begun to act almost like the communists—lots of people thought I was one—always "con-

sulting" about my work, looking for contact with factories, even
looking for "the next front." I had acquired their habits so
well that even Borodin had thought I knew what I was doing.
But I hadn't known. My efficient instinct had made a bluff of
being consciousness and had acted almost as well. But it had
acted slavishly. The chief difference now between me and the
communists seemed to be that they had the pleasure of knowing what they were doing. They analyzed the social classes
from which they sprang and from which they derived their
minds and impulses; then through analysis this instinct which
I followed blindly became in them a conscious will. That was
what one meant by "consciousness."

Why this, I said in growing wonder, this is freedom! Not
that endless fleeing from tyrants through the wilderness of
one's soul, more and more alone in shrinking spaces. Not that
endless finding and losing of editors who like my stuff till the
editor changes his mind or the owner changes the editor. Not
those scraps of life are freedom. But this conscious seeking
and finding over wider and wider areas, for ever more complex
creation, comrades with whom to consult and create.

It is more than freedom; it is an end forever to loneliness.
Not to "be chosen," but to choose with others. Freedom and
comradeship can grow wider always. Increasing organization
does not squeeze out freedom, but multiplies its vast variety of
choices!

What had I once meant when I said "freedom"? I could
hardly now recall. It was as if I had come over a great divide
and could no longer see that lower valley. Yet a moment before
I had not seen these new horizons. As I went further into the
range ahead it would grow ever harder to remember that past.
I had mocked at the man from the Ukraine yet now I was
speaking his language. I had said "a socialist ant-heap," but
where was that ant-heap? Would I some day be unable even
to hail across the hills all the old friends with whom I had so
recently been traveling?

Swiftly then I must seize this moment of passing; I must
delay briefly on these ridges to chart the path by which I had
come. A thousand ways rose to this high pass across the

ranges, and all of them were new and steep. Every map sent back helped those who followed; I must mark down the steep bits and morasses and the places where I managed to get through. Then there would be no time for looking back. There was such a long trail ahead and such great mountains.

Books and Pamphlets by Anna Louise Strong

Storm Songs and Fables (Chicago, Langston Press, 1904)

The Song of the City (Oak Park, Ill., Oak Leaves Press, 1906)

The King's Palace (Oak Leaves Press, 1908)

The Psychology of Prayer (Chicago, University of Chicago Press, 1909)

Boys and Girls of the Bible (Chicago, Howard-Severence Co., 1911)

Child Welfare Exhibits: Types and Preparation (Washington, D.C., Government Printing Office, 1915)

The Seattle General Strike, issued by the History Committee of the General Strike Committee; Anna Louise Strong, historian (Seattle, Seattle Union Record, 1918; reprinted by The Shorey Bookstore, Seattle, 1972)

The First Time in History; Two years of Russia's New Life—preface by Leon Trotsky (New York, Boni and Liveright, 1924)

Children of Revolution: the story of the John Reed children's colony on the Volga, which is as well a story of the whole great structure of Russia (Seattle, Pigott Printing Center, 1925)

China's Millions: the Revolutionary Struggles from 1927-1935 (New York, Knight Publishing Co., 1935, expanded from 1928 edition, Coward-McCann, Inc., New York)

Red Star in Samarkand (New York, Coward-McCann, Inc., 1929)

Modern Farming—Soviet Style (New York, International Pamphlets, 1930)

From Stalingrad to Kuzbas: Sketches of the Socialist Construction in the USSR (New York, International Pamphlets, 1931)

The Soviets Conquer Wheat; the drama of Collective Farming (New York, Henry Holt and Co., 1931)

The Road to the Grey Pamir (Boston, Little, Brown and Co., 1931)

Dictatorship and Democracy in the Soviet Union (New York, International Pamphlets, 1934)

I Change Worlds: the Remaking of an American (New York, Henry Holt and Co., 1935)

The Soviet Union and World Peace (New York, International Pamphlets, 1935)

The Soviet World (New York, Henry Holt and Co., 1936)

The New Soviet Constitution; a study in Socialist Democracy (New York, Henry Holt and Co., 1937)

Spain in Arms (New York, Henry Holt and Co., 1937)

One-fifth of Mankind (New York, Modern Age Books, 1938)

China Fights for Freedom (London, 1939)

My Native Land (New York, Viking Press, 1940)

The Kuomintang-Communist Crisis in China: a first-hand account of one of the most critical periods in Far Eastern History (New York, 1941)

The Soviets Expected It (New York, Dial Press, 1941)

China's New Crisis: The Kuomintang (London, Fore Publications, LTD, 1942)

Wild River (a novel) (Boston, Little, Brown and Co., 1943)

The Russians Are People (London, Cobbett Publishing Co., LTD, 1943)

Peoples of the USSR (New York, The Macmillan Co., 1944)

Soviet Farmers (New York, The National Council of American-Soviet Friendship, 1945)

Inside Liberated Poland (New York, The National Council of American-Soviet Friendship, 1945)

I Saw the New Poland (Boston, Little, Brown and Co., 1946)

The Chinese Conquer China (Garden City, N.Y., Doubleday, 1949)

The Stalin Era (Altadena, CA, Today's Press, 1956)

The Rise of the Chinese People's Communes (Peking, New World Press, 1959)

When Serfs Stood Up in Tibet; Report (Peking, New World Press, 1960)

Cash and Violence in Laos and Vietnam (New York, Mainstream Publishers, 1962)

Letters from China Nos 1-10 (Peking, New World Press, 1963)
Letters from China Nos 21-30 (Peking, New World Press, 1966)

China's Fight For Grain: Three Dates from a Diary in late 1962 (Peking, New World Press, 1968)

INDEX

Aberdeen, Lady: 46

Advance, the: 27-9

American Communist Party: 67, 127, 158

American Educational Workshops: early plans for 207-10; organization and dissolution 216-23

American Federation of Labor: 66,73-5,155

American Friends Service: offers to send ALS to Poland 89-90; Warsaw mission 90-5; famine relief 111, 121-2,126

American Relief Administration: 94, 102, 114-5, 128, 179-80, 182, 186

American Union Against Militarism: 62

"Anise":   73, 91, 127

Anti-Conscription League: 57, 61

Asahi, the: 236-7

Ault, Harry: editor of *Seattle Union Record* 66-7, 73, 84, 87-8

Axelrod, T.L.:   editor of *Moscow News* 305; disagreements with 307-12; reorganizes *Worker's News* 313-4; Stalin intervenes in dispute with 338-41; 343, 346, 350

Ayres, Leonard: 37, 43-5, 249,367

Babaieff, Akhun: President of Uzbekistan 273, 275-6

Barrow, Florence: 91, 93-5

Barton, Dante: 41-2, 152

Beals, Carleton: 27,238,247,249-50

Borodin, Fanny: 231-2

Borodin, Michael: 162,188; advisor to Chinese nationalists 231-5; 249, 253-4, 257, 260-1; discusses Chinese divisions 263-5; President of Paper Trust 300-1; 315, 343; chief of *Moscow Daily News* 350-2; 373-6, 378; conversation with ALS about *Moscow Daily News* 406-12; 421

British Labor Party: 69-70, 154

Bryant, Louise: 69-71

Bryn Mawr: 22, 25-6

Bullitt, William: 86-7, 378, 388

Calles, Plutarco: Mexican President 238; dealings with U.S. 242-3; 246, 248, 249, 254-5

Carr: 127, 153

Chang Tso-lin: 229-30, 237, 261